D1187177

The Complicity of Imagination examines the rich and complex relationship between four nineteenth-century authors and the culture and politics of seventeenth-century England. Challenging the notion that antebellum Americans were burdened by a sense of cultural inferiority in both their thought and their writing, this study portrays an American Renaissance whose writers were deeply enough read in the literature and controversies of seventeenth-century England to appropriate its cultural artifacts for their own purposes. American writers such as Emerson, Fuller, Thoreau, and Melville consciously absorbed literary, philosophical, and political strategies from their reading in the earlier period in order to interrogate the orthodoxies of American Whigs, as well as the agenda of the radical Democratic "Young Americans." By exploring the broader cultural implications of intertextual relationships, this book demonstrates how literary texts participate in the artistic, political, and theological tensions within American culture.

CAMBRIDGE STUDIES IN AMERICAN LITERATURE
AND CULTURE

The Complicity of Imagination

Books in the series

Continued on pages following the Index

THE COMPLICITY OF IMAGINATION

The American Renaissance, Contests of Authority, and Seventeenth-Century English Culture

ROBIN GREY
University of Illinois at Chicago

CAMBRIDGE
UNIVERSITY PRESS

PUBLISHED BY THE PRESS SYNDICATE OF THE UNIVERSITY OF CAMBRIDGE
The Pitt Building, Trumpington Street
Cambridge CB2 1RP, United Kingdom

CAMBRIDGE UNIVERSITY PRESS
The Edinburgh Building, Cambridge CB2 2RU, United Kingdom
40 West 20th Street, New York, NY 10011-45211, USA
10 Stamford Road, Oakleigh, Melbourne 3166, Australia

First published 1997

Printed in the United States of America

Typeset in Baskerville

Library of Congress Cataloging-in-Publication Data

Grey, Robin (Robin Sandra)
The complicity of imagination : the American renaissance, contests
of authority, and seventeenth-century English culture / Robin Grey.
p. cm. – (Cambridge studies in American literature and
culture ; 106)
ISBN 0-521-49538-5 (hc)
1. American literature – 19th century – History and criticism.
2. English literature – Early modern, 1500–1700 – Appreciation –
United States.   3. Fuller, Margaret, 1810–1850 – Knowledge –
England.   4. Emerson, Ralph Waldo, 1803–1882 – Knowledge –
England.   5. Thoreau, Henry David, 1817–1862 – Knowledge –
England.   6. Melville, Herman, 1819–1891 – Knowledge –
England.   7. American literature – English influences.   8. England –
Civilization – 17th century.   I. Title.   II. Series.
PS159.E5G74   1996
810.9'003 – dc20   96-2284
CIP

A catalog record for this book is available from
the British Library

ISBN 0 521 495385 hardback

CONTENTS

═══════

v

ACKNOWLEDGMENTS

For their scholarly assistance and guidance I would like to thank Christopher Grose, Barbara Packer, Jonathan Post, and Donald Weber. Special thanks are due to the staff at the William Andrews Clark Memorial Library, particularly to Librarian John Bidwell, and to Carol Briggs. I would also like to thank Stephen Ferguson, Curator of Rare Books and Assistant University Librarian for Rare Books and Special Collections at Princeton University, and a private endowment for their permission to inspect the original annotations written by Herman Melville in his text of John Milton's poetry.

To the others who contributed to this project, each in a different way, I extend my appreciation: to Greg Belcamino, Anna Berger, William Edinger, Pamela Legge, Richard W. F. Kroll, and Arthur J. Orlowski. For her friendship and valuable advice, I extend my special thanks to Victoria Silver. And to David Loewenstein I owe my deepest gratitude for his assistance, support, and expertise.

To the Department of English at the University of Illinois at Chicago I am indebted for support (through leave time and a semester sabbatical). And to my colleagues at UIC who read some or all of my manuscript and gave me invaluable suggestions, I wish to offer my gratitude – to Michael Anania, Brian Higgins, Kyoko Inoue, Michael Lieb, Donald Marshall, Christian Messenger, and Terence Whalen.

I also wish to acknowledge others in the profession who have assisted me by reading parts of the manuscript or by giving me advice, information, or materials: Harrison Hayford, Janel Mueller, Merton M. Sealts, and James Grantham Turner. I am grateful for permission to republish parts of Chapter 2 that originally appeared in *Modern Philology* (University of Chicago Press),

Volume 92, no. 1 (August 1994), and to *Milton Quarterly* for permission to republish parts of Chapter 6 that originally appeared in that journal in Volume 26, no. 4 (December 1992).

Finally, I wish to thank the anonymous readers of Cambridge University Press for their valuable suggestions, Eric J. Sundquist for his scholarly and professional assistance in bringing this manuscript to publication, and T. Susan Chang of Cambridge University Press for her thoughtfulness and guidance with the manuscript.

CAMBRIDGE STUDIES IN AMERICAN LITERATURE
AND CULTURE

The Complicity of Imagination

INTRODUCTION

ANTEBELLUM AMERICA AND THE CULTURE
OF SEVENTEENTH-CENTURY ENGLAND

————————

This study examines the significant relationship between four antebellum nineteenth-century American authors and the writers, culture, and politics of seventeenth-century England. The relationship is a rich and complex one, but critical treatment has been only intermittent, and the connections noticed by scholars have been disparate, or confined to instances of local and explicit literary indebtedness. Even when F. O. Matthiessen noted the "vogue" for seventeenth-century writers among "American Renaissance" authors, his analysis emphasized many of the New Criticism's preoccupations with "the metaphysical strain," and in the tradition of T. S. Eliot, focused upon the formal features of seventeenth-century poetry and its tendency toward Neoplatonic "transcendence" of history. However inadvertent, the enduring effect of Matthiessen's interpretation has been both to aestheticize and to dehistoricize the American authors' interest in seventeenth-century English culture.[1] Following Matthiessen, several commentators have suggested that seventeenth-century English writers offered American authors a source of transhistorical "humanist" values, or a convenient repository of arcane and antiquarian lore.[2] More recently, critics have noted Matthiessen's heavy reliance upon Shakespeare in the formation of his American literature canon: Elizabethan (and Caroline) literature became a "means of securing English Renaissance validity for American Renaissance figures."[3]

I would like to argue instead for an "American Renaissance" whose writers were sufficient in their own agency, confident in their own powers, and deeply enough read in the earlier period to revise those earlier cultural artifacts for their own distinctive aesthetic, social, and sometimes political purposes. This study in fact complicates the ways Americans defined their individual and

1

national identities, as well as their relationship with their historical predecessors, both English and American. My inquiry suggests that we should approach the nineteenth-century Americans' interest in seventeenth-century English culture less as the legacy of a single intellectual and Puritan religious tradition (Winters, Miller, Bercovitch, Chase), or as a literary "vogue" (Matthiessen), or as a psychological reaction to an "anxiety of influence" (Bloom, Weisbuch), or as a version of the English Romantic response to the Enlightenment (Chai).[4] Nor should the American authors' interest in early modern England be seen as one entirely informed by impulses toward containment or the restriction of radical impulses in America (Bercovitch, Stavely, Van Anglen).[5] Rather, I propose that their interest in the seventeenth century was initiated by common necessities rooted in the historical conditions of American society, but variously interpreted. Accordingly, nineteenth-century American writers consciously absorbed literary, philosophical, and political strategies gathered from their wide reading in the earlier period in order to interrogate both the orthodoxies of the American Whigs and the radical ("Young American") Democratic agenda in the antebellum Northeast.[6] The fact that nineteenth-century Americans were deeply conversant with the literature and controversies of early modern England and saw them as instructive has been largely overlooked, and now deserves to be reexamined.

Matthiessen's willingness to associate antebellum American literature with English literature of the sixteenth and seventeenth centuries derived from a desire to carve out a separate field of American literary study through an initial process of legitimating association with English culture. But the absence among Americanists of sustained examination of the connections between English and American literatures and cultures may also be the legacy of the "American Puritan origin" paradigm so ably defined by Perry Miller and later modified and extended by Sacvan Bercovitch.[7] Although Bernard Bailyn, in his important work on the American Revolutionary period, has emphasized transatlantic connections between American colonists and the spokesmen of the English Civil War period (Milton, Harrington, Algernon Sidney) and Opposition "Country" party politics in eighteenth-century England,[8] American Puritan covenant theology has been, through the continuing efforts of Bercovitch, credited (perhaps exaggeratedly so) as the dominant source of national mythology and, in turn, of national identity. Indeed, the American Puritan argument, as Americanists well know, both confirmed a desirable aesthetic autonomy from English culture and upheld nationalist boundaries within humanist academic fields of study, particularly in the American academy.[9] The extent of educational specialization expected in the American academy has only continued to obscure the once-intimate connections between the two cultures. Modern American scholars, moreover, continue to resist exploring direct links and to define American cultural identity apart from English culture because of their assumption that the only response on the part of antebellum Americans to British culture was one informed by a sense of inferiority. Without doubt, nineteenth-century American authors suffered some degree of intimidation by their English counterparts, as Albert von Frank has vividly demonstrated, but that response was far from unvarying.[10]

The four major American authors I examine exhibited an intense uneasiness concerning how accurately and assuredly the prevailing Whig notions about language, knowledge, and social conduct (promoted in such American universities as Harvard and enforced by criticism in such contemporary periodicals as the *North American Review,* the *Christian Examiner,* and the *American Whig Review*) shaped the dominant American discourse. Suspicious of the way in which Whig values reinforced and perpetuated each other, yet also dismayed by the lack of discrimination in the literary values of Democratic nationalists, Emerson, Fuller, Thoreau, and Melville did not, however, devise a shared idiom as an alternative to either the English neoclassicism proffered by the Whigs or the recourse to local idioms and Anglophobia practiced by many of the Young American literary Democrats.[11] Instead, they relied on their individual resourcefulness both in seeking out the writings of the earlier period and in appropriating their various strategies.

Some of the distinctive qualities of nineteenth-century American literary practices emerged as a result of the efforts of its writers to recover and assimilate seventeenth-century English heterodoxies in response to a particular nexus of circumstances in America perceived by them as an aesthetic as well as political predicament. "American Renaissance" prose is remarkable as much for its departure from the genial lucidity of eighteenth- and early nineteenth-century American prose as for its eclecticism and extravagance. These qualities arose in part from the American writers' assimilations of seventeenth-century heterodoxies – including prose styles, archaic epistemological categories, and doctrinal heresies – which they adapted and used to challenge a variety of values within their culture. American authors were quick to employ English texts that were associated with the discrediting of traditional authority. But they also revised texts considered "conservative" in their own time – like the writings of Sir Thomas Browne or Izaak Walton – for ironic or unsettling purposes. By disconcerting or provoking those nineteenth-century readers who relied on the conventional modes of discourse and categories of knowledge, these writers often challenged the educated and cultured conservative hegemony. At the same time, by selectively assimilating rather than eschewing English texts, they offered an alternative to the literary values of the unsophisticated Democratic nationalists (Cornelius Matthews, for example). In this way these authors provided a powerful critique of the philosophical and rhetorical foundations of the antebellum culture of the Northeast, and they engaged in reshaping the culture and reformulating its alternatives.

No doubt other nineteenth-century authors might have been included here – Emily Dickinson and Nathaniel Hawthorne come most readily to mind. Dickinson was steeped in the poetry of George Herbert and Henry Vaughan no less than the prose of Sir Thomas Browne; and Hawthorne profoundly assimilated Milton's writings. I have chosen these four, however, for the characteristic ways in which they illustrate engagement with early modern English culture: a "representative" eclecticism (as in the case of Thoreau); a personal identification with the circumstances of an earlier figure (Emerson and, more indirectly, Fuller); and an affinity of intellect and sensibility, however imaginatively interpreted (Melville).

My work differs from the recent studies of Thomas Gustafson, Michael Kramer, Donald Weber, and Philip Gura, who emphasize language theory and practice, rhetoric, and alternative canons, but do not share my emphasis upon the ways that the literature and politics of an earlier age are imaginatively exploited so as to interrogate nineteenth-century orthodoxies.[12] Other recent studies by Stavely and Van Anglen have sought to connect the cultures on both sides of the Atlantic, but these analyzed exclusively the Puritan theological basis for challenges to authority, or in the case of Van Anglen, the ambivalent Unitarian desire both to suppress and to accommodate "antinomian" impulses in a culture otherwise law-abiding, "Arminian," and optimistic about effectual individual agency. David Reynolds has valuably documented the tensions within American culture created by a competing canon of popular American literature and its stereotypes – but that canon arose within American society, not outside of it.[13]

I stress instead the broad interrelationship between the English and American cultures, and between American literature and politics that so much characterizes antebellum nineteenth-century America. I draw upon nineteenth-century political orations, reviews, political and literary journals, and selected sermons to understand the conditions that shaped antebellum literary texts and prompted American authors to turn – sometimes imperiously, sometimes reverently – to the English seventeenth century. As evidenced by the abundance of politicoliterary journals in the United States in the nineteenth century, literature and politics were not necessarily regarded as separate discursive modes. Indeed, Orestes Brownson announced in 1838 in the Democratic *Boston Quarterly Review,* "We would have no literary man avoid party questions, in politics, religion, or philosophy; but we would have every man who loves Humanity and craves progress, discuss those questions as a judge, not as a pleader."[14] Both through an examination of the cultural and intellectual conditions prevailing in the antebellum Northeast and through a series of close readings, my study highlights the strategic dimensions of literary texts, examining how the literary imagination helps to shape events, values, and assumptions in both the seventeenth and nineteenth centuries. Moreover, this study examines the aesthetic and rhetorical dimensions of the literary texts, as well as those of political and polemical texts.[15] Indeed, among Americans the popularity of Madame de Staël's treatise *De la Littérature Considerée dans ses Rapports avec les Institutions Sociales* (1800; trans. 1813) suggests that nineteenth-century writers were deeply concerned with the relation between political democracies and the production of vital national literatures.[16] The anonymous author of an 1847 article on "Nationality in Literature," published in the *Democratic Review,* noted that

> Madame De Stael's great work on the influence of literature upon society, was written . . . "to show that all the peculiarities in the literature of different ages and countries may be explained by a reference to the condition of society, and the political and religious institutions of each; and at the same time to point out in what way the progress of letters has, in its turn, modified and affected the government and religion of those nations among whom they have flourished."[17]

While the English Romantics – particularly Coleridge, Lamb, and Keats – were partly responsible for introducing nineteenth-century American writers to seventeenth-century English culture, it is also clear that the Americans' knowledge of the literature and events of this period was not exclusively refracted through the English Romantic writers. Rather, as I hope to demonstrate in this study, their familiarity was often gained through their own intensive and individualized reading in the period. James Freeman Clarke, an 1829 graduate of Harvard and a Transcendentalist, acknowledged in his autobiography his fellow classmates' sometimes overlapping but often discrete interest in both the Romantics and the seventeenth-century writers – all in opposition to the official classical and neoclassical Harvard curriculum:

> When I recall what my classmates were interested in doing, I find it was not college work, which might have given them rank, but pursuits outside of the curriculum ... We unearthed old tomes in the college library, and while our English professors were teaching us out of Blair's "Rhetoric," we were forming our taste by making copious extracts from Sir Thomas Browne, or Ben Jonson. Our real professors of rhetoric were Charles Lamb and Coleridge, Walter Scott and Wordsworth. I recall the delight which George Davis and I took in an old copy of Sir Thomas Browne which we stumbled upon in the college library. We had scarcely heard the name; but by a sure instinct we discovered the wit, originality, and sagacity of this old writer.[18]

Even more assiduously, Thoreau devoted nearly three years to reading and transcribing early modern English literature after graduating from Harvard. Melville brought back from his trip to England folio editions of Sir Thomas Browne's writings; and Emerson's journals are filled with excerpts from his readings in the prose and poetry (much of which he appears to have committed to memory), as well as the theology and history of the period. Moreover, observing that Margaret Fuller's "English reading was incomplete," Emerson took credit for expanding her familiarity: "I believe I had the pleasure of making her acquainted with Chaucer, with Ben Jonson, with Herbert, Chapman, Ford, Beaumont and Fletcher, with Bacon, and Sir Thomas Browne."[19] Fuller, quite on her own, read biographies of seventeenth-century authors, translated the Latin poetry of Lord Herbert of Cherbury, and sought out arguments for companionate marriage in Milton's divorce tracts.

Knowledge of seventeenth-century English culture and literature among educated Americans was in fact extensive and nuanced. A reviewer discussing Sir Thomas Browne's writings in the *American Whig Review* in 1848 (one among many such articles in the 1830s and 1840s) expected his audience to know that Browne's style had recently "been a topic of much animadversion" – presumably among Whig critics, who were more often admirers of neoclassical styles. He also assumed that they were so familiar with the writing of Browne's contemporaries, "Owen Feltham, Abraham Cowley, and John Milton," that a comparison of their styles was unnecessary.[20] Contemporary reviewers of Melville and Thoreau, moreover, frequently noticed what many scholars today have tended to overlook in these authors' writings – the many resonances, allusions, and explicit appropriations of seventeenth-century English texts.

The literature and politics, particularly of pre-Restoration England, were regularly enlisted in the debates about current events in antebellum America. Indeed, as late as the conclusion of the American Civil War, a commissioner appointed by Jefferson Davis entreated Lincoln to negotiate with the Confederate South rather than insist on complete surrender: "Mr. Hunter . . . in illustration of the propriety of the Executive entering into agreements with persons in arms against the acknowledged rightful public authority, referred to repeated instances of this character between Charles I, of England, and the people in arms against him." "All I distinctly recollect about the case of Charles I," replied Lincoln, "is, that he lost his head in the end."[21] Americans' acquaintance with such diverse texts as Milton's polemical tracts, Clarendon's *History of the Rebellion,* King Charles I's *Eikon Basilike,* Cromwell's speeches, Browne's *Religio Medici* and Harrington's *Oceana* is everywhere apparent in the nineteenth-century politicoliterary journals of both Whigs and Democrats, in orations, in personal libraries, and in the literary texts of the four writers highlighted in this study.[22] The library of Edward Everett, the Whig governor of Massachusetts, contained a number of seventeenth-century English texts (considerably outnumbering those of colonial American origin), including the writings of Donne, Herbert, Matthew Hale, Jeremy Taylor, Algernon Sidney, Milton, William Chillingworth, Locke, Hobbes, Cromwell, and, in seventeenth-century first editions, Milton's *Paradise Lost* and Charles I's *Eikon Basilike.*[23] Thoreau, in a lyceum lecture, heralded Carlyle's edition of Oliver Cromwell's letters and speeches, and later favorably compared John Brown at Harpers Ferry to Cromwell. Both Emerson, in "Woman" and "Courage," and Fuller, in *Woman in the Nineteenth-Century,* incorporated excerpts from Lucy Hutchinson's memoirs of her husband, the English regicide John Hutchinson, assuming the American public's familiarity with her *Memoirs of the Life of Colonel Hutchinson,* first published in 1806 and republished several times in the late 1840s.[24] The discovery and publication of Milton's *On Christian Doctrine* in 1825, moreover, became the occasion for new editions of his prose and reevaluations of the theological, social, and political implications of his prose tracts.

From the frequent references to seventeenth-century English literature and politics in American periodicals, we can infer that allusions to events and texts of that period, as well as the assimilation of seventeenth-century prose styles and epistemological practices, would be perceived by American antebellum contemporaries as an attempt to interrogate various forms of authority based on the experiences of that earlier period. For example, in an 1846 assessment of "Imaginary Commonwealths" for the *Democratic Review,* J. Sullivan Cox, a Democratic supporter of Manifest Destiny, adapted Milton's ecstatic vision of an impending civil millennium in England.[25] Cox borrowed imagery from Milton's *Areopagitica* both to highlight the *translatio* of freedom from England to America ("man for ever flying westward from civil and religious thraldom") and to sanctify the motives of a Jacksonian "western commonwealth in America" through association with Milton's famous text (Cox, 184).[26]

In *Areopagitica,* Milton had interpreted prophetically the increasing turmoil of London (that "shop of war") as a sign of the imminent approach of an earthly civil and spiritual millennium. He addressed the collective wisdom of Parliament in this state of heightened expectation: they must not suppress radical sectarian activity by imposing censorship, for that would impede the apocalyptic struggle between truth and falsehood. Similarly, in order to glorify America's Manifest Destiny and the Mexican War by associating both with an apocalyptic struggle for definitive democratic perfection, Cox addressed the collective wisdom of Democratic America with exalted expectations recalling those of Milton when he described his mystical vision of the godly English commonwealth. But in Cox's account, the hope has been transferred to the Americans, who have become, like the inspired Englishmen of Milton's day, reformers of worldly institutions and visionary aspirants to "the perfection of a purer existence, 'kindling their undazzled eyes at the full mid-day beam, purging and scaling their long abused sight at the fountain itself of heavenly radiance'" (Cox, 184; Milton, *CPW,* 2:558). Following Milton's prophetic model, Cox implies that with earthly fulfillment of ideal nationhood so near, the conflict must not be halted or impeded.

But the American commonwealth Cox envisioned differed in one crucial way from Milton's. Cox tellingly revised Milton's "Temple of the Lord" image, an architectural metaphor for the English church and commonwealth in the earthly millennium. Milton acknowledged the necessity – even in the millennium – of accommodating (sectarian) differences: "when every stone is laid artfully together, it cannot be united into a continuity, it can but be contiguous *in this world*" (*CPW*, 2:555; my emphasis). Milton claimed, "the perfection consists in this, that out of many moderat varieties and brotherly dissimilitudes . . . arises the goodly and gracefully symmetry that commends the whole pile and structure." He insisted that these differences were the very basis of collective effort and the best means of wresting truth from falsehood by conflict (*CPW*, 2:555; Cox, 185). Cox, however, replaced Milton's word "contiguity" in reference to the arrangement of building blocks in this ideal edifice of a church-state. Rejecting tolerance of acknowledged differences, and inscribing uniformity instead of unity in the image of a continent unbroken by national boundaries, Cox ultimately hoped for "not a mere 'contiguity' of materials, but one continuous pile of mild majesty and chaste magnificence" (Cox, 185). Indeed, Cox's final appropriation from *Areopagitica* is that of the "enraptured beholder" visualizing Truth's torn body reassembled as "one immortal feature of loveliness and truth" (and "perfection" in Milton's version) (Cox, 185; *CPW*, 2:549). For Cox, whose article is a paean to the nobility of expanding American values along with its territories – tacitly understood as Texas and Oregon – Milton's image of Truth restored may well have served to render imaginatively an American continent undivided by boundaries and eventually healed from the strife created by the Mexican War.

Some have argued that Jonathan Edwards was the exclusive source for Americans' hope for a "civil millennium" on earth; he invested "revolution" with sacred and providential implications and divested it of destructive connotations.[27] Yet clearly, in such seventeenth-century English texts as John Milton's prose works (*Of Reformation* [1641], *Areopagitica* [1644], and *The Tenure of Kings and Magistrates* [1649]), American radicals and dissenters, at least as early as the American Revolution, had found inspired visions of a future millennium.[28] And while Milton regarded history as sacred and providential, he did not eschew but rather embraced apocalyptic conflict and turbulence as necessary. Indeed, it seems that Cox turned to one of Milton's best-known texts – one associated with the English Revolution – precisely for its ability to render acceptable both conflict and disruption for an eventual earthly national fulfillment.

American Whigs and Democrats often adopted contrary views of early modern England to suit their competing political agendas. In fact, American periodicals (many of which were the organs of one or another of the political parties) chose different aspects of seventeenth-century English culture as sociopolitical and cultural touchstones. As Daniel Walker Howe has noted, the events of the English Revolution provided conservative American Whigs with a repertoire of figurations for anarchy and the perversions of absolute power, equating, for example, Andrew Jackson's and Martin Van Buren's use of executive power with the autocracy of Charles I and Charles II.[29] According to Sacvan Bercovitch, Reginald Horsman, and David Levin, many of these same Americans also conservatively reinterpreted the upheavals of the Great Migration (the emigration of English Puritans to America) and the American Revolution as events that instead represented a reassuring paradigm of progressivism and gradualism. They did so, according to these scholars, in order to bolster their own authority, defuse the incendiary implications of past rebellions, and maintain an ideology of "progress" led by an Anglo-Saxon, Puritan vanguard.[30]

Whigs and Democrats, moreover, constructed dramatically different arguments from the very same seventeenth-century English cultural artifacts. A case in point is James Harrington's utopian vision in *The Commonwealth of Oceana* (1656), read by such early Opposition ideologues as John Trenchard and Thomas Gordon, who were in turn read widely by the American colonists in *Cato's Letters* (1720s). In the same article on visionary commonwealths for the *Democratic Review* cited above, J. Sullivan Cox examined Harrington's *Oceana* along with Plato's *Republic* and More's *Utopia*. In the midst of the Mexican War over the annexation of Texas, Cox analyzes these three commonwealths to assert the nobility of high principles and visionary schemes that it is America's "destiny" to realize ("By us must these fair visions be realized" [Cox, 185]), and America has begun already to make them "manifest" (Cox, 184). Cox stressed the importance of *Oceana* as a model of republican ideals that, according to Democratic principles, America had implemented: agrarianism, the division and balance of powers in government, the secret ballot, equal rotation, and, by replacing primogeniture with labor capitalism ("that protecting arm which stimulates to labor by insuring reward" [Cox, 181]), an enhancement of Harrington's ideals of Agrarian Law.[31] Harrington's concept of a system that remains intact and self-regulating into perpetuity, however, seemed too conservative for this supporter of Manifest Destiny, who asserted instead the necessity of dauntless innovation: "modifications must be made – . . . improvements are always in order – and . . . the age is recreant to the past, and reckless of the future, that will not dare and do something beyond the confines of barren custom" (Cox, 182).

Daniel Webster, a Whig, also made Harrington's *Oceana* the basis of two of his most famous speeches, but hailed Harrington's more conservative features. In his speech on "The Basis of the Senate" (1820), Webster pronounces Harrington "one of the most ingenious of political writers" and cites *Oceana* in support of one of the Whigs' favorite principles: "that power *naturally* and *necessarily* follows property," that "a government founded on property is legitimately founded."[32] Webster, not surprisingly, omits mention of Harrington's prescriptive limits on the amount of property owned by each individual, which Harrington regarded as the crucial foundation of a stable society. Early modern English texts and events, in effect, helped to supply the vocabulary for a dialogue – and sometimes a heated contest – among Americans. These texts from seventeenth-century England shaped the American dialogue and were themselves shaped by their use in an American context.

David Simpson and Sacvan Bercovitch have suggested that oppositional discourse in antebellum America was supplanted by an Emersonian or Puritan discourse that universalized and thereby effaced regional, class, and racial differences previously registered in American speech. I argue instead that dissenting discourse was in part preserved and enacted in antebellum America through the appropriation and revision of seventeenth-century English styles, texts, and modes of knowledge.[33] Indeed, Orestes Brownson, a radical Democrat and sometime Transcendentalist, deeply admired the more heterodox and combative aspects of the seventeenth century. He commented on the relationship between literature and revolution: "When Orthodoxy reigns unquestioned, and all is reduced to uniformity of opinion, literature cannot flourish . . . The richest portion of English literature belongs to the seventeenth century; and what is that century in England but an epoch of political and religious revolutions, defeated, effected, or adjourned?"[34]

The four American authors selected for this study turned to

texts of the seventeenth century as they confronted a series of cultural "predicaments." Chapter 1 provides a fuller examination of the cultural predicaments that each confronted and to which each author creatively responded. For now, I will outline briefly those cultural circumstances in their most probable relation to the individual author's use of seventeenth-century English texts. In doing so, I will suggest the constitutive argument of each of the case studies offered in Chapters 2 through 6.

For Melville and Emerson, the culture's insistent expectations for clarity informed social and theological judgments concerning the unfamiliar no less than it shaped aesthetic judgments concerning modes of oratorical and literary discourse. Accordingly, unfamiliar, empirically unverifiable experiences, and such anomalous phenomena as prodigies and miracles represented, as did "oracular" eloquence, manifestations of epistemological opacity, which the culture sought to displace, suppress, or relegate to an inferior status.[35] As we shall see in Chapter 1, liberal Christian culture of the Whiggish antebellum Northeast turned particularly to Locke's epistemology and method for verifying religious experience in order to maintain a stable culture and to buttress the social hierarchy. We know that the Transcendentalists attempted to redress the culture's emphasis on Lockean sensationalism and empiricism.[36] But another important implication of Locke's epistemological presence in the American culture seems to have been overlooked – that it tended, especially when revised by the Scottish Common Sense philosophers, to promote an expectation of credibility based on predictability.[37] The neoplatonism of many of the Transcendentalists and the Cambridge Platonism of some Unitarians, however, did little to address social, philosophical, and literary values based to a significant extent on a process of identification (intelligibility and classification based on shared or familiar attributes.) The culture's commitment to identification as the basis of verification left many Americans with few or no provisions for processes of negotiation with the unfamiliar – processes that would permit degrees of acknowledgment for that which is (or those who are) less readily familiar or homologous.

By turning to the literary, philosophical, and political culture of seventeenth-century England, such writers as Emerson (examined in Chapter 2) and Melville (examined in Chapters 5 and 6) hoped to challenge or exploit subversively this distrust of that which appears unfamiliar, or not immediately intelligible. The dilemma, then, with which Melville struggled was the pervasiveness in America of John Locke's empiricist discourse and epistemology, which, while restrictive of what human knowledge is deemed "certain," is distrustful of all knowledge not gained through the "experience" of concrete particulars and suspicious of religious experience not verified by external evidence. And as we shall see in Chapter 5, Melville attempted to enhance his culture's awareness of the process by which their judgments – too often of unconsidered identification or dismissal – were made. To do so, Melville invested the speculations of the narrator of *Mardi*, as well as Ishmael's "extravagant speculation," with qualities fashioned from the seventeenth-century Anglican writings of Sir Thomas Browne (particularly *Pseudodoxia Epidemica*), qualities that call attention to the process by which a limited but still engaged rational faculty may acknowledge, accommodate, indeed negotiate unfamiliar phenomena, situating them within provisional categories of knowledge, and insisting upon gradations of probability to lend them degrees of credence. In so doing, Melville found an alternative to the Calvinists' discredited rational faculty, the glib presumption of Unitarian rationalism, and the naive Platonism of the Transcendentalists. As we shall see in Chapter 6, Melville confronted the frustration of inscrutability again, though this time he responded in annotations written in his copy of Milton's poetry, by intensifying that opacity as he identified with, and imaginatively transformed, Milton's rendering of such dubious characters as Samson, Dalila, and Satan.

Most troubling to Emerson's self-fashioning in his early career was a prescriptive, uniform rhetorical training at the universities extolling an aesthetics of lucidity in English neoclassical (particularly Addisonian) prose styles and in oratory. This aesthetic of lucidity (examined in Chapter 1) was founded on eighteenth-century Scottish Common Sense philosophy – a reductive rationalism that assumed both the adequacy of language to the task of communicating truths necessary for moral conduct and the accuracy of all human knowledge based on a consensus of understanding (but not implying that the status of knowledge is merely conventional). Emerson, I suggest, sensed that the Whig promulgation of a uniform aesthetic checked or devalued the varied and sometimes veiled prophetic eloquence he sought to employ. It seemed, moreover, unsuitable as the idiom of a reformer who increasingly did not share the assumptions of his culture. A uniform aesthetic implicitly discouraged political dissension in favor of the Whig status quo, as Emerson noted in 1841:

> The cause of education is urged in this country with the utmost earnestness, – on what ground? why on this, . . . if they [the people] are not instructed to sympathize with the intelligent, reading, trading, and governing class, inspired with a taste for the same competitions and prizes, they will upset the fair pageant of Judicature, and perhaps lay a hand on the sacred muniments of wealth itself, and new distribute the land. (W, 1:320)

Indeed, a decade earlier, Edward Everett, in a lecture entitled "Advantage of Knowledge to Workingmen," advanced this Whig educational agenda, observing that "the general ignorance of large numbers and entire classes of men, acting under the unchastened stimulus of the passions, and excited by the various causes of discontent which occur in the progress of human affairs, is often productive of scenes which make humanity shudder."[38]

As seen in Chapter 2, Emerson increasingly identified with the prophetic Milton of the early prose tracts. Emerson encoded his struggle with the Whig Harvard Unitarians through his revisionist reading of Milton, whom the Unitarians themselves had previously identified as a pivotal figure and interpreted for their own purposes. Emerson self-consciously shifted his model of verbal expression from the uniformity of Whig oratory to Milton's varied and vehement prophetic discourse, especially in Milton's early tracts. Emerson's aversion to "set forms" and static institutions has often been depicted as evolving exclusively from Coleridgean organicism and the Romantic opposition to neoclassicism, while his prophetic role has been largely associated with the American jeremiad tradition. Yet this American author's early familiarity with the seventeenth-century controversy over censorship and the Anglican–Puritan controversy about "set forms" played out in Milton's prose of the 1640s argues for a different justification for the linguistic diversity and complexity in Emerson's conception of inspired language. In crucial periods of forming his own identity and goals, Emerson turned to Milton's apocalyptic writings, as much for their displays of polemical agility or "manly" ad hominem ferocity as for the occasions they offer to explore and conceptualize inspired, efficacious language. Emerson's unorthodox insistence that "The Reason of Ch.[urch] Gov[ernment] & Areopagitica are better poems than whole books of P[aradise] L[ost]" attested to his distinctive belief in the power of varied and vehement prophetic eloquence to guide a nation toward renovation and ecclesiastical amelioration.

In Chapter 3, Margaret Fuller offers an interesting example of a nineteenth-century woman versed in and significantly engaged with particular "heterodox" aspects of seventeenth-century English culture – an aspect of Fuller that has received no critical attention. She finds the ecclesiastical institutions authorizing revealed religion audaciously challenged by English writers in the seventeenth century. Her recourse is often to imaginary dialogues like those of Walter Savage Landor, which become externalized projections of her own inner conflicts, as well as coded criticisms of her society and her difficult relationship with Emerson. Her artful imaginary dialogue between the "Two Herberts" (George Herbert, the religious poet, and his elder brother Lord Herbert of Cherbury, the Cavalier, diplomat, and philosophical proponent of natural religion) allows Fuller to argue, as Lord Herbert, for worldly action combined with spiritual contemplation: "the figure we most need to see before us now [in nineteenth-century America] is not that of a saint, martyr, sage, poet, artist, or preacher, or any other whose vocation leads to a seclusion and partial use of faculty, but 'a spiritual man of the world.' " I argue that Fuller depicts Emerson as a feminized, ethereal, and reclusive George Herbert – a poet whom Emerson so greatly admired and frequently cited that he regarded the mistaken attribution of one of his own poems to George Herbert as a high compliment. Fuller, who embarked for the political turmoil of Europe shortly after writing the imaginary dialogue, casts herself as the masculine, worldly, and audacious Lord Herbert, who courageously acknowledges that "none is so profoundly lonely, none so in need of constant self-support, as he who, living in the crowd, thinks an inch aside from, or in advance of it." As a Lord Herbert figure she challenges the "partial" nature of her society, one that makes the female the repository of moral virtue and spiritual refinement (especially the nineteenth-century American "cult of true womanhood"), yet does so at the cost of her worldly engagement. Fuller, moreover, adapts Lord Herbert's controversial treatise *De Veritate* to expose the "partial" nature of a revealed religion in which God favors "one race and nation, and not another," and so challenges the prerogatives of Christianity, but also the expectations of a society to be redeemed by feminine exemplary goodness and passive suffering. Fuller's Lord Herbert effectually eliminates dependency ("prayers") upon the will of a partial God for favors ("gifts of grace"), wresting the power to gain knowledge and immediate experience of the divine ("aspirations") instead for all individuals through an inborn faculty. Fuller's recuperation of the writings and thought of this seventeenth-century epistemologist, then, allows her both to play out a genial and ultimately conciliatory critique of Emerson and to align herself with other Transcendentalists against the "orthodox" Unitarian argument for revealed religion.[39]

Chapter 4 examines Thoreau's response to the cultural dilemma of a society with a penchant to "naturalize" the myth of the United States as a simple, rustic agrarian or pastoral society. Thoreau too often encountered among his countrymen a literalism that endowed the American landscape with powers and distinctions to confer national identity, which to him verged on a reductive idolatry. Indeed, as more recent sociohistorical work has recuperated the historical moment of Massachusetts and more generally of New England, it is now increasingly acknowledged, as it seems then to have been widely known, that a golden age of pastoralism or congenial and self-sufficient agrarianism was conspicuously unavailable in the comparatively barren soil of New England. It was assumed as fact in the *Boston Quarterly* of 1840 that "Massachusetts is a State where property depends almost wholly upon the flourishing condition of her navigation, commerce, the fisheries, and especially manufactures. Agriculture, in most other parts of the country the leading interest, is here of subordinate importance, and can only advance under the favorable influence of the other branches of industry to which we have adverted."[40] In the "Economy" chapter of *Walden,* Thoreau warns, "How vigilant we are! determined not to live by faith if we can avoid it; all the day long on the alert, at night we unwillingly say our prayers and commit ourselves to uncertainties. So thoroughly and sincerely are we compelled to live, reverencing our life, and denying the possibility of change . . . [Yet] all change is a miracle to contemplate."[41] By examining the natural world mediated by the artifice of the seventeenth-century literary pastoral and georgic, Thoreau sought to prevent his audience from indulging in nostalgic longing, or from lodging significance directly in the landscape. He urged them instead to discern the limits of their illusions and to welcome change rather than guarding vigilantly against it.

Although the decades preceding the publication of *A Week on the Concord and Merrimack Rivers* and *Walden* were filled with political and social instability – the Bank War and the panic of 1837, the influx of immigrants, the Mexican War, and the divisions wrought by slavery – Thoreau still asked an uneasy audience to resist the desire to dwell in an imaginary American landscape. He did this by appropriating the techniques of pastorals and georgics written by writers caught in the turbulence of the English Revolution (Walton's *Compleat Angler,* Milton's *Lycidas,* Cowley's *Essays in Verse and Prose*), as they resisted despair, remained vigilant, and exploited these modes to express judgments – sometimes explicitly, often covertly – about the values and circumstances of their own societies. Moreover, by appropriating the stylization and theatricality of certain seventeenth-century masques (Carew's *Coelum Britannicum,* Jonson's *Masque of Queens*) and the dramatic guises of distinctive characters (Carew's Momus and Mercury, Browne's extravagant persona in *Religio Medici*), Thoreau assumed the pose of unflinching audacity and gracious magnanimity for a dispirited and conforming "democratic" America that would have preferred to imagine for itself the pose of rustic simplicity.

There was a much higher degree of engagement on the part of these four major writers with contemporary nineteenth-century American culture and with the literature and events of England in the seventeenth century than has been previously recognized. Indeed, while modern literary and cultural studies have particularly inscribed – in fact enshrined – American national boundaries in the process of defining the distinctive and valuable features of its cultural artifacts, these authors of the "American Renaissance" readily crossed our hallowed boundaries to draw the writers of seventeenth-century England into a complicity of imagination.

1

CULTURAL PREDICAMENTS AND AUTHORIAL RESPONSES

It may seem little less than an American cultural heresy to suggest that Emerson, who demanded "an original relation to the universe," turned to seventeenth-century English culture as he confronted cultural and social dilemmas in his own country. Indeed, for all the public cries for nativist literature and a national culture, for all the insistence upon indigenous productions and the throwing off of an "aristocratic" or "feudal" English culture, there appears to have been no reticence among the authors of the American Renaissance in turning to the England of this earlier age.[1] For them it was an age that seemed to possess the inexhaustible vitality of uncompromising convictions and revolutionary urgency, of nervous energy and resourcefulness. As Robert Weisbuch has already established for the Romantic and Victorian periods, nineteenth-century Americans consistently distinguished among periods of English culture. Orestes Brownson, a radical Democrat with Transcendentalist leanings, articulated what seems to have been a truism to a number of other American authors regarding pre-Restoration seventeenth-century English culture: that its moments of religious, political, and philosophical controversy produced the richest literature and the flowering of what he identified as "culture." In an 1840 article on "American Literature," Brownson pointed out the importance of heterodoxy in advancing English culture, implicitly pointing to the potential for a flourishing national culture in the United States:

> The history of the Church shows, that its literature springs up in its seasons of controversy with paganism, heresy, philosophy, or infidelity. When Orthodoxy reigns unquestioned, and all is reduced to uniformity of opinion, literature cannot flourish ... The effort to maintain Pro-

18

testantism in England, and to give it supremacy over Cathol-
icism, is marked by the masculine literature of the age of
Elizabeth. The richest portion of English literature belongs
to the seventeenth century; and what is that century in
England but an epoch of political and religious revolutions,
defeated, effected or adjourned?"[2]

Without dissociating the polemical and the literary, Brownson
suggests here that strife, controversy, and dissent enriched English cultural artifacts.

In contrast, Joseph Buckminster, a conservative Unitarian re-
nowned for his eloquent preaching, earlier suggested that the
distinguishing feature of seventeenth-century English culture was
its embrace of historical continuity through deep scholarly learning – an accomplishment he urged his contemporaries to imitate
and use in the service of tempering the impulses and passions of
American society. Indeed, in his 1809 Harvard Phi Beta Kappa
address, "On the Dangers and Duties of Men of Letters," Buckminster blamed the intellectual "diffuseness" of American culture
and the decline of American society upon revolutions ("the world
is yet covered with the wrecks of its ancient glory") and the legacy
of egalitarianism in the American and French Revolutions – the
latter having left the "foul spirit of innovation and sophistry . . .
wandering in the very groves of the Lyceum, and [it] is not yet
completely exorcised."

Although Buckminster did not tell the Harvard graduating
class that the "man of letters" should reject political engagement
(to eschew social and political engagement for secluded study was
to allow one's "learning [to] become effeminate"), he did insist
upon restricting political power to the educated and stabilizing
elite, "who are to direct our taste, mould our genius, and inspire
our emulation." In lamenting the "temporary degradation" of
Milton's learning in the writing of his polemical tracts, Buckminster suggested that learning used for political purposes was justified only if it supported tradition, the learned ruling class, and
the establishment. Vindictively he remarks upon the connection
between Milton's blindness and his revolutionary writings: "those
fine orbs were quenched in the service of a vulgar and usurping
faction"; had "they not been thus early 'closed in endless night'
. . . that master spirit of England [would] have wasted in more
praises of Cromwell and more ribaldry against Salmasius." The
Harvard graduates had, like their English ancestors of the seventeenth century, the advantage of deep scholarly learning, which,

when correctly employed, would contrast sharply with their American contemporaries' shallow education and tendency toward demagoguery: "then men of letters were willing to study, and now they are in haste to publish. That the age of scholars; this of readers and printers."[3]

As I have suggested earlier, the differences among Americans in interpreting seventeenth-century English culture tended to correlate with the political and social ideologies of the author: whereas a radical Democrat and iconoclast like Brownson applauded the operations of individual conscience and the necessity of rebellion in the earlier period, a conservative Federalist like Buckminster approved instead its restraining antiquarian and traditionalist disposition. Indeed, looking back with a conservative's critical eye on the events of the 1840s, James Russell Lowell (who earlier in his life had more liberal sympathies) registered the ferment of "radical" social reforming trends in New England by comparing them unfavorably to the volatile, radical sectarian movements of revolutionary England:

> Every possible form of intellectual and physical dyspepsia brought forth its gospel . . . Plainness of speech was carried to a pitch that would have taken away the breath of George Fox [the Quaker leader], and even swearing had its evangelists [the Ranters] . . . Not a few impecunious zealots abjured the use of money [the Diggers], . . . professing to live on the internal revenues of the spirit . . . Communities were established where everything was to be common [the Diggers] but common sense . . . The belated gift of tongues, as among the Fifth Monarchy Men, spread like a contagion.

Similarly, in an essay on Milton's *Areopagitica,* Lowell compared the tumultuous England of the 1640s to the turbulent America of the 1840s: "Those who watched the strange intellectual and ethico-political upheaval in New England fifty years ago [the 1840s] will be at no loss for parallels to these phenomena."[4]

The Introduction suggested that antebellum Americans demonstrated social and political biases in assessing the prior periods of English culture. To these may be added their religious biases, which had social as well as philosophical implications. In an article on "Locke and the Transcendentalists" (1838), written in response to an article condemning Transcendentalism in the Unitarian organ *The Christian Examiner,* Orestes Brownson characterized the literature of Locke's age (the late seventeenth and early eighteenth century) as lacking in depth and complexity and having a tendency to engage in a secular reduction of sacred truths. In so doing, he reiterated what also seems to have been a commonplace in the American (particularly Democratic) periodicals of the time: that the great check in the development of England was the Restoration, which was associated with the resumption of political orthodoxy, consensus ideology, and the significant curtailment of religious experience.

For American political and cultural liberals, and especially for a radical Democrat like Brownson who also yearned for meaningful religious experience, Locke's philosophy was one more outworking of a process of political, cultural, and religious attenuation that had begun with the restoration of the monarchy. According to these Americans, the process of attenuation had begun even before eighteenth-century English cultural artifacts had been transported to America and had been assimilated in the first three decades of the nineteenth century. After remarking that Locke "helped to make others superficial, or rather he hindered others from becoming profound," Brownson asserted that "English literature, during the period of his reign, contrasts singularly enough with that of the epoch which preceded him":

> Saving the productions of those writers who were not of his school, of those whose hearts were touched with the coals from off religion's altar, or whose souls were kindled up by the great democratic movements of the time, English Literature of the eighteenth century is, . . . after the age of childhood, or early youth, absolutely unreadable. It is as . . . unproductive as the soil of one of our immense pine barrens . . . We grow weary of it, and pass it over in order to come at the richer and profounder and more living literature of the seventeenth century, – the literature of those "giants of old," as they have been called.[5]

Of course his characterization of a "light and shallow, cold and lifeless" eighteenth-century English culture brought with it the political and cultural justification for its rejection. Its artifacts had become trivial and sterile, suitable only for the spiritually and culturally indiscriminate and immature: "a different literature is never to be looked for, where [Locke's] philosophy is the dominant one" ("Locke and the Transcendentalists," 96).

American liberals, then, ascribed to Locke's age the reduction and dissipation of a previously integrated, complex, and occult originary power that typified the English culture of the seventeenth century. Often associated with the Young Americans of the Democratic Party, liberal American nationalists claimed they could not nurture their own culture by assimilating the alien and depleted culture of eighteenth-century England. But going back to the English culture of the seventeenth century evidently gave them the hope of a recoverable "renaissance" based upon contests of authority and conflict, upon heroic exertions against perceived orthodoxies. Indeed, that period was one already hallowed by previous generations of Americans for its "democratic" impulses, religious dissension, and a perceived integration of religious, political, and cultural experience. Not simply an affirmation of English Romantic values, the valorization of conflict and complexity articulated by Brownson was also a convenient accommodation of American circumstances in a period involving church disestablishment, territorial expansion, successive waves of immigration, class conflict, and growing tensions over slavery. According to American liberals, Locke and his heirs in the eighteenth century represented not only the insistent demand for intelligibility but also the loss of authentic complexity and uncommon spiritual experience for the sake of a specious clarity: "We ask every man to make it a matter of conscience, to speak and write as intelligibly to even the undisciplined mind, as the nature of his subject will admit," Brownson insisted. "But ... the interests of science, literature, philosophy, are never to be sacrificed for the sake of adapting ourselves to the apprehension of men of no spiritual experience" ("Locke and the Transcendentalists," 97). In his comments, Brownson has in fact been diagnosing cultural, spiritual, and social dilemmas in his own society, but not in the terms of the jeremiad tradition, extolling the virtues of the early colonists and lamenting his contemporaries' departure from those standards.[6] Rather, he has expressed the cultural and political liberal's disposition to view some of America's predicaments in terms of an English legacy of spiritual and cultural attenuation and the disengagement of skills needed in dealing with conflict.

The American liberal's valorization of dissent and conflict in seventeenth-century English culture challenges some of our assumptions about antebellum American culture and national identity. It has become the accepted wisdom in American studies that antebellum authors adopted an Emersonian approach, arriving at "an intensification of consciousness so powerful that the material universe dissolves into ... a[n individual] knowledge that claims, beyond interpretation, to be simply vision."[7] However-much these authors' desired to "dissolve the material universe," and however much we, their heirs, might wish to imagine an American culture that sprang full-grown from the American soil, these authors did not in practice believe entirely in the efficacy of "consciousness" utterly to resolve conflicts in a meaningful way, nor in an American national culture developed in isolation from a kindred ancestral culture. Instead, American cultural liberals studied and enlisted the earlier English culture of the seventeenth century, acknowledged the complexities presented by the circumstances of their society, and sought to negotiate with their culture's circumstances through the exertion of individual judgment. Seventeenth-century English culture seemed to represent to them – perhaps for the last time in their ancestral culture's history – not only a powerful attempt to challenge orthodoxy but also the necessity of negotiating differences, either overtly or covertly. Brownson does characterize the seventeenth century in England as one of "revolutions, defeated, effected or *adjourned*" – adjourned presumably in order to reassess and to renegotiate circumstances and strategies.

This chapter examines in greater detail how certain antebellum cultural assumptions and expectations (the significant inheritance of post-Restoration English culture) informed American aesthetic, social, and theological values, and involved tacit commitments in the American culture that were challenged by Emerson, Fuller, Thoreau, and Melville. Each author engaged a different facet of his or her culture's assumptions, and so subsequent chapters will consider more fully how each of these American Renaissance authors distinctively and creatively drew upon seventeenth-century English culture to engage antebellum American culture. The purpose of the present chapter, then, is to establish through a series of selective illustrations the antebellum Northeastern culture's dilemmas as perceived by these authors and by a number of their contemporaries.

Melville, the American Investment in Locke's Epistemology, and the Distrust of Epistemological Opacity

In a chapter of *Democracy in America* called "Philosophical Method of the Americans," Alexis de Tocqueville observes:

[Americans] readily conclude that everything in the world may be explained, and that nothing in it transcends the limits of the understanding. Thus they fall to denying what they cannot comprehend; which leaves them but little faith for whatever is extraordinary and an almost insurmountable distaste for whatever is supernatural. As it is on their own testimony that they are accustomed to rely, they like to discern the object which engages their attention with extreme clearness; they therefore strip off as much as possible all that covers it; they rid themselves of whatever separates them from it ... This disposition of mind soon leads them to condemn forms, which they regard as useless and inconvenient veils placed between them and the truth.[8]

Taken in conjunction with Tocqueville's observation above, Captain Ahab's attempt to strip off "the pasteboard mask" in "The "Quarter-Deck" chapter of *Moby-Dick*, no less than Ishmael's attempt to make whiteness intelligible, might be read as allegories of the profound frustration with epistemological opacity within the American culture. This frustration was not confined to the Calvinists with whom Melville's sensibility – perhaps for the very reason that Calvinists emphasized divine inscrutability – is most often associated.[9] As Tocqueville's observation implies, the relentless insistence upon empirical, utilitarian lucidity exists within the broader culture, though more pervasively among the elite Whigs with whom Tocqueville most associated. In fact, John Locke's empirical requirements for the foundation of knowledge and the giving of assent – even for events deemed miraculous – so informed liberal Christian American society that Unitarian Joseph Buckminster could say to his congregation that the true believer "is indeed, like [doubting] Thomas, on recognition of the Savior, ready to exclaim, 'My Lord and my God.'"[10] In his widely read Unitarian tract "Reason and Revelation," Abiel Abbot Livermore announced in 1838 that, "so far as [God's] existence is a fact, I believe in it; so far as it is a mystery, I cannot believe in it, because I have no grounds for belief." By 1859 Unitarian Henry Whitney Bellows could assert that "the rationality of method, the freedom of inquiry ... are ... so rapidly conquering the mind of our American Christendom, that it is no longer felt to be necessary to maintain a stringent denominational [Unitarian] organization for their sake."[11] Yet these empirical prejudices also informed the broader culture as well. Orestes Brownson corroborated Tocqueville's observation about broad empirical biases by praising his countrymen in 1838 for signs that they "are beginning to lose some portion of their hereditary contempt for abstract thought, and . . . are preparing themselves to raise hereafter the study of metaphysical science to the rank it deserves" ("Locke and the Transcendentalists," 85). Robert Burton's observation about empiricists in *The Anatomy of Melancholy* (1638) seems to apply to American culture: "in spiritual things God must demonstrate all to sense, leave a pawn, or else seek some other creditor."[12]

The implication of this demand for clarity, evidentiary "proof," and certainty, I suggest, is that it tacitly committed the culture (particularly the rationalist liberal Christian culture) to knowledge claims based heavily on immediate intelligibility. This commitment left many Americans with few or no processes for negotiation with the unfamiliar – processes that would have permitted degrees of acknowledgment for the unfamiliar. The culture's insistence upon clarity and its associated wish to deny epistemologically and sometimes morally "opaque" phenomena had disturbing and unsettling implications for Melville, for whom experience, as his seafaring narratives suggest, did not always assume such readily intelligible forms. His response was to turn to what are, as we shall see in Chapter 5, the still empirical but more accommodating Anglican categories of knowledge (based on degrees of possibility or probability) and the considered, "charitable" procedures of authentication in Sir Thomas Browne's *Pseudodoxia Epidemica*.

The distrust of the epistemologically "opaque" is illustrated both in the culture's reliance upon Locke's and Scottish Common Sense philosophy's dismissal of unverifiable religious experiences and in the culture's impulse to naturalize the extraordinary or the miraculous. For example, in an article condemning the influence of German transcendentalism in America, both the Princeton Calvinists who wrote it in 1839 and Andrews Norton, the conservative leader of the Unitarians who reprinted it in 1840, concur on the limits of human knowledge and the dangers of unconfirmed and unverified religious experiences. Using Locke's epistemology as the standard, the Princeton Calvinists complained, "As there are certain limits to intellectual powers, which the immortal Locke endeavoured to ascertain, and beyond which we float in the region of midnight, so those who have forgotten these cautions have in their most original speculations only reproduced the delirium of other times."[13] Not surprisingly, the Calvinists highlighted Locke's reservations about the extent and certainty of human knowledge. Yet the passage also implies, as Unitarians might have desired, Locke's associated acknowledgment of degrees of knowledge based upon external verifications in contrast to the antinomian implications of "original speculations" and "direct knowledge of the absolute" – the delirium of other times ("Two Articles," 87–8). As Locke scholars have noted, his emphasis on verifiable religious experience was itself a response to the politically and socially destabilizing authority of knowledge gained by the unverifiable "inner light" of religious experience among sectarians in mid-seventeenth century England.

If only in their fears about these forces acting within their society, the Unitarians and Calvinists were united in warning of the dangers to both society and religion in permitting transcendental philosophy in American colleges: "our young men shall have been taught to despise the wisdom of their elders, and renounce the reverence and submission which the human intellect owes to God; . . . the Holy Bible shall be treated as the mere play ground of antic and impious fancies" ("Two Articles," 94–5). In signaling the breakdown of the established social hierarchy and religious orthodoxy, this passage reveals a fear of knowledge claims not circumscribed, as Locke required, by a consensus based on historical testimonies. Francis Bowen, another admirer of Locke and an outspoken Whig conservative, made explicit his fears of social upheaval in an 1839 article for the *North American Review:* Kantianism had initiated epistemological uncertainties, had "brought a reproach on the very name of philosophy," and had "given too good cause for regarding a system of philosophical radicalism as a mere cover for an attack on all the principles of government and social order."[14] These conservatives realized that knowledge claims – particularly of divine and moral truths – gave power within their society. Competing knowledge claims (which seemed to the conservatives opaque, audacious, and unverifiable) had the potential to enfranchise the individual in ways that might erode the hierarchies of Whig paternalism, "tradition," and even the privileged status of Christianity. More particularly, such claims had the power to destroy the checks on social and political change that epistemological consensus provided.[15]

Indeed, George Bancroft and Orestes Brownson, supporters of "democratic" (universal) intuitionism, charged the Whigs with the co-optation of Locke's epistemology to further their agenda of elite rule. In an attack against Francis Bowen, Brownson complained that Locke's paradigm of the human mind as a *tabula rasa* promoted a politics of accumulation: "It depends wholly on the external circumstances, the quality of the masters secured, whether the mind's blank sheets shall be written over with truth or falsehood. The masses . . . are surrounded with unwholesome influences, and provided with most wretched teachers. They must then be filled with evil thoughts and false notions" ("Locke and the Transcendentalists," 101).[16] Brownson observed that when pressed into the service of American Whig values – of preserving property, social hierarchy, and elite rule – Locke's premium upon the accumulation of wholesome "sensible experiences" supported paternal governance by the better-educated, more worldly, and evidently more morally upright American patricians, while the less fortunate were caught in an infinite regress of disadvantage.[17] Speaking on behalf of popular sovereignty during the last year of Andrew Jackson's administration, George Bancroft, the historian and Democratic boss of Massachusetts, responded: "I speak for the universal diffusion of human powers, not of human attainments," for "There is a *spirit in man:* not in the privileged few; not in those of us only who by the favor of Providence have been nursed in public schools: . . . not one is disenfranchised."[18] Bancroft's speeches – especially those published in Brownson's radical-leaning *Boston Quarterly Review* – employed a more decidedly radical Democratic rhetoric than the more moderate language of his own popular *History of the United States* (Boston, 1837). Yet strains of this more radical egalitarianism (based on his Transcendentalist sympathies) are threaded through his conservative myth-making efforts in his *History of the United States.*[19]

In an extended comparison favoring Quakers George Fox and William Penn over John Locke in his *History,* Bancroft engaged in an act of historical synchronism, eliding the differences between Quaker supernatural illumination of the Holy Spirit and Transcendentalist universal (innate) intuitionism, co-opting Quaker history to show that Locke's epistemological precautions had been unnecessary.[20] In a letter to Emerson, Bancroft stated his agenda: "the public at large [might] start at the truth" after reading his *History,* but "if Locke did actually embody his philosophy, political and moral, in our American Constitution . . . and if the Quakers were wiser than he, why not say that too? Do you remember Locke's chapter on enthusiasm [in *The Essay on Human Understanding*]? Pennsylvania is the practical refutation of his argument."[21] Like Brownson, Bancroft identified with the egalitarian spiritism and emphasis on individual conscience of such seventeenth- and eighteenth-century English (and American) dissenting sectarians as the Quakers. Bancroft in fact devoted a significant share of chapter 16 (volume 2) of his *History* to praise of the Quakers: "almost for the first time in the history of the world, a plebeian sect proceeded to the complete enfranchisement of the mind."[22] Neither Brownson nor Bancroft had much interest in the empirical (or skeptical) strain represented by Locke's epistemology.

By subscribing to such an epistemology as Locke's, however, Whigs like Andrews Norton and Francis Bowen committed themselves to less "certain" foundations for belief, knowledge, morality, and political policy than they otherwise might have wished. The absence of certainty in Locke's theory of knowledge (which disallowed innate ideas) did not go unexploited by Democrats and Transcendentalists: Bancroft intimated in his *History* that Locke's epistemology and moral philosophy in the *Essay Concerning Human Understanding* – relying on opinion and probability (Book IV) and pain and pleasure (II.20.2 and II.21.42) and in harmony with the artifice and impermanence of his political contractualism – offered only the most precarious and uncertain foundation for moral obligation, political motive, or political union.[23] Locke's epistemology, as Bancroft understood it, undermined *both* private conscience and tradition as reliable guides: "To Locke conscience is nothing else than our own opinion of our own actions," and "the system of Locke lends itself to contending factions of the most opposite interests and purposes" (*History*, 2:377). Brownson similarly wondered, "if common sense, the universal beliefs of mankind, the instinctive beliefs of Humanity, the teachings of the spontaneous reason, be discredited, as they must be by a disciple of Locke, we ask, how is it possible to establish the certainty of any thing whatever?" ("Locke and the Transcendentalists," 106).[24]

The Unitarian Whigs' equal desire for "certainty" required that they revise the skeptical aspects of Locke's epistemology by turning to Scottish Common Sense philosophy for both its enhanced confidence in sensory data and for its insistence upon a "common sense," an innate (and confident) moral faculty in the structure of the human mind. Their recourse to the notion of an innate common sense reveals, then, as did the Transcendentalists' advocacy of "spontaneous reason," a similar desire to secure their beliefs and values against the liabilities of fallibility, skepticism, and moral relativism to which Locke's epistemology was heir.[25] Indeed, Whigs sought to shore up their source of authority as well by locating it in "tradition" and the Constitution rather than in potentially disruptive processes based on mere "opinions" and renewable Lockean social contracts. Whereas the Whig Party, an anonymous Whig defender wrote in 1848, regarded "government as unchangeable except by a solemn decision of the nation in convention," the other party treated it "as inferior in authority to the public opinion of a day ... Ultra Democratic doctrine ... indulges men in a perpetual revolution, cutting off the past from the present, and the present from the future."[26] Playing satirically upon the Whigs' frequent recourse to the U.S. Constitution, Brownson, referring to the French Revolution, warned of the dangerous consequences of Enlightenment social contracts not based upon an "inherent" and "democratic" moral rectitude and spiritual illumination:

> "Locke ... deduces government from Noah and Adam, and announces its end to be the security of property." His philosophy, if it decide in favor of freedom, can do it only on the ground of some contract, express or implied, made between the people and their rulers ... Its Magna Charta is preserved in the archives of state, not engraven on the heart, and preserved in the very constitution of man. Hence, the notion of a *Contrât Sociale* so famous in French revolutionary history.[27]

Yet Locke's evidentialist demands modified by the Scottish Common Sense philosophy's notion of an "innate sense" tacitly committed the American culture to give assent to the evidence and testimonies – even of miracles, or "God's seal" – based upon what was already familiar. That is, this combination of philosophies committed Americans to a process based to a significant extent upon an intuitive identification, *a congruence of the object with a prior understanding in the subject*. No less than the Transcendentalists, Unitarians increasingly questioned whether "To a consistent follower of Locke's philosophy," as Brownson asked,

> we can ... have in ourselves no power of apprehending religious truth, of apprehending the glory of God, the divinity of Christianity, the binding nature of Duty; for all these are neither operations of our own mind, nor objects recognisable by the senses ... But suppose, as every disciple of Locke must suppose, that we have no *a priori* knowledge of God's seal, that we have never seen it, and have in our possession no fac-simile of it, how are we to recognise it when presented? ("Norton on the Evidences," 106–7)

In the *Essay Concerning Human Understanding* and the *Reasonableness of Christianity,* Locke required a series of certifying circumstances and qualifications to determine the authenticity of miracles. But he did not require that validation come entirely from immediate "recognition" based on an inward affinity. That revision was shared by Transcendentalists, and, I suggest, the Unitarians.

Clearly the Whig Unitarians' desire to fortify Christian revelation against the effects of Continental hermeneutical practices, Transcendental intuitionism, and Deist "infidelity" drove them to Locke's evidentialist discourse, arguing from his *Essay* and his *Reasonableness of Christianity* that miracles provided "certain," empirical certifications of the authenticity of revelation, since presumably only God could perform miracles.[28] "There can be no intuition, no direct perception, of the truth of Christianity, no metaphysical certainty," insisted Andrews Norton. Instead, one must, with the exception of revelations validated by miracles, rely on "probabilities alone."[29] But however much Norton insisted upon the miraculous aspect of Christianity, his urgency derived from the need to secure a guarantee of the bona fides of Christian revelation in a Lockean epistemology otherwise entirely constituted by and reliant upon "probabilities alone." Norton's acknowledgment of the limits of postlapsarian human reason compelled him to seek the evidence of miracles "above human reason." But in adopting Locke's evidentialist and empiricist discourse to defend the biblical miracles, Norton in fact employs the vocabulary of both the German Higher Critics and those "infidels" promoting natural religion, and cedes nearly as much ground as he gains.[30] Antebellum historian Richard Hildreth astutely observed that Norton had "undertaken to strip Religion of the transcendental and supernatural character which it has ever borne; to reduce it to the rank of a natural, historical science": "you make the truths of Religion, a mere civil question of the credibility of witnesses."[31]

And yet Unitarians themselves were not comfortable with the notion that the evidence of epistemologically opaque, historical miracles provided the guarantee of Christianity's authenticity.[32] Fearing that the desire to perceive nature's uniform phenomena as registers of spirit could result in deformations of the spirit, Norton issued the staunchest exhortation to recognize miracles as wholly "other." Yet he also acknowledged the human disposition – not unlike Captain Ahab's – to see the supernatural as intelligibly mediated and informed by some meaningful relation to one's self: "Man, indeed, in his low estate, loves the supernatural; but ... as ... belonging to some form of faith more connected with this world than the future; or regarded as the operation of limited beings, presenting a semblance of human nature, on whom man can react in his turn" ("Infidelity," p. 19). By contrast, the complete otherness of God as exhibited in an "un-questionable miracle . . . breaking through the secondary agency, behind which the Deity ordinarily veils himself," would more than likely inspire "awe, [and an] almost appalling feeling," and "from the revulsion of feeling, that must take place . . . it is natural that many should shrink, and endeavour to escape from the view" ("Infidelity," pp. 20–1). Norton's observations seem to be corrob-orated by the practitioners of the visionary mode in literature in nineteenth-century America. According to David Reynolds's study of faith in fiction, those who wrote in this mode applied Lockean sensationalism and Scottish Common Sense to "divest faith of its enigmatic, metaphysical aspects," shifting piety "away from dangerous metaphysical realms" and instead directing it toward the "palpable" and "joyfully real," those vivid and sentimentalized depictions of angelic visitations.[33]

Within the liberal Christian culture, the need to confer authen-ticity by recourse to a supernatural phenomenon appears to have been at odds with the intense desire for a rational, thoroughly in-telligible religion, one corresponding to the pious intimations of the individual. In fact, while insisting upon the "awe" and "mys-tery" of divine truths, Unitarians, using Locke's *Reasonableness of Christianity*, tended to curtail the mysterious and miraculous by re-stricting the context for validating authentic miracles: they must have been performed by an agent whose life was deemed holy, mo-tives pure, and whose espoused revelations conformed with the morality and spiritual expectations of the Christian religion. To many Unitarians a miracle in the historical past seems to have been little more than an event that confirmed the conscience's beliefs and intimations. Even the Lockean Unitarian Francis Bowen comes close to this in his comment, "The law written on the heart expounds the law graven on tables of stone."[34]

And so Emerson's antipathy toward the miraculous in his infa-mous Divinity School "Address" could actually be seen as a length-ened shadow of Unitarian rationalist thinking: for him, as for many Unitarians, what was truly divine and "miraculous" was self-reflexive – it was (perceptually) anticipated in, and intelligible to, the individual.[35] While he imputed to Unitarians a grotesque narrowness in their theology, as his own Blakean proverb "All is miracle, & the mind revolts at representations of 2 kinds of miracle" suggests, he tellingly *shared* with the broader culture an abhorrence of that which neither corresponds to the familiar natural world nor to the self.[36] His iconoclastic equation of "mira-cle" with "monster" ("But the word Miracle, as pronounced by

Christian churches, gives a false impression; it is Monster") reiterated the Reformation problem of distorted mediations of divine
truths: "the [iconic] word Miracle . . . gives a false impression" of
spirit. It also reveals Emerson's intensification of a desire already
within his culture to naturalize that which constitutes an adequate expression of divine truth. "The miraculous is the measure
of our alienation from him [God]," noted Sampson Reed several
years earlier.[37]

In his sermon "Likeness to God" (1828), William Ellery Channing similarly insisted that "The divine attributes are first developed in ourselves, and thence transferred to our Creator. The
idea of God, sublime and awful as it is, is *the idea of our own
spiritual nature, purified and enlarged to infinity* . . . God, then, does
not sustain a figurative resemblance to man. It is the resemblance of
a parent to a child, the likeness of a kindred nature" (my emphasis).[38] Here Channing clearly asserted a resemblance between
man and God that is not the expression of the doctrine of accommodation to human understanding. In his essay on Milton's *De
Doctrina Christiana* (1826), Channing had suggested that during
the infancy of Christianity, "religion was administered with a wise
and merciful conformity to the capacities of its recipients," but
with "the progress of intelligence, and the developement [sic] of
the moral faculties, Christianity is freeing itself, and ought to be
freed, from the local, temporary, and accidental associations of
its childhood"; that is, the doctrine of accommodation (based on
figuration and analogy) would no longer be necessary.[39] In his
sermon "Likeness to God," then, the relationship between man
and God was one of synecdochic identification, based on the
emanation of divine attributes to man.[40] Even if Emerson disa-
vowed the "personation" of God as too exclusive and trivializing,
the method for acquiring certainty of the evidence of spiritual
experience was through anthropomorphic identity – assimilation
to human feeling and perception, however much enhanced. Emphasizing identification as the basis of verification, Emerson's
version in one of his own Unitarian sermons explicitly suggested
an assimilation to God, but implied a process of understanding
based on the human as the touchstone: with regard to "the manner of spiritual discernment[,] . . . The whole secret is in one
word, *Likeness*. The way to see a body is to draw near it with the
eye. The way to perceive a spirit is *to become like it. What is unlike
us, we cannot perceive*" (sermon no. 120).[41] The tension here paradoxically propels the participant both toward reconciliation with

the otherness of spirit and away from it, toward the corporeal and the self-referring. The balance is, however, not quite sustainable, for the analogy mediating this act of "spiritual discernment" valorizes human sensory powers and assumes, finally, an act of anthropomorphic identification.

Although Unitarians and Transcendentalists diverged on the issue of certain and probable knowledge, the recent revisionist assessments of Lawrence Buell, Wesley T. Mott, and Daniel Walker Howe more closely align Unitarianism with Transcendentalism, suggesting that both attempted to diminish the discrepancies between external evidence (historical miracles) and internal evidence (scriptural testimonies, as well as personal intuition).[42] The implication in each instance is to diminish the need and usefulness of the miraculous, and this may be interpreted as an antipathy within the culture toward epistemological opacity and anomaly. American Unitarians and Transcendentalists tended to employ synecdoche in relating to the holy as a way of distancing themselves from orthodox Calvinist concepts of grace and revelation with all their implications of God's alien qualities and arbitrary sovereignty. Yet even the Calvinists, Sydney Ahlstrom has shown, were increasingly adopting a rationalist discourse as a defensive measure.

Moreover, recent studies revising Perry Miller's emphasis on the internal forces working within American theology have shown that "the 'liberalization' of Calvinist orthodoxy in New England was promoted by the importation of Latitudinarian Anglicanism such as was embodied in the sermons of Tillotson," as well as by the theology and philosophy of Locke. In the eighteenth century, third-generation Harvard ministers encouraged a vogue (associated with the cosmopolitan, Anglo-American ruling elite) for Anglican learning, culture, and religious toleration in opposition to the stern theology and Calvinist dogmatism of the New England dissenting tradition.[43] According to O. B. Frothingham's retrospective account of his nineteenth-century contemporaries, many Whig Unitarian divines were "more familiar with Tillotson than Cudworth." That is, they shared a greater esteem for the rational, moral, and practical aspects of English Protestantism than for the mystical aspects of seventeenth-century Cambridge Platonists.[44] A journal like the Harvard-based *American Monthly Review* tended to review new American editions of the lives of such Latitudinarians as Sir Matthew Hale, offering extracts and commending the religious values espoused as "an example not of romantic but of practicable virtue and religion.[45] In a society drawn to increasingly secular, moral, well-balanced rationalist apologetics, both Unitarians and Transcendentalists revealed a desire to rehabilitate the anomalous, to naturalize the miraculous – except as an authority of last resort in the polemics against Deism and atheism.[46] If, as Jonathan Bishop has commented, "Miracles and otherness stand or fall together," both Transcendentalist and Unitarian might have wished these extraordinary sanctities a brisk farewell.[47]

Evert Duyckinck, editor of the *Literary World* (and a mentor of Herman Melville), participated in many respects in his culture's conservative ideology supported by a Lockean epistemology – despite his Democratic affiliations with the Young Americans involved in promoting a national literature.[48] Duyckinck in fact retreated from the more subversive implications of Melville's art. While he recognized the more speculative aspects of Melville's fiction and identified elements of Sir Thomas Browne's reflections and style in Melville's writings, Duyckinck exhibited his own High Church Episcopalian and socially conservative prejudices both in his interpretation of Browne and in his reviews of Melville's writings. Like other critics, Duyckinck linked *Mardi* and *Moby-Dick* to several seventeenth-century Anglican texts: Browne's *Religio Medici* and *Pseudodoxia Epidemica;* Jeremy Taylor's treatise *Ductor Dubitantium* (Duyckinck called *Moby-Dick* "a folio Ductor Dubitantium"); and Robert Burton's *Anatomy of Melancholy.*[49] Whigs admired these texts as representatives of a beloved English tradition that they also regarded as America's inherited tradition. Each of these texts, however, engaged in searching inquiries that, while acknowledging the power of human reason, carefully circumscribed its efficacy. Like many Whigs, Duyckinck consistently misconstrued the potentially unsettling rationalist inquiries and skeptical tendencies in the very seventeenth-century "pious" and "quaint" "old masters" he himself most admired and encouraged Melville to read, and which, in Melville's hands, turned into yet another assault on Locke's epistemology.

According to contemporary eulogies by Samuel Osgood and William Allen Butler, Evert Duyckinck "clung closely to the old English standards of culture," "was something of a partizan in his conservatism among the church champions of the New York Review," "tried to bring the cultured side of the English church to match and also to modify Puritan scholarship," and "As early as 1836 . . . was the champion of the old English literature ["The Old Prose Writers"] against the new radicalism."[50] Indeed, Duyckinck, a devout Episcopalian (no less than his brother George, an Episcopalian clergyman who co-edited the *Literary World*) read seventeenth-century Anglican texts by Sir Thomas Browne, Jeremy Taylor, and George Herbert with clearly defined religious and ideological biases.[51] It was surely with an ideological agenda – and a glancing blow to those "Apostles of the Newness" in Concord – that Duyckinck in 1838 prefaced his article on George Herbert's poetry for the *New York Review* with a paean to "the Past." Whereas Emerson had appropriated George Herbert's poem "Man" (shorn of its concluding stanza expressing obedience to God) to prophesy the unbounded and unmediated "Prospects" of man once institutions have been dissolved in the wake of nature, Duyckinck reinscribed Herbert in the service of his – and Herbert's – venerable institution, the English church (in America, the Episcopal church). In his article on Herbert's poetry, Duyckinck quoted all of Herbert's poem "The British Church," noting, "How Herbert loved the Church with an affection based not on indiscriminate zeal, but well-grounded judgment, may be read in these stanzas, which point to the golden mean of Christianity in the *reasonable* service at our altar."[52] For Duyckinck, Herbert's Anglican religion – clearly including his own Episcopal church ("our altar") – involved epistemological and ideological choices, ones associated with serene rational assent to the "reasonable service" linking past with present in the continuity of outward forms of an historical church – in Osgood's words, the "hallowed faith and firm institutions which Duyckinck loved."[53]

Not surprisingly, the Duyckinck brothers insisted upon dissociating their beloved, irenic Sir Thomas Browne from *Mardi*'s speculative volatility and self-conscious inventiveness. In their *Cyclopedia of American Literature* (1855), their entry for Melville evinced that separation: "In the first half of the book there are some of the author's best descriptions, wrought up with the fanciful associations from the quaint philosophy and other reading in the volumes of Sir Thomas Browne, and such worthies, upon whose pages . . . the author had thrown himself with eager avidity," but in the latter section of the book, "he wanders without chart or compass in the wildest regions of doubt and scepticism." Nor is it surprising that Evert Duyckinck was particularly troubled, as he read Melville's fiction, by what he considered Melville's "rash daring in speculation" and Ishmael's "extravagant daring speculation": "this piratical running down of creeds and opinions," noted Duyckinck, "is, we will not say dangerous in such cases, for there are various forces at work to meet more powerful onslaught, but it is out of place and uncomfortable."[54] While granting a "dramatic" dimension to Ishmael's behavior in his critical review of *Moby-Dick,* Duyckinck's figurative language ("piratical running down") condemned as exotic and lawless Ishmael's renegade activities, his assault on the "sacred associations of life." Duyckinck's suspicions – that Ishmael's pernicious habits of speculation were associated with "the conceited indifferentism of Emerson, or the run-a-muck style of Carlyle" – demonized, as we have seen, the same agents as did Whig conservatives.[55] Writing in 1848 for *the American Whig Review,* Joseph Hartwell Barrett similarly condemned Transcendentalist speculation while distinguishing it from Browne's speculations. Browne, he said, though "of a temper naturally visionary," "even with all [his] wild vagaries – his speculations upon the final cause of eclipses, and his wanton reveries over the oracles of old – he never once overstepped . . . the limits prescribed by his education and the laws." Even had Browne's "mind but swung aloof from these moorings, we might have looked for extravagances, less wild and antic, perhaps, than we are doomed to witness among our transcendental *savans.*"[56]

While condemning Transcendentalist speculation, Duyckinck pointed admiringly in his review of *Moby-Dick* to Melville's "humorous touches," "quaint suggestion," and "picturesque" descriptions of the whale fishery – presumably referring to those fabulous and arcane myths, those "monstrous" and "less erroneous pictures of whales" documented by F. O. Matthiessen and others as Melville's debt to Sir Thomas Browne's *Pseudodoxia Epidemica, or Vulgar Errors.*[57] Earlier, too, during the final stages of Melville's composition of *Mardi,* Duyckinck wrote to his brother, "I visited [a ship] with Melville, another representative of the old Arminius. Melville reads old Books. He has borrowed Sir Thomas Browne of me and says finely of the speculations of the *Religio Medici* that Browne is a kind of 'crack'd Archangel.' Was ever any thing of this sort said before by a sailor?" For Duyckinck, Melville's interest in reading these "old books" became associated with his being, like Evert and his brother George, "another representative of the old Arminius" – a turn of phrase alluding to Melville's similar Dutch genealogy and praising, in the words of Duyckinck's own eulogist, Osgood, the "[Dutch] Remonstrant spirit" of "civic wisdom" and "generous theology," as distinguished from "their adversaries who triumphed at the synod of Dort," the stern Dutch Reformed Calvinist predestinarians from whom Melville actually descended. Duyckinck, who made a pilgrimage to the monument to Grotius in Delft, was himself described by his eulogist as "a cross between Hugo Grotius and Jeremy Taylor" – "the remonstrant side of the old Dutch mind in alliance with the tolerant and comprehensive spirit of the English Church."[58] And so Duyckinck benevolently envisioned Melville as the enlightened and urbane comrade who eschewed Calvinist obscurantism and dogmatism in favor of educated, rational inquiry and social amelioration through the cultivation of letters.

Thus Duyckinck's mixed responses to Melville's two most Brownean novels (*Mardi* and *Moby-Dick*) reflect his distinctly nineteenth-century American anxieties: he wished to have a "Democratic" native literature, at once as dynamic and daunting as the American landscape and yet as Whiggishly poised, self-possessed, and "cultivated" as any traditional and socially stabilizing literature. It seems that the "Whiggish" High Church Episcopalian scholars and litterateurs of the *New York Review* and the *Literary World* did enlist their old English authors, with whom they identified, as champions of a cautiously circumscribed ideology. It was one responding, not unlike the American followers of Locke, to the bulwarks of Anglican stability – reasonableness, tradition, human consensus, and, to a lesser extent, rituals, "the Hedge that fence the Substance of Religion"[59] – rather than to the epistemological uncertainties and opacities (explored so avidly by Browne in *Pseudodoxia Epidemica*) that rendered those buttresses necessary.

The culture's apparent distrust of the unfamiliar and its insistence on immediate intelligibility, then, posed the problem of how to come to terms with the unknown, the marvelous, the unfamiliar, that which fits no readily available epistemological category. The blighted faculty of reason acknowledged by the Calvinists could offer Melville no assistance. Untested and glibly confident Transcendentalism was worthy of mockery and contempt, as he demonstrated in "The Mast-Head" chapter of *Moby-Dick*. Moreover, the facile confidence that Unitarians and Episcopalians placed in reason and its analogies based on the benevolent individual seemed insufficient to the task of explaining the "opaque" or the terrific – a task they seemed clearly unwilling to engage. Thus it was, as we shall see in Chapter 5, to Sir Thomas Browne's encyclopedia of the marvelous, *Pseudodoxia Epidemica, or Vulgar Errors*, that Melville turned to find a mind congenial to the improbable, yet probing and systematic enough to reconfigure categories of knowledge and reclaim the degrees of probability that Locke's heirs canceled in their pursuit of certainty and predictability.

The Aesthetics of Lucidity

In a celebration of Milton's prose writings in 1826, William Ellery Channing, the eloquent and revered Boston Unitarian minister who bridged Unitarianism and Transcendentalism, acknowledged a defect in American aesthetic tastes: "To be universally intelligible is not the highest merit . . . We must not expect in the ocean the transparency of the calm inland stream . . . Impose upon it no strict laws . . . Let it speak in its own language . . . If not understood and relished now, let it . . . utter oracles which futurity will expound." [60] Channing's response to Milton was partially prompted by the same concerns about the superficiality of American education, absence of a national literature, and tendency on the part of American readers toward complacency ("a great mind cannot . . . shrink itself to the grasp of common passive readers" [21]) that we saw in Joseph Buckminster when he praised the scholarly depth of learning in seventeenth-century English culture. Channing observed disparagingly that "There are writings which are clear through their shallowness," but what Americans need, he argued, is not ease and clarity but rather "to have our faculties tasked by master spirits" (22). And yet Channing's particular articulation of what was desirable in the "profundity" of Milton's prose also set him apart from the prevailing rhetorical and belletristic practices at American universities and in many American periodicals. Channing insisted, "Let such writers as Addison . . . 'bring down philosophy from heaven to earth.' But let inspired genius fulfil its higher function of lifting the prepared mind from earth to heaven" (22). "In the moment of inspiration," he explained, "[the 'full mind'] will often pour forth ['thick-coming thoughts and images'] in a splendid confusion, *dazzling to common readers, but kindling to congenial spirits*" (21–2; my emphasis). Here Channing echoed Milton's own words in *Areopagitica* prophesying the greatness of the English nation in the vanguard of the ongoing spiritual and political reformation ("Methinks I see her as an eagle muing [moulting] her mighty youth, and *kindling her undazzled eyes at the full midday beam;* purging and unscaling her long-abused sight at the fountain itself of heavenly radiance" [my emphasis]). Channing's allusion suggests that *Areopagitica* was a favorite with Americans: we have already seen in the Introduction that J. Sullivan Cox employed it to dignify the Democratic agenda of Manifest Destiny. Here Channing implicitly associated the common American reader with the tradition-bound clerics and censoring Parliamentarians disparaged by Milton ("timorous and flocking birds . . . amazed at what she means"). These Channing contrasted with those whose "prepared mind" would allow them to respond to the inspired genius with true vision. Channing intimates that America's demand for "universal intelligibility" indicated the failure of a willingness to be tried and tested. But he also signals, as Emerson seems to have understood, an inspired speech understood by certain readers, while others must be content to be "dazzled."

Contrasting with the literary values Channing admired were the prevailing values promoted in the first decade of the nineteenth century by the *Monthly Anthology, and Boston Review* (at one time edited by Emerson's father). Its writers and editors promoted an aesthetics of lucidity, rationality, morality, and conservative social consensus. Like other periodicals, it attempted to shape American aesthetic judgments based on Locke's epistemology, Scottish Common Sense philosophy, and that model of lucidity, Joseph Addison's prose style.[61] *The Christian Examiner,* the *North American Review,* and the *American Whig Review* took up the cause through the middle of the century. The *Monthly Anthology,* especially, encouraged deference to eighteenth-century English models rather than to "provincial" American writers: "were we to adopt the opinions of these gentlemen [nationalists], we might proudly proclaim that [Americans] can write better verses than Pope, and more elegant essays than Addison."[62] Together with John Quincy Adams's *Lectures on Rhetoric and Oratory,* Hugh Blair's *Lectures on Rhetoric and Belles-Lettres,* an eighteenth-century Scottish compendium of rhetorical lectures, were among the most influential rhetorical texts at Harvard and other American universities. Blair's *Lectures* was, moreover, largely prescriptive and neoclassical in its values, acknowledging emotional affect to some extent, but largely urging "refinement," "correctness," "strict unity," and "simple clarity." Indeed, like other writings of the Queen Anne period so esteemed by many conservatives, a reviewer commented, "Power was not its characteristic. It was comparatively, timid and constrained, not free and bold." The same reviewer, citing an article from the *Edinburgh Review,* confirmed that writers of that period "are sagacious, no doubt, neat, clear, and reasonable, but for the most part cool, timid, and superficial."[63]

"Blairing-it," as it was called, required an Addisonian perspicuity of language and a style that "frees us from all fatigue of searching for [the author's] meaning." Recent rhetoricians have suggested that in Blair's *Rhetoric* "political discourse is given far less attention than literary issues," and that Blair's approach was essentially "apolitical" or at most espoused "moderation."[64] But this modern taxonomic separation of the literary and political into discrete rhetorical categories works against nineteenth-century American rhetorical practice.[65] As I have suggested about Locke's epistemology in America, Blair's aesthetic values took on decidedly social and political implications and had embedded within them particular sociopolitical assumptions and behavioral directives, especially when imported to and promulgated in America by a Unitarian "class of educated gentlemen, who substituting polite letters for theology . . . set the tone for society and regulate[d] public tastes."[66]

When we look closely at the style deemed the "safest" for emulation, we can infer from Blair's adjectives that "smoothness [rather] than strength," "limpid[ity]" rather than "obscurity," "simplicity [rather] than affectation," and "modesty and politeness" rather than boldness meant that self-discipline and social consensus within an unambiguously structured and stable society was the "natural" order.[67] "Obscurity" seemed often to signify "obfuscation" rather than, as Channing suggested of Milton's prose, "profundity." The charge of "obscurity" entailed the frustration of communitarian goals and the obstructing of precise social evaluation. Blair forbade writers from attempting certain innovations of style, particularly the coining of new words, "except by such, whose established reputation gives them some degree of dictatorial power over Language" (1:188). While this language suggested a masterly skill on the part of that author, it also permitted – particularly in the new context of America – the university-educated critics to establish the writers' reputations, and determine which among them would have this "dictatorial power over Language." As Albert von Frank has suggested, the exaggerated emphasis on "correctness" evinced by some Americans may have been a compensation for anxieties about their country's provincialism.[68] Yet the enforcers of a normative grammar, vocabulary, and style – in fact, a canon of literature – also had the authority and the means to reinforce and perpetuate the kinds of tastes and styles that would in turn perpetuate their desired values of elite rule and moral guidance of the nation.[69] Indeed, the abundance of periodicals in antebellum America attested to the desire to guide values and tastes: "It has been often remarked," noted Unitarian Andrews Norton for the conservative *Monthly Anthology*, "that periodical publications more than any other, contribute toward forming the manners of a people . . . The papers of Addison, as Dr. Johnson informs us, added not a little to the civility of England."[70]

Nor were such aesthetic values as offered in Blair's *Rhetoric* confined to New England universities. In 1849 the New York-based *American Whig Review* (founded by Wiley & Putnam) offered its audience a medley of extracts from Cicero, Quintilian, and Blair's *Rhetoric* under the title "The Principles of Rhetoric."[71] Readers were instructed that an orator must obey the rules of simplicity; he must use "such words as are best calculated to express our ideas most clearly" (602); under the category of "correctness of language," "No useless or ambiguous words should be permitted" (603). "The rules of grammar should be particularly observed"; "nor should the orator labor, by an affected style and ridiculous contortions, to utter sentences which are unnatural" (603). And in the previous year, in the article on Sir Thomas Browne for the *Whig Review,* Joseph Hartwell Barrett, had defended Browne, not only, as we saw, exculpating him from the charge of speculative wildness, but also, on the aesthetic level, defending his "peculiar" style ("the topic of much animadversion") by claiming that Browne never willfully transgressed the bounds of politeness and decorum. Although "The obscurity of many of his expressions . . . are features of his style that grow . . . out of his own peculiar nature" ("a reserved habit, manifestly, and a covert manner of thinking"), yet "there is nothing in his writings like a studied contempt of conventional forms, or an attachment to oddity for its own sake." The assumed values that are the standard of good writing are articulated entirely in terms informed by the values of social community and complaisance:

> That a writer should avoid any eccentricities of manner, in so far as it is possible, is a no less evident requisite to good standing in letters than to a favorable reception in society. Egotism of manner as well as of speech – and much more any degree of indifference to the sentiments and feelings of those about us that exceeds this – amounts to positive impoliteness, and betrays the want of a gentle disposition and breeding. (20)

We are reminded here of Evert Duyckinck's charge that Ishmael assaulted the "sacred associations of life" and perhaps exhibited the "conceited indifferentism of Emerson." Even in Browne's autobiographical account of his religious faith, Barrett continued, if "he is certainly chargeable with some degree of egotism [particularly in *Religio Medici*], we cannot attribute it to him as a predominating characteristic – softened and shadowed as it is, by a respectful deference to the opinion of others, and a mild and habitual charity."[72] Chapter 4 demonstrates that Thoreau exploited Browne's narrative persona in *Religio Medici* for exactly the extravagance that this reviewer disavows.

Even less tolerant of "obscurity of . . . expression" or stylistic extravagance, a reviewer writing in 1853 on "Our Young Authors" protested Melville's appropriation of Browne's style in *Mardi*. A notorious bohemian, but one capable of writing to suit the politically conservative audience of the New York-based *Putnam's Monthly,* Fitz-James O'Brien seemed annoyed by the exaggeration of Browne's aureate style in Melville's productions: "Of course, we give Mr. Melville every credit for his deliberate plagiarisms of old Sir Thomas Browne's gorgeous and metaphorical manner. Affectation upon affectation is scattered recklessly through its pages. Wild similes, cloudy philosophy, all things turned topsy-turvy, until we seem to feel all earth melting away from beneath our feet, and nothing but Mardi remaining."[73] After passing through the rarefied and alien medium of Browne's "magnificent diction," Melville's metaphorical rhapsodies failed to describe experiences correspondingly refined, and subtle in their sublimity rather than in their apparent incoherence. Browne has failed to civilize Melville. Instead, Melville exploited Browne's "gorgeous and metaphorical manner" and "deep meaning" but rendered them uncivilized – "reckless," "wild similes" and "cloudy philosophy." O'Brien in fact employed the language of Locke and his heirs' empirical assumptions of external referentiality and predictability – that is, knowledge "identical with verifiability or with likelihood based on past observation."[74] Although in *Moby-Dick* "There was so much truth," O'Brien complained, in an 1857 review entitled "Our Authors and Authorship," that "we were excessively vexed with him for darkening his counsel by words which we could not but esteem to be words without knowledge."[75] All the narrative's oddities, anomalies, supernatural occurrences and speculations, when subjected to the criteria of the senses and increasingly to the requirements of the social, the probable, and the predictable, were rendered "vague" and "fantastic." Melville himself, O'Brien feared, may have "plunged headlong into the vasty void of the obscure, the oracular, and the incomprehensible" ("Our Authors and Authorship," 389). O'Brien insisted that Melville is "a man born to create, who resolves to anatomize; a man born to see, who insists upon speculating" ("Our Authors and Authorship," 389 – 90). The language he employed to describe Melville's *Mardi* and *Moby-Dick* highlighted his annoyance with Melville's paradoxical tendencies both to court reason ("dissect and divide") and to subvert rational apprehension ("cauterize and confound," "amaze and electrify").[76]

O'Brien voiced the conservative Whig aesthetic preference for lucidity in the service of social and moral amelioration.[77] As a reviewer for *Putnam's Monthly*, O'Brien was expected to encourage new American writers and national literary efforts, yet he was also expected to applaud the more secularized and masculinized domain, the much-diminished scale – "the clearness of narrative . . . and the simplicity of style" – of *Typee* and the "clear, wholesome satire, and . . . manly style" of *White-Jacket*. It seems that O'Brien's earlier prescription in his review of *Mardi* – "Let him diet himself for a year or two on Addison, and avoid Sir Thomas Browne, and there is little doubt but that he will make a notch on the American Pine ("Our Young Authors," 164) – was not exclusively a Whig stylistic prescription for the "pellucid prose" of Addison, Steele, or Irving. In the later assessment of Melville's writings in *Putnam's Monthly*, he restated his recommendation: "We desire him to give up metaphysics and take to nature and the study of mankind" ("Our Authors and Authorship," 391).

Emerson, whose own style would be increasingly characterized by his contemporaries as "oracular," "obscure," "indistinct," and resembling parables, urged in an early lecture that the student be "entirely wean[ed] from traditionary judgment," pleading, "will you not save him wholly that barren season of discipline which young men spend with the Aikens and Ketts and Drakes and Blairs acquiring the false doctrine that there is something arbitrary or conventional in letters?[78] As we shall see in more detail in Chapter 2, Emerson saw in Milton's apocalyptic prose of the 1640s a model of how prophetic discourse might with spiritual justification be used to renounce his culture's demand for a narrowly and humanly defined "decorum." He also saw how he might negotiate his culture's intrusive expectation of lucidity: veiled prophetic discourse could protect the sacred from those who would desecrate it and require exertion from those who would arrive at its true meaning. Indeed, Emerson's expectation for the intelligibility of sacral language was very different from that of the Harvard Unitarian professor of rhetoric who had assigned Hugh Blair's *Rhetoric* to him. That professor, Sidney Willard, wrote a review in 1832 of the newly reprinted American edition of Locke's posthumous *A Paraphrase and Notes on the Epistles of St. Paul* (1705) that offered Locke's procedure – using the more lucid passages of the Epistles as exegetical keys to the more obscure – as a model that "may be applied by every reader of the Epistles himself." Using Locke's own words, Willard alerted each reader to the necessity of exercising individual judgment in scriptural exegesis (acknowledging that Locke exercises fallible reason, not inspired prerogatives), but tacitly he suggested one should have considerable confidence that these obscurities will eventually be rendered intelligible.[79] The sort of prophetic language Emerson admired acceded to no demands for genteel decorum, Augustan lucidity, or polite complaisance.[80] Rather, Emerson desired an inspired, sacral language that unsettled, ranged across the broadest of spectrums, and at times, in its polyphonic density, veiled itself from those who would diffuse its power.

In 1834 Emerson proclaimed in his journal that "a religion of forms is not for me" (*JMN,* 4:282). What is interesting is his association of this pronouncement with Milton's words from his notorious tract *The Doctrine and Discipline of Divorce* (1643). "To the parishes in my neighborhood," Emerson writes, "Milton would seem a freethinker when he says 'they (the Jews) thought it too much licence to follow the charming pipe of him [Christ] who sounded & proclaimed liberty & relief to all distresses'" (*JMN,* 4:282).[81] Most obviously, in linking himself with Milton's words, Emerson accused American Unitarian exegetical practice of a pharisaical literalism: in this tract Milton emphasized an exegetical practice that involved no exaction of an "alphabetical servility" (*CPW,* 2:280) to the scriptural text. Instead, Milton claimed to see a "plainness" in Christ's *intent* in interpreting Mosaic law, not in his explicit words. Accordingly, to the "many licentious and hard-hearted men [who] took hold of this [divorce] Law to cloak thir bad purposes," Christ would "answer these tempting Pharises, according as his custom was, not meaning to inform their proud ignorance what Moses did in the true intent of the Law." "Our Saviour corrects not in them whose pride deserv'd not his instruction," Milton insisted, but rather "only returns them what is proper to them" (*CPW,* 2:307). Christ sought, according to Milton, to confound and "dazle them and not to bind us" with his apparent but not actual prohibitions on divorce (*CPW,* 2:308). According to Milton's exegesis, to those who would not abuse "that wise and ingenious liberty which *Moses* gave" (*CPW,* 2:286) in his divorce law, its intent and limits were discernible and self-evident. Chapter 2 discusses how Emerson saw himself as similarly challenging American society upon the society's investment in decorum, univocality, and literalist exegesis. At first his challenge involved fantasies of profound verbal powers capable of disrupting and renovating society; gradually, however, Emerson acknowledged the powers and demands of his culture by exploiting a deliberate obliquity by which some are engaged by his truths, while others are baffled.

Fuller and "Feminine" Sequestered Virtue

Melville responded to the glib rationality and exaggerated anthropomorphism of antebellum culture. Not unlike Melville, Margaret Fuller reacted to a New England culture that defined human experience in polarized and reductive terms, a culture that bifurcated an integral whole into a secularized and masculine realm of practical action and a femininized domain of passive spiritual and moral "influence."[82] Sarah Hale, the socially conservative editor of *Godey's Lady's Book* and significant arbiter of feminine roles and literary tastes, explained and justified such a social and spiritual division in her article on "Eve" in *Woman's Record,* an elaborate compendium of "all distinguished women from the Creation to A.D. 1854." According to Hale, Eve, who was the "crowning work of creation, . . . a nearer assimilation with the angelic, a link in the chain connecting earth with heaven," perfected Adam's "lower" nature: "Endowed with superior beauty of person and a correspondent delicacy of mind, her soul was to help him where he was deficient, – in his spiritual nature." Together they made "the perfect Adam." Given Hale's conservatism, her willingness to elevate Eve and to exculpate her by insisting upon the nobility of Eve's motives for disobedience at first seem curiously uncharacteristic: "In the act of disobedience the conduct of the woman displayed her superior nature. The arguments used by the tempter were addressed to the higher faculties of her mind as her predominant feelings, namely, the desire for knowledge and wisdom," whereas Adam showed "no higher motive than gratifying his sensuous inclinations" and "probably did not covet or estimate ["gaining heavenly wisdom"] as she did."

But in pointing to Eve's superior moral powers and spiritual aspirations, Hale had, in fact, been establishing the basis for Eve's distinctive, more noble punishment – a theme she continued through many of her biographical articles, including her article on Margaret Fuller in *Woman's Record*. Adam was "condemned to hard labour for life," but Eve (and all women after her) was to "suffer" according to her "deep affections and acute sensibilities," with her only hope of escape "centered on winning, by her love, gentleness and submission, his heart."

The polarities of the American social arrangement were not, as far as this conservative apologist was concerned, based on any harmonious or complementary design, but rather were the just outworkings of divine punishment appropriately correlated to the different powers of Adam and Eve. While this division of human experience was evidently perceived by Hale as punishing, it was eventually to be overcome through woman's exemplary goodness and submission ("her moral sense might be effective in the progress of mankind"). Christlike, Eve must submit to and suffer under the punishment, but also "minister" to her husband, for Adam had "not a ray of hope ... save through the promise made to the woman!" If "Christ was made of a woman" as Hale emphasized in the preface to her volume (p. ix), the reciprocal implication was also unmistakable. As in her article on Margaret Fuller, Hale throughout the volume consistently praised the virtues of patient, self-sacrificing responsibility, such as that shown by Fuller toward her mother and siblings. In an earlier sketch called "The Old Maid," in her *Traits of American Life* (1835), Hale established that it was not exclusively marriage, but a woman's cheerful acceptance of self-sacrifice in the performance of her domestic duties (in this case caring for an elderly father) that defined her highest good to society and her happiness.[83] If a woman was a mother, then "through the influence of her purer mind, infused into their children, [she would] finally spiritualize [man's] harder and more earthly nature." Indeed, although the Lockean paradigm of the human mind had been blamed for creating a social hierarchy, as the socially and politically liberal-minded insisted ("it depends wholly on external circumstances ... whether the mind's blank sheets shall be written over with truth or falsehood"), such conservatives as Hale and Lydia Huntley Sigourney embraced that model of the human mind as enabling woman to shape morally and refine spiritually her children (while also countering the bad influences of the marketplace upon men): "Write what you will upon the printless tablet with your wand of love," Sigourney noted in her popular *Letters to Mothers* (1838).[84]

But for Fuller the gendered polarities identified and rationalized by Sarah Hale were an artificial reduction of integrated human experience; moreover, the very basis of such a revealed religion as Christianity seemed exclusionary, in that it was revealed to some and not to all. But not even the Transcendentalists' investment in natural religion adequately redressed the society's divisions of human experience. In an 1840 letter commenting upon both Christianity and Transcendentalism, Fuller insisted that "No true philosophy will try to ignore or annihilate the material part of man, but will rather seek to put it in its place, as servant and minister to the soul."[85] Fuller's accommodation of the "material part of man" both strategically employed Hale's hierarchy and inverted Hale's depiction of the passive and spiritualized woman who must be a "servant and minister" to a lower masculine nature. Indeed, in *Woman in the Nineteenth Century*, Fuller often tactically appropriated the culture's language of feminine "influence" and the "fall" into divided spheres for her own purposes.

On occasion, however, Fuller genuinely tried to accept the position of Christian suffering and subjection, embracing her feminine ordeal by trying to make the justification of helplessness of George Herbert – a seventeenth-century supplicant religious poet – her own. But as we shall see in Chapter 3, Fuller more often attempted to bring the culture's "feminine" spiritual role into meaningful relationship with the "masculine" domain of efficacious exertion, identifying herself also, and more deeply, with Herbert's elder brother Lord Herbert of Cherbury, a proponent of natural religion as well as the power of the individual's own agency.

Indeed, the promise of effectual individual agency prompted Fuller to complain, in her comments on children's books, that many books gave too much attention to (feminine) "moral influence" instead of a "large proportion of the facts of natural and human history," which would "speak for themselves." She is highly critical of a culture "so fond of instruction, that we forget development": "the infant needs to stretch its limbs," and children need "difficulties to overcome, and a sense of the vast mysteries which the progress of their intelligence shall aid them to unravel."[86] While other women sought to leave their spiritual impress upon the passive, "printless tablet" of their children, Fuller approved of actively grappling with limitations, with circumstances. Utopian enterprises, she thought, were actually another form of artificially sequestering individuals from conflict and strife. While Fuller admired the Transcendentalists' aspirations, she asserted that "Utopia is impossible to build up ... I accept the limitations of human nature, and believe a wise acknowledgement of them one of the best conditions of progress." Her more general indictment of American culture involved a similar complaint about a want of exertion among her contemporaries: "Since the Revolution, there has been little in the circumstances of this country, to call out the higher sentiments" (*Letters,* 2:108). Indeed, the shallowness of learning and literary culture typical of her countrymen was also apt to leave their nobler faculties undeveloped ("The infrequency of acquaintance with any of the great fathers of English lore marks this state of things"). Like Joseph Buckminster, who warned the graduating class at Harvard earlier in the century not to "seek in ... seclusion that moral security, which is the reward only of virtuous resolution," Fuller sought an integration of the material and spiritual that eschewed her culture's artificial and gendered divisions. In Chapter 3, we shall see how Fuller's essay "The Two Herberts" depicted the potential integration in the twin (and gendered) spirits of the two brothers, the supplicant Christian and ethereal George Herbert with the assertive, natural religionist who acknowledged positively "the material part of man," Lord Herbert.

In *The Feminization of American Culture,* Ann Douglas has argued, in the Milleresque tradition, that during the nineteenth century "masculine" (Calvinist) theology and "feminine" fiction merged in liberal Christian culture, and that in the process theology was trivialized. She exploited this essentializing premise to explain Margaret Fuller's rejection of feminine fiction for the masculine domain of history. But Fuller did not quite forsake fiction for history: her imaginary dialogue between the two Herberts, like her depiction of Miranda in *Woman in the Nineteenth Century,* and like Walter Savage Landor's elaborate compendium of *Imaginary Conversations,* imaginatively explored and elaborated from historical figures and events. Moreover, her interest in Lord Herbert suggests no clear rejection of Christian faith on Fuller's part, but rather a rejection of the nexus of associations connected with Christianity in her culture – exclusivity, passive suffering, and sequestered virtue. The writings and figure of Lord Herbert represented a prior and potent integration of the sacred and secular. Fuller tried, as Emerson had urged, "to annul the adulterous divorce between intellect and holiness" in her culture.

Thoreau and the Enshrinement of Nature

Whereas Melville responded to the culture's reductive empiricism and Emerson to an exaggerated complaisance and a literalist exegesis, Thoreau encountered in his countrymen a similar literalism that endowed the American landscape – in a manner verging upon idolatry – with powers and distinctions to confer a facile American national identity. Early in the century, political conservatives and liberals alike were worried that the philistinism of Americans, as well as their earnest attention to the material aspects of their continent, were retarding the nation's cultural development: "Invention and effort have been expended on matter, much more than on mind," noted William Ellery Channing in "Remarks on National Literature" (1823).[87] And of course Emerson's ascending scale, in *Nature*, from "Commodity" to "Spirit," stipulated the proper priorities in the "uses of nature," but also implied the necessity of setting such priorities for the culture.

Yet by mid-century, indeed in the same year Thoreau published *A Week on the Concord and Merrimack Rivers*, James Russell Lowell registered a somewhat different problem with respect to Americans and the natural resource of their landscape. In a review essay for the *North American Review* that focused largely on "Nationality in Literature," Lowell remarked upon a characteristic tendency among Americans: "When anxious European friends inquire after our Art and our Literature, we have nothing to do but to refer them to Mount Washington or Lake Superior."[88] Exaggerating the absurdity of the mimetic relationship perceived by Americans between the landscape and national cultural artifacts, Lowell insisted that "we should remember to the credit of the Mississippi, that, being the longest river in the world, it has very properly produced the longest painter, whose single work would overlap by a mile or two the pictures of all the old masters stitched together" (198). With tongue in cheek, Lowell disparaged the degree to which environmental determinism or naive mimeticism had taken hold of the American mind: "since it seems to be so generally conceded, that the form of an author's work is entirely determined by the shape of his skull, and that in turn by the peculiar configuration of his native territory, perhaps a new system of criticism should be framed. Want of sublimity would be inexcusable in a native of the mountains, and sameness in one from a diversified region" (198).[89] Lowell perceived the self-deception and desperation in this attempt to lay claim to a distinctive American culture based upon the peculiar effects "the New World" landscape had upon its inhabitants. More precisely, he recognized the maneuver as one that appealingly shifted the responsibility of national culture to the "broader back of the continent itself." Whether blaming the absence of culture on the more immediate necessity of subduing the land, as Channing suggested, and Margaret Fuller affirmed in her essay on "American Literature"; or whether ascribing the glory of America to its untapped natural resources, as William Cullen Bryant did in his poetry and his book of essays *Picturesque America;* or whether delegating to the landscape the responsibility for a national culture, as Lowell lamented, the implication was the same. The cultural and social labor – of engaging individual judgment, of adapting to specific and changing circumstances, and of defining an American culture in relation to an ancestral culture – was being evaded by Americans or was being passively abdicated to the power that had been mythically invested in the land itself.

Chapter 4 discusses how Thoreau challenged his countrymen's mythic investment in the American landscape. But he did this neither by eschewing pastoral literary conventions altogether, nor by appealing exclusively to the refining, restorative spirit immanent within nature, as the landscape painter Asher B. Durand urged in 1855 in one of his "Letters on Landscape Painting" in the *Crayon.* In his advice to painters, Durand instructed them to paint with utmost fidelity and without mediation, that "If abused and adulterated by the poisons of conventionalism, the result will be the corruption of veneration for, and faith in, the simple truths of Nature, which constitute the true Religion of Art, and the only safeguard against the inroads of heretical conventionalism."[90] While Thoreau might have found Durand's definition of conventionalism appealing – "the substitution of an easily expressed falsehood for a difficult truth"[91] – his own practice of mediating his landscapes through the conventions of literary texts suggested neither a categorical rejection of traditional literary conventions nor an unquestioning belief in the power of unmediated nature to inform and renovate the social world ("let him scrupulously accept *whatever* [nature] presents him," Durand had urged). Rather, as we shall see, Thoreau appropriated seventeenth-century English pastoral conventions for his own purposes, exploiting their artifice to call attention to the limits of pastoralism – an ideal that in America had encouraged an abdication of individual exertion and judgment ("an easily expressed falsehood for a difficult truth"). Indeed, many of these texts from the English seventeenth century, including those of the English Revolutionary period, exhibited in a heightened way the precariousness already associated with pastoralism. Not a provocation to synchronism or idealization, his act of connecting the landscape of America to that of Revolutionary England was rather an attempt to encourage a necessary engagement with American circumstances. Through the mediation of these English texts, Thoreau introduced a degree of compensatory skepticism toward the American landscape.

The ensuing chapters examine the inventive ways in which each of the four authors of the American Renaissance appropriated the culture of seventeenth-century England in response to the cultural dilemmas we have considered here.

2

"A SERAPH'S ELOQUENCE"

EMERSON'S INSPIRED LANGUAGE AND MILTON'S APOCALYPTIC PROSE

The Reason of Ch.[urch] Gov[ernment] & Areopagitica are better poems than whole books of P[aradise] L[ost]

Emerson[1]

After resigning from his ministerial post and deciding on a literary career, Emerson attempted to calm his anxieties of "going to the bottom" during a winter storm at sea by reciting Milton's elegy about vocation and premature death as a perverse talisman against his own possible death and foreclosed career: "I remembered up nearly the whole of Lycidas, clause by clause, here a verse & there a word, as Isis in the fable the broken body of Osiris."[2] Milton's elegy, however, did not seem to allay Emerson's fears of dissolution and artistic oblivion, fears perhaps all too vividly associated with the haunting presences of the drowned pastor-poet Lycidas, the dismembered vatic poet Orpheus, and the struggle with vocational ambition in Milton's poem. Yet Emerson's impulse to wrest these "treasures of the memory" from the oblivion of death or forgetfulness suggests that this act of recollection was tied in some powerful way to his desire to survive. In that moment of crisis, Emerson also recalled the enabling apocalyptic vision of *Areopagitica,* where Milton figures scattered Truth as Osiris gathered up by Isis in order to provide a palpable image of loss recuperated in the millennium. In recollecting this passage, Emerson attempted to effect his own rescue and secure his own artistic as well as physical survival. As in the "Masters second comming," Emerson himself assumed the power to re-unite the fragmented corpus of the *Lycidas* text, the torn body of the poet Orpheus, and the "broken body" of Truth (Osiris).[3] By shifting his identification from the Lycidas poet (who recalls Orpheus and Osiris) to Isis and from the elegiac poetry of *Lycidas* to the jubilant apocalyptic prose of *Areopagitica*, Emerson revealed his conflicting impulses toward terrifying dissolution and mastering empowerment. He confirmed, moreover, his ultimate investment in the apocalyptic power that subsumes division into wholeness and, when channeled into language, ensures the saving power of words. We shall see that these ambivalent impulses, which Emerson found expressed in Milton's poetry and apocalyptic prose, not only reveal his intense identification with Milton but also illustrate his own complex contrariety, and together they inform his notions of prophetic language and identity.

Emerson's earliest writings reveal a thorough knowledge of Milton's apocalyptic prose tracts – more so than critics have previously recognized.[4] He in fact copies into his journals or incorporates into his essays long passages from *The Reason of Church-Government* (1642), *An Apology Against a Pamphlet* (1642), and *Areopagitica* (1644). These prose works, as interpreted by Emerson, offer resounding testimonies of extraordinary expectations, verbal empowerment, and epistemological disclosure. While assuming a series of Miltonic personae, Emerson imagined power as efficacious language, an achieved eloquence that was not only a stay against annihilation but also an assertion of the dominion of spirit made manifest through his speech. Ambitious and impatient with negotiating the obstacles of the phenomenal world, this Emerson imagined himself in full possession of prophetic discourse, surmising all the while the vexed prospects for retaining this power in the fallen world. And so while Michael Colacurcio has recently emphasized an Emerson earnest, pure in motive, and ultimately diffident in his prophetic duty to proclaim the (self-evident) universal obligation to moral virtue,[5] there is yet another Emerson who more than once savors the grandiose possibility of omnipotent speech and vies for the singular status of a prophet, as when he fantasizes in his journals that "the high prize of eloquence may be mine[,] the joy of uttering what no other can utter & what all must receive" (*JMN*, 4:324 [1834]; 5:219 [1836]). Emerson's despairing depiction of language in *Nature* (as unable to "cover the dimensions of what is in truth") has led Barbara Packer and Julie Ellison to highlight Emerson's exploitation of such hallmarks of postlapsarian linguistic distrust as lacunae, parables, and epigrammatic ellipticism. Within a month of the publication of *Nature*, however, Emerson depicted inspired discourse in his journal as both all-powerful and utterly intransigent: "Eloquence [is] always tyrannical never complaisant or convertible" (*JMN*, 5:219).[6] This is not the Emerson of *Nature*, whose hope for mild, synthesizing linguistic accommodations of nature and spirit is most associated with Coleridgean organicism and Wordsworthian rhapsodies. *Nature*, in fact, fails to intimate a teleology that makes powerful, overmastering language itself the focus of Emerson's desires. Moreover, Emerson is not always and utterly convinced of the poverty of words and the evanescence of thoughts. To his brother Charles's skepticism about language, Emerson replied, "Yet I maintained that the Lycidas was a copy from the poet's mind printed out in the book, notwithstanding all the mechanical difficulties, as clear & wild as it had shone at first in the sky of his own thought" (*JMN*, 5:109 [1835]).

In crucial periods of his own self-fashioning, then, Emerson turned to Milton's apocalyptic prose works, as much for their displays of polemical agility or "manly" ad hominem ferocity as for the occasions they offer to explore and conceptualize inspired, efficacious language.[7] Fascinated with catastrophic apocalypses and an avid reader of Milton's impassioned prose, this Emerson fantasized himself in possession of a univocal, "Samson-like" speech that was irresistible in its renovating power. Accordingly, Emerson reduced Milton's complex temporal and circumstantial accommodations of divinely infused language. But as he became increasingly disappointed with his vocation in the well-established Unitarian ministry, he was more and more drawn to the promise of prophetic linguistic diversity and literary fulfillment that he saw characterized in Milton's own aspiration to be "enriched with all utterance and knowledge." Emerson reconceived inspired discourse – as infinitely complex and overwhelming in its aggregate powers, and devised fictions of inspired discourse that signaled his correspondingly complicated attempts to outmaneuver threats to his linguistic power. If "the problem of the poet," as Emerson increasingly understood it, was "to unite freedom with precision" (*W*, 8:72), the "problem" also turned out to be a solution. Uniting freedom with precision requires constant verbal inventiveness, and so the prophetic poet-orator both asserts and preserves his multiform powers, for "the slippery Proteus," according to Emerson, "is not so easily caught" (*W*, 4:121). Not surprisingly, the early tracts of the 1640s – the prose writings that most attracted Emerson's attention, both in his journals and in his essays – trace Milton's growing assurance of his prophetic task and display the integrity and verbal virtuosity that confirmed his inspired status.

But Emerson's fascination with Milton involved more than his own self-fashioning: Emerson encoded his contest with the Whig Harvard Unitarians through his revisionist reading of Milton – the pivotal figure whom, as Kevin Van Anglen has shown us, the Unitarians themselves had previously identified as their own and interpreted for their own purposes.[8] Emerson desired Milton's prophetic authority as a counter authority to the powerful national orators of his day whom he most admired – Edward Everett and Daniel Webster – but who were equivocal models at best, since their motives involved preserving the Whig status quo, and Webster's support of slavery eventually led Emerson to the judgment that he was no national hero. Their elegant speech, moreover, could not ultimately elude his suspicion, since Emerson regarded a truly eloquent speaker as "a man whom college drill or patronage never made" ("Eloquence," *W,* 2:761). Yet it was also Milton's inspired language, a language in the Hebrew mode, that Emerson wished to emulate. As Emerson understood it, this was a language that observed no Unitarian genteel decorum, Augustan lucidity, or polite complaisance; rather, in Emerson's equation of eloquence with the absence of epistemological limits, this sacral language unsettled, ranged across the broadest of spectrums, and at times, in its polyphonic density, veiled itself from those who would diffuse its power. Emerson's unorthodox insistence that "The Reason of Ch.[urch] Gov[ernment] & Areopagitica are better poems than whole books of P[aradise] L[ost]" attests in part to his inheritance of the Whig Unitarian legacy reverencing Milton's virtuous moral character – as did William Ellery Channing's tribute to Milton in the Unitarian *Christian Examiner* upon the publication of Milton's *Treatise on Christian Doctrine,* as well as Unitarian F. W. P. Greenwood's review of a new edition of Milton's prose for the Whig *North American Review.*[9] But it also bears witness to Emerson's more distinctive belief in the power of this prophetic leader to guide his nation through particular reforming renovations and ecclesiastical amelioration. And so Milton's writings, revised by Emerson, provided the forum for an account of the interconnection between literary, religious, and socio-political motives as Emerson struggled with contemporary Whig Unitarian values.

"Eloquence [is] always tyrannical
never complaisant or convertible":
The Violent Power of Godly Language

Emerson's journals, especially when analyzed as literary texts, reveal his use of many experimental Miltonic personae with their various modes of inspired discourse. Emerson's earliest allusion to Milton's prose occurs in an 1820 passage on "Pulpit Eloquence," where he searches for noble "themes," "grand subjects," and a "fine topic of sublimity" to stimulate his own prophetic eloquence.[10] Emerson's dramatic enactment of such eloquence associates Milton's prophetic speech in *The Reason of Church-Government* with his own and with the Apocalypse depicted in the Book of Revelation.[11] Emerson creates a fantasy scenario of "pulpit eloquence" in which a young, "untried" orator – almost certainly an empowered surrogate for the shy Emerson himself – addresses an "august convocation of a nation's *wise* on a subject where the passions are awake & knowledge is full & power is strong."[12] In his invocatory catalogue of requests for this "wise Christian orator," Emerson specifies the orator's ambitions for apocalyptic disclosure and efficacious speech: "let him unfold the stupendous designs of celestial wisdom," "let him gain the tremendous eloquence which stirs men's souls, which turns the world upside down, but which loses all its filth & retains all its grandeur when consecrated to God" (*JMN*, 1:8). The explicit causality between his orator's eloquence and the renovating events of the Apocalypse reveals that Emerson has situated himself, following Milton's example, in the long line of prophets that extends to the Last Days. Moreover, Emerson's desire for an all-powerful speech that "will *valde* tremefacere *eos* (really make them tremble)," that "will chain attention" and will cause "every hearer to dilate & contract, . . . triumph & droop, as he shall desire," reminds us of the injunction in Hebrews 12:25, "See that ye refuse not him that speaketh." In asking for the profound verbal power that "turns the world upside down," Emerson conflates three texts, all of which focus on the performative power of divine language to devastate and cleanse: Isaiah's stern prophecy ("Behold, the Lord maketh the earth empty . . . and turneth it upside down . . . for the Lord hath spoken this word" [Isaiah 24:1–3]); Martin Luther's reforming words ("such a kingdom [Popedom] must be turned upside down and destroyed by the word of truth"); and the apocalyptic warning in Hebrews 12:26–27 founded on the inescapable power of Christ's language at the

Second Coming ("Yet once more I shake not the earth only but also heaven . . . removing . . . those things that are shaken . . . that those things which cannot be shaken may remain").[13] What starts at the beginning of the passage as a desire for rhetorical effectiveness (a speech that "will chain attention") gives way to the desire for an irresistible language that promises renovation in the wake of its cosmic destruction. Emerson is evidently drawn to the violent power of godly language. One even detects behind his orthodox anticipation of prophetic inspiration a less orthodox longing, an aggressive will to power not unlike that of Milton's fallen Archangel in the Council of Hell.

Emerson goes on to suggest in this passage on pulpit eloquence that the orator is rewarded with true eloquence, for he signals both the influx of the divine and the beginning of the world's renovation in that moment when the orator-prophet looks at his audience and sees that they "have yielded up their prejudices to the *eloquence* of the lips which the archangel purified & hallowed with fire & this first sacrifice is the sin offering which cleanseth them" (*JMN*, 1:8 my emphasis). Here Emerson appropriates Milton's own words (and those from Isaiah) in *The Reason of Church-Government* that ascribe to the future poet a divine empowerment that Milton implies is already enfranchising the young prophetic polemicist for the reformation of the Anglican church during the turbulent "Last Days" of the 1640s. In *Church-Government,* Emerson discerns Milton's self-portrayal as one summoned by God to denounce, through the reforming activity of prophecy, the spiritual decay of the English church under Archbishop William Laud. In order to cleanse the church of its privileged clerical hierarchy, Milton interrupts his course in self-education, but anticipates inspiration "by devout prayer to that eternall Spirit who can *enrich with all utterance and knowledge,* and sends out his Seraphim with the hallow'd fire of his Altar, to touch and purify the lips of whom he pleases" (*CPW,* 1:820–1; my emphasis). So evocative to Emerson is this passage from the medial preface of *Church-Government* that he obsessively copies or writes from memory long segments of it no less than four other times in his commonplace book, journals, and lecture on Milton, and refers to it in his early journals and lectures on four additional occasions. Calling the autobiographical section of *Church-Government* "that eloquent chapter," he confers upon it the highest distinction: "Nothing of ~~prose~~ human composition is so akin to inspiration" (*JMN,* 2:109; scored word deleted by Emerson). It has not escaped Emerson that Milton the polemicist appears already to have been enfranchised with divine verbal powers. Indeed, for Emerson, prose polemics must not exclude inspiration; unlike Orestes Brownson, Emerson desires no dialectic, nor anything less than nobility of motive. Accordingly, Emerson complains that in Milton's *A Defence of the People of England* (1651), "There is little poetry, or prophecy, in this mean and ribald scolding. To insult Salmasius, not to acquit England, is the main design" (*EL*, 1:47). And so although Emerson cancels the word "prose" and replaces it with "human composition," he seems as pleased to have found the rare illustration and model of what inspiration might look like in prose as he is certain of his ability to identify it as such.

In this particular segment on utterance, Milton draws upon Isaiah 6:6–7. Isaiah's emphasis, however, is on the purging of the prophet's sins to make him worthy of the vision of God with which he has been entrusted and to prepare him for his harsh prophetic task:

> Then flew one of the seraphims unto me, having a live coal in his hand, which he had taken with the tongs from off the altar: And he laid it upon my mouth, and said Lo, this hath touched thy lips; and *thine iniquity is taken away, and thy sin purged.* (my emphasis)

Although Milton's allusion to the Isaiah passage implies his own special status as a denouncing prophet, he revises Scripture, shifting the emphasis away from the prophet's "iniquity" and "unclean lips" (Isaiah 6:5) toward the powers of the "eternall Spirit" to grace him with what is central to his vocation – eloquent speech "enrich[ed] with all utterance and knowledge." Emerson condenses Milton's phrase "enriches with all utterance and knowledge" into the single word "eloquence," the crucial focus of his own vocational decisions as well.[14] And although Milton makes an orthodox nod in the direction of purification ("to touch and purify the lips"), he clearly relishes the endowments of speech to be bestowed in conjunction with his own intense literary preparation, rather than the deficiencies of any sins to be lifted.

Emerson's version, shaped to suit his fantasy orator's moment of apocalyptic triumph, denies altogether imputation of sin to his orator; instead, he shifts the requirement of ritual purification from the orator-prophet to the listeners themselves who "yield up their prejudices" ("human passions & folly & ambition & interest & hope") to the orator. They can now be said to have made "this first sacrifice . . . the sin offering which cleanseth them."

Although both authors make eloquence (sacred speech as well as literary achievement) the distinctive feature of their divine infusions, it becomes increasingly clear that Emerson feels the need to exaggerate the power and perfection of his orator well beyond the bounds of even Milton's significant claims. Accordingly, while he incorporates from Milton's version the sense of prerogative to "purif[y] the lips of whom he pleases," he revises the nature of that prerogative as well as its agent. What had been the eternal Spirit's mysterious choice of a fit vessel is now the Emersonian orator's arbitrary determination to "lead [his audience] whithersoever he will," yet without any imputation of such personal "sins" as "ambition & interest & hope." Not surprisingly for an author who would later locate God within rather than above, Emerson has collapsed Milton's careful distinctions of agency in this fantasy figure of the eloquent orator.[15]

Although he retains the sense that his orator, like Milton, has received "the inspired guift of God rarely bestow'd" (*CPW*, 1:816), Emerson effaces Milton's sense of distance from an inscrutable divine force whose choice of persons and modes of expression cannot be fully or easily anticipated. Milton prays for the linguistic facility to accommodate a God who is unimaginably magnificent but also inscrutable; Emerson shows his orator already gaining access to divine power through speech untroubled by issues of an alien prerogative or even the necessity of accommodating it. If, many years later, Emerson refuses to imagine God (the Neoplatonic One) by imaging him anthropomorphized in the individual ("I deny Personality to God because it is too little not too much. Life, personal life is faint & cold to the energy of God" [*JMN*, 5:467]), he does not at this point seem troubled by conversely enhancing himself and arrogating to his orator-persona divine powers of astonishing scope, power, and impersonal motive.

The youthful Emerson designates as the "noblest theme for eloquence" the Apocalypse ("to picture the world destroyed & all the peoples thereof & whole human race assembled") and "the judgement," when "the archangels shall marshal them to the stupendous tribunal of inexorable Justice" (*JMN*, 1:8–9). Here he demonstrates that he has learned well the lessons of his oratorical culture, culling from his reading, college declamation contests, and Sunday sermons such grandiose verbal depictions of cataclysm as the fall of Jerusalem, "the fire tempest which overshadowed Sodom & Gomorrha [*sic*]," and the intimations of the final Apocalypse when "Time shall be no more" (*JMN*, 1:38, 6).[16]

Emerson transcribes into his commonplace book of the same year a longer segment from the medial preface to *Church-Government,* including not only Milton's evolving spiritual dedication, but also Milton's contemplations about the specific literary genre *best suited* to serve as "doctrinal and exemplary to a Nation." Although Milton considers several genres, Emerson, in his transcription, omits all but the epic and, significantly, "the Apocalyps of Saint John" as "the majestic image of a high & stately tragedy, shutting up & intermingling her solemn scenes & Acts with a sevenfold chorus of Hallelujas & harping Symphonies" (*JMN*, 1:374; *CPW,* 1:815). As in the Renaissance, when the literary dimensions of scriptural genres were matters of great interest,[17] Emerson considers the aesthetic possibilities of the Apocalypse. His own comments about the best themes and subjects for eloquence show Emerson clearly impressed with the grand, operatic theatricality of the Apocalypse, something that Milton's description, with its "sevenfold chorus of Hallelujas & harping Symphonies," surely confirms. But Emerson also must consider the epic and tragic possibilities of the Apocalypse because these genres are most clearly associated in his mind with prophetic abilities. Yet, significantly, whereas Milton considers the Book of Job (along with the works of Homer, Virgil, and Tasso) to be an important epic model, Emerson seems to avoid such human issues as trials of loyalty or ordeals of affliction, for he omits this choice entirely from those he transcribes and contemplates. Emerson seeks to experience unblighted moral purity, a divine afflatus, and the prophetic enhancement of his speech – not terrifying vulnerability or troubling manifestations of divine will.

Culminating this entry on "Pulpit Eloquence" is Emerson's own version of the Last Days. He shifts abruptly from considerations of striking topics and powerful genres to depict the Apocalypse itself as initiated by the orator's inspired words. As in the earlier jarring juxtaposition of rhetorical considerations with efficacious utterance, the effect here is one in which the extraordinary event issuing from impersonal inspiration seems to suppress his self-consciousness and supersede his personal ambitions for supreme rhetorical efficacy. What one perceptive critic observed about the consistently exaggerated power of Emerson's style might apply more generally to the source of Emerson's interest in apocalyptic power: "the style gives no hint" of Emerson's probable moments of "reluctance, diffidence, or hesitation" while engaged in the act of writing, "or hints at it only in the heightened energy which the conquest of that reluctance involved."[18] Emerson's equivocations, doubts, and fears about his own abilities and ambitious motives – the specters of *Lycidas* that he himself summoned – must be suppressed by an overpowering and empowering influx. The experience of being overwhelmed by an afflatus then becomes his paradigm for the relationship between the inspired orator and his audience. But no mere "channel of supernatural powers" nor site of possession by some alien force, this orator savors his heightened verbal powers and appreciates his enhanced perception too much to relinquish selfhood entirely. "It is not, as some of the fathers imagined," remarks Emerson in one of his sermons, "that he [the prophet] utters he knows not what. He sees his predictions to be true and necessary, exactly with the same evidence that he discerns any other truth.[19] Instead Emerson conceives the relation between the inspired orator and his audience as analogue to the divine's relation with him, and so he imagines this orator's speech as overpowering his auditors and the world, cleansing all of personal "prejudice" – including ambition. Emerson's Apocalypse is captured first in the image of the congregation's figurative release from spiritual and epistemological blindness, then depicted as a literal vision of devastation opening into a glimpse of transmundane glory. His apocalyptic language strongly echoes Revelation 6:14: when the "blinding influence of prejudice pass[es] away . . . behold the loud clamour of rejoicing nations is hushed – astonishment hath made them dumb," and

> the heavens & all their host rolled together as a scroll, the world is blazing beneath them . . . the pillars of the universe are falling to decay & creation's fabrick is mouldering away hitherto deemed eternal in vain. All all is vanishing but the throne of the everlasting. (*JMN*, 1:9)

Evidently the Emersonian orator's prayer to "let him unfold the stupendous designs of celestial wisdom" has been answered, for he has effected the holy transaction: the "prejudices" of the congregation, equated with their "sacrifice" and "sin-offering," are figured as defects of sight that are lifted ("the blinding influence of prejudice [shall] pass away from all eyes; and things shall be seen as they are when human passions & folly & ambition & interest & hope are removed"). Yet the orator with unimpaired vision has all along seen and spoken without limits. Indeed, only unusual vision permits the orphic poet of *Nature* to know that the "ruin or the blank that we see . . . is in our own eye" (*W*, 1:73), or Milton to assert that "The very essence of Truth is plainnesse, and brightnes; the darknes and crookednesse is our own . . . If our understanding have a film of ignorance over it, or be blear with gazing on other false glisterings, what is that to Truth?" (*CPW*, 1:566). In the case of Emerson's prophetic orator, inspired eloquence appears to coincide with the absence of epistemological limits, figured here as visual limits or distortions. Emerson's substitution of "eloquence" for Milton's "all utterance and knowledge" seems to hinge upon the clear correspondence between the two expressions in Emerson's mind. And if the facility for "all utterance" or "eloquence" arises from "all knowledge," then Emerson once again not only effectively stifles his own anxieties about any partiality of his own but also renders superfluous other interpretive perspectives, and other voices.

The implications of such linguistic and epistemological equivalence also emerge in Emerson's 1841 essay "History." There he appropriates and revises Milton's words in the conclusion of *An Apology Against a Pamphlet.* Milton distinguishes oratory shaped by rules the "best Rhetoricians have giv'n" from his apparently self-referential definition of true eloquence:

> yet true eloquence I find to be none, but the serious and hearty love of truth: And that whose mind so ever is fully possest with a fervent desire to know good things, and with the dearest charity to infuse the knowledge of them into others, when such a man would speak, his *words* (by what I can express) *like so many nimble and airy servitors trip about him at command, and in well order'd files, as he would wish, fall aptly into their own places.* (*CPW,* 1:949; my emphasis)

By contrast, Emerson's version boldly substitutes "facts" for Milton's "words":

> But if the man is true to his better instincts or sentiments, and refuses the dominion of facts, as one that comes of a higher race; remains fast by the soul and sees the principle, then *the facts fall aptly and supple into their places; they know their master, and the meanest of them glorifies him.* (*W,* 2:33; my emphasis)

Milton envisages the felicity of moral virtue and divine order infusing and arranging his words. His simile comparing his words to obedient seraphic regiments is not simply an image of effective rhetorical display. Perhaps alluding to the seraphim in Isaiah who attend the altar of the throned God, Milton conveys an image of divine fiat implemented by angelic words – words capable of affecting the outcome of historical events beyond the ordinary power of persuasion. Yet, although he may believe that his words can have an extraordinary power in these Last Days, Milton still patiently searches historical events for interpretive confirmations – and the events in the English Revolution, we are told in *An Apology*, were affirming Milton's exegesis of contemporary history as well as his prophecies. Only on this mediated basis does he claim the ability to render historical events intelligible.

Emerson's claim, however, is more comprehensive and aggressive. The words suggesting a duty to higher principles – "refuses the dominion of facts, as one that comes of a higher race" – may allude to William Ellery Channing's 1826 observation (which Emerson himself later appropriated) that "Milton ['The poet'] observes higher laws than he transgresses." Emerson copied and praised Channing's comment in his 1842 journal as the "true doctrine of Inspiration" (*JMN*, 8:283; *W*, 8:21).[20] (As scholars have shown, Emerson was drawn to Channing partly because his aesthetics and his theology bridged the gulf between Unitarians and Transcendentalists.)[21] Significantly, in the passage from Milton's *Apology* that he himself associates with eloquence (he uses the entire quotation as an epigraph to his essay "Eloquence" [1867]), Emerson implies by substituting "facts" for "words" that the condition that allows for Milton's efficacious eloquence also permits the heightened and clarified perception of actuality. For Emerson historical "facts" obey "their master" by becoming immediately and completely *intelligible* from the vantage point of Reason's higher intuitions.[22] Disorderly, interconnected worldly relations instantaneously give way to an apocalyptic clarity revealing the moral and spiritual principles informing existence, or, in Emerson's later terminology, there is a sharp change from the Understanding to the Reason. From Reason's perspective, "facts" no longer need interpretation, and interpretations no longer need confirmation. Accordingly, in an 1836 journal passage that would become part of the "Prospects" chapter concluding *Nature*, Emerson asserted that the operations of Reason demonstrate man's "resumption of power by vaulting at once into his seat" rather than "recovering his world an inch at a time" through the Understanding. In his list of Reason's operations in the world, he cites "the Miracles of enthusiasts ... prayer, eloquence ... [as] examples of the Reason's momentary grasp of the sceptre." Eloquence, one of the "exertions of a power not in time or in space but an instantaneous in-streaming causing power," renders resourcefulness, experimentation, accommodation, and interpretation superfluous (*JMN*, 5:180). For Emerson, inspired utterance is inextricably tied to complete epistemological disclosure, and as such, attains the incontrovertibility of absolute truth.

By tethering eloquence to the sudden epistemological disclosure of the Apocalypse or the Reason, Emerson assures eloquent language of an elocutionary force that eludes the risk of interpretation by rendering it superfluous. The early Emerson seems interested in the sheer, unequivocal force of prophetic speech, independent of the temporal circumstances that diffuse or deny its power by asking what it *means*. In the dedication of his 1823 college journal, for example, he creates a fable of man's genesis which figures man's "articulate voice" and "Eloquence" as "a Sceptre of irresistible command, by whose force, the great & wise should still the tumult of the vulgar million, & direct their blind energies to a right operation . . . And he that had it . . . turned their actions whithersoever he would" (*JMN*, 2:105). We hear the echoes of Emerson's earlier words on the prerogative of the orator to lead his audience "whithersoever he will" – a prerogative that had belonged in Milton's passage to the "eternall Spirit." No plurality of interpretations (which could then became negotiations) is possible in this depiction of a mastering eloquence that "sounded like the language of the gods." Emerson alludes to an "irresistible" Orpheus, whose song civilized barbarians ("still[ed] the tumult of the vulgar million"). And we know from his mention of the Isis and Osiris myth during the storm at sea that he associated the dismembered Orpheus with the "torn body of our martyred saint," "Truth," in *Areopagitica* (*CPW*, 2:549). Emerson, like Milton, well knows the risks of the Orpheus-Osiris figure. Both connect godly, inspired language – "martyred Truth" – with its vulnerability in a fallen world.[23] If Emerson himself, in "The Lord's Supper" sermon, could diffuse the performative force of Christ's words at the Last Supper by interpreting them as culture-bound, ritualistic artifacts and utterly dismiss them with the challenge of indifference, then the only kind of language that would be all-powerful is the one that is susceptible neither to multiple interpretations nor to denial. Emerson's tendency to suppress rhetorical considerations as soon as they emerge reflects not only a desire to be mastered by a powerful influx that supersedes his personal ambitions but also a desire to reject any rhetorical restraints upon his ideal speech.

Significantly, then, Emerson's earliest reworkings entirely suppress the uncertainties of interpreting history that so troubled Milton – the convolutions of history corresponding to the inward "mazes and *Labyrinths* of dreadfull and hideous thoughts" from which Milton prays for deliverance in *Of Reformation* (*CPW*, 1:213).[24] Milton's prophetic powers, involving the ability to render intelligible the historical events of his nation, have instead acquired, in Emerson's earliest writings, an iconic status: there Milton's prophetic powers appear static rather than dynamic, and exaggerated in their *potentia*, while utterly shorn of their terrors and burdens.[25] Emerson's Milton turns from the circumstantial struggle for national purification and spiritual renovation to await instead an apocalypse of abrupt displacement and universal intelligibility, to be signified by the sudden access of vision and efficacious speech. This sharp revisionary turn away from Miltonic historical process to Emersonian epistemological disclosure informs Emerson's ideal language: it is a kind of mighty "eloquence" by which his fantasy orator triumphs, like that other reformer, Martin Luther, who proclaims the "Samson-like" power of his own words to vanquish papists (*EL*, 1:129). Milton's supreme exertions – a profound verbal responsiveness appropriate to the contingencies of historical circumstances, but also to the revelations of God in all their possible linguistic diversity (to be "enriche[d] with *all utterance* and knowledge") – are transformed by Emerson into effortless performances of oracular power that give words a "forceful & appalling sublimity" (*JMN*, 1:39). The turbulent power of the Apocalypse itself can be taken as Emerson's metonymy for the sublime, undeniable upheaval precipitated by the prophetic orator when his sacred word gains the substantial power that renders the material world insubstantial. "Thunder and lightning," according to Emerson, "are faint & tame descriptions of the course of astonishing eloquence" (*JMN*, 1:39 [1820]).

Bold Ambition and the "Talent Which is Death to Hide"

It seems that both Emerson's decision to enter the ministry and his decision to leave it were significantly tied to his "passionate love for the strains of eloquence" (*JMN*, 2:239). Yet the boldness that had permitted him to imagine himself an all-powerful, prophetic orator not only fails but appears to recoil upon him during the period leading to his ministerial ordination. Strong ambitions mixed with a heightened and explicit mistrust of the source of his motivation, clash and compete inside him: "Strange the succession of humors that pass through this human spirit. Sometimes I am the organ of the Holy Ghost & and sometimes of a vixen of petulance" (*JMN*, 7:9). A subdued, benign, and orthodox tenor now pervades Emerson's expression more consistently than the aggressive presumption that had characterized his apocalyptic orator. Now he particularly longs for the assurance that his own motives are pious:

> The office of a clergyman is twofold; public preaching & private influence. Entire success in the first is the lot of few, but this I am encouraged to expect. If however the individual himself lack that moral worth which is to secure the last, his studies upon the first are idly spent. The most prodigious genius, a seraph's eloquence will shamefully defeat its own end, if it has not first won the heart of the defender to the cause he defends, but the coolest reason cannot censure my choice when I oblige myself *professionally* to a life which all wise men freely & advisedly adopt ... But I would learn to love Virtue for her own sake, I would have my pen so guided as was Milton's when a deep & enthusiastic love of goodness & of God dictated the Comus to the bard, or that prose rhapsody in the 3rd Book of Prelaty [*The Reason of Church-Government*]. (*JMN*, 2:240 [1824])

Emerson's palpable anxiety that his "seraph's eloquence will shamefully defeat its own end" – if his motives are impure – draws him to what he believes to be the enabling purity and integrity of Milton's motives. (In a comment certainly read by Emerson, William Ellery Channing remarked in his essay on Milton, "Milton we should rank among seraphs" [37]). I have suggested that Emerson countervails his feelings of depletion and self-doubt through revisionist impersonations of the prophetic Milton exercising his verbal powers. Yet Emerson does not sustain that satisfying sense of enormous power in himself, perhaps not simply from inability but also from unwillingness to do so.

At times his self-mistrust, provoked by the bold aggressiveness of his own ambitions, is not entirely without warrant. In one of his earliest delivered Unitarian sermons (on 1 Thess. 5:17: "Pray without ceasing"), two years after the 1824 journal entry, Emerson tellingly describes a fervent spiritual aspirant – presumably himself – by appropriating Milton's description of the ruined Archangel in Book IV of *Paradise Lost*. Disdainful of the cherubs who seem not to recognize him, Satan is suddenly forced to acknowledge his own tarnished glory and changed appearance when he sees the contrasting "grace invincible" of the beautiful cherub Zephon standing before him: "abasht the Devil stood, / And felt *how awful goodness is, and saw / Virtue in her shape how lovely*, saw, and pin'd / His loss; but chiefly to find here observ'd / His lustre visibly impair'd; yet seemed / Undaunted" (*Paradise Lost*, IV: 845; my emphasis). We might expect that in Emerson's appropriation the emphasized words would serve to highlight what Satan foreshadows here in Eden – the promise that despite its fallen condition, humanity may still recognize and revere true virtue. Yet Emerson's borrowing of the description of Satan is considerably more equivocal. While one critic has suggested recently that Emerson's early self-fashioning is "conventionally Unitarian" and only much later becomes "antinomian,"[26] we can see in the passages we previously analyzed, and in the sermon we are about to examine, substantial evidence of Emerson's heterodox and unconventional motives, which set him apart from the Unitarians starting with his college years, earliest journal entries, and earliest sermons. And so while the larger argument of Emerson's sermon passage identifies and urges the worthiest and most conventional spiritual goals for prayer, Emerson's language expressing peerlessness, unchecked aspiration, limits surpassed, and powerfully efficacious prayer – in conjunction with the description of the Archangel, who, we should note, remained "undaunted" – hint more darkly at Emerson's spiritual sprezzatura and bold ambition:

> If there be, in this scene of things, any spirit of a different complexion, who has felt, in the recesses of his soul, "how awful goodness is, and virtue in her own shape how lovely," who has admired the excellence of others, and set himself by the precepts of the wise, and by imitation . . . to assimilate himself to a model, or *to surpass the uncertain limit of human virtue*, and *found no model in the Universe, beneath God, level with his venerated idea of virtue*, who looks with scorn at the cheap admiration of crowds, and loves the applause of good men, *but values more his own*; and *has so far outstripped humanity, that he can appreciate the love of the Supreme*; if he aspire to do signal service to mankind, by the rich gift of a good example, and by unceasing and sober efforts to instruct and benefit men; will this man wholly fail, and waste his requests on the wind: Assuredly he will not. His prayers, *in a certain sense, are like the will of the Supreme Being*: "His word leaps forth to its effect at once, / He calls for things that are not, and they come." (*CS*, 1:58 [1826]; my emphases)

Emerson's articulation here dwells little upon the "borrowed new strength" that, according to William Ellery Channing's already significant departure from Unitarian moralism, allows that "many a virtuous man has borrowed from the force, constancy, and dauntless courage of evil agents," and which Channing claims Satan emblematized as the "energy which resides in mind" – "the power of mind" and "spiritual might made visible by the racking pains which it overpowers" (16). Instead, this passage discloses a barely concealed tension and precariously maintained balance between Emerson's earnest longing for virtue and his immoderate pride in his own unmatched spiritual gifts and aspirations. He shifts from attempting to "assimilate himself to a model" to finding "no model in the Universe, beneath God, level with his venerated idea of virtue," from "lov[ing] the applause of good men" to "valu[ing] more his own," and from feeling an appreciation of virtue deep "in the recesses of his soul" to competitively "so far outstripp[ing] humanity, that he can appreciate the love of the Supreme." We might be tempted to see the young Emerson's Milton as the Unitarian hero – a sublime moralist, anti-Trinitarian, and general defender of libertarian values – were we to focus our attention exclusively upon Emerson's mention of Milton's name and character.[27] But in his earliest writings, Emerson's appropriation of Milton's words in his poetry and in his prose, his telling verbal revisions, his intense focus on Milton's conception of inspired language, and his acute awareness of the seventeenth-century theopolitical contexts of Milton's writings all reveal a more unorthodox, more daring, and at times more combative Emerson engaged in Miltonic self-fashioning than critics have acknowledged.

Given this ongoing internal struggle, it is not surprising that ten months after writing the 1820 passage on pulpit eloquence we examined earlier, Emerson turned again to Milton's *Church-Government,* seeking assurance as much about the inevitability of his own prophetic powers as about his moral duty – and hoping to experience Milton's profound assurance of still unproven literary powers. Emerson attempts to pacify his intermittent uneasiness and self-mistrust by appropriating the ways Milton in his prose legitimizes his vast prophetic and literary ambitions. Accordingly, Emerson remarks that Milton was "yearning for the destiny he was appointed to fulfil" (*JMN*, 1:41 [1820]). While impersonating the young Milton confident in his literary "talents," Emerson says of himself, "My talents (according to the judgement of friends or to the whispered suggestions of vanity,) are popular, are fitted to enable me to claim a place in the inclinations & sympathy of men" (*JMN*, 1:41 [1820]). Emerson rehearses here (and transcribes or paraphrases elsewhere [*JMN*, 1:374, 1820; 2:107, 1823]) Milton's "covnant with any knowing reader" for the future fulfillment of his literary ambitions. Emerson's certainty that Milton refers to great future literary achievement emerges in his characterization of this covenant as "The *Shadowing*-out / Promise / of the 'Paradise Lost' " (*JMN*, 1:373 [1820]). Milton himself represents his sense of futurity in terms of 2 growing

> assent both to them [the scholars at private Italian academies] and divers friends here at home, and not lesse to an inward prompting which now grew daily upon me, that by labor and intent study . . . joined with the strong propensity of nature, I might perhaps leave something so written to aftertimes, as they should not willingly let it die. (*JMN*, 1:374 [1820]; *CPW*, 1:810)

Emerson understands Milton's "inward prompting" to "leave something . . . written" as literary-prophetic inspiration, for Emerson later (paraphrasing these words) described Milton as "continually summoned & inspired by a Spirit within him . . . to do God's work in the world by sending forth strains which 'aftertimes would not willingly let die' " (*JMN*, 2:107). Emerson's cynical claim to be urged by no greater inward prompting than the "whispered suggestions of vanity" may signal a moment of self-abasement elicited by his admiration for Milton.[28] But it also reveals an attempt to mitigate or minimize to himself his grand ambitions, for his cynicism about his source of hope hardly obscures his greater audacity – his impulse to apply to himself Milton's already presumptuous assurance of great literary promise and lasting fame. "Every act," Emerson would later say, "betrays the ill-concealed deity" (*W*, 3:78).

In turning this time to *Church-Government*, Emerson also transcribed a section of the preface to Book II that catalogues the reproaches with which Milton's conscience would chastise him if he failed, as God's zealous servant, to sound his trumpet and denounce the corrupt practices of the Anglican prelates. Emerson quotes Milton's rationale for speaking out, one that makes Milton's prophetic leadership and defense of the oppressed church in prose both urgent and inescapable. Unlike the young Emerson, paralyzed by shyness and self-reproachful about his "lassitude" and "desultory habits," Milton is a prophet who has

been freed, in Milton's words, of his "disposition" to be "too
inquisitive or suspicious of [him]self" in his "green years," and
who must now exercise the "honest liberty of free speech from
[his] youth" lest "stories" of "discourage & reproach" ring within
him for forbearing to use *"those few talents which God hath lent me"*
(*JMN*, 1:41–42; Emerson's emphasis; *CPW*, 1:804). The rousing
urgency of Milton's call to action here is evidently far more
attractive to Emerson than Milton's resigned submission to the
inscrutable divine will in that other poignant expression of anxiety about the "Talent which is death to hide." Like Margaret
Fuller, similarly anxious about her own poetic ambitions,[29] Emerson will not now be satisfied with the advice of Milton's Sonnet
19, "They also serve who only stand and wait."[30]

Significantly, for an Emerson hesitant about the magnitude
of his ambition, Milton in *Church-Government* sanctions his own
ambition not only by appealing to events but also by invoking his
own divinely inspired conscience. The imaginary dialogue between the "slothfull," "timorous and ingratefull" Milton and Milton's own berating conscience may have sounded decisive and
irrefutable to the Emerson who knew *Paradise Lost* well, for the
language and tone of Milton's internal colloquy may have seemed
to reveal that Milton associated his inspired conscience with
God's will. This is evidenced by the correspondences between the
voice of Milton's conscience and the holy language of recrimina-
tion voiced by God in *Paradise Lost* in disparaging "ingrate" man
(III.96), by Abdiel in chastising "ingrate" Satan (V.811); and by
the Miltonic narrator condemning the fallen angel Belial, who,
like Satan and the young Milton in *Church-Government*," fails to
use his "persuasive accent" piously: "For dignity compos'd and
high exploit . . . To vice industrious, but to Nobler deeds / Timorous and slothful" (II.115 –16). In Emerson's mind, Milton's vast
linguistic ambitions to defend the church and to "justify the ways
of God to men" may be exonerated from presumption because
they are responses proportionate to the divine promptings within
him. To fail to respond to an "inward prompting" with appropriate verbal performance, as Milton's Satan later dramatizes, is
to choose to become a fallen angel – or, as Emerson fears, to have
"a seraph's eloquence . . . shamefully defeat its own end."

Emerson desires exactly this goad to his bold verbal ambitions,
since he copies down only the reproaches for failing to use his
verbal "talents," omitting Milton's "charter and freehold of rejoicing" if he were to take on his prophetic responsibilities. Moreover,
the Emerson who would later write the Divinity School "Address"

and *Self-Reliance* could not have missed this argument from "an inward prompting which now grew daily upon me." Indeed, when Emerson later read in Channing's review Milton's words from *Christian Doctrine* ("the Spirit which is given to us is a more certain guide than Scripture, whom, therefore, it is our duty to follow"), he must have been struck by Channing's attempt to revise their unorthodox appreciation of immediate inward illumination into Unitarian rationalism: "This, in words, is genuine Quakerism," observes Channing, "but whether Milton understood by the Holy Spirit that *immediate* revelation, which forms the leading doctrine of that creed, we doubt . . . We imagine that Milton believed, that the Holy Spirit works with and by our own understanding, and, instead of superseding reason, invigorates and extends it" (58). Above all, for Emerson, who is seeking to increase his powers and to dispel anxiety about the impiety of his ambitions, the resonances of godly language in the words of Milton's inspired conscience were more likely to suggest identity than correspondence between divine and human powers.

Emerson has been examining the modes by which Milton transformed his vast verbal ambitions into indispensable obligations to God, the reformed church, and the nation. Sixteen years later, Emerson reflected upon the powerful effect that Milton's *Church-Government* had upon him. In doing so, he may well have been looking forward to writing *The American Scholar* and the Divinity School "Address," in the following two years, where he, like Milton, attempted to prod the consciences and provoke to "manly" action the clerical scholars often perceived as "effeminate" in their reticence and reclusion: "The second Book of his Tract called Reason of Church Government urged against Prelaty is a provocative to a manly and pure ambition such as was never addressed to scholars" (*EL,* 1:363 [1836]).[31] For Emerson, the tract may have indeed not only inspired young clerical scholars but also sanctioned his own bold plans as "manly and pure ambition."

But if the desire for inspired language and the hope of accommodating his "talents" drew Emerson to the ministry, his growing uneasiness with Unitarian liturgical and homiletic discourse also provided a strong impetus for his departure from the ministry. After suffering through the oratorical infelicities of one Rev. Barzillai Frost, Emerson announces,

> there is no better subject for effective writing than the Clergy. I ought to sit & think & then write a discourse to the

> American clergy showing them the ugliness & unprofit-
> ableness of theology & churches at this day & the glory &
> sweetness of the Moral Nature out of whose pale they are
> almost wholly shut. (*JMN,* 5:464 [1838])

Emerson here seems to be proposing his Divinity School "Address," which he would deliver four months later. But in designat-
ing "the Clergy" as the best "subject for effective writing," he also
seems to be suggesting that this loyal admirer of Milton's "Prelaty"
tracts would now write his own post-Reformation tract. Like Milton, Emerson views the condition of his Unitarian church – one
that had also ceased its reforming activities and become en-
trenched in its own rituals and traditions – as irresistibly oppor-
tune for the exercise of his talents. No longer biding with his
equivocations or fears of impiety, Emerson now strongly registers
the external circumstances that make his ambitions both noble
and inevitable.

Emerson expressly aligns himself with Reformation tradition
when he proclaims in the "Address," "That which shows God in
me, fortifies me. That which shows God out of me, makes me a
wart and a wen. There is no longer a necessary reason for my
being" (*W,* 1:132). Like such Protestant polemicists as Milton,
William Prynne, and Alexander Leighton before him, Emerson
here applies to himself a common Reformation trope for the
superfluous and parasitical clergy – that of the disfiguring, lethal
"wart" or "wen" that must be excised from the body ecclesiastic.[32]
For both Emerson in the Divinity School "Address" and Milton in
Of Reformation, the clerical "growth" (including its doctrines and
phraseology) has the potential to usurp divine authority when it
claims only to mediate on its behalf. So while Milton viciously
calls the Anglican prelacy "a monstrous Wen," "a foul disfigure-
ment and burden," which, "when I have cut thee off, and open'd
thee, as by the help of these implements I will doe, all men shall
see" (*CPW,* 1:584), Emerson in the "Address" more discreetly
laments the passing away in the Unitarian church of the reforming "creed" of "Puritans in England and America." They-
found "scope for their austere piety" in the "Christ of the Catholic
Church, and in the dogmas inherited from Rome." He instead
offers his own "Address" as just such a "remedial" Reformation
tract "to find the causes of a decaying church and a wasting
unbelief" (*W,* 1:142–3). In the "Address," Emerson seems to object to mediated religion, and to the idolatrous worship of Jesus's
personality and words. Michael Colacurcio has ably traced in the

"Address" Emerson's "agon" with Jesus, his bias against Unitarian Christology, which (inadvertently) resembles the "Christ of the Catholic Church," and Emerson's allegation of the "fallacy of linguistic presence" inhering in Unitarian worship of Christ's words.[33] Yet curiously, Emerson's own intense identification with the prophetic Milton – his rehearsal of Milton's exact words as if they had some extraordinary power – combined with his own prophetic and literary ambitions, suggest that Emerson may well be substituting Milton, the more sympathetic and effective prophetic model, for Christ.

"Free and Unimpos'ed Expressions" and Unitarian Decorum

Like the Milton of *An Apology,* Emerson is particularly provoked by the issues of verbal decorum and ritual phraseology as they restrict the pulpit orator. Milton argues in *An Apology* against the bishops' plea for the established liturgy, calling instead for "free and unimpos'd expressions ... Which to dresse up and garnish with a devis'd bravery abolisht in the law, and disclam'd by the Gospell addes nothing but a deformed uglinesse" (*CPW,* 1:941–2). Milton objects as much to the ornate superfluity as to the stifling accretion of forms: both threaten to extinguish inspiration and usurp worship. Emerson (ironically, given the issue at stake) echoes Milton's exact words in pointing to the "ugliness" of the Unitarian church's practices in the 1838 journal entry on the clergy, and, in the Divinity School "Address," to its "deformity." In suggesting that "free and unimpos'd expressions from a sincere heart unbidden come," Milton highlights the pure motive that enables inspired preaching and prayer. But also at the center of *An Apology's* polemics are concerns crucial to Milton's literary and prophetic ambitions: "scripted" sermons and "set forms" prevent authentic prophetic speech in all its variety and vehemency; they also deny exercise of the individual's "talents."[34] Similarly, at the heart of Emerson's polemics in his Divinity School "Address" are issues essential to his own ambition for eloquence.

Three months before Emerson delivered his address, he revealed in a journal entry that the clergy's substitution of formulaic speech for inspired verbal gifts was at the center of his discontent:

I told them [the Harvard Divinity School youths] that the preacher should be a poet smit with love of the harmonies

of moral nature: and yet look at the Unitarian Association &
see if its aspect is poetic. They all smile No . . . The fire of
the minstrel's eye & the vivacity of his word is exchanged for
intense grumbling enunciation of the Cambridge sort, &
and for scripture phraseology. (*JMN*, 5:471)

The best sort of priestly language, in Emerson's view, is vivid,
varied, inspired, poetic. Here Emerson echoes Milton in his invocation to Book III of *Paradise Lost* ("Yet not the more / Cease I to
wander where the Muses haunt / Clear Spring, or shady Grove,
or Sunny Hill, / *Smit with the love of sacred Song*" [lines 26–9]; my
emphasis). Milton's invocation refuses the restrictions imposed
by physical blindness; instead it celebrates the intensification of
his prophetic and creative powers, as well as his receptivity to the
source of his inspiration. Emerson translates Milton's "sacred
Song" into his own idiom – "the harmonies of moral nature," or,
in the entry two weeks earlier, "the glory & sweetness of the Moral
Nature." No longer only an issue of "theology & churches," the
Unitarians' sin is now also their willingness to exchange the
vivacious (Miltonic) word for "scripture phraseology" that is "the
plainest prose, the prose of prose." Emerson is deeply troubled
by Unitarianism's "pale negations" of a Miltonic poet-priest who,
Emerson intimates, he himself might be. The Christ Emerson
portrays in his Divinity School "Address" may indeed be, as one
critic suggests, "the doomed poet, whose words of truth are be-
trayed into dogma by the treachery of language."[35] Emerson, no
less than Milton, fears such a doom, yet Emerson places his
highest hopes upon Milton.

Central to the Divinity School "Address" is Emerson's fear of
the "nigh quenched fire on the altar" that once hallowed "chiefly
. . . those Hebrews, and through their lips spoke oracles" (*W*,
1:149, 151). Emerson describes the Unitarian church's failure of
faith in ongoing inspiration: this "injury to faith throttles the
preacher," and the "goodliest of institutions becomes an uncertain and inarticulate voice" (*W*, 1:134). Yet Emerson suggests, as
Milton also asserts in *An Apology*, that the true orator may still
have access to sacred speech: "Courage, piety, love, wisdom, can
teach; and every man can open his door to these angels, and they
shall bring him the gift of tongues" (*W*, 1:135). As in his anguished 1824 journal entry about the source of his ambition in
public preaching, Emerson here creates an antithesis between
the minister who, relying on human institutions, only "babbles,"
and "every man," who, by opening his door, may receive "the

gift of tongues" – the Pentecostal reparation of linguistic ruin precipitated by the building of the Tower of Babel. This polarity corresponds significantly to one that Milton himself poses and that Channing affirmed in his 1826 essay on Milton's *Christian Doctrine*, with which Emerson was familiar. Seconding Milton, Channing himself suggests that "public instruction, instead of continuing to be a monopoly of ministers, may be extended freely to men of superior intelligence and piety," resulting in "the substitution of a more natural, free, and various eloquence, for the technical and monotonous mode of treating subjects, which clings so ... obstinately to the performances of the pulpit" (62).[36]

In both Milton's *An Apology* and his *Christian Doctrine*, Emerson sees Milton as attempting to broaden the range of inspired discourse, in part by extending the range of who may preach and prophesy beyond established ecclesiastical restrictions. Among the passages Channing excerpts and Emerson reads from the *Christian Doctrine*, Milton insists that "each believer in turn should be authorised to speak, or prophesy, or teach, or exhort, according to his gifts" and that "the Spirit which is given to us is a more certain guide than scripture, whom, therefore, it is our duty to follow" (58). From Reformation history, Emerson would have known that Milton himself could ascribe access to prophetic utterance to a belief that in "those cases where religion has fallen into decay, evangelists [including Apostles and Prophets] are raised up in an extraordinary manner, to restore the pure doctrine which had been lost."[37] Certainly Emerson had been quick to see the implications for himself of the open-ended operations of poetic prophecy in Milton's writings: "What shall forbid us to universalize the operations of God & believe the operation of the Holy Spirit is the same in kind in the prophet Isaiah as in the poet Milton?" (*JMN*, 3:240 [1831]).

Milton proposes in *An Apology* not only a greater inclusiveness regarding who may prophesy but also a reordering of Christian obligation that expands the range and character of inspired discourse. He vows that "I ... shall always be of this opinion that obedience to the Spirit of God rather then to the faire seeming pretences of men, is the best and most dutifull order that a Christian can observe" (*CPW*, 1:937). The very strictures of Anglican "decency" – the "faire seeming pretences of men" – have created, according to Milton, a "Liturgy all over in conception leane and dry, of affections empty and unmoving, of passion, or any heigth whereto the soule might soar upon the wings of zeale,

destitute and barren" (*CPW*, 1:937, 939). This zeal, however, may
on occasion require denunciatory vehemence. Milton authorizes
the appropriateness of vehemence in "true Prophets" by appeals
to the example of Christ's and Luther's "ardent spirit" (*CPW*,
1:901). In so doing, he redefines what is "decent" in inspired,
passionate language according to the requirements of the Holy
Spirit: "those free and unimpos'd expressions which from a sincere heart unbidden come into outward gesture is the greatest
decency that can be imagin'd" (*CPW*, 1:941–2). Thus when Emerson confesses, in his "Lord's Supper" sermon, that "I am not
engaged to Christianity by decent forms" (*W*, 11:21), the phrase
"decent forms" has gained for Emerson an allusive force. It alludes to the Unitarian injunction while also evoking one of the
key linguistic issues in the Anglican argument that the impassioned, prophetic Milton had refuted.

Not surprisingly, five months after Channing published in the
Christian Examiner his tribute to Milton, which entertained the
possibility of substituting in the pulpit "natural, free, and various eloquence, for the technical and monotonous mode" (62)
and acknowledged the need for vehement language under certain circumstances (24–5),[38] Emerson, employing Miltonic resonances from *An Apology*, defined what constituted true prayer in
his own sermon on 1 Thessalonians 5:17 ("Pray without ceasing"). This was the same sermon in which Emerson revealed
himself as the fervent spiritual aspirant with bold ambitions.
"[T]hese are not prayers, but mockeries of prayers," insisted Emerson, "which begin with the ordinary appellatives of the Deity
and end with his son's name, and a ceremonial word . . . if they
utter no one wish of our hearts, no one real and earnest affection,
but are formal repetitions of sentiments taken at second hand."
He was clearly echoing Milton's complaint of "a Liturgy all over
in conception leane and dry, of affections empty and unmoving,
of passion." As Milton defines the "greatest decency," so Emerson
proposes "true prayers," which "are the daily, hourly, momentary
desires." Like Milton's "free and unimpos'd expressions which
from a sincere heart unbidden come into outward gesture," prayers "come," according to Emerson, "without impediment without
fear, into the soul, and bear testimony at each instant to its
shifting character. And these prayers are granted" (*CS*, 1:57
[1826]). The "shifting character" of the soul and the "testimony"
of subtly responsive prayers and various eloquence suggest that
Emerson's redefinition of what constitutes true, efficacious prayer
may well attempt – like Milton's plea for unscripted liturgy and

Channing's suggestion of "free, and various eloquence" in pulpit preaching – to remove the institutional ecclesiastic "impediments" to the exercise of individual (Milton's, Channing's, and Emerson's) verbal talents.

Indeed, in the Emersonian version of Milton's conflict, the terms of opposition as rendered in a journal entry pit the Whig party (the party of the Harvard Unitarians) against "Exaggeration [which] is the law of nature." Even after his final resignation from the Unitarian ministry, Emerson still expressed exasperation and disappointment with their methods.[39] In a passage that later became part of his essay "The Conservative," Emerson complains that the Whig party

> concedes that the radical enunciates the primal law but makes no allowance for friction and this omission makes their whole doctrine impertinent ... [The Whigs'] legislation is for the present distress, – a universe of slippers & flannels, with bib & pap-spoon, swallowing pills & herb tea, whig preaching, whig poetry, whig philosophy, whig marriages. No rough truth telling Miltons, Rousseaus. (*JMN*, 8:87[1841])

Although Emerson has been accused by at least one recent critic of co-opting the voices of difference and dissent in his "hegemonic" discourse, he here arouses the Whigs and seems to suggest that the party has made itself irrelevant by avoiding the "friction" produced by dissent that characterizes the stridency of the Miltonic mode.[40] Emerson instructs us, earlier in the entry, that "the air would rot without lightning" (presumably that "radical [who] enunciates the primal law"), and we must therefore "Aim above the mark to hit the mark," since only such "violence of direction" compensates for the inadequacy of a certain kind of language – the enervated language ("whig preaching, whig poetry") he associates with Unitarians. Rather than an argument for the categorical inadequacy of language, in this entry he suggests that in order to approach adequacy, language requires a sharpness, boldness, and heterogeneity that by the rules of Whig Unitarian decorum (which he associates with conservative politics) would be faulted for impropriety or exaggeration. If, in Emerson's words, "the infinite diffuseness refuses to be epigrammatized, the world to be shut in a word" (though Emerson, a lover of epigrams, would frequently try), it is the passionate, "rough truth telling Miltons" who expand the range of language and exaggerate enough to "soar upon the wings of zeale."

Having studied *An Apology,* Emerson gradually revised his sense of inspired language to contrast with the polite, pellucid discourse of the Whig Unitarians. The rhetoricians at Harvard, drawing upon, as we saw in Chapter 1, John Quincy Adams's *Lectures* and Hugh Blair's *Lectures on Rhetoric and Belles-Lettres,* demanded a style more elegantly and transparently Addisonian – a style that "frees us from all fatigue of searching for his meaning," "flows always like a limpid stream, where we see to the bottom," is "easy, agreeable . . . carrying a character of smoothness more than strength . . . [a] character of modesty, and politeness."[41] Blair and Adams were willing to grant that Milton's poetry exemplified "grandeur of imagination."[42] But Blair complains that "obscurity . . . reigns so much among many metaphysical writers . . . for the most part, owing to the indistinctness of their own conceptions" (1:186). Unitarian tastes, influenced by Blair, Locke, and the Scottish Common Sense philosophy, accordingly promoted an "excellence of language in the sense of effective communication of ideas. Crucial to such effectiveness was perspicuity of language."[43] Blair specifically laments the syntactical inversions and "forced constructions" that "Milton in his prose works, and some other of our old English writers endeavored to imitate" from the example of Latin and Greek, but "the genius of our Language, as it is now written and spoken, will not admit such liberties" (1:234). Chapter 1 examined the broader social implications of these values adopted by Whig Unitarians, particularly those expressed by the Monthly Anthologists presided over by Joseph Buckminster and later by Emerson's father William. Channing, in his essay on Milton, addresses Blair's complaints and may have confirmed Emerson's growing sense that Milton's inspired prose is an alternative to Whig Unitarian (and Emerson's own father's) approved discourse:

> [I]t is objected to his prose writings, that the style is difficult and obscure, abounding in involutions, transpositions, and Latinisms; that his protracted sentences exhaust and weary the mind, and too often yield it no better recompense than confused and indistinct perceptions . . . [W]e cannot but lament the fastidiousness and effeminacy of modern readers. We know that simplicity and perspicuity are important qualities of style; but there are vastly nobler and more important ones, such as *energy and richness,* and in these Milton is not surpassed . . . To be universally intelligible is not the highest merit . . . There are writings which are clear through

their shallowness. We must not expect in the ocean the transparency of the calm inland stream ... We delight in long sentences, in which a great truth, instead of being broken up into numerous periods, is spread out in its full proportions, is irradiated with variety of illustration and images, is set forth in a splendid affluence of language, and flows, like a full stream ... Let abundant provision be made for the common intellect. *Let such writers as Addison, an honored name, "bring down philosophy from heaven to earth."* But let inspired genius fulfil its higher function of lifting the prepared mind from earth to heaven. Impose upon it no strict laws, for it is its own best law. Let it speak in its own language, in tones which suit its own ear ... If not understood and relished now, let it ... utter oracles which futurity will expound. We are led to these remarks, not merely for Milton's justification, but because our times seem to demand them. Literature, we fear, is becoming too popular. (21–3; my emphasis)

Channing defends Milton's prose against Blair's exact objections and precise prescriptions. But he also defends a richer, more complex, and more varied language – the language of the "inspired genius" that overwhelms the "effeminacy of modern readers" and requires instead preparation ("lifts the prepared mind") and exertion.

In the period leading up to his Divinity School "Address," Emerson had transcribed in his journal an excerpt from Milton's argument in *An Apology* that justifies not only invective but also scurrilous language. Milton asserts that "we may finde in Deuteronomy and three of the Prophets" places where God speaks in a "terme immodest to be utter'd in coole blood," and that elsewhere in Scripture events are to be related "not without an obscene word." According to Milton, we must recognize that "God who is the author both of purity and eloquence, chose this [scurrilous] phrase as fittest in that vehement character wherein he spake." To render God's expression in more discreet terms would be to "teach men to read more decently then God thought good to write" (*CPW*, 1:902–3). Among a series of maxims on the irrelevance of quotidian values to the expansive, virtuous life, Emerson transcribes Milton's final point, which warrants the use of "unwonted manner" of words in certain circumstances: "Ye may know, not only as the historian speaks 'that all those things for which men plough build or sail, obey virtue,' but that words &

whatsoever may be spoken, shall at some time, in an unwonted manner wait upon her purposes" (*JMN*, 6:385; *CPW*, 1:903). The often fastidious Emerson increasingly imagines a variety of sacred language that may well have been authorized by this section on immodest language in *An Apology*. This is a godly language compendious enough to fulfill – oxymoronically – all the requirements of "virtue." In describing the language of the poet, for example, Emerson suggests that, as divine language inscribed in the Book of Nature is indifferent to "the distinctions which we make in events and in affairs, of low and high, honest and base," so the poet must encompass all manner of words, for

> The vocabulary of an omniscient man would embrace words and images excluded from polite conversation. What would be base, or even obscene, to the obscene, becomes illustrious, spoken in a new connexion of thought. The piety of the Hebrew prophets purges their grossness. ("The Poet," *W*, 3:17)

In the early passage on pulpit eloquence, we saw Emerson as the Miltonic orator whose devastating eloquence bespoke the absence of epistemological limits. Now we see Emerson as the would-be prose rhapsodist or poet whose heterogeneous eloquence corresponds to his Archimedean perspective. Emerson now desires a divine language that represents the gathering together of all modes of speech, "the gift of tongues" in eloquent, varied prophetic discourse.

The Panharmonicon of Language

The ferment of reform movements and experimental communities in the New England of the 1840s clearly excited Emerson: in his 1841 "Lecture on the Times" he often speaks of New England in words that resoundingly echo Milton's apocalyptic excitement in *Areopagitica* about the London of 1644, that "mansion house of liberty." There Milton had argued that with accelerated reforms already demonstrating England's privileged position at the vanguard of the millennium, the indiscriminate imposition of censorship was urgently to be avoided. Censorship of printing would impede the gathering together of the "thousand peeces" of "virgin Truth" "scatter'd . . . to the four winds" (*CPW*, 2:549). Emerson himself, though dismayed by the partial, eccentric, and misguided nature of current reform movements, also sees signs of a greater day approaching in the increased outpouring of the print-

ing presses, which would correct current biases through its comprehensiveness: "By the books it [society] reads and translates,
judge what books it will presently print. A great deal of the
profoundest thinking of antiquity, is now re-appearing in extracts
and allusions, and in twenty years will get all printed anew" (*W*,
1:275). And when Emerson heralds all this new activity – "See
how daring is the reading, the speculation, the experimenting of
the time" – his voice resonates with the exhilaration of Milton's
words:

> there be pens and heads there, sitting by their studious
> lamps, musing, searching, revolving new notions and idea's
> wherewith to present, as with their homage and their fealty
> the approaching Reformation: others as fast reading, trying
> all things, assenting to the force of reason and con-
> vincement. (*CPW*, 2:554)

But Milton's emphasis is a plea for toleration in a collective,
national effort, however fraught with tensions: since "there of
necessity will be much arguing, much writing, many opinions . . .
prudence, forbearance, charity might win all these diligences to
joyn, and unite into one generall and brotherly search after
Truth" (*CPW*, 2:554). Emerson's revised version, however, reveals
his vesting of all hopes in one individual: "If now some genius
shall arise who could unite these scattered rays" (*W*, 1:275). That
single "genius" would need to have gathered in himself all the
powers of speech that would otherwise also lie scattered. Moreover, that single genius would render superfluous the need for
"trying all things, assenting to the force of reason and con-
vincement."

Emerson's notion of the eloquent orator encompasses just
such a panoply of prophetic verbal abilities, corresponding to
those on which Milton also insists in *An Apology*, and that Milton
may have embodied for Emerson. As William Kerrigan observes,
Milton in *An Apology* presents "a magnificent description of the
[existing] kinds of ministry, a description which closely resembles
the myth of divided Truth in *Areopagitica*." Kerrigan proceeds to
note that, for Milton, those gifts are explicitly related to language:
"Christ possessed all the gifts of prophetic speech. When Christ
departed, these verbal gifts were divided among the various ministers . . . The finest servants of God will gather together, as occasion requires, the dismembered portions of the perfect ministry."[44] When Emerson resigns the ministerial pulpit for the more
expansive forum of the lyceum podium, we gain a glimpse of

precisely that prophetic, apocalyptic "genius" who gathers together once again the "dismembered portions of the perfect
ministry," and who speaks a correspondingly compendious language. In the following 1839 journal entry, Emerson's expression
reveals the familiar conflict between the strictures of Unitarian
discourse and true eloquence. He proclaims, under the twin titles
"Eloquence" and "Lyceum," the liberties of the lyceum "pulpit"
in facilitating his much-desired eloquence:

> Here is all the true orator will ask, for here is a convertible
> audience & here are no stiff conventions that prescribe a
> method, a style, a limited quotation of books, & an exact
> respect to certain books, persons, or opinions. No, here
> everything is admissible, philosophy, ethics, divinity, criti-
> cism, poetry, humor, fun, mimicry, anecdotes, jokes, ventril-
> oquism. All the breadth & versatility of the most liberal
> conversation highest lowest personal local topics, all are
> permitted, and all may be combined in one speech; it is a
> panharmonicon, – every note on the longest gamut, from
> the explosion of cannon, to the tinkle of a guitar. Let us try
> if Folly, Custom, Convention & Phlegm cannot hear our
> sharp artillery. Here is a pulpit that makes other pulpits
> tame & ineffectual – with their cold mechanical preparation
> for a delivery the most decorous, – fine things, pretty things,
> wise things, but no arrows, no axes, no nectar, no growling,
> no transpiercing, no loving, no enchantment. Here he may
> lay himself out utterly, large, enormous, prodigal, on the
> subject of the hour. Here he may dare to hope for ecstasy &
> eloquence. (*JMN,* 7:265 [1839])

This "prodigal" orator seems to contain within himself the same
vast diversity of language by which Emerson characterizes the
inspired poet and prophet. Here Emerson begins as a theatrical
performer but ends in a *furor poeticus.* In the mounting denunciation of "pulpits tame & ineffectual – with their cold mechanical
preparation" and their "exact respect to certain books, persons,
or opinions," as opposed to the "growling . . . transpiercing" he
desires, there is an audible translation of the earlier "Life, personal life is faint & cold to the energy of God" (JMN, 5:467
[1838]).

Moreover, in the mastery of language displayed, Emerson resembles the Milton of *An Apology,* who is solicitous to "entertaine
my selfe and him that list," (*CPW,* 1:922). Emerson, in fact, had
in an earlier lecture emphasized Milton's "mastery of language,"

his "performance on the instrument of language," which ranges from the "delicate melody" of his "pastoral ... fancies" to "the harsh discords of his polemic wrath" gathered from "the kennel and jakes as well as the palaces" (*EL*, 1:153). Emerson has probably registered Milton's own announcement that his prophetic roles modulate from the "harsh discord" of the *tuba dei* to the "smoother string" of the praising harp. In the care he must take, Milton compares himself to "some Musicians [who] are wont skilfully to fall out of one key into another without breach of harmony" (*CPW*, 1:922, 928). But in the journal passage just quoted, Emerson substitutes the "panharmonicon" for the traditional metaphors of inspiration – the trumpet, flute, harp, or lyre – all of which modulate within ranges narrower than Emerson's choice. The inspired Emersonian orator's speech is "a panharmonicon," an organlike instrument especially popular in the early nineteenth century. The panharmonicon that Emerson would have heard in Boston was a tour de force of musical instrument technology, one that was touted as being able to imitate "over 206 instruments"; it was even said of an earlier version that "every one of those metallic and wooden tubes has an eloquent speaking voice."[45] Indeed, this Emersonian orator seems capable of performing solo the "sevenfold chorus of Hallelujas & harping Symphonies" that herald the Apocalypse in Milton (*CPW*, 1:815). By means of substitution of tropes, Emerson's inspired orator becomes capable of polyphonic speech. The sheer power and plentitude of Emerson's polyvocality contained in this "one speech" overwhelms the daintily "decorous" and "pretty" language of Unitarian pulpits.

The apocalyptic power of Emerson's ideal discourse resides not only in its ability to assault ("Let us try if Folly, Custom, Convention & Phlegm cannot hear our sharp artillery") but also, and more distinctly, in its power to displace and supersede. Indeed, Emerson's behavior here might be deemed an act of verbal iconoclasm – a fanciful, faintly mocking, dismantling usurpation of Unitarian "pulpit" discourse usually defined by a particular sort of ritual and governed by certain conventions ("stiff conventions that prescribe a method, a style, a limited quotation of books, & an exact respect to certain books, persons, or opinions"). Undoubtedly the iconoclasts of Milton's age displayed far more vehement contempt for Anglican ceremony and decorum than does Emerson of the Unitarians. According to the (Anglican) Bishop Joseph Hall, during the English Civil War "a Lewd Wretch" showed blasphemous contempt by "walking before the Train in his Cope trailing in the Dirt, with a Service Book in his Hand, imitating, in an impious Scorn, the Tune, and usurping the Words of the Litany," and still others showed their scorn by "Piping on the destroy'd Organ Pipes."[46] Yet the "prodigality" of the Emersonian orator's discourse ("everything is admissible, philosophy, ethics, divinity, criticism, poetry, humor, fun, mimicry, anecdotes, jokes, ventriloquism") suggests a disregard for class boundaries: the well-educated Unitarian elite would find only the first half of the topics suitable to the sort of "self-culture" promulgated in the lyceums of the 1830s in the Northeast, while the popular, provincial, and pragmatic lyceum audiences would find only the latter half of the topics agreeable. This "prodigal" orator, moreover, issues a challenge to the culture of self-restraint and practicality – which lyceum lectures were meant to inculcate – proposing instead the culture of inspired self-abandon signaled by Emerson's language of "ecstasy" ("arrows, "axes," "nectar," "growling," "transpiercing," "enchantment").[47]

It is odd too that Emerson's "convertible audience" is felt to require such astonishingly diverse verbal skills. Presumably Emerson need not win them away from allegiance to a particular creed. The addition here of linguistic diversity to his earlier conception of an all-powerful language does not suggest that the orator commands enhanced powers of rational or emotional suasion. Just as Milton's notion of immediate revelation in *Christian Doctrine* elicited Channing's objection, so might Emerson's notion of suprarational, inspired eloquence have invited Channing's complaint that "it disparages and discourages our faculties, and produces inaction of mind, leading men to expect from a sudden flash from Heaven, the truth which we are taught to seek by the right use of our own powers" (58). Indeed, in this "panharmonicon" passage, Emerson experiments with being an orator whose verbal diversity once again declines concern for rhetorical effectiveness in its usual sense. Although Emerson imagines a sacred discourse circulating within a fallen world, its sound is neither the "babble" of confused tongues nor the various organ tones of Pandemonium's fallen angels, though it shares with both enterprises the desire for usurpation. Instead, it is a panlinguistic eloquence, one that resembles the Pentecostal "gift of tongues" Emerson so longs for in the Divinity School "Address." In his 1847 essay "Eloquence," Emerson describes a multiplicity of listeners lying dormant within each audience member; each listener waits to be touched by the consummate orator. That orator, Emerson explains, has within him a divine comprehensiveness: he is the prophetic Osiris/Truth/Christ figure who has gathered within him the "gift of tongues" diffused among the apostles but spoken simultaneously at the Apocalypse prophesied in Joel 2:28–29 and reiterated by Peter in Acts 2:16–21. When Emerson's "eloquent" orator speaks, the members of his audience "now hear their own native language for the first time, and leap to hear it (*W*, 7:67). Emerson echoes Milton's confidence in being inspired by the "eternall Spirit who can enrich with all utterance and knowledge" when he reassures his audience in *Self-Reliance* that "There is at this moment for you an utterance brave and grand as that of . . . the pen of Moses or Dante, but different from all these. Not possibly will the soul, all rich, all eloquent, with thousand-cloven tongue, deign to repeat itself" (*W*, 2:83–4). Thus Emerson's orator personae anticipate divine infusions that are not simply one unique and distinct utterance. Rather, they expect to exercise the full complement of verbal powers analogous to that of "the soul" or "the eternall Spirit" – "all rich, all eloquent, with thousand-cloven tongue."

By appropriating "the gift" of extraordinary Pentecostal powers for his ideal orator, Emerson not only repairs the linguistic ruins of Babel but contrives to prevent the diffusion of his verbal powers in acts of interpretation. This is perhaps a lesson he learns, not only from German Higher Criticism but also from that portion of Milton's *Christian Doctrine* quoted by Channing: "It is difficult to conjecture the purpose of Providence in committing the writings of the New Testament to such uncertain and variable guardianship," notes Milton, "unless it were to teach us by this very circumstance, that the Spirit which is given to us is a more certain guide than Scripture, whom, therefore, it is our duty to follow" (58). Moreover, we know from the "mocking" responses to the apostles' glossolalia as drunkenness in Acts 2:13, and from Paul's clear caveats in 1 Corinthians 14:5–19, that those who speak in tongues are unintelligible to the community unless their speech is interpreted. We may surmise, then, that the Emersonian orator's "panharmonicon" speech is meaningful to the individual addressed in her "native tongue," yet simultaneously unintelligible to all others until they in turn are addressed in "their own native language for the first time" (*W*, 7:67). What Emerson proposes, then, in his list of topics for the ideal "lyceum pulpit" where "everything is admissible," is not really a broadening of audience tastes from elitist to populist in opposition to Channing's complaint that "Literature . . . is becoming too popular." Rather, the

Emersonian orator's speech functions as prophecy to the individual who finds it intelligible, and as miraculous sign to those who do not. Emerson employs to his own purpose – indeed combines – what were two different kinds of ministry as articulated by Paul: "Wherefore tongues are for a sign, not to them that believe, but to them that believe not: but prophesying serveth not for them that believe not, but for them which believe" (1 Cor. 14:22).

When we think of the multiple personae or voices that constitute any one of Emerson's essays, we may do well to remember his panharmonicon, as well as Paul's words. Finally, we should remember the significance for Emerson of possessing these cumulative verbal powers. He sees that even while insisting upon the rhetorical necessity of heterogeneous discourse to sustain the ongoing Reformation, Milton simultaneously demonstrates his own artistic powers as well as his putative inspiration in his superb verbal responsiveness and pyrotechnical skills. Emerson now imagines himself the orator whose sacral language, like Milton's prophetic speech in his apocalyptic prose, exhibits a verbal range and virtuosity that is both the sign and seal of his fitness as a divine instrument in his American Reformation. On this basis, Emerson can "dare to hope for ecstasy & eloquence."

3

MARGARET FULLER'S "THE TWO HERBERTS," EMERSON, AND THE DISAVOWAL OF SEQUESTERED VIRTUE

I have been reading the lives of Lord Herbert of Cherbury, and of Sir Kenelm Digby. These splendid, chivalrous, and thoughtful Englishmen are meat which my soul loveth, even as much as my Italians. What I demand of men, – that they could act out all their thoughts, – these have. They are lives; – and of such I do not care if they had as many faults as there are days in the year, – there is the energy to redeem them. Do you not admire Lord Herbert's two poems on life, and the conjectures concerning celestial life? I keep them.

Margaret Fuller to Emerson

I have a great share of Typhon to the Osiris, wild rush and leap, blind force for the sake of force.

Margaret Fuller, Memoirs

Dante, thou didst not describe, in all thy apartments of Inferno, this tremendous repression of an existence half unfolded; this swoon as the soul was ready to be born.

Margaret Fuller to Caroline Sturgis[1]

While Margaret Fuller's alienation from "provincial" American culture has been compellingly delineated and her flight from "feminine" sentimental fiction to "masculine" republican history has been provocatively posed, her sense of being out of place in her own age has gone unremarked, although it is everywhere apparent in the nostalgia that pervades her depictions of seventeenth-century English culture.[2] In the first epigraph to this chapter, her admiration of Lord Herbert of Cherbury and Sir Kenelm Digby – both courtiers and pious philosophers in the age of James I and Charles I – reveals the scope of the active life that she herself craves ("meat which my soul loveth").[3] A new American edition of Milton's prose works provokes her wistful envy: "he was fortunate in an epoch fitted to develop him to his full stature – an epoch rich alike in thought, action and passion, in great results and still greater beginnings." Her verbal portraits of Lord Herbert of Cherbury (1583–1648) and his brother George Herbert (1593–1633) in her artful imaginary conversation "The Two Herberts" (1844) accentuate the individuality of the men and lament the attenuation of the once vital but now blighted aristocracy of England – "an external life grown out of proportion with that of the heart and mind."[4]

Fuller's fascination with seventeenth-century English culture and her dissatisfaction with contemporary American culture, in fact, appears to have been well-founded: in 1820 a New England reviewer of an edition of Madame de Staël's life and writings noted that contemporary American culture, while conducive to moral restraint and seeming to promote social amelioration, also had "powers of assimilation, the direct tendency of which is to destroy all high individuality of character, alike the good and the bad."[5] This process, Fuller insists, must be reversed by a bold figure who will redefine her age: "we need a new expression, peculiarly adapted to our time time" (18). For this role it is Emerson with whom Fuller most ries.[6]

Lord Herbert, Fuller, and the "Spiritual Man of the World"

In "The Two Herberts" Fuller declares, "the figure we most need to see before us now is not that of a saint, martyr, sage, poet, artist, preacher, or any other whose vocation leads to a seclusion and partial use of faculty, but 'a spiritual man of the world,' able to comprehend all things, exclusively dedicate to none . . . In the past it will be difficult to find one more adequate than the life and person of Lord Herbert" (18). These words bear a significant resemblance to her own words, reprinted in her *Memoirs*, describing what she desires to be: "It is a mockery thus to play the artist with life, and dip the brush in one's own heart's blood. One would fain be no more artist, or philosopher, or lover, or critic, but a soul ever rushing forth in tides of genial life" (*M*, 1:294). In the imaginary dialogue, her identification with Lord Herbert is sustained, moreover, by her corresponding concern with issues important to him – for example, religious toleration and companionate marriage. She reveals her own wistful desires for a deep, binding union in acknowledging, through Lord Herbert, that so far "I had postponed all hopes except of fleeting joys or ideal pictures" (32). Indeed, she repeats similar words about Lord Herbert in *Woman in the Nineteenth Century*, quoting lines from one of his poems appended to his autobiography ("Were not our souls immortal made, / Our equal loves can make them such") and offering details about his arranged marriage to suggest the ideals of companionate marriage never to be surrendered, if infinitely postponed.[7]

By employing in "The Two Herberts" the genre of a Landor-like imaginary conversation, Fuller is able to acknowledge resemblance yet emphasize the polarity between Emerson and herself in the guise of the two brothers, each of whom attempts to reduce the other's subjectivity to his own identity, though each is ultimately able to resist the other's impulse. Throughout her long and highly artful imaginary dialogue, written in her prose and the two brothers' verse, the richer dimensions, bolder aspirations, and tested convictions of Lord Herbert, with whom she appears to identify, contrast with the less compelling though sweetly admirable life of his reclusive brother, the famous religious poet. The contrast is, moreover, informed by a Transcendentalist value system based on self-culture and consequently depicted in language so fraught with disdain for and fear of the individual's arrested development, whether from "repression" or lack of inspiration ("this swoon"),[8] that such a state might constitute a kind of hell worthy of being added to Dante's Inferno, as the third epigraph to this chapter suggests. Though imputed by each brother to the other, this disparity in development is rendered most convincingly, albeit genially, between "the brother and the child" (19).

Fuller's depiction of the relationship between the elder brother, Lord Herbert, and George Herbert becomes even more evocative of her relationship with Emerson (despite his seniority) when we realize that some of Emerson's early poems were highly reminiscent of George Herbert's poetry. Indeed, one of other editors of Fuller's *Memoirs* used Emerson's poem "Grace" as one of the epigraphs for his own chapter on Fuller, mistakenly believing the poem to be Herbert's. (Emerson responded with a mixture of pleasure and humility: "For your mottoes to your chapter, I saw that the first had the infinite honor done it of being quoted to Herbert! The verses are mine, – 'Preventing God,' etc. – so I strike them out."[9] Not coincidentally, I suggest, Emerson's impressions of Margaret Fuller in the *Memoirs* are fraught with similar insinuations of *her* cultural puerility but also with his uneasy assumption of the "right to lead her." Although her knowledge of foreign languages and literature was remarkable,

> her English reading was incomplete . . . she was little read in Shakespeare; and I believe I had the pleasure of making her acquainted with Chaucer, with Ben Jonson, with Herbert, Chapman, Ford, Beaumont and Fletcher, with Bacon, and Sir Thomas Browne. I was seven years her senior, and had the habit of idle reading in old English books, and, though not much versed, yet quite enough to give me the right to lead her. (*M*, 1:204)

The section in *Woman in the Nineteenth Century* in which Fuller depicts the "possibilities of woman" and companionate relationships in the English Renaissance (in the writings of Shakespeare, Spenser, Ford, Massinger, Lovelace, Col. John Hutchinson, Donne, and Lord Herbert) may well be her rebuttal to Emerson's charge of an insufficiently mastered canon of English texts. Fuller's "Two Herberts" in part reenacts her rivalry with Emerson – one he reciprocated in his ambivalent and often captious rendering of Fuller in the *Memoirs*. If "in a passionate love-struggle she wrestled with the genius of De Stael, of Rousseau, . . . of Petrarch" (*M*, 1:113), as her friend and editor James Freeman Clarke wrote of her, Fuller engaged with Emerson in a mutual struggle, each to attain the authority to "lead" the other and their age.

Moreover, Fuller tactically emphasizes the "subversive" and inclusive aspects of Lord Herbert's philosophy of natural religion to articulate her own troubled sense of revealed Christianity's exclusivity and of liberal New England Christianity's "feminization." Fuller resurrects in her dialogue between two brothers – one the "representative of natural religion," the other the representative of the "Son of Man" – the seventeenth-century debate on natural and revealed religion. Indeed, while she frames her imaginary conversation with the claims that it was written as a setting for her translation of Lord Herbert's sacred poems (15) and that it was an affirmation of affinity between the two brothers just before George Herbert's death ("one true hour of friendship" [34]), she focuses the dialogue on their very different ways to faith and their irreconcilable differences over the extent of human agency. Encoded in Lord Herbert's promulgation of natural religion is Fuller's assessment of Transcendentalism as more highly evolved than its Unitarian source, and Lord Herbert's as the more "mature" and enabling expression of belief, the one that more fully teases out the social implications of these two systems of belief. As the proponent of natural religion and the efficacy of human agency, the historical Lord Herbert exhibited inclusive and enabling propensities in his epistemological treatise *De Veritate* (1624) "against revealed religion": he inferred the existence of an innate faculty and "common notions" within the human mind that permitted to all sane individuals access to truth and true religious knowledge.[10] (It was in fact to this treatise that Locke addressed the argument against innate ideas in the first book of *The Essay on Human Understanding*.) Fuller, through Lord Herbert's speeches, expresses the issue in terms of the disenfranchised, stressing the partial, exclusionary, and prejudicial nature of a revealed religion in which God favors "one race and nation, and not another" with extraordinary demonstrations of his grace and will "at the expense of another." Fuller's Lord Herbert, whose values nicely coincide with Transcendentalist values (which encouraged self-culture in all),[11] eliminates infantilizing dependency ("prayers") upon the will of a partial and personal God for favors ("gifts of grace"), wresting the power to gain knowledge and immediate experience of the divine ("aspirations") instead for all individuals through their inborn faculty.

Fuller's depiction of Lord Herbert's attitude toward his life as a courtier, soldier, and diplomat, her emphasis on his egalitarian access to divine truths, and her translation of his Latin (Neoplatonic) poems of aspiration become for her the creative means by which she dissociates "aspiration" from moral and spiritual nonage, and spiritual growth from dependency, "effeminacy" (a term her Lord Herbert uses), and sequestration. (In one of her most depleted moments, she speaks of herself in a letter in terms of aspiration nearly thwarted, as one of those "who are but the hieroglyphics of their future being. Souls which must be all before they can speak one word, Destinies strangely mismatched with the ungrateful Hermes, travel to the mount of life through fields of graves, and nothing is heard but the slow tread of their footsteps" [*L,* 2:199].) She contests with Emerson for the role of Lord Herbert, a philosopher with whom Emerson clearly had much in common and whose voice in this dialogue often sounds like the familiar Emerson. She, in fact, chooses to acknowledge the Lord Herbert within herself while distancing herself from George Herbert – the devotional poet most often characterized as "the supplicant" – instead relegating Emerson to that role.

In *The Feminization of American Culture,* Ann Douglas has demonstrated that women, the clergy, and authors were similarly socially and politically disenfranchised in antebellum New England, relegated to the professedly central but actually peripheral and secluded roles of "refining" the culture morally and spiritually ("the figure we most need to see before us now is not that of a saint . . . sage, poet, artist, preacher, or any other whose vocation leads to a seclusion and partial use of faculty").[12] Fuller's disdain for the benighted "partiality" of Christianity and her uneasiness with the symbolically feminized roles of authorship and the religious ministry (something we saw also troubling Emerson in Chapter 2) originate in the same problem: the culture's attempt to make spiritual enrichment and moral refinement the task of particular groups strategically esteemed by their society for their "cloister'd virtue" – virtue removed from all temptations and challenges. In "What Soft – Cherubic Creatures – / These Gentlewomen are," Emily Dickinson similarly registers the result in her contempt of a Christianity "so refined" ("Such Dimity Convictions – A Horror so refined / of freckled Human Nature–/ Of Deity – ashamed"), and insists instead upon its robustness: "It's such a common – Glory – / A Fisherman's Degree – / Redemption – Brittle Lady / Be so – ashamed of Thee." And Madame de Staël, whose life and writings Fuller carefully studied, justified not offering models of good behavior in her novels as was expected in the sentimental fiction associated with women, based upon the necessity of seeing virtue tested and provocations to growth and choice offered: "the best thing to be done to him, who wishes to be good and wants not correctness but firmness of purpose, is to inspire a dread of faults, which they whose feelings are pure and delicate and whose intentions are good, commit when placed under tempting circumstances and stimulated by passion." Although de Staël rhetorically implies that this is an accommodation of the accepted moral paradigm associated with fiction written by women, she also implies a criticism of sequestered virtue. And indeed, de Staël's largely sympathetic reviewer for the *North American Review* exhibited some uncertainty about how precisely to gauge her achievements, since "her sex increases the difficulty of judging her aright as an author," and in a just assessment, we need to remember, though we are apt to forget, "that she was one of a sex whose minds are trammelled and attenuated by the customs of society."[13]

Fuller's Lord Herbert even more conspicuously insists upon the combative way to truth: "we need the assaults of other minds to quicken our powers, so easily hushed to sleep, and call it peace. The mind takes a bias too easily, and does not examine whether from tradition or a native growth intended by the heavens" (24). Fuller appropriates Lord Herbert's voice to argue that both individual effort and the "exercise" of judgment are needed for the individual to ascend to spiritual and psychological maturity. (We are reminded here of Emerson's comment in "Quotation and Originality": "It is a familiar expedient of brilliant writers, and not less of witty talkers, the device of ascribing their own sentence to an imaginary person, in order to give it weight, – as Cicero, Cowley, Swift, Landor, and Carlyle have done.")[14] Her Lord Herbert insists that while some who enjoy worldly prosperity are made "effeminate and slothful by want of that exercise which difficulty brings . . . this is not the case with me"; "the goal which my secret mind, from earliest infancy, prescribed, has been high enough to task all my energies" (24). If worldly graces came too easily to Lord Herbert and intellectual accomplishment too easily to Fuller, the trials and buffetings of ever broadening experiences and the internal catalyst of a "goal which my secret mind . . . prescribed" would ensure Fuller's desiderata of ever-deepening spiritual, psychological, and intellectual maturity. She imagined that goal in the image of "a well-tempered wine," which, says her Lord Herbert, with what now seems prescient irony for the woman who was to die in a shipwreck, "has been carried over many seas, and escaped many shipwrecks"(25).

In the Image of Emerson: Fuller's Reclusive George Herbert and "Effeminate" Dependency

A reviewer for the *Democratic Review,* commenting upon Margaret Fuller's portrait of George Herbert in the dialogue, praised her "reverent study of his sacred poems," and noted more generally of "The Two Herberts" that she "does justice to the temperaments of both these literary heroes – reconciling differences, showing like results under different names."[15] While differences between the brothers are not so muted or "reconciled" in the dialogue as this reviewer suggests, Fuller does indeed fluently incorporate into her imaginary dialogue untitled excerpts from George Herbert's poems ("Prayer (I)" [20], "The Pearl" [21–22], "Affliction (I)" [25], "A True Hymn" [30]) and alludes cleverly to the titles of many others ("The Collar" [20], "The Pearl" [22], "Church Music" [32], "The Elixir" [33], and "The Flower" [34]). But her choice of excerpts and the remarks she voices through the reclusive poet create the impression of a meek, ethereal, and serene man, who differs considerably in temperament from the emotional and tormented persona that emerges from Herbert's sacred poems. Hers is neither the dramatic, rebellious sinner anguished by his own sinfulness and self-doubt nor the priest who savors the sensuousness and consolation of Anglican sacraments. Instead, she creates George Herbert in the image of the Emerson she perceives. Accordingly, she neutralizes Herbert's orthodox sacramental symbolism, displacing his eucharistic images – "that liquour sweet and most divine," / Which my God feels as bloud; but I, as wine" (in "The Agonie")[16] – with the more secular "banner of my Master" and the more natural (or neoplatonic) act of taking "drink at what I have found the fountain of pure wisdom" (21).

Her George Herbert in fact bears a considerable resemblance to her impressions of a dispassionate and emotionally withholding Emerson, to whom she once thought of sending as a "literary curiosity" a description in verse and prose of "one of my naughtiest moods," but then thought better of it: "this might destroy relations, and I might not be able to be calm and chip marble with you any more, if I talked to you in magnetism and music" (*M*, 1:230).

Given her view of Emerson (one quite different from the privately self-conflicted Emerson we saw in Chapter 2), it is not surprising that in her portrayal of the reclusive younger brother the striking tensions in Herbert's poetry between his own anxious agency and God's will disappear, to be replaced with what seems an amiable complaisance and placidity on the part of Fuller's Emersonian Herbert. Although she alludes to the dramatic colloquy of Herbert's "The Collar," in which God sharply checks the reckless rebelliousness of his exasperated supplicant, Fuller herself depicts George Herbert's "choleric temper" as reasonably and gently corrected by God, involving hardly more than being counseled to abjure "magnetism and music" and instead to "be calm and chip marble": "My Master has been very good to me in suggestions of restraining prayer, which come into my mind at the hour of temptation" (20). Certainly, Emerson's own early poem "Grace" (the one that was mistaken by W. H. Channing as Herbert's) justifies Fuller's depiction in its thankful assurance of effectual grace – one that lacks the anxiety, restlessness, constant vigilance, and frequent nervous despondency of Herbert's actual poems.[17] Instead, Emerson proclaims, "How much, preventing God, how much I owe / To the defences thou hast round me set!

. . . The depths of sin to which I had descended, / Had not these
me against myself defended."[18]

But clearly Emerson is complex and many-sided, and the Emerson to whom Fuller imagined she could not speak of naughty
moods or "magnetism and music" in 1839 is not quite the same
Emerson whose observations, also written in 1839, on the "panharmonicon" of lyceum eloquence were examined in Chapter 2. Emerson's journal passage, we will recall, exhibited neither what Fuller interprets as his habitual emotional economy nor what she
believes is his characteristically diligent craftsmanship ("to be calm
and chip marble with you"). Rather, it expressed the dramatic pro-
fusion and "prodigality" of eloquence. That affirmation of the
range, liberality, and bountifulness of his new-found "eloquence"
may in fact be Emerson's rendition of Herbert's poem simultaneously defining and enacting "Prayer." "All the breadth & versatility
of the most liberal conversation highest lowest personal local topics . . . every note on the longest gamut, from the explosion of
canon, to the tinkle of guitar . . . [lacking] no arrows, no axes, no
nectar, no growling, no transpiercing, no loving, no enchantment." Similarly, Herbert's "Prayer (I)" offers an abundant collocation of epithets ranging from the mild, "the Church's banquet,
Angels' age / God's breath in man returning to his birth" to the
dynamic music of apocalyptic power: "The Christian plummet
sounding heav'n and earth; / Engine against th'Almighty, sinners'
towre, / Reversed thunder, Christ-side-piercing spear / The six-
daies' world transposing in a houre, / A kinde of tune, which all
things heare and feare" (*EPGH*, 51; Fuller, 21). Emerson's concluding assertion that the lyceum orator "may dare to hope for ecstasy & eloquence" has within it the sense of an expectation fulfilled similar to Herbert's concluding line, "The land of spices;
something understood." Despite all the emotional and verbal dy-
namism exhibited in Emerson's journal entry and in Herbert's
poem, and despite their expectations of efficacious communion,
Fuller's George Herbert recites the entirety of "Prayer (I)" in the
imaginary conversation only to find that Lord Herbert has heard
in it largely the difference between his brother's spiritual dependency and his own self-possession: "you have expressed yourself
nearest mine own knowledge and feeling, where you have left
more room to consider our prayers as aspirations, rather than gifts
of grace; as – Heart in pilgrimage; . . . A kinde of tune, which all
things heare and fear . . . Something understood" (21).

One critic has compellingly demonstrated Emerson's "agon"

with George Herbert's poetry. In *Nature* (where he uses excerpts from Herbert's "Man") and in the Divinity School "Address" (a response to the allure of apostasy in Herbert's "The Collar") Emerson was "very precisely rewriting and unwriting Herbert in a single gesture of imitative cancellation." That gesture involved not only "a naturalistic redefinition of Herbert's entire sacramental system" but also Emerson's assumption of a "psychology of adult apostasy," one superseding Herbert's obedient, theistic theology of immaturity.[19]

Evidently, in the years between 1836 and 1839, the early years of Emerson's and Fuller's acquaintance, Emerson struggled with the power of Herbert's poetry and an ongoing self-authorization to reject a personal God. Fuller captured something of that early Emerson in her portrayal of George Herbert – the poet with whom she too shared certain similarities of sensibility and position, among them, the anxiety of waiting for inspiration.[20] Fuller here depicts both an Emerson and a Herbert shorn of much of their private anxieties, self-doubts, and exertions – as if, not buffeted by external circumstances, they had no internal challenges to meet. (Perhaps this is the only side of Emerson he allowed her to see.) Her George Herbert is shown to have arrived at an acceptance of his circumscribed and dispossessed existence as a country parson, primogeniture having given the elder brother all the worldly goods and its attendant forum (25). The lines she quotes from "Affliction (I)," however, do not present the dynamic struggles and cross-currents that alone distinguish George Herbert's consent and mature acceptance of God's will from disillusioned resignation.

Emerson's Fuller, Lord Herbert, and the Victory of Exertion

Fuller is sparing in her willingness to endow Emerson or George Herbert with the power conferred by victory over heroic challenges and prefers instead to depict their reclusiveness as qualifying their successes. Similarly, Emerson, through his selections of her writings, shapes Fuller in her posthumous *Memoirs* in ways that sometimes enhance the limitations he perceived in her. And yet one recent critic is quite right to note the frequency with which Emerson allows Fuller some considerable autonomy in the *Memoirs* by juxtaposing his own interpretations of her with excerpts from her letters and other personal writings clearly contradicting or undermining his words.[21] Emerson explicitly terms her fascination with coincidences "puerile" ("this catching at straws of coincidence"), but then goes on to supply instances from her letters justifying her belief, and to add his own reconsidered response that "her own experiences, early and late, seemed strangely to justify" this "propensity" (*M*, 1:221–2). Further, Emerson includes her remarks on Lord Herbert (in the first epigraph to this chapter) to dramatize her struggle in choosing between fallible human relationships and the art of the ideal in writing – an art, he suggests by his selections, uncongenial to her disposition. Yet her own words suggest instead a hunger ("meat which my soul loveth") for a larger stage, like Sir Kenelm Digby's and Lord Herbert's, upon which "to act out all [her] thoughts": she grasps what the "art" of these men was–"they are lives . . . there is the energy to redeem them" (*M*, 1:295). In excerpts Emerson arranges on the same page, her own verses contrastingly display a self-acknowledged meretriciousness, disconnected from the life that would give them authenticity: "I am ashamed when I think there is scarce a line of poetry in them, – all rhetorical and impassioned, as Goethe said of De Stael" (*M*, 1:295). In many instances, then, Emerson intimates that her profound frustrations with her writing were a sign of something in writing uncongenial to her (female) nature, but he also allows her own words to suggest that she was dissatisfied with authorship not exercised, as was Lord Herbert's, by the fullest range of experience in life and within oneself.

Emerson similarly arranged the passages (the second and third epigraphs to this chapter) in her *Memoirs* to convey something of Fuller's "temperament," a term he uses in his essay "Experience" to denote limitations of character. In the section of the *Memoirs* that he entitled "Temperament," he depicts her haunted restlessness, her "inscrutab[ility]" ("her strength was not my strength – her powers were a surprise" [*M*, 1:228]), and her "nocturnal element" involving states of painful excitement and claims of occult powers. Yet her own words about Typhon and Osiris as well as about Dante's *Inferno* in the epigraphs to this chapter reveal no overwrought energies – no "nocturnal element" barely dignified by "as fine names as it would carry" (*M*, 1:230). Instead, the words confess her titanic, overwhelming power, thresholds and conflicts nearly surmounted, and anguished, arrested force. Emerson implies that Fuller's idiosyncrasies often overwhelm her powers of discernment, leading her to find something of "true portraiture in a disagreeable novel of Balzac's *Le Livre Mystique*, in which an equivocal figure exerts alternately a masculine and feminine influence on the characters of the plot" (*M*, 1:229). The evocative lines he next quotes from her poem "To the Moon" virtually proclaim, it seems from his setting, her eccentric perceptions: "But if I steadfast gaze upon thy face, / A human secret, like my own, I trace; / For, through the woman's smile looks the male eye" (*M,* 1:229). Although Emerson ascribes to her an unbecoming, indeed immature, belief in mystical forces ("somewhat a little pagan about her" [*M,* 1:219]), and hints that provincial gullibility made her "a willing listener to all the uncertain science of mesmerism and its goblin brood, which have been rife in recent years" [*M,* 1:229]), her allusions to the menacingly powerful and the occult and her blending of the masculine and the feminine in the passages he quotes reveal a desire for comprehensiveness that excludes no ranges of experience. Indeed, Lord Herbert's poems – particularly his "conjectures concerning the celestial life" – probably appealed so much to her ("I keep reading them") because they attempt to imagine what lies beyond established thresholds bounded by the human body. In combination with Fuller's own words, what emerges from Emerson's depiction of a Fuller who has "somewhat a little pagan about her" is a portrait of Fuller whom he obliquely acknowledges could be a Lord Herbert figure.

Strategies of Reconciliation

Most interesting in the dynamics of Fuller's two brothers' relationship is their respective gendered strategies for eliminating difference within Fuller's larger plan for acknowledging difference. In the larger plan, Fuller chooses two seventeenth-century figures for her dialogue, implying likeness yet teasing out the gendering consequences of Renaissance primogeniture, which elevates the eldest son (Lord Herbert) "at the expense" of the younger (George Herbert), who is largely reduced to disenfranchised feminine dependency and envy of the elder's privilege of worldly action: "Whereas my birth and spirits rather took / The way that takes the town; / Thou didst betray me to a lingering book, / and wrap me in a gown" (lines 37–40) (*EPGH,* 47; Fuller, 25). Fuller takes these words from George Herbert's poem "Affliction (I)," where they are addressed to God, whose power is manifested in the innumerable reverses the poet has suffered, eliciting his uncomprehending anguish ("Thus doth thy power crosse-bias me" [line 53]). Fuller, however, portrays Lord Herbert repeating these words of imagined reproach from his younger brother's poem (25), words that Herbert implies must surely resonate with accusations of stolen agency, and even infantilization ("betray me to a lingering book / and wrap me in a gown"). George Herbert's acknowledgment of God's power has become, in Fuller's dialogue, an implied indictment of the system of primogeniture and the inequities and dependencies it creates.[22] Fuller's version tellingly shifts the source of arbitrary power and inequity to human institutions, the inadequacies of which she felt keenly in her own culture (particularly as they affected women), but against which she felt human action might be efficacious.

In her personal letters, Fuller does allow herself to identify with George Herbert in speaking of the pain of her domestic, quotidian burdens ("I feel like Herbert, the weight of 'businesse to be done,' but the bird-like particle would skim and sing at the sweet places" [L, 3:80]) and in writing to another woman about her lack of control over her own life, even as she tries to content herself with what compensations are given: "Destiny which still 'cross biases me' as Herbert said it did of him, refusing me what I desired, solitude and quiet in which to concentrate my powers, has rewarded my submission to her guidance with . . . many new and sweet thoughts, and extending hope, a clearer faith" (L, 3:56–7 [1842]). Herbert's "Affliction (I)" again comes to her mind when she expresses to yet another woman her frustration with outward circumstances, even as she is proffered compensations:

> My inward life has been rich and deep . . . It seems to me that Heaven, whose course has ever been to "cross-bias me," as Herbert hath it, is no niggard in its compensations . . . [and yet] I have indeed, been forced to take up old burdens . . . the pen has been snatched from my hand just as I longed to give myself to it . . . forced to dissipate when I wished to concentrate, to feel the hourly pressure of others mental wants when it seemed otherwise I was just on the point of satisfying my own. (L, 3:40 [1842])

To the extent that Fuller allows herself to feel the burdens of George Herbert's "Affliction," she has secularized the source as the will of society, the vagaries of her familial domestic circumstances, or the unfathomable will of a lover – not the inscrutable will of Herbert's God. Indeed, in a letter to her lover James Nathan, who had abandoned her, Fuller uses lines from Herbert's poem "The Temper" in a desperate attempt to mitigate the discord in their relationship as "but the tuning of the breast / To make the music better" (L, 4:117 [1845]). In so doing, she

shifts the strife between Herbert and his God to her very human
conflict, trying to accept the torture, and to make Herbert's
justification of helplessness her own ("Yet take thy way; for sure
thy way is best," insists Herbert, "Stretch or contract mee / thy
poor debtor" [lines 21–2]),[23] hoping all the while for a reconciliation and a greater concord. Her moments of identification with
George Herbert, then, are moments when she is most chastened
by circumstances: when her energies are most depleted, her goals
most jeopardized ("the pen has been snatched from my hand"),
and when she is most cajoled to accept the limitations of a "woman's sphere" with the lure of a compensatory inner life of imaginative power and personal love. It is the crushing limitations George
Herbert suffered at every turn that she most identifies with – and
wishes most to escape.[24]

Indeed, her own sympathy for the disenfranchised informs her
portrayal of the feminized and ethereal George Herbert, who
has learned, as she sometimes fears she might, to embrace the
ambiguous benefits of his circumstances. Her George Herbert,
for example, poses the possibility – one which her own culture
strategically endorsed but which her Lord Herbert dismisses –
that worldly demands make true contemplation and spiritual
discernment impossible, that only seclusion permits spiritual rip-
ening: "My brother does not think the mind is free to act in
courts and camps," remarks Lord Herbert (24). And her George
Herbert distrusts Lord Herbert's confidence in the power of human agency – a confidence prominently displayed in Lord Herbert's two sacred Latin poems of aspiration included in translation by Fuller. Indeed, she portrays a George Herbert who
affiliates himself through his religious beliefs with characteristics
associated with women in Fuller's culture: with human weakness
(29–30) (recall here Fuller's ironic, Shakespearean epigraph to
Woman in the Nineteenth Century: "Frailty, thy name is Woman");
with the need for support and association (29); and with the
Victorian polarized associations of the "heart" rather than the
"mind." "Let me answer in a strain," says Fuller's George Herbert,
"which bespeaks my heart as truly, if not as nobly as yours answers
to your [Lord Herbert's] great mind" (30). It is with some conde-
scension as well as affection that her George Herbert insists that
his elder brother, implicitly the prodigal son, will eventually receive "every conviction which a human needs, to be reconciled to
the Parent of all" (30).

Just as Fuller, in *Woman in the Nineteenth Century,* exhorts women
not to accept, much less embrace, their infantilized position, so

her Lord Herbert asks his younger brother to reconsider his theistic-orientation and his dependent position as a child to "the Parent of all."[25] Lord Herbert urges his brother not to speak in terms of an interposing higher power that helps him curb his temper (like the "Preventing God" of Emerson's "Grace," who anticipates and defends him from "The depths of sin to which I had descended / Had not these me against myself defended"). Instead, her Lord Herbert rephrases his brother's language to emphasize his brother's abdicated power: "Why do you not say, rather, that your own discerning mind and maturer will show you more and more the folly and wrong of such outbreaks" (20). Moreover, to his brother's question whether he ever doubted or wavered in his beliefs, Lord Herbert admits that his confidence sometimes alternates with misgivings, but "I do not count those weak moments, . . . they are not my true life" (30). And in his Latin poem translated by Fuller as "Conjectures Concerning Heavenly Life," he argues strongly for human agency: "the sleeping minds which heaven prepares from the beginning – / Only our labor and industry can vivify, / Polishing them with learning and with morals"; moreover, it is "by the use of our free will, we put to rout those ills / Which heaven has neither dispelled, nor will hereafter dispel" (28). This poem, as well as "Life," are the very poems Fuller praised to Emerson in her letter of 1842 (the first epigraph to this chapter), and which she translated for her American readers, blending her voice with Lord Herbert's.[26] Evidently, she so completely appropriated one of the English authors to whom Emerson introduced her that she could ask him, as if she had forgotten, "Do you not admire Lord Herbert's two poems on life, and the conjectures concerning celestial life? I keep reading them."[27] And so it seems that each brother in her dialogue sees the other as poised for the spiritual growth that he himself has attained, and each urges the other to "grow up" – intimations that echo in Emerson's response to Fuller in the *Memoirs* no less than in Fuller's response to Emerson in this dialogue.

Yet for all these acknowledgments of differences, when Fuller employs the test of religious tolerance (perhaps the most crucial issue developing in England at the time in which this imaginary dialogue is set [1633]), she reveals each brother's gendered strategy for reducing the subjectivity of the other to resemble his own. Paradoxically, it is the feminized George Herbert who employs the most aggressive and mastering maneuvers, insisting upon orthodox religious absolutism at exactly the moment when Lord Herbert is trying to interpret his brother's words as expressing a religious tolerance that avoids such mastering absolutism. (Lord Herbert's *De Veritate* was in fact intended to end religious conflict and priestcraft by demonstrating a universal access to the truths necessary for salvation [five "common notions"] and by basing the certainty of knowledge, which is otherwise only probable, on the consensus of all sane individuals, rather than upon the words of an elect few.)

Initially, in an attempt to show his appreciation of his brother, Fuller's George Herbert offers a gesture of inclusiveness, alluding to the argument of Lord Herbert's posthumously published *De Religione Gentilium* (1663).[28] There Lord Herbert maintained, as an extension of his thoughts in *De Veritate*, that the historical record of the religion of the Gentiles showed that Greek and Roman religious beliefs, when stripped of sacerdotal superstition, were identical with his five "common notions," and may even represent them more clearly than later religious phenomena. Fuller's George Herbert appears at first to accept the ancients by speaking lines from Herbert's poem "The Pearl. Matt. 13:45" that suggest an acceptance of natural religion: "I would not blot from the book of life the prophets and priests that came before Him, nor those antique sages who knew all '[T]hat reason hath from nature borrowed, / Or of it self, like a good huswife, spunne / In laws and policie; what the starers conspire, / What willing nature speaks; what, forc'd [freed] by fire: / Both th'old discoveries, and the new-found seas, / The stock and surplus, cause and history' " (lines 3–8: *EPGH*, 88; Fuller, 21–2). He goes on to embrace his brother in these words: "As I cannot resign and disparage these, because they have not what I conceive to be the pearl of knowledge, how could I you?" (22). But the original poem in fact does "resign and disparage" human exertion, including human learning, in an unequivocal acknowledgment of a spiritual hierarchy and the priceless treasure gained in accepting revealed religion: "I know all these, and have them in my hand: / Therefore not sealed, but with open eyes / I flie to thee, and fully understand / Both the main sale, and the commodities / And at what rate and price I have thy love" (lines 31–5: *EPGH*, 89). For those familiar with George Herbert's poems, as she suggest many of her American readers are, George Herbert's acknowledgment of natural reason and his acceptance of the ancients are established only in order to be undermined by the reversal expected at the poem's "turn" toward God.

Yet given Fuller's complete excision of George Herbert's hierarchy placing revealed religion above natural religion, Lord Herbert is not entirely misguided in initially attributing to his brother an egalitarian charitableness: "Were all churchmen as tolerant, I had never assailed the basis of their belief. Did they not insist and urge upon us their way as the one only way, not for them alone, but for all, none would wish to put stumbling-blocks before their feet" (22). Deploring dogmatism and sectarian self-righteousness, Lord Herbert would refashion his brother in his own image. But his younger brother resists, insisting unequivocally and unabashedly, "None, more than I, can think there is but one way to arrive finally at truth" (22). Still, Lord Herbert refuses to concede he has misunderstood his brother; instead he behaves toward George with the tolerance he prefers and exemplifies the kind of pluralism he would encourage: "feeling that you are one who accept[s] what you do from love of the best, and not from fear of the worst, I am as much inclined to tolerate your conclusions as you to tolerate mine" (22). Lord Herbert resists acknowledging what seems to him his brother's dogmatism.

But Fuller's George Herbert responds with a composure and brusque assurance that the poet's persona rarely evinces in George Herbert's actual poems: "I do not consider yours as conclusions, but only as steps to such. The progress of the mind should be from natural to revealed religion, as there must be a sky for the sun to give light through its expanse" (22). However much Fuller's George Herbert employs the secular vocabulary associated with his brother's natural religion, the younger brother still reckons spiritual maturity by the scale of spiritual hierarchy; indeed, he uses this naturalistic language to trap Lord Herbert, who exclaims, "The sky is – nothing!" To this George Herbert artfully rejoins, "Except room for a sun, and such there is in you" (22). With a Christic pun, he brings closure to the debate on tolerance and implies revealed religion's superiority.

Just as Lord Herbert attempts to ascribe to his brother his own tolerant values and make him speak his language of efficacious will and independent intellectual discernment, so George Herbert would refashion his brother in his own image. George Herbert insists that Lord Herbert's prayer to God requesting a divine sign approving the publication of *De Veritate* was a true if inadvertent acknowledgment of self-distrust and of the need for spiritual dependency: "Of your own need of such, did you not give convincing proof when you prayed for a revelation to direct whether you should publish a book against revelation?" (22). George Herbert's phrasing here so clearly raises the specter of Lord Herbert's inconsistency that Fuller includes, along with Lord Herbert's actual, verbatim account of the incident in which his prayer was miraculously answered, an assertive footnote supporting Lord Herbert's resorting to prayer: "It should be respected as evidence," Fuller insists in her own voice, "of his [Lord Herbert's] integrity, being, like the rest of his memoir, a specimen of absolute truth and frankness towards himself and all other beings" (22).

Her George Herbert attempts to undermine Lord Herbert in pointing to this event as evidence not only of his self-delusion in thinking human reason sufficient to salvation but also of his implicitly egotistical expectation that the "customary order of nature . . . be deranged in your behalf. What miraculous record does more?" (23). Fuller resurrects at this point the seventeenth-century debate on revealed and natural religion, which, as seen in Chapter 1, reemerged in the Unitarian and Transcendentalist controversy over miracles. Emerson figured prominently in that controversy by appropriating miracles as the daily bounty of life ("one with the blowing clover and the falling rain") rather than the anomaly cited by the Unitarians as evidence of Christianity's revealed status and consequent assurance of its certainty and supremacy among the world's religions. Whereas Emerson was concerned to naturalize the miraculous no less than the sacramental aspects of revealed religion, and to establish intuition as the source of certain knowledge, Fuller's focus in this dialogue coincides more with the socially radical Transcendentalists' concerns (such as those, as seen in Chapter 1, of Orestes Brownson): she focuses on the potentially devastating effects – spiritual, social, and political – of revealed religion's exclusiveness. Indeed, her Lord Herbert strikes at revealed religion on behalf of those it disenfranchises. He professes "disbelief in a partial plan of salvation for the nations, which, by its necessarily limited working, excludes the majority of men up to our day" (23), and explains that he can accept his miracle only because it was at no one else's "expense" ("it was at the expense of none other . . . nothing special, nothing partial wrought in my behalf, more than if I had arrived at the same conclusion by a process of reasoning" [23]).

Fuller's Lord Herbert argues implicitly for self-enabling access to truth, insisting that as long as no one is excluded, there are many ways to truth, even the miraculous: "each individual soul, wherever born, however nurtured, may receive immediate response, in an earnest hour, from the source of truth . . . A spirit asked, a spirit answered" (23). George Herbert's strategy is to show his brother that his (Lord Herbert's) real convictions are something other than those he professes, and that his elder brother has simply failed to listen to his true instincts acknowledging God's power and his own dependency. So, although the brothers attempt to acknowledge their differences genially, they do so by attempting to efface those differences by reducing the other's subjectivity to his own. (Yet they are aware, as were Fuller and Emerson, that authentic and meaningful differences cannot be compellingly denied.)

Fuller ultimately tips the balance in favor of Lord Herbert, whose values and beliefs are to be valorized by her readers. His long speech on the importance of spiritual achievements in the midst of worldly trials goes unanswered by his brother, particularly since her George Herbert, limited by his cloistered existence, has neither the wherewithal to do so, nor the will to disparage a life he would have chosen: "I can the less gainsay you, my lord and brother, that your course would have been mine could I have chosen" (25). It is one of the most impassioned speeches in the dialogue, one focusing on the importance of choice and discernment neither foreclosed nor constricted by seclusion:

> if my road, leading through the busy crowd of men, amid the clang and bustle of conflicting interests and passions, detain me longer than would the still path through the groves, the chosen haunt of contemplation, yet I incline to think that progress so, though slower, is surer. Owing no safety, no clearness to my position, but so far as it is attained to mine own effort, encountering what temptations, doubts and lures may beset a man, what I do possess is more surely mine, and less a prey to contingencies. (25)

Fuller's Lord Herbert refuses to secure his values and beliefs by eliminating temptations or limiting choices.

When Fuller calls for a "spiritual man of the world" as her ideal for all – including women – the split identities of female and author are reconciled in the heroic exertions of her Lord Herbert.[29] Although Fuller viewed her own efforts to triumph over domestic responsibilities as significant, she longed to triumph in greater worldly trials. And so when she writes, in a letter to her friend and German tutor Frederick Hedge, that what she finds so appealing about Lord Herbert is that "He had a strong and bold wing in thought, and in character a union of purity boldness and variety that has not many times been seen" (L, 3:108–9), her nearly oxymoronic conjunction of "purity" with "boldness" is a clear rejection of her culture's polarities and of the cloistered virtue to which women were relegated. Implied, moreover, in the image her Lord Herbert employs to characterize his spiritual treasure – "a well-tempered wine that has been carried over many seas, and escaped many shipwrecks" (25) – is not just durability but enrichment by time and the buffetings of life.

Fuller's phrase describing Lord Herbert's thought as having "a strong and bold wing" suggests an epic Miltonic and Satanic audaciousness ("Thee I revisit now with bolder wing" [*Paradise Lost*, III.14]). Indeed, like the Miltonic narrator in Book I of *Paradise Lost*, who "with no middle flight intends to soar," she seems to disdain the "middle range" of thought, experience, and writing, which has been the range assigned to women writers. Indeed, in an article on "Female Novelists" that Fuller may well have read in the *Democratic Review* (it follows directly after the 1844 article on "The Legal Wrongs of Women" that she cites in *Woman in the Nineteenth Century*),[30] William A. Jones affirms, "A middle range, between high passion and indifference, the pathos of domestic tragedy, the prose imagination of the poet, depicting scenes of ordinary or even of humble life, appear to fall within the sphere of female genius ... Whole classes of society are thus excluded from the vision of the fair author, and the motley manners of many men. We have had no female Ulysses or Homer."[31] Jones goes on to suggest that this middle range is most appropriate for women because it calls upon neither the powers of discernment needed to distinguish good from evil nor upon the moral power to withstand vice's example: "many should learn only the best characters, as they want strength and penetration to see the good in evil." Indeed, certain authors (including Goethe, one of Fuller's favorites) are "dangerous writers, inasmuch as their works are fraught with deleterious influences, which require a strong intellect and a vigorous moral sense to withstand."[32] When Fuller's Lord Herbert asserts to his younger brother, "encountering what temptations, doubts and lures may beset a man, what I do possess is more surely mine, and less a prey to contingencies," she assumes the adult's "right to lead" Emerson and her age, as well as the pious Renaissance courtier's polymathic powers, which call into question her culture's gendered divisions between feminine spiritual refinement and masculine worldly engagement.

4

"AS IF A GREEN BOUGH WERE LAID ACROSS THE PAGE"

THOREAU'S SEVENTEENTH-CENTURY LANDSCAPES AND EXTRAVAGANT PERSONAE

All the distinguished writers of that [Renaissance] period, possess a greater vigor and naturalness than the more modern ... and when we read a quotation from one of them in the midst of a modern author, we seem to have come suddenly upon a greener ground, a greater depth and strength of soil. It is as if a green bough were laid across the page, and we are refreshed as by the sight of fresh grass in mid-winter or early spring.

Thoreau, "Sunday," *A Week on the Concord and Merrimack Rivers*[1]

As readers of Thoreau's *Walden* and *A Week on the Concord and Merrimack Rivers,* we respond most immediately to his engagement with the sensuous particularity of the New England landscape, to his recuperation of an earlier linguistic vitality, and to his presentation of a coherent, purposeful, and mystically suffused world. We tend to forget that his newly created landscape is just that – an invention of his own imagination that frequently comes before us at the expense of the actual New England landscape.[2] If we lose sight of Thoreau's active hostility toward institutionalized religion as well as toward the conventions of American law, government, and society, and if we overlook the high degree of literary allusiveness in his texts, we are apt to forget that the landscapes he presents are often highly artificial ones.[3] For all the individualizing descriptive nuances Thoreau records of the Concord and Merrimack rivers, for all the features of the particular scenes of Walden Pond he conveys, the actual landscapes often disappear to be replaced by a montage of literary ones. This supposed chronicler of the here-and-now, this admirer of the statistics of gazettes, turns not only to classical eclogues, as has been well documented, but also to seventeenth-century texts that have gone largely unremarked: masques, pastorals, georgics, and religious anatomies, out of which he fabricates a new landscape.[4] Reminders of the nineteenth-century New England landscape – mills, cash crops, and immigrant workers – are periodically displaced by a tapestry of archaic landscapes evoked by allusions to and quotations from earlier texts.[5]

Indeed, the multiple frames of reference that are part of the allusive framework immediately suggest that the landscape he envisions is not a continuous, unmediated event, but rather a landscape so highly mediated by literary texts and so serial that it recedes farther from him than the one he has forsaken in the present world. More than one critic has observed of Thoreau's responses to the landscape that "the pedantry of a bookworm underscores the insincerity of the rapture."[6] But Thoreau in fact shows no consistent desire entirely to conflate the voices in quotations with his own, nor to banish all distance from the landscape, as those who read Thoreau as a Romantic naturalist imply.[7] In the epigraph to this chapter, Thoreau's central image clearly acknowledges the disjunction between the quotation and its new setting ("come suddenly upon a greener ground") and emphasizes the incongruous juxtaposition of "a green bough ... laid across the page," or seen preternaturally in the "mid-winter or early spring" – the artificial presence of the natural, in fact. But it is not nature that is the subject there. Rather, the natural is a trope for the Renaissance writer's perceptions and prose style, which Thoreau has just been discussing, as at once dynamic and capable of changing with the exigencies of circumstances as compared with the rigid and ornamental styles of Thoreau's contemporaries: "The sentences are verdurous and blooming as evergreen and flowers, because they are rooted in fact and experience, but our false and florid sentences have only the tints of flowers without their sap or roots" (*Week*, 104). Although this seems to be an exhortation against imitation conjoined with a myth of progressive historical declension, it is more deeply an endorsement of Raleigh's exertion, his grappling with the contingent: "You have constantly the warrant of life and experience in what you read [by Raleigh]." The pastoralism of the passage, moreover, intimates a transparent mode through which glimpses of historical tensions and the pastoral's own limits may be glimpsed, for we are not left to alight in a cleared, settled, static, and easeful preserve. Instead, Thoreau explicitly and self-consciously undercuts that illusion: "[Raleigh's] chapters are like English parks, or say rather like a western forest, where the larger growth keeps down the underwood, and one may ride on horse-back through the openings" (*Week,* 104).

Many scenes in both *A Week* and *Walden* are distinctly mediated by seventeenth-century English literary texts – indeed, more so and in different ways than commentators have previously recognized. His authors range from Ben Jonson, early in the century, to Thomas Carew, John Milton, and Sir Thomas Browne (in *Religio Medici*) in the mid-century, to Izaak Walton and Abraham Cowley during the Commonwealth and Restoration periods. But it is the nature of Thoreau's choice of early modern English texts (pastorals, georgics, allegorical masques, and autobiographical anatomies) with all the artifice and static qualities of these *modes* – qualities thrown into sharp relief by the developing crisis of the English Revolution and its aftermath – that tells us something about his purposes. Thoreau draws significantly upon the nervous energies arising from the political and economic instability of this earlier period (when land might be seized and religious and political careers abruptly terminated), not to join in a communal, nostalgic longing for pastoral settledness but rather to signal the artifice of such fantasies and desires. By highlighting the imposition of literary texts upon the landscape, Thoreau prevents the possibility of lodging significance directly and resolutely in the depicted idyllic scene, however "pastoral" or appealing.[8] Rather, he locates significance peripherally, in the margins where nature is sometimes depicted as unassimilated and inassimilable ("Here was no man's garden, but the unhandselled globe"), and where the limits of his culture's myths are exposed in all their reductiveness and pre-emptiveness of contingency and individual judgment ("We need to witness our own limits transgressed, and some life pasturing freely where we never wander").[9] The seventeenth-century English texts that he appropriates and re-vises, then, are not seamlessly assimilated into transhistorical, synchronic visions, extensions of his own pastoral impulses or metaphysical yearnings, as Leo Marx, F. O. Matthiessen, or Sherman Paul once implied.[10] Nor do gleanings from the earlier texts in Thoreau's writings represent, as has been more recently suggested, the last vestiges of his apprenticeship to Emerson – cullings from an unfinished homage to English literature, an anthology project suggested by Emerson, begun by Thoreau, but later abandoned for more original, Adamic enterprises, and eventually quarried simply to "embellish and adorn his prose."[11]

Instead, in *Walden* and *A Week,* Thoreau fashions landscapes from a tissue of pastoral fictions, and a narrative voice from the borrowed pastoral longings of seventeenth-century "uncouth swains" or theatrical voices of masque characters. He does so in order to resist yielding, not simply to the American ideology of modernity and "progress" (which has often been argued), but more particularly to the conservative seductions of "naturalizing" a nostalgic pastoral myth of an agrarian America. So in what seems an act of intellectual atavism commingled with nostalgia, Thoreau in *A Week* and *Walden* substitutes an anachronistically integrated and harmonious seventeenth-century landscape – as did his Cavalier counterparts, Izaak Walton and Abraham Cowley, in response to the disruptions of the English Revolution – for the alienating and reified landscape of his contemporary New England.[12] Corresponding to his archaic landscape, Thoreau re-populates the land with prior, archaic selves, which are figural "types," for example, of Walton's "compleat angler." In this way Thoreau fills the landscape, not only with marginalized "Former Inhabitants" ("with such reminiscences I repeopled the woods and lulled myself asleep" [*Walden,* 264]) who call into question the values of the predictable "successes" of the Concord land-scape, as Lawrence Buell suggests.[13] He also creates a fictional population of "aboriginal" selves patterned on heroes from the literary and historical past. Yet these projections are such distinc-tive literary landscapes, are so thoroughly saturated with particu-lar literary characters, that they function as intensifications, creat-ing a heightened sense of artifice that prevents the reader from entirely forgetting their imposition on the natural scenes. In-deed, the extended allusive play is often punctuated by an explicit quotation, making the submerged presence of the particular ear-lier text, its landscape, and its characters all the more difficult to escape.

In the midst of what appear to be nostalgic fantasies, Thoreau, moreover, calls into play literary landscapes and fictional selves that are often freighted with the tensions of their own historical moments, the artifice of their modes, and the signs of their own precariously imposed pastoralism. He does so in order to prevent the domestication of the nostalgic fantasies, and to prevent the "sojourner" from putting down roots, even in the midst of the bower. As Stanley Cavell once suggested of Thoreau's task in *Walden:* "the difficulty is keeping us at the point of departure, and on our own."[14] This point of departure, Thoreau intimates, is a position from which individual critical judgment and conscience may be exercised – and dissent enfranchised.

The very allusiveness of Thoreau's enterprise is, then, an insistent reminder of the distance between the man and his landscape. Through the mediation of seventeenth-century texts, *Walden* rebukes those philistine, property-owning, mercantile Whig entrepreneurs, as well as those "ultra-reforming" radicals and Jacksonian empire-building contemporaries who would impose competing myths on the landscape. The Thoreauvian persona in *Walden* correspondingly interweaves various seventeenth-century voices, including Thomas Carew's insouciant Momus and eloquent Mercury from the Caroline masque *Coelum Britannicum* and the theatrical, extravagant narrative persona from Sir Thomas Browne's *Religio Medici*, in order to exaggerate his iconoclastic, baiting, or subversive responses to his contemporary American culture. Thoreau's disenchantment with both nineteenth-century Democratic reform movements and Whig commercial schemes prompts him in *Walden* to appropriate these seventeenth-century literary characters as his own prior, archaic selves: he skillfully employs these voices to offer ironical commentaries and subtle critiques of his contemporaries' social agendas. Whereas Sacvan Bercovitch reads Thoreau, as he does Emerson, as a "representative" American ethos and latter-day American Puritan saint, I suggest that the presence in Thoreau's writings of many seventeenth-century English texts (many secular and non-Puritan) signals his critical distance from America's dominant ideologies.[15]

Thoreau's Seventeenth-Century Pastorals and Georgics: Precarious Gardens and Haunted Fields

In the "Saturday" chapter of *A Week on the Concord and Merrimack Rivers,* the statuesque form of a solitary fisherman on the shore of the Concord River evokes in Thoreau the memory of his own youthful pastime and the memory of another solitary English fisherman who had emigrated to America, and whom he describes as the "Walton of this stream" (*Week,* 24). The imaginative progression, then, is typically from the actual figure in the landscape (the fisherman on the Concord shore), to the recollected image formerly in the same landscape (the young Thoreau or the old, silent fisherman), to the literary allusion that provides the paradigm for the scene, to the imaginative recuperation of the archaic worldview embedded in the literary text – and the apparently seamless relationship between the literary persona and his double, the landscape.[16] The idyllic scene (actual and remembered), the fishing that is "not a sport, nor solely a means of subsistence, but a sort of solemn sacrament and withdrawal from the world" (*Week*, 25), culminates in the Waltonian seventeenth-century landscape on the banks of the Concord River.

And so Izaak Walton's integrated, sacramental relationship with nature is available to Thoreau in nineteenth-century New England only in certain youthful stages of a young man's life, in certain hidden recesses in the riverbank secluded from the mercantile world, and in certain uncommon periods of intense, withdrawn contemplation. Recollections of Walton's seventeenth-century text, a text so popular that it went through 164 editions in the nineteenth century alone, allow Thoreau to recuperate, almost in the interstices of his world, the archaic harmony, the tender communion with the landscape that is nearly gone from the world.[17]

In the very next section of the "Saturday" chapter, Thoreau envisions his native Concord as a Waltonian world of gratifying abundance, reassuring order, and benevolent civility. Indeed, he casts his pastoral world in Waltonian language. Walton's direction for baiting a frog ("use him as though you loved him") is echoed through a Thoreauvian world where "our finny contemporaries" swim gracefully, "expressive of their humble happiness, ever "[w]illing to be decimated for man's behoof" (*Week*, 27, 37).[18] Walton's tender and familiar tone finds its way into Thoreau's descriptions of the native fish of the Concord region. Once again available in Thoreau's Concord are the benevolence and reciprocity of Walton's world, where Walton's angler instructs, "give him [the chivin] play enough before you offer to take him out of the water" (*CA*, 46–7), and the compliant fish nearly jumps into his net. That Thoreau has interposed Walton's vision of nature between the reader and the Concord landscape is suggested not only by Thoreau's catalogue of fishes described in sensuous detail but also by such observations as "He who has not hooked the red chivin is not yet a complete angler" (*Week*, 29) and "It enhances our sense of the grand security and serenity of nature, to observe the still undisturbed economy and content of the fishes of this century, their happiness a regular fruit of the summer" (*Week*, 26). Emerson's description of *A Week* seems particularly apt: "a seven days' voyage in as many chapters, pastoral as Izaak Walton, spicy as flagroot, broad and deep as Menu." Emerson's remark on *A Week*'s structure, moreover, both highlights the cyclical symmetry typical of the pastoral and suggests the volume of Walton Thoreau read, for the 1836 edition by Sir Nicholas Harris Nicolas is the only one that takes the liberty of dividing Walton's *Compleat Angler* into the days of the week. Bronson Alcott similarly noted the pastoral and Waltonian elements in *A Week*, describing a draft he had seen in March of 1847 as "Virgil and White of Selborne, and Izaak Walton, and Yankee settler all in one."[19]

Thoreau had prefaced his reminiscence of the angler on the shore with the dictum, "The characteristics and pursuits of various ages and races of men are always existing in epitome in every neighborhood" (*Week*, 23). Thoreau's notion of "in epitome" operates in several ways. The lone fisherman on the Concord shore who is "still a fisher, and belongs to an era in which I myself have lived" (*Week*, 23) is the angler phase of Thoreau's youth writ large, for in a certain early stage of life, all men partake of a Waltonian simplicity and harmony with nature that has now "become the inheritance of other men" (*Week*, 23). Similarly, the old fisherman of Thoreau's memory who had "passed the period of communication with his fellows," who "was always to be seen in serene afternoons haunting the river, almost rustling with the sedge . . . almost grown to be the sun's familiar" (*Week*, 24) typifies the class of archaic pastoral dwellers of which the man on the Concord shore is a member. But it is Izaak Walton's "compleat angler" who defines the class: he is the type of them all. Thoreau's interpolation of Walton's fictive angler, as well as his explicit mention of seeing an "epitome" (which clarifies but also abridges and intensifies), and his evocation of an outmoded period "the inheritance of other men") work against an easy assimilation into a timeless pastoral existence or a Wordsworthian palimpsest of memories charged with a revelation.[20] Although the ritualistically repeated fishing scenes appear to transcend the flux of history, the consciously static pastoral mode at the same time seems tenuous and precariously poised in the midst of a bustling and contentious environment. Thoreau situates his American anglers in the midst of Jacksonian expansion; Walton places his pastoral Anglican anglers in the midst of strife and the instabilities of the Puritan Commonwealth. Even the opening of the "Saturday" chapter, perhaps an echo of Walton's piously expanded revision of "Come live with me, and be my Love / And we will all the pleasures prove" in *The Compleat Angler* (*CA*, 57–8), simultaneously alludes to the pastoral and spiritual modes but concedes they are nearly vitiated. The epigraph Thoreau chooses, "Come, come, my lovely fair, and let us try / These rural delicates" (from Francis Quarles's "Christ's Invitation to the Soul," in *Emblemes* [1635]), is soon followed by the comment that Concord is "a port of entry and departure for the bodies as well as the souls of men; *one shore at least exempted from all duties* but such as an honest man will gladly discharge" (*Week*, 15; my emphasis). Although the potential intrusion of a complex, mutable, and corrupt world is part of the pastoral mode itself, Thoreau's renditions of the mode call particular attention to its fragility, its artifice, and its limits.

In *Walden*'s "Higher Laws" chapter, moreover, it becomes impossible to overlook the mediating use to which Thoreau puts the pastoralism of *The Compleat Angler*. It is Walton's particular antidogmatic theological stance, camouflaged in part by his pastoralism, that Thoreau calls upon and exploits. Scholars have noted that when *The Compleat Angler* appeared in 1653, during the Puritan Commonwealth, it was "originally a subversive book, hiding under its general air of innocence and simple piety a sharp criticism of the Puritan and Parliamentarian ethos."[21] ("Subversive" is a relative term, and probably too strong for what Walton's editors and contemporaries discerned as his coded manner of writing: a prefatory poem by Walton's friend Christopher Harvey alerts the reader of *The Compleat Angler* that "Here sits in *secret* blest Theology."[22] Even if Thoreau had not known that in Walton's day the Brotherhood of the Angle was a figurative term for Anglicans, there are enough pointed asides and digressions within Walton's text to signal his theologically antidogmatic position; furthermore, the edition Thoreau most likely read, that of Sir Nicholas Harris Nicolas, emphasized Walton's political and religious climate. For example, Thoreau would have read directly in *The Compleat Angler* the frequent disavowal of contention (*CA*, 63, 173–5); the praise of "harmlessness" in the unvexed "simplicity" of an angler (*CA*, 12); the description of the angler's freedom "from the unsupportable burden" of a sectarian's, "accusing, tormenting, Conscience" (*CA*, 173); the lines in praise of the controversial Anglican Book of Common Prayer (*CA*, 81–2); and the depiction of a deceased clergyman and angler whose monument "stands yet undefaced" (by Puritan iconoclasts), a cleric of great learning who, "(knowing that God leads us not to Heaven by many nor by hard questions) like an honest Angler, ma[d]e that *good, plain, unperplexed* Catechism" which was still in use (*CA*, 32).[23] Moreover, if Thoreau had read the introductory "life of Walton" in the Nicolas edition, he would have seen in Walton's own words (prefacing an associate's poem, "Thealma and Clearchus") the clear alternative of the Anglican pastoral to contemporary religious contention:

> And the reader will here also meet with passions heightened by easy and fit descriptions of joy and sorrow; and find

also such various events and rewards of innocent truth and undissembled honesty, as is like to leave in him (if he be a good-natured reader) more sympathizing and virtuous impressions, than ten times so much time spent in *impertinent, critical, and needless disputes about religion.*[24]

If "All things necessary to salvation are, by definition, non-controversial," as Walton and his Anglican associates believed,[25] and as Piscator (the fisher) implicitly instructs Venator (the hunter) in Walton's text, then it seems that in "Higher Laws" Thoreau's criticism of his contemporaries in the vocabulary of Walton's text focuses only at the most obvious level on America's reification of its natural resources.

More importantly, Thoreau's subtle and pointed criticism turns upon his countrymen's underlying tendency toward false mediations of the divine ("They might go there a thousand times before the sediment of fishing would sink to the bottom and leave their purpose pure" [*Walden,* 213]), as well as the nation's penchant for exegetical or doctrinal legalism (another form of unwarranted human mediation): "If the legislature regards it [Walden pond], it is chiefly to regulate the number of hooks to be used there; but they know nothing about the hook of hooks with which to angle for the pond itself, impaling the legislature for a bait" (*Walden,* 213). (Like Walton, who includes Donne's parodic pastoral "The Baite" in his work [*CA,* 127–8], Thoreau may have in mind here Donne's line "For thou thy self art thine own bait," from the poem's conclusion.) Moreover, like Walton's "civil, well governed, well grounded, temperate, poor Angler" (*CA,* 75), the self-disciplined Thoreauvian narrator of "Higher Laws," as well as the antinomian of *Civil Disobedience,* obviate the need for such institutional legislation as it becomes mediatory and inevitably the object of undue respect. By recalling Walton's rejection of sectarian theological sophistry, Thoreau prevents his audience from simply naturalizing Walton's *locus amoenus* within Concord. His, or Piscator's, retreat to a pastoral pleasance, however ideal, is not the issue; rather, a vigilance against false spiritual mediation is.

In the "Brute Neighbors" chapter, Thoreau offers a Waltonian dialogue between "Hermit" and "Poet" that uses satire and stylization to distance further the pastoral mode from the natural landscape. The satiric element recalls Walton's text. In the *Compleat Angler,* Walton's depiction of arguing beggars seems to be a parody of Puritans: they argue their points "with as much beggarly Logic and earnestness, as was ever heard to proceed from the mouth of the most pertinacious Schismatic" (*CA*, 85). Elsewhere Walton complains "of a sour complexion, money-getting-men" whose "corroding cares" are so pervasive that "if he would find content in any of his houses[,] he must leave himself behind him" (*CA*, 11, 175). And just as Walton probably begins Piscator's pastoral and instructional adventures on May Day as a protest against the Puritans (*CA*, 36) who held the mirth of May Day celebrations in particular contempt as sacrilegious,[26] so Thoreau begins his experiment by the pond on Independence Day, and gives to Hermit a speech that ridicules the Puritan legacy of industry: "And O, the housekeeping! to keep bright the devil's door-knobs, and scour his tubs this bright day! Better not keep a house. Say, some hollow tree" (Walden, 223). In both texts the parodic is focused upon a regnant Puritan ethos – English and American – invested in the tacit (and ironic) idolatrous mediations of doctrinal legalism and financial prosperity. In both Walton and Thoreau, pastoral leisure and religious simplicity are offered as tactical affronts only partly disguised as innocent alternatives.[27]

Thoreau's Waltonian dialogue in "Brute Neighbors," however, reveals not only a satiric vein but also a considerable degree of stylization similar to that in Piscator's speeches in *The Compleat Angler* about the idyllic life. Piscator, for example, twice describes in the most conventional and nearly identical terms contemplative moments "when [he] was last this way a-fishing": he is seated upon "Cowslips-banks" beneath a "broad Beech-tree" (like "Virgil's *Tityrus* and his *Meliboeus*" [*CA*, 82]), listening to "birds . . . have a friendly contention with an Echo," viewing "the silver-streams glide silently," "beguil[ing] time by viewing the harmless Lambs, some leaping securely in the cool shade, whilst others sported themselves in the cheerful Sun" (*CA*, 56). A third iteration comes in the "Angler's wish" poem, filled with conventional pastoral scenery and alluding to a poem about a "Hermit poor" (attributed to Raleigh); the lonely narrator of Walton's poem would fish to "raise my low pitched thoughts above / Earth" and "meditate my time away" (*CA*, 83).[28] Thoreau's Hermit also loses himself in a pastoral meditation expressed in very conventional terms: "I wonder what the world is doing now. I have not heard so much as a locust over the sweet-fern these three hours. The pigeons are all asleep upon their roosts" (*Walden*, 223). Moreover, Thoreau's Poet and Hermit utter their thoughts in obvious Waltonian archaisms ("Hark!," "Methinks," "a-fishing," "Come, let's along" [*Walden*, 223–4) and echo Walton's idiom ("Angle-worms are rarely to be met with in these parts," "The sport of digging the bait is nearly equal to that of catching the fish," "I think I may warrant you one worm to every three sods you turn up" [*Walden*, 223–4]). Just as Walton's Piscator cites a poet's conventional couplet to depict his elated contentment (" 'I was for that time lifted above earth; / And possessed joys not promised in my birth' " [*CA*, 56]), so Hermit's musings are offered in conventional, self-conscious, and nearly schematic terms:

> Methinks I was nearly in this frame of mind; the world lay about at this angle. Shall I go to heaven or a-fishing? If I should soon bring this meditation to an end, would another so sweet occasion be likely to offer? I was as near being resolved into the essence of things as ever I was in my life. (*Walden*, 224)

The conventional in the Thoreauvian passage functions to call attention less to a Waltonian conservative rootedness in tradition than to the pastoral pleasance and *otium* as artificial stasis, not an actual desideratum. We are warned by the Thoreauvian Hermit's self-consciousness and by Thoreau's stylization of Walton's already conventional description that the fixity that Hermit and Poet attempt to impose on the transient and natural results in affectation ("a true Mediterranean sky," Poet observes of the clouds [*Walden*, 223]) and in grotesque transformation, indeed mummification ("I know not whether it was the dumps or a budding ecstasy," complains the confused and uninspired Hermit [*Walden*, 225]), of what is otherwise in Theocritus and Virgil a dynamic leisure and animated tranquillity.[29] Rather than offering a parody of Transcendentalism, as has sometimes been suggested, this stylized Waltonian dialogue offers a satire on pastoralism's artificial stasis and purity.[30]

Following this Waltonian dialogue, Thoreau offers depictions of his brute neighbors with minute details expressive of tenderness as well as fascinated alienation.[31] Yet in the peculiar paralysis of the partridge chicks, in the elusive and vaguely insidious behavior of the loon, and in the grisly battle of the ants, his depictions betray an element of the grotesque, a heightening and distortion of what occurs in nature that does not let us forget his interpretive impositions upon the landscape. We are called upon to recognize a fact already signaled by the heightened stylization of the introductory Waltonian dialogue, that his brute neighbors described here indeed "are all beasts of burden . . . made to carry some portion of our thoughts" (*Walden*, 225).

Walton's muted religiosocial polemics, disguised and coded as pastoralism, or by means of a highly conventional pastoral idiom, thus allow Thoreau to exploit the subtexts of Walton's pastoral fantasy even as he appears to depict the idyllic in *A Week* and *Walden*. Similarly, in his "Ponds" chapter, Thoreau adopts the patent artifice of Milton's pastoral mode in *Lycidas*, blended with parts of *Paradise Lost*, to suggest social and religious criticisms and intimate his own prophetic obligation to his nation.[32] In *Lycidas*, Milton juxtaposes pastoral conventions and fierce satire to offer an allegory of true poet-shepherds (Edward King and Milton) contrasted with corrupt Anglican prelatical "shepherds" ("Blind mouths! that scarce themselves know how to hold / a sheep-hook" (lines 119–20). The collection of critical commentaries that Thoreau compared and copied into one of his commonplace books in 1837 ("Miscellaneous Extracts," Morgan Library, Ms. 594) shows that he was clearly aware that the poem's satire was directed at the English nation's corrupt prelacy (lines 110–31): Thoreau copies, "[Milton's] design [in "Admitting Peter to be a bishop" (referring to Lycidas, line 112)] was to sharpen his satire by making the prelacy to be condemned by one of their own order." Moreover, Thoreau knew Milton's elegy played upon the idea of the "pastor" as one obliged to provide spiritual nourishment to one's "flock": "*Lycidas* is with great judgment made of the pastoral kind, as both Mr. King and Milton had been designed for holy orders and the pastoral care, which gives a peculiar propriety to several passages in it."[33] Critics have noted the near-anonymity of the elegiac narrator's lament for the death of Edward King, a requiem expressed largely in conventional pastoral terms. They suggest that all the emotional intensity was reserved for Milton's drama of vocation as vatic poet or denouncing reformer.[34] Unlike the more personalized pastoral lament of Milton's *Epitaphium Damonis* (which Thoreau also knew and transcribed in Latin), the Thoreauvian narrator of "The Ponds" adopts the pastoralism of Milton's *Lycidas* precisely because the convention is already patently transparent and accordingly suitable for chastising an American nation of such false "pastors" as the spiritually impoverished farmer Flint.[35]

At the beginning of "The Ponds," Thoreau signals his shift away from contemporary Concord society to a composite Miltonic world of his own making:

> Sometimes, having had a surfeit of human society and gossip, and worn out all my village friends, I rambled still

farther westward than I habitually dwell, into yet more unfrequented parts of town, "to fresh woods and pastures new," or, while the sun was setting, made my supper of huckleberries and blueberries on Fair Haven Hill ... It is a vulgar error to suppose you have tasted huckleberries who never plucked them. (*Walden*, 173)

This passage, echoing both the opening and closing lines of *Lycidas*, is a distillation of Milton's pastoral elegy. The decision of Milton's "uncouth swain" to turn to the pastoral mode and his own premature artistic expression for sustenance in the face of loss and disappointment ("Yet once more ... I come to pluck your berries")[36] is also Thoreau's decision to gather sustenance by plucking berries and by completing while at Walden Pond what becomes, as critics have suggested, the pastoral elegy of *A Week* for the brother who had accompanied him on his trip up the Concord River.[37] But Thoreau's allusive perambulation "to fresh woods and pastures new" also suggests his acceptance in *Walden* of a literary vocation entailing the "mantle" of pastoral care – of a national flock and prophetic obligation in corrupt times.

A sense of broader national obligation and promise, moreover, is implicit in the final lines of Milton's pastoral poem (lines 190–4), which Thoreau copied in full into *Walking* (his 1851 lecture later revised as an essay): "And now the sun had stretched out all the hills, / And now was dropped into the western bay; / At last *he* rose, and twitched his mantle blue; / Tomorrow to fresh woods and pastures new."[38] Thoreau cites these lines to create a collocation of associated images: of Milton's "uncouth swain" with Columbus at the vanguard of exploration and westward movement toward America, and the sun's progress over the horizon toward a paradisiacal site (emphasizing Milton's own ambiguous antecedent for the "he" that "rose"). To these he adds the notion of the symbolic "wild" of the New World, and associates all with the spirit of "westering" in himself. In view of Thoreau's claim at the opening of *Walking*, that "sauntering" or walking westward "is a sort of crusade, preached by some Peter the Hermit in us, to go forth and reconquer this Holy Land from the hands of the Infidels (*Writings*, 5:206), the Thoreauvian uncouth swain's pastoral motive in *Walden* to wander "still farther westward ... 'to fresh woods and pastures new' " is not one of withdrawal into a serene and stable pastoral retreat, nor one of condoning America's land-grabbing Manifest Destiny. Nor is this the motive of an American

Jeremiah exhorting a backsliding nation to reclaim the myth of an ideal "city on the hill." Rather, it is one of assuming the role of a prophetic pastor anticipating authentic earthly renovation of ecclesiastical and political institutions, as did the polemical Milton of the 1640s, who linked *Lycidas,* in the headnote to the 1645 edition, to such earthly triumphs over a corrupt clergy and a misguided Parliament as had already been celebrated in the revolutionary London of *Areopagitica* (1644).[39]

It has been suggested that the opening of the chapter titled "The Ponds" intimates the deline of the pastoral that attends ascendance of the the marketplace, and reveals Thoreau's disgust with the reification of the Concord landscape, as in his comment, "The fruits do not yield their true flavor to the purchaser of them."[40] But Thoreau's language in this section ("who never plucked them," "bloom," "ambrosial and essential part of the fruit," "Eternal Justice") suggests that he employs the Miltonic idiom from *Lycidas* and *Paradise Lost* ("I come to pluck your berries," "blooming," "ambrosial fruit," "quintessence pure," "Eternal Justice") more to allude to exilic separation (prelatical or satanic) from the divine and to moral deformation than to lament the disappearance of the pastoral or to signal the presence of a positive evil in the land.

Indeed in the late fall and early winter of 1836–7, just before he copied the critical comments on *Lycidas,* Thoreau copied into another of his college commonplace books ("Index Rerum," Huntington Library, Ms. 945) numerous extracts from Milton's works, including phrases from Book IV of *Paradise Lost* cataloguing Eden in all its pastoral euphony and sensuous detail.[41] Milton's descriptions of Eden, moreover, repeatedly lie behind Thoreau's descriptions of White and Walden Ponds. Milton's rivers run through Eden "under pendant shades" and then "in a Lake, / That to the fringed bank with Myrtle crown'd, / Her crystal mirror holds, unite thir streams" (IV.239, 261–3). Walden, in particular, is "a perfect forest mirror" (*Walden,* 188); Thoreau sees the trees that line the shores of Walden as "eyelashes which fringe it, and the wooded hills and cliffs around are its overhanging brows" (*Walden,* 186), and describes the lakes themselves as "great crystals on the surface of the earth, Lakes of Light" (*Walden,* 199). Eden's "Universal Pan . . . Led on th' Eternal Spring" (IV.266–8), while Walden is "not an intermitting spring"(*Walden,* 179). Yet while other pre-Christian gardens to which Milton compares Eden are used proleptically to intimate edenic violation (Dis and Proserpine, Apollo and Daphne, Ammon and Amalthea

[IV.274–5]), Thoreau declines to insinuate violation into the midst of natural purity.[42] Instead he selects from Milton's catalogue of gardens ("not that fair field of Enna ... nor ... th' inspired Castalian Spring might with this Paradise of Eden strive") features that are pure and inspiring ("who knows in how many unremembered nations' literatures this has been the Castalian Fountain?"), that suggest a pagan ideal ("what nymphs presided over it in the Golden Age?"), or that connote the pristinely originary ("gem of the first water"). Thoreau appropriates Milton's Eden to locate a center of purity, then situates his own pond outside the temporal and spatial perimeter of the garden, attempting to circumvent the Original Sin as entailing nature: "Perhaps on that spring morning when Adam and Eve were driven out of Eden Walden Pond was already in existence, ... and covered with myriads of ducks and geese, which had not heard of the fall" (*Walden*, 179). In "Slavery in Massachusetts" the disconnection is highlighted all the more by contemporary events: "Nature has been partner to no Missouri Compromise. I scent no compromise in the fragrance of the water-lily. It is not a *Nymphoea Douglassii*."[43]

The pastoral "fruit" – Thoreau's huckleberries of Fair Haven Hill, the uncouth swain's berries, or the edenic apple – have in themselves no inherent moral significance but are indices to the discernment and judgment entailed by them. According to Milton, "It was necessary that one thing at least should be either forbidden or commanded, and *above all something which was in itself neither good nor evil,* so that man's obedience might in this way be made evident."[44] Similarly, the pastoralism of "The Ponds" pleads for no actual retreat away from market economy into a nostalgic Jeffersonian agrarianism. Rather, Thoreau combines the satiric "pastoralism" of *Lycidas* with *Paradise Lost's* geography of moral discrimination and infernal exile (*Paradise Lost,* I.70–74) to sharpen his own apparently divine decree at the beginning of "The Ponds" that "As long as Eternal Justice reigns, not one innocent huckleberry can be transported thither from the country's hills" (*Walden*, 173). Accordingly, resonating behind the explicit language of commerce in "The Ponds" is Milton's monotheistic language of injunction against pollution and idolatry signaled by the vocabulary of prohibition and judgment, desecration and defilement. Farmer Flint, like the rapacious prelatical "blind mouths" of *Lycidas,* is described as someone "who exhausted the land around [the pond]," whose "presence perchance cursed all the shore," who is himself "unclean," who prefers the image of his own "brazen face" reflected in the dollar, and who would carry his God, to market, if he could get anything for him." His "fields bear no crops . . . trees no fruits, but dollars"; indeed, he "goes to market *for* his god as it is" (*Walden,* 195–6).

No doubt, as has been suggested, Thoreau had been reading with contempt popular manuals on efficient capital agriculture.[45] But Thoreau's language particularly condemns his nation's model farmers in sacral "pastoral" terms: Flint "never *saw* [the pond] . . . never loved it, . . . never protected it, . . . never spoke a good word for it, nor thanked God that he had made it" (*Walden,* 196) . Just as Milton's vehement language regarding the prelatical shepherds focuses on their misuse of priestly duty in infecting their flock ("The hungry sheep look up, and are not fed / But swoll'n with wind, and the rank mist they draw, / Rot inwardly, and foul contagion spread" [lines 125–7]), so Thoreau's intense revulsion is expressed in Milton's language of contamination and desecration involving both the physical and the spiritual: the model farm is "where the house stands like a fungus in a muck-heap, chambers for men, horses, oxen, and swine, cleansed and uncleansed, all contiguous to one another! . . . redolent of manures and buttermilk! Under a high state of cultivation, being manured with the hearts and brains of men! As if you were to raise your potatoes in the church-yard! [*Walden,* 197]). This fierce outburst condemning "skin-flint" farmers and "model farms" (*Walden,* 195–6) in the midst of Thoreau's pastoral chapter "The Ponds," then, may be seen as a parallel to the intrusion of ecclesiastical satire in *Lycidas,* which Milton, no longer refraining from triumphalism in 1645, retrospectively described as a prophecy foretelling the "ruin of our corrupted clergy then in their height." And therefore, Thoreau's imposition of Milton's transparent pastoralism upon the Concord landscape signals his own prophetic call and points to an alternative pastorship of chastened discretion: "There is but one way to obtain ['their true flavor'], yet few take that way" (*Walden,* 173).

In other seventeenth-century pastoral landscapes that he evokes, like those in the essays of Abraham Cowley, the royalist author of the English Revolutionary, Commonwealth, and Restoration periods, Thoreau identifies more with the ironies of transvaluing what constitutes "civilization" in the midst of menacing turmoil and forgotten loyalty than with the fantasy of a pastoral retreat. Indeed, the bower imagined by Cowley is always tinged with melancholy – already a signal of the limits of the pastoral.[46] And in fact the darker, haunting presence of the English "Grand

Rebellion" and its aftermath is unmistakable to the reader of Cowley's *Several Discourses by Way of Essays, in Verse and Prose*.[47] Intertwined with the personal reminiscences, observations, poetry, and classical epigrams in the essays in the pastoral and georgic modes ("Of Solitude," "Of Obscurity," "The Garden," "Of Myself," "Of Agriculture") are more grim reflections on the verities of moral, civil, and political power, gleaned from the wisdom of the ancients and some moderns (Montaigne and Bacon) and from Cowley's own experiences ("Of Liberty," "Of Greatness," "Of Avarice," "The Danger of an Honest Man in much Company").[48] From his transcriptions, Thoreau makes it clear that he read Cowley's advice on expedient behavior in uncertain times ("The Dangers of Procrastination," "The Shortness of Life, and the Uncertainties of Riches"), his caveats against the entanglements and abuses of power ("Of Greatness"), and his personal frustrations with worldly affairs and the promises of the court ("Of Myself").

Interestingly, Cowley's long, dreamlike, "visionary" dialogue between Cowley and Cromwell's fallen angel excoriating the "Protector" for the havoc he wrought upon England draws an ambiguous response from Thoreau, who is half sympathetic to each: "He thinks that Cromwell attained his ends 'because his ends were so unreasonable, that no human reason could foresee them.' "[49] Thoreau could in fact sympathize with earlier figures who were themselves historical adversaries, since he was more often attracted, as he suggests in his review of Carlyle and Cromwell, to the defining features of an individual sensibility in the midst of historical crisis than to an "historical justice" of depiction arrived at "by nicely balancing the evidence" ("Carlyle" [1847], 243). Nor does it seem contradictory to the Democratic-leaning writer raised among Whigs to admire a defeated royalist while also praising Carlyle's edition of *Oliver Cromwell's Letters and Speeches* in a lyceum lecture and review. Indeed, Thoreau would later favorably compare John Brown at Harpers Ferry to Oliver Cromwell.[50] Thoreau admires that "there was joined in [Cromwell], too, such a divine madness, though with large and sublime features, as that of those dibblers of beans on St. George's Hill" – that is, the agrarian communist Diggers, who began cultivating the common lands in April 1649.[51] "The great danger," Thoreau insists in his article on Carlyle and Cromwell, "is not of excessive partiality or sympathy with one, but of a shallow justice to many, in which, after all, none gets his deserts" ("Carlyle" [1847], 243, 245). For Thoreau, the Puritan regicide, the radical sectarian communist, and the defeated Anglican royalist are all worthy of remark in proportion to the transformative principles they exhibit in the unpropitious moment.

The essays in Thoreau's volume of Cowley's writings, then, are Cowley's prose "gardens," the last resort of the much-tried and sorely defeated royalist poet who thought that in his time it was in poetry "so uncustomary, as to become almost *ridiculous*, to make *Lawrel* for the *Conquered*."[52] Cowley's essays explore the impulse of the Cavalier who had once called himself "The Muses' Hannibal" for quietism and retreat after he had served as an official secretary and cryptographer in exile, after his arrest upon his return to England, and after the Restoration brought him fresh disappointment with the meager rewards for his (perceived) clouded royalist loyalty:[53]

> My desire has been ... to retire myself to some of our American plantations, not to seek for gold, or enrich myself with the [slave] traffic of those parts, which is the end of most men that travel thither; so that of these Indies it is truer than it was of the former ... but to forsake this world for ever, with all the vanities and vexations of it, and to bury myself there in some obscure retreat, but not without the consolation of letters and philosophy. ("Author's Preface to the 1656 folio," pp. 7–8)

Samuel Johnson famously chastised Cowley for his apparent naïveté and "cowardice," despite a mind "exalted by genius," in imagining that such a "chimerical provision" would settle an unquiet mind – as if "content was the inhabitant of particular regions."[54] But by his reference to "American plantations" in the West Indies (to which he never fled), Cowley hints that self-aggrandizement and worldly entanglement, represented by the gold and African slave trades, are actually foils for his quest for personal "liberty" during the uncongenial Cromwellian Commonwealth.[55] Similarly, Thoreau exhorted an antebellum America to imitate the example of the abolition of slavery in the West Indies obtained by Wilberforce (as Emerson's 1844 address "Emancipation in the British West Indies" suggests) by seeking a "Self-emancipation even in the Western Indian provinces of the fancy and imagination" (*Walden*, 7–8). Dismissing the convention of inspiration in retreat, Cowley hopes to find no poetic muse in such a place: "Doctor Donnes Sun Dyal in a grave is not more useless and ridiculous then Poetry would be in that retirement" ("Author's Preface," p. 8). Yet Cowley's desire to celebrate in prose the "commodities" of private liberty, freedom from public opinion, and chastened values at the very site of colonial avarice and worldly ensnarement may well have encouraged Thoreau to employ, in a double allusion, this site of exploitation in his call to envision one's self in a nation of self-enfranchised individuals – "*even* in the Western Indian provinces of the fancy and imagination" (my emphasis). Cowley's choice of a retreat and Thoreau's allusion ironically portray the far-flung retirement as already so pervaded by corruption that a campaign of self-possession and transvaluation – not the pursuit of an artificial *otium* or pleasance – is the true achievement and consolation.

Granted, at times both Thoreau's "forest" and Cowley's "garden" suggest a vivid sense of besieged values, partially protected or "enclosed" by cautiously planned defensive measures: "if we engage into a large acquaintance and various familiarities," observes Cowley in "Of Obscurity," "we set open our gates to the invaders of most of our time: we expose our life to a quotidian ague of frigid impertinencies, which would make a wise man tremble to think of" (p. 138). Yet in view of the choice of the West Indies as the locus of self-emancipation for both writers, Thoreau's suggestion in "Slavery in Massachusetts" (1854) that geographical retreat had once seemed a viable alternative to him ("I dwelt before, perhaps, in the illusion that my life passed somewhere only *between* heaven and hell" ([*Reform Papers*, 106]), seems to be a retrospective reworking of his life to rouse others from complacency, not a new realization arrived at since the writing of *Walden*. In fact, both Cowley and Thoreau, even at their respective emotional and professional nadirs, never quite seem to envision retreats that are either attainable or satisfactory. Cowley's "The Garden" (once part of a 1666 letter to John Evelyn lauding his effort to write a history of gardens) reveals that

I never had any other desire so strong . . . as that one which I have had always, that I might be Master at last of a small House and large Garden, with very moderate Conveniences join'd to them, and there dedicate the Remainder of my Life only to the Culture of them, and the Study of Nature;
"And there (with no Design beyond my Wall) whole and entire to lye
In no unactive Ease, and no unglorious Poverty."
. . . But several Accidents of my ill Fortune have disappointed me . . . of that Felicity . . . I am gone out from *Sodom*, but I am not yet arriv'd at my Little *Zoar* . . . I do not look

back yet; but I have been forc'd to stop, and make too many
Halts. ("The Garden," 170)

While Cowley's impulse is to see himself as Lot among the cities
in the plain of Jordan, fleeing the sinfulness of political life
(and perhaps the court of Charles II) to save his soul, he also
acknowledges that only the promise of Evelyn's book sustains in
him any hope of the pastoral: Cowley's own "garden" is figuratively surrounded by sinful cities, and is literally "a hired House
and Garden, among Weeds and Rubbish" (p. 170). In "Slavery in
Massachusetts," Thoreau even more clearly depicts the devalua-
tion of the once desirable garden retreat: "Suppose you have a
small library, with pictures to adorn the walls – a garden laid out
around – and contemplate scientific and literary pursuits, &c.,
and discover all at once that your villa, with all its contents, is
located in hell . . . – do not these things suddenly lose their value
in your eyes?" (*Reform Papers,* 107).

It is in Thoreau's most despairing chapter of *Walden,* the opening "Economy" chapter, that Cowley's "garden" of chastened values, elaborated in his essay "Of Liberty," is most clearly interposed
in the Thoreauvian landscape, signaling an assertion of the
threatened values of the honest, private man in the midst of the
encumbrances of an elaborate and dissolute life (as in the court
of Charles II). In "Of Liberty" – "the liberty of a private man, in
being master of his own time and actions" – Cowley begins his
series of essays, as Thoreau does *Walden,* by condemning the
courtier's loss of personal autonomy in the language of land
tenancy as it blurs into enslavement: "Now for our Time," notes
Cowley, "the same God, to whom we are but Tenants-at-will for
the whole, requires but the seventh Part to be paid to him as a
small Quit-Rent in Acknowledgment of his Title. It is man only
that has the impudence to demand our whole time, though he
neither gave it, nor can restore it, nor is able to pay any considerable value for the least part of it" ("Of Liberty," pp. 105–6). Such
a royalist as Cowley would express the oppressive burdens of
courtly life in the georgic language of exploitive land-tenancy
practices because, as Thoreau would have known from reading
"Of Agriculture" and "Proposition for the Advancement of Experimental Philosophy," Cowley was a "propagandist" for the new
science's land reformers, who were sensitive to the plight of exploited tenants and assumed that if science could reform land
use, "then human nature and politics would somehow follow."[56]
The Thoreauvian version in *Walden* issues a similar call to self-

emancipation and reformed attitudes toward the land in the idiom of nineteenth-century American slavery and the blasphemy of enslavement to the land: "It is hard to have a southern overseer; it is worse to have a northern one; but worst of all when you are the slave-driver of yourself. Talk of a divinity in man!" (*Walden*, 7). A much diminished farmer, moreover, is depicted as "creeping down the road of life, pushing before [him] a barn seventy-five feet by forty . . . and one hundred acres of land, tillage, mowing, pasture, and wood-lot!" (*Walden*, 5).[57]

Similarly, just as Cowley identifies the curiously inverted system of valuation by which "the greatest part of men make such a bargain for the delivery-up of themselves, as Thamar did for Judah; instead of a kid, the necessary provisions for human life, they are contented to do it for rings and bracelets" ("Of Liberty," p. 106), so Thoreau addresses his *Walden* in part to the reordering of values among the members of the Whig mercantile class. "I also have in my mind that seemingly wealthy, but most terribly impoverished class of all, who have accumulated dross, but know not how to use it, or get rid of it, and thus have forged their own golden or silver fetters" (*Walden*, 16).

Cowley's conventional pastoral and georgic criticisms of the luxury and servility of the court are deepened by the specific inflections of his life. His descriptions of the court's "ensnarements" of the table and its obsequious ceremonies – "The half hat, the whole hat, the half smile, the whole smile, the nod, the embrace, the positive parting with a little bow, the comparative at the middle of the room, the superlative at the door" ("Of Liberty," p. 114) – serve Thoreau well for his criticisms of the supposedly democratic but actually degrading concessions necessary to thrive in America's "Economy." As Thoreau expresses it, one must be continually "seeking to curry favor, to get custom . . . lying, flattering, voting, contracting yourselves into a nutshell of civility, or dilating into an atmosphere of thin and vaporous generosity" (*Walden*, 7).

Cowley's praise, moreover, of the husbandman's relative contentment, "innocence," and purposiveness, in his georgic paean "Of Agriculture," is an explicit gesture of civic gratitude: "In our late mad and miserable Civil Wars, all other Trades, even to the meanest, set forth whole troops . . . : But, I do not remember the Name of any one Husbandman who had so considerable a Share in the twenty Years Ruin of his Country, as to deserve the curses of his Countrymen" (pp. 145–6). Cowley's high valuation of the husbandman during the upheavals of the "Great Rebellion" comports well with another text Thoreau clearly knew – Thomas Jefferson's *Notes on the State of Virgina.* Jefferson's praise of farmers was similarly expressed in the midst of a later historical moment when an established way of life was threatened by the advent of a manufacture-based economy.[58] Jefferson likewise suggested no known instance of "the corruption of morals among the mass of cultivators," corruption being instead "the mark set on those, who not looking up to heaven, to their own soil and industry, as does the husbandman, for their subsistence, depend for it on the casualties and caprice of customers."[59] For his renovated "economy" in "Of Agriculture," Cowley accordingly creates an imaginary coat of arms – noted and transcribed by Thoreau, who sometimes exploits the doubly allusive vocabulary of Cowley's as well as Jefferson's "pastoral" agrarian idiom:

> Behold the original and primitive nobility of all those great persons, who are too proud now, not only to till the ground, but almost to tread upon it. We may talk what we please of lilies, and lions rampant, and spread-eagles, in fields *d'or* or *d'argent:* but, if heraldry were guided by reason, a plough in a field arable would be the most noble and ancient arms. ("Of Agriculture" 1664–5, p. 147)

Yet Cowley's "Of Agriculture" and "Proposition for the Advancement of Experimental Philosophy," published together in *Essays, in Verse and Prose,* are not unequivocally pastoral and nostalgic; they are also clearly prospective and, in a restricted sense, reformist texts: Cowley's playful punning on the idiom of georgic heraldry is his response to a gentry that prefers to educate its youth in dance instruction rather than agricultural experimentation. Promoting programs of land and educational reform grounded in the ideas of the new science (including Francis Bacon's and Samuel Hartlib's) and implementing practical instruction in agriculture, Cowley's two essays may well have inspired Thoreau's suggestions, in "Economy," for a similar reform of such colleges as "Cambridge College" (*Walden,* 49–52). But perhaps the central point of Cowley's georgic heraldry to which Thoreau responds is its conjunction of heraldic emblems and meaningful behavior, the desire to assert coherence and vigilantly seek out significance – here played out in the georgic and courtly modes – in what seems an all too bleak, tumultuous, indeed nominalist world.

Thus, the sane and fresh landscape of georgic moderation that Cowley offers Thoreau is, upon closer inspection, actually an illusory retrenchment, haunted by threats to its existence, composed of inwardly focused values, reassessments, exclusions, and renunciations – a sometime sanctuary vigilantly defended against real or imagined treacheries as well as against the impingements of civility's forms and pretensions. Tinged with the travails of war, intrigues, petitions, suits, and betrayals, such a landscape and such a courtier's pastoral and georgic codes serve Thoreau well to challenge the desirability of a "courtier-like success" (*Walden*, 15) in a New England presided over by the Whiggish elite of property, commerce, and industrialism in the 1840s and 1850s.[60]

Like Cowley, who was "employed all his days and half his nights ciphering and deciphering,"[61] Thoreau exploits Cowley's pastoral and georgic codes to proffer values not always strictly pastoral or georgic. Indeed, the "pastoralism" of Walton's, Milton's, and Cowley's England has shown Thoreau no stable, serene, or pristine refuge; instead, their transparent pastoralism and their partially veiled counsels suggest the ordeal of engaging with a turbulent world. Each pastoral participant is "tried," as Cowley was once described, "in the business of the highest consequence, and practised in the hazardous secrets of court and cabinets."[62] Enduring through changing centers of power and shifting values, these English Civil War survivors appealed to an antebellum Thoreau, who sometimes felt like a foreigner in his own land and similarly summoned up the pastoral, but not altogether as an actually proffered refuge. If on occasion Thoreau saw himself as a reformer raised before the public eye by circumstances, selections in his literary notebook imply that he also felt himself entrusted with the sanctity of a clandestine and private commission, as when he copied a remark of Cowley's from "Of Solitude": "The first minister of state has not so much business in public as a wise man has in private." Cowley continues, "the one has but part of the affairs of one nation, the other all the works of God and Nature under his consideration" (Cowley, *Prose Works,* p. 132). In light of his earlier reading in his volume of Cowley, Thoreau's 1852 journal remark that "as Cowley loved a garden, so I a forest"[63] intimates a landscape of desire as well as of melancholy, one partly sequestered yet poignantly informed by the distresses and disillusionment of public life. Because he employed the language of the pastoral and georgic modes, Thoreau has sometimes been viewed as participating in a deeply nostalgic conservatism most often associated with the old Federalist party in America. Yet his appropriation of the devices of pastoral and georgic codes from these embattled seventeenth-century authors – two royalists (Walton and Cowley) and one republican (Milton) – should remind us that however much he wished to preserve the purity of a divinized nature and blame bad "pastors" for its desecration, he explored *both*, the assets as well as the liabilities of the rhetoric of pastoralism and retreat. This rhetoric more often signals his sense of personal displacement than indicates an ideological alternative of compromising with conservative impulses. Vigilance must be exercised so that the idyll will not become the idol. Most of all, as we have seen from the example of pastoralism in the midst of civil war in Milton's, Walton's, and Cowley's texts, Thoreau's language of the spirit cannot be severed from the language of sociopolitical debate.

Patriotic Pastoralism and a Landscape of Mausoleums

There is, moreover, a tension in Thoreau between his apparent intent literally to dwell in the rustic pastoral bower or sow his georgic bean field and his implicit allegiance to sophisticated cultivation, evinced by the density of allusion and complexly wrought quality of his own literary artifact ("Most men . . . are so occupied with the . . . superfluously coarse labors of life that its finer fruits cannot be plucked by them" (*Walden,* 6). Thoreau's apparent locus of values in the rustic pastoral or georgic seems to be at odds, moreover, with his desire to urge a national identity based neither upon pastoral natural resources nor upon technological mastery or land acquisition, but upon the cultivation of its "abstract thought," its cultural national genius.[64]

In the "Economy" chapter of *Walden,* for example, Thoreau imagines – perhaps in homage to Thomas Cole's paintings *The Course of Empire* – Arcadian pastoral America as displacing the landscape of plundered mausoleums, crumbling temples, and defaced epitaphs depicted in the powerful final chapter of Sir Thomas Browne's *Hydriotaphia.* Yet Thoreau expresses, to an audience familiar with Browne's popular text,[65] what should represent a distinctive American national identity in the conspicuously aureate style of Browne. Mankind's deplorable error in the "art of perpetuation" and the laudable endurance of less opulent but more worthy artifacts of the human spirit are translated from Browne's Christian terms into Thoreau's terms of American cultural identity:

> It should not be by their architecture, but why not even by their power of abstract thought, that nations should seek to

commemorate themselves? How much more admirable the Bhagvat-Geeta than all the ruins of the East! Towers and temples are the luxury of princes. A simple and independent mind does not toil at the bidding of any prince. Genius is not a retainer to any emperor, nor is its material silver, or gold, or marble, except to a trifling extent. To what end, pray, is so much stone hammered? In Arcadia, when I was there, I did not see any hammering stone. Nations are possessed with an insane ambition to perpetuate the memory of themselves by the amount of hammered stone they leave. What if equal pains were taken to smooth and polish their manners? One piece of good sense would be more memorable than a monument as high as the moon . . . The grandeur of Thebes was a vulgar grandeur. More sensible is a rod of stone wall that bounds an honest man's field than a hundred-gated Thebes that has wandered farther from the true end of life. (*Walden,* 57–8)

A quarter of a century earlier, in his "Remarks on National Literature" (1823), William Ellery Channing had expressed what was then already conventional wisdom about American culture:[66] "Invention and effort have been expended on matter, much more than on mind. Lofty piles have been reared; the earth has groaned under pyramids and palaces. The thought of building up a nobler order of intellect and character, has hardly crossed the most adventurous statesman."[67] The Thoreauvian version clearly contains pastoral and georgic elements that Channing's does not: "a rod of stone wall that bounds an honest man's field," for instance, stands in clear opposition to the "ambitious" opulence of the ancients; moreover, "a simple and independent mind does not toil at the bidding of any prince." Yet Thoreau declines Channing's accommodating insistence that he intends only to "correct what we deem a disproportional attention to physical good, and not at all to condemn the expenditure of ingenuity and strength on the outward world."[68] Instead, using architecture metonymically, as he often does in "Economy," Thoreau proceeds to chastise American philistine materialism when he condemns the American "religion" that made the privately owned United States Bank its shrine, and when he comments reproachfully upon the conservative New York Episcopalians' magnificent edifice ("What reasonable man ever supposed that ornaments were something outward . . . [gotten] by such a contract as the inhabitants of Broadway their Trinity Church?" [*Walden,* 47]).[69] Thoreau appropriates Browne's towering vision in

Hydriotaphia – as one who looks back over history from a point very near the end of time and sees things in a just light – to offer a rebuke to Whig ambition and arrogance:

> The religion and civilization which are barbaric and hea-
> thenish build splendid temples; but what you might call
> Christianity does not. Most of the stone a nation hammers
> goes toward its tomb only . . . As for the religion and love of
> art of the builders, it is much the same all the world over,
> whether the building be an Egyptian temple or the United
> States Bank. It costs more than it comes to. The mainspring
> is vanity, assisted by the love of garlic and bread and butter.
> (*Walden*, 58)

Thoreau uses Sir Thomas Browne's leveling *vanitas* theme to condemn, like Andrew Jackson, the institution most symbolic of Whig corporate power, land speculation, and arrogant autonomy in the 1830s: Nicholas Biddle's privately owned United States Bank. Orestes Brownson repeatedly attacked the bank in the early issues of his *Boston Quarterly Review,* which Thoreau read.[70] Thoreau's concern is not to know about the aristocracies that built "the monuments of the West and the East," but to know "who were above such trifling" (*Walden*, 58).

Browne's highly alliterative prose (the "minor monuments" of human bones sequestered in urns, for example) both echoes behind and informs Thoreau's reproach to the "Towers and temples . . . of princes." Browne's retrospective wisdom makes an example of the ancients' misguided efforts in finely wrought epigrammatic phrases ("Had they made as good provision for their names, as they have done for their relicks, they had not so grossly erred in the art of perpetuation") and informs Thoreau's rebuke, "what if equal pains were taken to smooth and polish their manners? One piece of good sense would be more memora-ble than a monument as high as the moon." To Browne's marmo-real landscape imagery filled with vainglorious "Pyramids, Arches and Obelisks," Thoreau not only adds "towers and temples" and "a monument as high as the moon," but he intensifies the artifice still more with the "vulgar grandeur" of the "hundred-gated Thebes" (*Walden*, 57). Thoreau, moreover, imitates the cumula-tive effect of Browne's descriptions of monuments to compound the effect of the incessant "hammering of stone" resounding earlier in the passage. He likewise appropriates Browne's habit of paradoxically juxtaposing spirit and matter in balanced cadences. Browne balances "St. Innocent's church-yard" with the "sands of

AEgypt," the "Read[iness] to be any thing" with "the ecstacy of being ever," and "six foot [of earth] with the *moles* of Adrianus". Thoreau counterposes the "Bhagvat-Geeta" with "all the ruins of the East," and "a rod of stone wall that bounds an honest man's field" with the "hundred-gated Thebes that has wandered farther from the true end of life."[71]

Thoreau often subtly and sometimes obviously exploits Browne's highly patterned seventeenth-century style – a style, as seen in Chapter 1, that was considered for its "eccentricities" "a topic of much animadversion" by a reviewer for the *American Whig Review*. Thoreau's use of Brownean stylistic features permits a creative tension between a patriotic investment in American national identity and an implicit but conspicuous participation in early modern English culture. The Thoreau who can, in *A Week*, complain of "idle learning" ("We are amused to read how Ben Jonson engaged, that the dull masks with which the royal family and nobility were to be entertained, should be 'grounded upon antiquity and solid learning' " [*Week*, 105]), can simultaneously advise Americans to "Learn to split wood" and display his knowledge of masques. Indeed, his knowledge of masques extended to an awareness of the periodic contest between Jonson's poetry and Inigo Jones's "transitory devices" of spectacle; he cites Jonson's own words from the preface to the masque *Hymenaie*, which he had earlier transcribed in his journal for 1841.[72]

By stressing the artifice and limits of the pastoral and georgic modes while engaging them, Thoreau alerts his audience to the boundaries of America's own pastoral myth, signaling it as one among other cultural artifacts. Complementing his emphasis on the artifice of the pastoral mode, Thoreau, as we shall see next, fashions an ethos from the theatrical characters of masques as well as from the playful narrative persona of Sir Thomas Browne's *Religio Medici*. Thoreau's landscape, moreover, retains its potential as the locus for the rearticulation of virtuous ideals for conducting both public and private life on a higher plane, as we shall see next in his use of Thomas Carew's masque *Coelum Britannicum*.

Thoreau's Theatrical and Extravagant Personae: Seventeenth-Century Masques and the Autobiographical Anatomy

In the "Economy" chapter of *Walden*, Thoreau employs Thomas Carew's antimasque character Momus, as well as Mercury from the Caroline masque *Coelum Britannicum* (1633), to inaugurate the ethopoesis of his own narrative persona.[73] Like Momus and Mercury, his highly theatrical, witty blend of voices offers a critique, alternately satiric and idealized, of contenders for the title of "virtue" in Thoreau's own renovated and purified "economy." The creation of his persona's ethos, then, is shaped partly by his engagement with these prior texts and partly by his dialogue with his own society. Thoreau's identification with Chanticleer, in the epigraph to *Walden* preceding the "Economy" chapter ("to brag as lustily as chanticleer in the morning ... if only to wake my neighbors up"), as well as with prophetic cockcrowing in the "Sounds" chapter (*Walden*, 127), may well signal a connection early in the text, not only with American folklore's Gamecock of the Wilderness[74] but also, for the paganized Thoreau, with Mercury in Carew's *Coelum Britannicum*. At the opening of the masque, Mercury, the god of language, arrives with a message for English society. He arrives in a chariot upon which "stands a cocke, in action of crowing" (lines 41–2).

Carew's masque, which Thoreau partly transcribed in his literary notebook and later in *Walden* and thought remarkable for its "wit and rhetoric," attempts nothing less than the renovation of heaven based on the pattern of Charles I's and his consort's chaste virtues. (Thoreau knew that the masque celebrated the values of the court, commenting in his literary notebook, "It was written at the request of the King and performed by his majesty and his lords," and observing that "Carew was an ornament of the court of Charles I and the friend of Jonson, Suckling, Davenant, and Clarendon.")[75] After the masque's profligate Jove promises reform and the bestial constellations are expelled from the (king's) "Starre-Chamber" of Heaven, contenders for celestial ascendancy – Riches and Poverty, Fortune and Pleasure – offer their own respective claims to fill the void in a heavenly sphere soon to reflect the felicitous reign of Charles and Henrietta Maria. Momus's and Mercury's witty, skeptical judgments about these contenders and their expulsions of antimasque figures also clear the way for the harmonious, pastoral order of the main masque. They may also inform the audacity and extravagance of the Thoreauvian narrative voice in the "Economy" chapter, as it clears the way for the more pervasively harmonious natural descriptions in *Walden* beginning in the next chapter, where Thoreau imperiously announces himself as presiding over and claiming the landscape as a monarch (*Walden*, 82). Just as Momus and Mercury judge and expel personified voluptuaries, vices, and "pretenders" to virtue from Charles's renovated realm, so Thoreau begins with the satiric and irreverent Momus's ridicule of the property-encumbered, rejecting them from his ideal "economy" (*Walden*, 33). He then concludes the chapter with Mercury's contemptuous, high-handed dismissal of Poverty's false claims to virtue ("The Pretensions of Poverty" [*Walden*, 80]), banishing contemporary American reformers and philanthropists as well as the straitened virtues of the poor from his renovated domain of *Walden*.

The aspect to which Thoreau seems most drawn in *Coelum Britannicum* – particularly in the figures of Momus, god of blame, and Mercury, god of eloquence – is the dramatic, transformative power of their language. Thoreau evidently admires the witty arguments, satiric debates, and eloquent rhetoric capable of both expelling vices and "pretenders" to virtue from the realm and reforming society. Clearly he saw his own *Walden* as a reforming text, and imagined himself, like Mercury, as one intending to "trade in messages from heaven" (*Walden*, 70), hoping to be one of "the benefactors of the race, whom we have apotheosized as messengers from heaven, bearers of divine gifts to man (*Walden*, 36).

Mercury's response to Poverty – the "Complemental Verses" that constitute the "Pretensions of Poverty" at the end of Thoreau's "Economy" chapter – has been, in fact, mistakenly viewed by scholars as a "complement" to (that is, "contrasting" with) Thoreau's own thoughts. The editors of the *Norton Anthology of American Literature* suggest that these lines are "offered ironically as a retort to [Thoreau's chapter] 'Economy.' "[76] In fact, as in Carew's masque, Thoreau actually offers Mercury's "complemental verses" (in the archaic sense of "accessory" and "additional") to corroborate his own values and provide a poetic accompaniment to the prose perspective he offered as the Momus figure. The Momus figure vulgarly ridicules the ill-humor and character deformations of the degraded poor as well as the idiosyncratic leaders of reform movements. He complains, "If any thing ail a man, so that he does not perform his functions, if he have a pain in his bowels even, – for that is the seat of sympathy, – he forthwith sets about reforming – the world" (*Walden*, 77).[77] Mercury's eloquent and powerful verse speeches throughout *Coelum Britannicum* serve as the representations of wisdom paired with Momus's satire, as elegant poetic depictions of the new order's ideals paired with Momus's prose criticism of the old order's lapses. The corresponding speeches of Momus and Mercury in Carew's masque, I suggest, serve Thoreau well as alternating, theatrical voices that offer equally appropriate criticisms of Thoreau's society. Thoreau appropriates Carew's Momus to chastise the regnant gods "stellified" by his own Concord society;[78] Mercury's verse speech at the end of "Economy" serves to commend ideals after exorcising emphatically and poetically the debased and joyless pretensions to virtue of the involuntarily poor, the misguided philanthropists, and the radical reformers.

The first draft of *Walden* (1846–7), written within three years of Thoreau's reading of *Coelum Britannicum*, reveals his identification with Momus, god of "witty mischiefes," blame, satire, and ridicule. Announcing in the first version of *Walden* that "I have often been struck by that fable of Momus," and citing Lempriere's classical dictionary on Momus's criticisms of the gods and consequent banishment from heaven, Thoreau poses the question, "What, think you would Momus say if he were living in our day? And I am not sure but what [that] he is."[79] In the final draft of *Walden*, Thoreau retains only a single quotation about Momus's criticism of Minerva's wisdom in building a house that was not portable "by which means a bad neighborhood might be avoided" (*Walden*, 33). Yet he distinctly regards himself as confirming and extending Momus's criticism, no longer simply hinting at social criticism but, like Carew's Momus, acting as a social provocateur. Thoreau eschews paying poll taxes and writes *Civil Disobedience* to register his complaints against the U.S. government. Correspondingly, Carew's Momus, the "Woollsacke god" (highest officer of the judiciate), who is without power to "vote in the sanction of new lawes," does have "yet a Praerogative of wresting the old to any whatsoever interpretation" (lines 147–8). With his irreverent analysis and impudent perspective, Carew's Momus (and Thoreau's) demystifies the claims of the old order and its attendant embodiments of worldliness. Taking issue with property-minded Whigs and land-grabbing Democrats, the Thoreauvian narrator in *Walden* insists, with Momus' self-acknowledged rudeness, that Momus's criticism "may still be urged, for our houses are such unwieldy property that we are often imprisoned rather than housed in them; and the bad neighborhood to be avoided is our own scurvy selves" (*Walden*, 34). Most explicitly, Thoreau's allusions in *Walden* are to the Momus not yet banished from heaven, but daring to find fault with each of the gods. Implicitly, however, as the Thoreauvian narrator surveys the contemporary state of New England, he seems to adopt the bold, sardonic pose and marginal status of Carew's Momus – "hypercrittique of manners, protonotarie of abuses, arch-informer, dilator-generall, universall calumniator, eternall plaintiffe, and perpetuall foreman of the grand inquest" (lines 136–9).[80]

Attired (not inappropriately for a skeptical and irascible Thoreauvian persona) in "a robe, all wrought over with ponyards, serpents' tongues, eyes, and eares; and upon his head a wreath stucke with feathers, and a porcupine in the forepart" (lines 104–6), Carew's Momus offers a dazzling, parodic catalogue of Charles I's austere statutory reforms curbing the excesses and licenses of James I's reign. These assert Charles's direct control over all areas of life in the realm: "Monopolies are called in, sophistication of wares punished, and rates imposed on Commodities. Injunctions are gone out to the Nectar Brewers, for the purging of the heavenly Beverage . . . Ganimede is forbidden the Bedchamber . . . Pan may not Pipe, nor Proteus juggle, but by especiall permission . . . In briefe, the whole state of the Hierarchy suffers a totall reformation" (lines 233–62).[81] In this tongue-in-cheek catalogue of reforms (only a small part of which is quoted here), Carew's Momus presents Charles's consolidation of power and affirms divine right and prerogative rule as part of the purification and renovation of the heavenly realm.[82] Thoreau's disenchantment with the debasement associated with commerce and the bogus individualism it encouraged in nineteenth-century America issues in a playful reworking of Momus's proclamation – Thoreau's parodic reformation of "business" practices in his enterprise at the pond. Indeed, with tongue in cheek, the Thoreauvian narrator insists, "I have always endeavored to acquire strict business habits" (*Walden*, 20). Employing the rhetoric of reforming business transactions, Thoreau enacts the consolidation of his own powers for a more noble trade – "with the Celestial Empire" – for you have to

> oversee all the details yourself in person; to be at once pilot and captain, and owner and underwriter; to buy and sell and keep the accounts; to read every letter received, and write or read every letter sent; to superintend the discharge of imports night and day; to be upon many parts of the coast almost at the same time; . . . to be your own telegraph, unweariedly sweeping the horizon . . .; to keep up a steady despatch of commodities, for the supply of such a distant and exorbitant market; to keep yourself informed of the state of the markets, prospects of war and peace every where, and anticipate the tendencies of trade and civilization . . . It is a labor to task the faculties of a man, – such problems of

profit and loss . . . as demand a universal knowledge. (*Walden*, 20–1).

While Carew's Momus both carries out and playfully mocks the autocratic power of Charles's decrees ("It . . . seemed meet to Our Omnipotency, for causes to Our selfe best knowne" [lines 440–4]), the Thoreau narrator playfully exploits and subverts the awe and power accorded to business in American culture, while incorporating into himself its many delegated powers, though for a more grand and worthy "transaction" with the divine.

Not only does the Thoreauvian narrator offer critiques of the household gods of American property and commerce, he also issues, in the manner of Carew's masque, a peremptory verdict upon popular novel and romance writers of his time. With Charles's delegated authority, Momus issues a proclamation rescinding the traditional practice of commemorating the profligate gods' "famous enterprizes" in constellations (lines 424–40) and demanding that they henceforth "unfurnish and dis-array Our foresaid Starre-Chamber of all those Antient Constellations which have for so many Ages beene sufficiently notorious" and replace them with those "onely as shall be qualified with exemplar Vertue and eminent Desert" (lines 444–9). In the "Reading" chapter of *Walden*, an imperious Thoreauvian narrator similarly decrees a parodic, reverse apotheosis, purging from his counsels of "the best English books" (*Walden*, 106) those among his contemporaries who fail to be provocative in their writing, yet, unlike Thoreau, "find a surer market" (*Walden*, 105).[83] "I think that they had better metamorphose all such aspiring heroes of universal noveldom into man weathercocks, as they used to put heroes among the constellations, and let them swing round there till they are rusty, and not come down at all to bother honest men with their pranks" (*Walden*, 105). Like the bestial constellations of Carew's masque that are purged from "this adulterate Spheare" by a wave of Mercury's magical caduceus ("Divested of your gorgeous starry robes, / Fall from the circling Orbe . . . Then to Fens, Caves . . . Fly, and resume your native qualities" [lines 294–303]), these nineteenth-century pretenders to literary stardom are relegated to a more appropriate existence as relics and registers of the public's prevailing literary whims.

So too are licentious Pleasure's claims dismissed from Thoreau's renovated realm. Thoreau copied into his literary notebook Mercury's retort to the "Bewitching Syren" Pleasure, in *Coelum Britannicum*, acknowledging her powers: captains and nations have been rendered "effeminate," and "Empires, that knew no limits but the Poles, / Have in thy wanton lap melted away" (lines 828–9). The Thoreauvian narrator similarly finds the emasculating powers of Pleasure easily dismissed in the "Economy" chapter and in the conclusion of "Where I Lived, and What I Lived for," where he identifies with the heroic Ulysses tied to his ship's mast (*Walden*, 97). In "Economy" he, like Mercury, condemns "the luxurious and dissipated who set the fashion," and disdains to become "a Sardanapalus, and if he resigned himself to their tender mercies he would soon be completely emasculated" (*Walden*, 36–7). Just after citing Mercury condemning Pleasure's "wanton lap," Thoreau notes of Carew himself that "in his life he was dissipated."[84] Yet for the ascetic temperament of Thoreau, the "Pretensions of Poverty" are more compelling, and require his more careful consideration since she claims as her progeny artistic invention (line 601) and the freedom necessary for spiritual contemplation (line 609). Indeed, Poverty's pretension to virtue is so strong that Mercury must exert his poetic skills to defeat her claims.

Thoreau copies into his literary notebook part of Poverty's speech from *Coelum* declining all titles to dominion based on her numerous subjects as well as her offsprings of virtue, wit, and invention:

> . . . I decline those titles, and lay clayme
> To heaven, by right of Divine contemplation;
> Shee is my Darling; I, in my soft lap
> Free from disturbing cares, bargaines, accounts,
> Leases, Rents, Stewards, and the feare of theeves,
> That vex the rich, nurse her in calme repose,
> And with her all the Vertues speculative,
> Which, but with me, find no secure retreat.
>
> (lines 609–16)

The temptation to yield to this argument of Poverty's must have been considerable for the spartan Thoreauvian temperament, who curses trade (*Walden*, 70) and denounces America's belief in its Manifest Destiny, Mexican War (*Walden*, 160–1), and the land-grabbing speculation of the late 1830s and 1840s. But judging from the note he had written to himself in the earliest draft of *Walden* – "Mercury's Reply to Poverty in Carew" – Thoreau had decided to include in *Walden* Mercury's banishment of "The Pretensions of Poverty," dismissing her claim to a place in his own "new enlightened sphere" (*Walden*, 80; line 667).[85] Moreover, in language that corresponds to Momus's and Mercury's appraisals of claims to virtue in Carew's masque, Thoreau announces that "Philanthropy is almost the only virtue which is sufficiently appreciated by mankind. Nay, it is greatly overrated" (*Walden*, 76). Carew's Momus impudently rejects Poverty's faulty logic, her "grosse . . . inference" that if the claims of Plutus (Riches; in Thoreau's terms, the "degraded rich") were not valid, then hers must be the alternative of choice ("the degraded poor"). But Mercury's assessment, like Thoreau's analysis, instead denounces Poverty's tendency to offer counterfeits of virtue.[86] Her frauds are exposed by Mercury, as well as by Thoreau, who quotes Mercury's entire speech at the end of "Economy." Her frauds are revealed as the disguised forms of dejected indifference ("Tearing those humane passions from the mind, / Upon whose stocks fair blooming virtues flourish, / Degradeth nature, and benumbeth sense, / And, Gorgon-like turns active men to stone"); straitened dispiritedness ("We not require the dull society / Of your necessitated temperance, / Or that unnatural stupidity / That knows nor joy nor sorrow"); reticent docility ("Falsely exalted passive fortitude / Above the active"); and uninspired meekness ("This low abject brood, / That fix their seats in mediocrity, / Become your servile minds" [*Walden*, 80]).

In the place of these pretenders to virtue and stellification, Thoreau, as a Mercury figure, offers his own pattern of "extravagant," "heroic virtue" – in Mercury's words, "but we advance / Such virtues only as admit excess, / Brave, bounteous acts, regal magnificence, / All seeing prudence, magnanimity that knows no bound" (*Walden*, 80).[87] Like Mercury, who banishes pretenders to virtue in favor of authentic kingly virtues, Thoreau had, earlier in the chapter, complained of and rejected "the success of great scholars and thinkers [which] is commonly a courtier-like success, not kingly, not manly. They . . . are in no sense the progenitors of a nobler race of men" (*Walden*, 15). Here, then, at the end of "Economy," appropriating Mercury's exact words from *Coelum Britannicum*, the Thoreauvian narrator would replace their successes with "that heroic virtue / For which antiquity hath left no name, / But patterns only, such as Hercules, / Achilles, Theseus" (*Walden* 80).[88] Mercury's language displays the power both to banish the inauthentic and to surpass the verbal appeals of worldliness, and even Momus's criticisms, by presenting the ideal. Whereas Carew's Momus, an antimasque figure (child of night and chaos), suddenly departs after the banishment of the last claims of worldliness (lines 836–42), Mercury is permitted to introduce the heavenly visions of harmony that follow (lines 843ff.). Mercury, then, is presented not only in *Coelum* (lines 392–9) but also in *Walden* as the verbally powerful agent of renovation who commends the ideal.

Thoreau would replace the plebeian reform virtues and bourgeois complacencies with his own patrician virtues offered, too, with the flourish of Mercury's eloquent verse. Familiar with both the masque tradition and Charles I's reign, Thoreau revises Carew's sumptuous depiction of Charles' and his consort's virtue (based on the Platonic correspondence between outward fairness and inward grace and virtue). In *Walden,* Thoreau insists instead upon "bounteous" virtues "that admit excess" and "magnanimity that knows no bound," to reflect the "extravagance" of his rustic pose and his own spartan economy of "simplicity, independence, magnanimity, and trust" (*Walden,* 15). Thoreau's images of the good, the ideal, as well as his many images of metamorphosis (also abundant in Carew's masque) are testimonies to his own Platonic belief in their socially transformative power, rather than signs of his retreat from a reforming social agenda.[89] Nor is this entirely surprising in someone with such a lively awareness of the symbolic resonance of the place-name "Concord." The New England Jeremiah may well intersect here with the function of the kingly ideal in English Renaissance Platonism: Thoreau does seem to offer, in the place of the masque's Albion and the monarchial ideal, the ideal of America incorporated in himself, "Wherever I sat, there I might live, and the landscape radiated from me accordingly" (*Walden,* 81). The visions of harmonious order presented in *Coelum Britannicum* are depicted as evolving in the course of the nation's history: Mercury introduces archaic visions of Britain's ancient past. As Stephen Orgel and Roy Strong have suggested, once having banished the old mythology, Carew has the task of creating and celebrating a new national mythology descending from the "antient Picts, Scots, and Irish" (line 881), who appear in the antimasque, so that "from its origins . . . the kingdom is recreated."[90] Several commentators have suggested that Thoreau juxtaposes scenes from Edward Johnson's *Wonder-Working Providence* depicting Concord's settlement with his own Concord reenactment of the nation's "moment of origin . . . in order to do it right."[91] If this is true, Thoreau might be offering, in the manner of Carew's courtly masque, his own native gods and unsung heroes for national celebration.

Indeed, Thoreau seems captivated by the Platonic validation of the power of the ideal to transform society in both Carew's and

Jonson's masques.[92] Drawn to depictions of "Virtue" and "good fame" triumphing over worldly menaces, power, and glory, Thoreau transcribes into his literary notebook entire songs and speeches from masques that begin with such lines as "Who, Virtue, can thy power forget" (*The Masque of Queens,* lines 515–27), and "How near to good is what is fair! / Which we no sooner see, / But with the lines and outward air / Our senses taken be" (*Love Freed from Ignorance and Folly,* lines 301–4). Thoreau's penchant for appropriating and revising allegorical idealizations and their antitheses from the masques (Love and Wisdom or Ignorance and Folly) corresponds to his own concern with ideals and his own taste for such allegorical idealizations as "the West" and "the Wild":

> Ben Jonson exclaims, "How near to good is what is fair!" So I would say, "How near to good is what is *wild!*" . . . The most alive is the wildest. Not yet subdued to man, its presence refreshes him. One who pressed forward incessantly and never rested from his labors, who grew fast and made infinite demands on life, would always find himself in a new country or wilderness. (*Writings,* 5:220)

Here, in *Walking,* Thoreau revises a speech of one of Jonson's wise and prophetic priest figures in the masque *Love Freed from Ignorance and Folly.* The priest figure confirms Love's solution to the Sphinx's (Ignorance's) riddle by recognizing and proclaiming the unique ideal of King James (Phoebus) and Albion (England) and thus "Bowing to the sun throned in the west" (line 234). Thoreau appropriates the speech to commend his ideal of walking to "the West" ("westering") and into "the Wild" ("a new country"), that is, progressing toward an ideal expressed not in America's misguided Manifest Destiny, but in a symbolic geography of the ideal: "We would fain take that walk, never yet taken by us through this actual world, which is perfectly symbolical of the path which we love to travel in the interior and ideal world; and sometimes, no doubt, we find it difficult to choose our direction, because it does not yet exist distinctly in our idea" (*Writings,* 5:220).

As evidenced from the other masques he read and partly transcribed into his literary notebook, *A Week, Walden,* and *Walking,* Thoreau finds Platonic transformation more compelling than dramatic entanglements and confrontations. Vice, melancholy, and the privations of virtue are simply dispelled by the actual presence of virtue in Ben Jonson's *Hymenaie* (1606), *The Masque of Queens* (1609), *Love Freed From Ignorance and Folly* (1611), and *The Golden Age Restored* (1616), and in James Shirley's *Cupid and Death* (1653). He alludes, for example, to Jonson's *Masque of Queens* in his depiction of the screech owls' strains in the "Sounds" chapter ("Their dismal scream is truly Ben Jonsonian. Wise midnight hags!" [*Walden*, 124]). Just as Jonson's witches and hags represent, we are told in the masque, the vices of bad fame or scandal (lines 50–65) and chant their seventh "charm" ("Black go in, and blacker come out, / At thy going down, we give thee a shout: Hoo . . . Thou shalt have ten, thou shalt have a score. / Hoo, Har, Har, Hoo" [lines 230–3, 236–7]), so too Thoreau creates of the screech owls, hooting owls, and bullfrogs his own tragic grotesque and comic grotesque antimasque figures and "infernal groves" (*Walden*, 124), with his own explanation of what they represent. Whereas the screech owls are the "low spirits and melancholy foreboding, of fallen souls that once in human shape night-walked the earth and did the deeds of darkness," the "hooting owls" call out:

> Hoo hoo hoo, hoorer hoo . . . It is a sound admirably suited to swamps and twilight woods which no day illustrates, suggesting a vast and undeveloped nature which men have not recognized. They represent the stark twilight and unsatisfied thoughts which all have. All day the sun has shone on the surface of some savage swamp . . .; but now a more dismal and fitting day dawns, and a different race of creatures awakes to express the meaning of Nature there. (*Walden*, 125–6)

Yet just as with Jonson's masque, where the hags of ill fame and disorder are suddenly and magically banished by the personification of Heroic Virtue, the Ben Jonsonian Walden owls (though more appreciated by Thoreau than were the midnight hags by Jonson) are similarly displaced by day and Chanticleer (*Walden*, 127).

Not simply "an embellishment," then, Carew's masque, and to some extent Jonson's, inform sections of Thoreau's texts, particularly *Walden*. And the bold, insouciant voices of Momus and Mercury, displaying the power through speech to demystify the old order and celebrate the new, respectively, introduce the bravado of the narrative persona that Thoreau maintains through much of *Walden*. Indeed, the Thoreauvian persona in *Walden* interweaves the voices not only of sardonic Momus and eloquent Mercury, but also Sir Thomas Browne's voice from *Religio Medici* –

a voice that is exuberant, often theatrical, and also magnanimous.[93] The intermittent presence in *Walden* of a narrative voice
of playful self-assurance has struck critics as anomalous, obtrud-
ing itself in the midst of Thoreau's anxious defensiveness about
his literary vocation, which, as we have seen in his banishment of
novel writers from the constellations, also emerges intermittently.
But if Browne's theatricality and humor function as implicit criticisms of the zeal and strident prejudice that characterized the
Puritan mode of expression during the English Civil War period
of *Religio Medici*,[94] Thoreau's extravagance, the sheer hyperbole
of these voices, serves to challenge and defy the very American
deference to conformity and to communal values that allowed
the Whig reviewer, whose comments were examined in Chapter
1, to remark uneasily upon the "egotism" of *Religio Medici*. Thoreau offers, as almost an overcompensation, an exaggerated ideal
to displace what he has discerned in nineteenth-century Americans: "Some are dinning in our ears that we Americans, and
moderns generally, are intellectual dwarfs compared with the
ancients, or even the Elizabethan men." Thoreau impatiently
responds, "Shall a man go hang himself because he belongs to
the race of pygmies, and not be the biggest pygmy that he can?"
(*Walden*, 325–6).

Thoreau's oxymoronic image of "the biggest pygmy" suggests
the exaggeratedly defiant quality and the strained, artificial dilation of the narrative persona – the "I" that is "strongly tempted to
seize and devour [a woodchuck] raw," the "I" that "roves freely"
and "extravagantly" over the landscape, or the "I" that would
heroically "stand right fronting and face to face to a fact . . . and
feel the sweet edge dividing you through the heart and marrow."
Thoreau copied into his commonplace notebook ("Miscellaneous
Extracts," Ms. 594) long passages from *Religio Medici* – exactly
those passages that most suggest the theatrical, playful, and genially combative persona assumed by Browne in his appeal for
toleration as well as for the efficacy and moderate independence
of the individual conscience. Like the apparent political conservatism of Walton's pastoralism, Browne's extravagant persona partially disguises, in its exaggerated equanimity and magnanimity, a
distinctly liberal Anglican theological position – of charitable
inclusiveness and an antidogmatism that eschews sectarian contention. Whereas the American Whig reviewer excuses Browne's
"egotism" in *Religio* because he appears to accede to the dictates
of the English church and English society (as a good conservative
should), Thoreau responds instead to Browne's triumphant disre-

gard for creeds too humanly conceived, and to Browne's examination of his own individual faith and conscience. It is difficult,
in fact, to locate precisely where Thoreau's appropriation of
Browne's ethos modulates from a true ideal into a rhetorically
constructed, artfully poised persona.

Probably his most sustained and acrimonious attack on the
conventional Christianity of his day, the "Sunday" chapter of *A
Week* also offers Thoreau's most explicit reference to Browne.
Browhe's *Religio* echoes strongly in this chapter, for Browne's
boldness, his broadminded magnanimity, and his sense of the
immanence of the divine in the individual exactly epitomize Thoreau's ideal man of faith and the ethos Thoreau would like to
project in his own narrative. Here too Thoreau calls for both a
more broadly conceived notion of what constitutes true religion
and a more daring assertiveness on the part of all men in acknowledging the divine, the fabulous, the inspired aspects of life.
Thoreau allows that the "Concord is a dead stream, but its scenery
is the more suggestive to the contemplative voyager, and this day
its water was fuller of reflections than our pages even" (*Week*, 61).
Up to this point his emphasis has been on the heightened pastoral quality of that day's landscape, on the choral harmony with
which the human race has assembled a collective mythos, and on
the possibility of a Platonically ideal world suggested by the inverted and perfected world reflected in the river's surface. A
procession of churchgoers on the shore all too quickly disrupts
this "heathenish" observance of the Sabbath, and Thoreau protests that he and his brother are actually the "truest observers of
this sunny day" (*Week*, 63). The intrusion of conventional religion
into the landscape prompts an attack on the institutions of the
church, in which Thoreau calls the church the "ugliest looking
building in [a village], because it is the one in which human
nature stoops the lowest and is most disgraced" (*Week*, 76). Thoreau then offers as an alternative Browne's assertion in *Religio
Medici* that his life had been a "miracle of thirty years" as the
credo of a truly religious man. In so doing, he takes issue with
Samuel Johnson's reproach, in his "Life of Sir Thomas Browne,"
that "whatever [his life] may have of miracle, [it] will have nothing of fable . . . Of these wonders, however, the view that now can
be taken of his life offers no appearance" (*Week*, 68).[95] Whereas
Johnson quibbles with the accuracy of Browne's words, Thoreau
relishes the exuberance and audacity of Browne's assertion: "that
is a superfluous wonder, which Dr. Johnson expresses at the assertion of Sir Thomas Browne, that 'his life has been a miracle of

thirty years, which to relate, were not history, but a piece of poetry, and would sound like a fable.' *The wonder is rather that all men do not assert as much*" (*Week,* 68, my emphasis). Whereas Thoreau's response enshrines the *ethopoeia* of Browne's statement, Johnson's response overlooks the rhetorical mode that Browne himself signals at the beginning of *Religio.* Indeed, the Browne who boasts that "Men that look upon my outside, perusing only my condition and fortunes, do err in my altitude; for I am above *Atlas's* shoulders"; the Browne who "take[s his] circle to be above three hundred and sixty," who claims that "That mass of flesh that circumscribes me limits not my mind. That surface that tells the heavens it hath an end cannot perswade me I have any" (*Religio,* 2:110); the Browne who humorously claims that he "could digest a salad gathered in a church-yard as well as in a garden" or could "study, play, or sleep, in a tempest" (*Religio,* 2:86) – are all projections of the ethos of heightened magnanimity he has created.

Thoreau applauds – and appropriates – the sprezzatura that characterizes the ethos of the *Religio* narrator.[96] Indeed, in one of his most playful chapters ("Where I Lived, and What I Lived For"), Thoreau imperiously walks over each farmer's "premises"; he recounts how he might have owned property, if only to preserve the natural beauty of the land and "To enjoy these advantages I was ready to carry it on; like Atlas, to take the world on my shoulders, – I never heard what compensation he received for that" (*Walden,* 83). Thoreau's "altitude," like Browne's, is "above Atlas his shoulders" and men "perusing only [his] condition, and fortunes, do err in [taking his] altitude." In another of his most ebullient moments, Thoreau develops his notion of "extravagance" (in the "Conclusion" of *Walden*). One might recall that Browne used the same root sense of that word to describe himself in the beginning of *Religio,* where he comments on his belief in certain obsolete heresies during his "greener studies" and notes that these were such that could only have been revived by "such extravagant and irregular heads as mine" (*Religio,* 2:10). Thoreau, while capturing the grandiosity of Browne's persona, deletes the restraining modesty, calling instead for the greatest boundlessness: "I fear chiefly lest my expression may not be *extra – vagant* enough . . . so as to be adequate to the truth of which I have been convinced" (*Walden,* 324).

Indeed, Thoreau copied into his commonplace book a passage from *Religio* that is perhaps the most extended and exaggerated rendering of this extravagant pose, and the one that also seems in its exaggerated ideal to compensate for the absence of such virtue in Browne's contemporaries. Introducing the long discourse on charity in Book II of *Religio,* the Brownean narrator reacts to "those national repugnances" of his contemporaries that cause them to "behold with prejudice the French, Italian, Spaniard, or Dutch." Implicit in Browne's self-portrait of one whose "constitution [is] so general, that it consorts and sympathizeth with all things" (*Religio,* 2:85) is a catalogue of the many national customs (among others, eating frogs and locusts) and prejudices, the many "common antipathies that [he] can discover in others" but "feel[s] not in [him] self." The hyperbole in this section of *Religio,* referring exclusively to the human arena, is clearly Browne's response to the constrictions of his culture as well as an amplification of his desire for national and cultural equanimity. The *Religio* narrator offers the paradigm of extravagant compensation when he suggests that in response to the much-maligned foreigners, "where I find their actions in balance with my countrymen's, I honour, love, and embrace them, *in the same degree*" (*Religio,* 2:86; my emphasis): he embraces them to the same extent as he does his countrymen, *and* in proportion to their contrariety.

Thus Thoreau records the *Religio* passage that most addresses his own concern with the restrictiveness of habit and custom and that offers an alternative model of compensatory expansiveness – one that is "yarded" "every where" and "under any meridian." This passage, which so struck Thoreau in the year of his graduation from college, finds its way into the final draft of *Walden* many years later. The conclusion of *Walden* echoes this section of *Religio* as well as Browne's pronouncement elsewhere in the work that "There is all *Africa,* and her prodigies in us. We are that bold and adventurous piece of nature, which he that studies wisely learns, in a compendium, what others labour at in a divided piece and endless volume" (*Religio,* 2:21):

> Our voyaging is only great-circle sailing . . . What does Africa, – what does the West stand for? Is not our own interior white on the chart? . . . explore your own higher latitudes . . . If you would learn to speak all tongues and conform to the customs of all nations, if you would travel farther than all travellers, be naturalized in all climes . . . obey the precept of the old philosopher, and Explore thyself. (*Walden,* 321–2)

Although the "metaphysical" compendium or epitome that finds in the individual a transcendental abridgement of the cosmos was long ago noted by F. O. Matthiessen, for Thoreau, I think, the dramatic copiousness, the dilation of the self to its extreme limits, offers an exaggerated and defiant ideal, not necessarily in the pastoral bower, but "every where" and "under any meridian." Moreover, it is not with hagiography that Thoreau quibbles, but, as we have seen, with its too narrow canon. Nor is it with faith that he takes issue, but with religious creeds conceived in too human and too exclusive terms.

Thus Thoreau's pastoral and georgic fantasies and their religiously and politically engaged subtexts exploit the models of particularly equivocal pastorals and georgics and particularly extravagant narrative personae from the period of the English Revolution and its aftermath. Perhaps Thoreau saw in this period the clearest disjunction between the pastoral mode and historical circumstances. Certainly he saw that the pastoralism, or the exaggerated playfulness of even such political conservatives as Walton, Cowley, Carew, and Browne, could serve as the tactical disguises that allowed them to remain engaged in the political debates of their culture. But also by deftly assimilating and adapting particular English texts, Thoreau attempts to provoke self-consciousness on the part of Americans, to warn his audience to resist the naturalization of the pastoral mode – a temptation to which they were particularly prone, for Americans often resorted to the pastoral splendors of their natural resources as the basis for reckoning their national value and national identity. He uses English texts to drive a wedge between the American pastoral's surface delights and satisfactions – little more than reifications of a culture's desire – and the contingent circumstances of American life, which require constant discernment and judgment. Thoreau demonstrates, moreover, with what skill he can assimilate and subordinate particular English texts to his own cultural purposes, exhibiting no provincial imitativeness but rather suggesting that an American Renaissance participating with English culture need not be an act of filial deference.

5

Melville's Mardi *and* Moby-Dick, *Marvelous Travel Narratives, and Seventeenth-Century Methods of Inquiry*

The Poetics of Probability: John Locke, Sir Thomas Browne, and the Marvelous

Recent critics have examined how Melville's fiction and the American political "romance" exploited a common ideological language, one converging on such issues as national expansion, the frontier, and race relations. Others have investigated the participation of Melville's novels and mid-century popular fiction in social reform discourse subversive of conventional and elite values.[1] But we have yet to discern how Melville's writings, by engaging with the mid-century Northeastern culture's rationalist assumptions – its nexus of empirical biases, liberal theological values, political agendas, and literary tastes – were able to fashion critiques of Whig values in the culture's own rationalist vocabulary. Evert Duyckinck's fears about Ishmael (see Chapter 1) illustrate the social and political "dangers" that Americans perceived in transcendentalism and in the rationalist extremes of European deism and atheism. But Melville, disposed neither toward Locke nor toward transcendentalism, explores the implications and reveals the dangers of Britain's "safer" rationalism (both English and Scottish) embraced by America. Indeed, we should remember that in his analogy of two whales hoisted and secured to either side of the Pequod, Ishmael laments the burden of both Lockean and transcendental philosophical biases: "So, when on one side you hoist in Locke's head, you go over that way; but now, on the other side, hoist in Kant's and you come back again; but in very poor plight. Thus, some minds for ever keep trimming boat. Oh, ye foolish! throw all these thunder-heads overboard, and then you will float light and right."[2] Ishmael's speculations dramatically enact certain rationalist

methods – those associated with seventeenth-century liberal Anglicans with whom not only John Locke but also American Whig Unitarians had much in common[3] – in order to interrogate the adequacy of those very Lockean categories of knowledge and methods of arriving at conclusions that buttressed American conservative Whig politics.[4] Available to Melville in the writings of Sir Thomas Browne, whom Melville had read thoroughly, and encoded in his use of Browne's "gorgeous" style and probabilist methods, those "extravagant daring speculations" that Duyckinck ascribes to Ishmael depict the enfranchisement of reason while also exposing its limits.[5] Browne's is a method of inquiry that, while engaged in making judgments about the alien or marvelous, asks its investigator to reevaluate the criteria by which judgment is usually determined. By adopting a Brownean method of inquiry – one sensitive to contingency and reliant upon private judgment – Melville exposes the limitations of Lockean rationalist assumptions in antebellum American culture. He in fact highlights in those assumptions the severely restricted conditions under which the anomalous and the alien, indeed the very notion of alterity, may be recognized.[6] Yet Ishmael's and the Mardian narrator's speculations are also meant to contrast with the radical egalitarian Democrats' and Transcendentalists' susceptibility to a Starbuck-like credulous faith or an Ahab-like delusion in their willingness to abandon rational methods – their "romance" with the experience of immanence and certain knowledge which informed their politics. Indeed, through Ishmael's Brownean speculations, Melville calls attention to the conspicuous exclusion of all that is not quite intelligible by pointing to incongruities, to the vestiges of disturbing phenomena that have been systematically purged from the world depicted in the "best" American literature. Discussed in detail later in this chapter, Ishmael among the cenotaphs in the whalemen's chapel finds neither spiritual nor worldly assurances, but instead is haunted and terrorized by the "knocking in a tomb" that refuses to be hushed. And as we examine Melville's imaginative recuperation of a seventeenth-century method of inquiry canceled by the Enlightenment, we see not only its intensely unsettling epistemological and political implications, but also the imaginative stimulus to which it leads – and the aesthetic challenge it enables Melville to make.

I am not necessarily claiming that the American authors were the dutiful descendants of the Anglicans, Browne, or even Locke, though Americans certainly read them. Rather, I demonstrate that these early modern writers were appropriated to help formulate and legitimate issues in nineteenth-century America. The writings of these seventeenth-century theologians, philosophers, and "experimentalists" provided an already articulated resource to be shaped and understood as contemporary circumstances required.

We first examine how John Locke's epistemology supplied the means and conceptual force (strengthened considerably by Scottish Common Sense realism's heightened trust in empirical data) by which the recognition of the anomalous could be diminished or entirely extinguished by conservatives who preferred, like O'Brien and Duyckinck, to banish or naturalize the miraculous and the marvelous, and to abhor such prodigies as a white whale. Locke's response to the wondrous and marvelous – both sacred and secular – contrasts with Sir Thomas Browne's, whose works preserve the equipoise of the sacred and the secular, permitting Melville to bring the epistemological, theological, literary, and political together in a way that challenged those Americans who embraced Lockean assumptions. After a brief examanation of Locke, we will better see how Browne, completing *Pseudodoxia Epidemica* less than twenty years before Locke's *Essay Concerning Human Understanding* was published, offers Melville an alternative. This is particularly apparent when we view Browne as Melville understood him to be, as engaged with the methodology and investigations of those pious Anglican empirical probabilists whose inquiries into the marvelous and whose commissioned travel narratives explored and reconfigured the boundaries of knowledge. We will then see, in an extended analysis of *Mardi* and in a more selective analysis of *Moby-Dick,* that Melville, through his Brownean inquiries, is able to offer readers sometimes playful but often terrifying confrontations with the anomalous both in the sensuous world and in the spiritual. These function as challenges to interpretive practices and as tests of interpretive judgments. Moreover, by illustrating the many domains in which human judgment must be exercised and open inquiry engaged in, Melville emphasizes the interconnection of philosophy, theology, science, politics, and aethetics in antebellum America and demonstrates the adjustments to judgment and inquiry crucial to America.

* * * * * *

In both the *Essay* and *The Reasonableness of Christianity,* Locke carried on the moderate empiricism of Robert Boyle and Joseph Glanvill and the probabilist epistemological tradition of Anglican Latitudinarians William Chillingworth and John Tillotson.[7] "Probabilistic empiricism," according to Barbara Shapiro, the

"most distinctive feature of seventeenth-century [English] intellectual life," emerged in part from the Baconian program out-
lined in *The Advancement of Learning* and implemented by the
Royal Society and in part from the Anglican Latitudinarian epistemological debates on the uncertainty of human knowledge regarding divine truths.[8] Questions of the probability and certainty
of knowledge were concurrently pursued in religion, natural history, and philosophy; probable judgments were, according to
Shapiro, frequently at issue in seventeenth-century travelers' reports, merchants' investment decisions, historical accounts, religious disputes, and courts of law. Culminating in Locke, these
empirical probabilists desired to define clearly the shifting
boundaries between faith and reason and the elusive distinctions
between opinion, faith, and knowledge that were among the
central preoccupations of the culture. Categories of knowledge
were increasingly developed and refined throughout the seventeenth century, each with its own method of discernment, requi-
site criteria, and corresponding degree of assent accorded it.[9]
Locke, however, influenced by Cartesian assessments ("*Knowledge*
is nothing but *the perception of the connexion and agreement, or
disagreement and repugnancy of any of our Ideas*" [my emphasis])[10]
and less confident about human knowledge than many earlier
seventeenth-century "naive empiricists," suggested that most of
what passes for knowledge is less than "absolutely" or "demonstra-
tively certain" and rarely even attains what some called the highly
probable or "morally certain" (the closest category in practice to
"knowledge"). Therefore, according to Locke, as well as such
liberal Anglicans as William Chillingworth, that which is not really
certain "knowledge" is unworthy of religious dispute or political
divisiveness, and deserves toleration: "Since," according to Locke,
"a man can never have so certain a knowledge, that a proposition
which contradicts the clear principles and evidence of his own
knowledge was divinely revealed, or that he understands the
words rightly . . . he . . . is bound to consider and judge of it as a
matter of reason, and not swallow it, without examination, as a
matter of faith" (*Essay,* IV.18.8).

More than to discriminate among degrees of assent, Locke
strove to demonstrate that certain and probable knowledge may
be known, with varying efficacy, by the *same* mental operations."[11]
One implication important for our purposes is that Locke required of the transmundane much the same method of verification as mundane propositions and phenomena: though not quite
subject to conformity with our prior experience (IV.16.13), reve-

lations must be accorded assent ("faith is nothing but a firm assent of the mind" [IV.17.24]), "for faith can never convince us of anything that contradicts our knowledge" (IV.18.5). Indeed, Locke stipulated the criterion of external evidences to guarantee the authenticity not only of revelations, but also of miracles and extraordinary wonders against both demonic counterfeit and the "certain" knowledge of religious enthusiasts. Locke insisted that "though faith be founded on the testimony of God (who cannot lie) revealing any proposition to us: yet we cannot have an assurance of the truth of its being a divine revelation greater than our own knowledge" (IV.18.5). But this restriction could be used, as some nineteenth-century Unitarians did, both to undermine Calvinist dogma and spiritists' (whether Quaker or Transcendental) private revelations and to cancel the very supernatural and the anomalous phenomena that so fascinated Melville.

Indeed, Locke felt compelled to require "something extrinsical to the persuasions themselves" to give revelations the mark of authenticity, otherwise "inspirations and delusions . . . will not be possible to be distinguished" (IV.19.14). Accordingly, after severely restricting what properly belongs in the category of revelation (that which is neither "against reason" [IV.18.8] nor "according to [unaided] reason" [IV.19.11]), Locke then relegated miracles to an evidentiary role; they became "outward signs" (IV.19.15) to measure independently the veracity and substantiate the "credit of the proposer of this revelation" (IV.18.2), "convince them of the Author of those revelations" (IV.19.15), and guarantee them as properly belonging to the category of that which is "above reason" (IV.17.23) and incontestably true (IV.16.14). But the "evidence" of miracles themselves would be subject to much the same rational criteria as ordinary ideas of sensation and the same mental operations. Moreover, the revelations they confirmed cannot be, as he later stated in his *Discourse of Miracles* (1703), "inconsistent with natural religion and the rules of morality."[12]

Although miracles may appear to be "contrary to the established course of nature" (*Discourse,* 79), to avoid the contextual and perceptual subjectivity of impressions to which this definition leans or the supposition of a universe in which anomalies can happen, and at the same time to preserve the mystery by which miracles gain their compelling power, Locke suggested that they are "above reason" but not truly against it. "Above reason" are those propositions or phenomena for which a deductive pattern linking them with idea particulars is not to be found. Existing without that link, a miracle, however, must be discerned from what is merely "against reason," or the imposture of the Devil, according to the power of God it displays ("marks of his over-ruling power" accompany it [*Discourse*, 84]), and its inward com-pelling force, both of which call upon the operations of reflection and intuition.[13] Yet Locke confesses that "we have, from the observation of the operations of bodies by our senses, but a very imperfect, obscure idea of active power" (II.21.4). In fact, he described in the *Essay* and *Discourse* a largely passive and material-ist epistemology of sensation incapable of clearly discerning God's "active power," then made subjective conviction of that active power the criterion that distinguishes a true miracle from demonic simulation or human *piae fraudes*. The polemical vigor with which Locke attempted to make both revelation and miracle verifiable by reason ("Reason must be our last judge and guide in everything" [IV.19.14]) effectively makes the authenticity of revelations and miracles as "signs" from God – indeed the possi-bility of wonders above the regular laws of nature – never quite demonstrable or trustworthy according to the mental operations, categories, and criteria he credited and most approved. Locke himself, unlike Deists John Toland and Anthony Collins or skep-tic David Hume, never pursued the notion of the intrinsic incred-ibility of miracles or revelations, nor admitted any intention to discredit religious mysteries. Yet he saw prodigies, miracles, and revelations as posing threats to intelligibility, rational assent, and natural laws, in much the manner that Melville's critic Fitz-Hugh O'Brien (see Chapter 1) regarded them. The necessity of intelligi-bility as a prerequisite to assent (IV.16.14) and the very standards of Locke's empirical discourse (insisting upon "not entertaining any proposition with greater assurance than the proofs it is built upon will warrant" [IV.19.1]) tended to make such phenomena suspect: "For if the mind of man can never have a clearer (and perhaps not so clear) evidence of anything to be a divine revela-tion, as it has of the principles of its own reason," then quite obviously, "it can never have ground to quit the clear evidence of its reason, to give a place to a proposition, whose revelation has not a greater evidence than those principles have" (IV.18.5). Though he considered human reason limited and miracles indis-pensable to the Christian religion, he articulated criteria that so curtailed what properly belongs in the categories of miracle and revelation, and so subjected them to the assessments of reason and experience, that despite his cautious and delicate discriminations, the category of miracles and wonders tended to collapse under the cumulative burden of his empirical requirements.

In contrast to Locke's increasingly secularized, rationalist discourse and more rigorously exclusive method was Sir Thomas Browne's earlier, pious empiricist discourse and capacious method. Browne's method was available to Melville in the gargantuan compendium of exotic natural wonders, extravagant superstitions, and errant iconographic traditions that constitutes *Pseudodoxia Epidemica.* Even more than *Religio Medici* and *Hydriotaphia,* Browne's *Pseudodoxia Epidemica, or Vulgar Errors* intensely fascinated Melville, providing him (as has now been well documented) with arcane details about spermaceti and narwhale horns. But more importantly, *Pseudodoxia* provided him with a method of inquiry that informs and structures the many speculative chapters of *Moby-Dick* as well as the flights of speculation of the narrator in *Mardi.* Browne's pious empiricism steadfastly avoided the equation of credibility with predictability, an issue raised by Locke in the *Essay* (IV.15.5) and insisted upon by his heirs. To Melville, Browne must have appeared to set aside the demands of precedent (increasingly a criterion for what constitutes "evidence") and verisimilitude (defined in Melville's age as that which happens with the greatest frequency and increasingly a criterion for determining what was aesthetically credible). Browne seems to set aside these demands to investigate the improbable – such travel accounts, myths, and stories of prodigies and marvels as may be the repository of divine motives or natural imperatives not yet understood. Indeed, the peculiar power of Melville's *Mardi* – its frenzied abundance, unrelenting speculative acquisitiveness, and lunatic sophistry – owes much to Browne's "libertie" and license for imaginative speculation enabled by reason, as well as to his susceptibility to "vulgar" (popular) and "democratical" credulousness in his attempt to accommodate the extraordinary and the improbable.[14]

In acknowledging Browne's desire to accommodate faith, some scholars have jumped to the opposite conclusion that Browne eschews reason altogether, resigning it in a fideistic leap of faith.[15] I suggest, however, that the Browne Melville appreciated neither abdicates the act of judgment nor entirely undermines the basis for human agency – rhetorical, salvific, political, or scientific.[16] Browne's enfranchisement of human reason underwrites the act of speculation in Melville's two novels, while Browne's chariness about the limitations of reason suggests the basis for Melville's cautious scrutiny of the process of speculation. A glance at the 1835–6 Simon Wilkin edition of Browne's writings, which Melville consulted while writing *Mardi* and *Moby-Dick,* will illustrate the precise nature of Browne's moderate skepticism.[17]

Through interpretive commentary mitigating what appear to be the most extreme skeptical expressions in Browne's writings, the Wilkin edition consistently attempts to shape Browne in the image of rational, liberal Anglicans who were moderate skeptics. Orchestrated by editor Wilkin in the prefatory and marginal commentaries on Browne's religious apologia *Religio Medici,* seventeenth-century Catholic and liberal Anglican polemicists are made to argue over Browne's epistemology. Suspicions of Browne's fideism were occasioned by his remarks in *Religio* (I.9) about desiring rational impossibilities upon which to exercise his faith, as well as his quotation of Tertullian's comment *"Certum est, quia impossibile est"* ("It is certain because it is impossible"). (As we shall see, this phrase is appropriated and revised by the Melvillean narrator of *Mardi* to mark a suspension of disbelief in the ensuing marvels related in the novel.) Wilkin stages the debate in which anti-Catholic polemicist John Jortin indignantly accuses Sir Kenelm Digby, a Catholic, of being "full of hopes, that this young author [Browne] might at last *unreason* himself into *implicit belief,* and go over to a church, which would feed his hungry faith with a sufficient quantity of impossibilities." Anglican Latitudinarian John Tillotson, "judging that the Papists would make an ill use of this [Browne's expression], and such passages as this [from *Religio*], in *Protestant* writers, was willing," according to Jortin, "to pass a gentle animadversion upon it." Tillotson boasts that he himself "could never yet attain to that bold and hardy degree of faith, as to believe any thing for this reason – *because it is impossible.*"[18] The debate is concluded by Jortin, who resolves the misunderstanding about Browne by shifting the terms of the discussion to Browne's extravagant rhetorical performance, proposing that Browne's desire, like Tertullian's, is for "*seeming*[,] not *real* impossibilities," and that his expressions "should be looked upon as a *verbum ardens,* a rhetorical flourish, and a trial of skill with Tertullian."[19] Ultimately the Anglicans are shown to deny Browne's apparent fideism, because it was seen as Catholic apologists' justification for vesting the "infallible" Roman Catholic church with the authority that the individual's blighted and ineffectual reason could not merit.

As displayed in the Wilkin edition, Browne's epistemology in fact conforms well to the modified skepticism of liberal Anglican theological method. Scholars of this method tell us that it relies strongly upon reason to infer principles from those religious truths clearly expounded by Scripture. But given the uncertainty of human knowledge regarding divine truths less plainly explained in Scripture, as well as the incompleteness of knowledge about the natural world, "probabilities" plausibly if not actually describing the world must suffice (especially if confirmed by consensus) to fulfill life's obligations.[20] Individual discretion exercised with "latitude," "toleration," or "charity" (as Browne calls it in Book II of *Religio*), is advised on all issues known only with uncertainty. Browne is willing to accede to the church's dictates on salvific knowledge, yet insists "whatsoever is beyond, as points indifferent [to salvation], I observe *according to the rules of my private reason,* or the humor and fashion of my devotion" (*Religio,* I.5; my emphasis). Indeed, whereas Sir Kenelm Digby thought Browne owed his church implicit faith, "without arrogating to [him]self a controlling ability in liking or misliking the faith, doctrine, and constitutions, of that church," Browne instead, "approveth the church of England, not absolutely, but comparatively with other reformed churches."[21] And Browne himself makes the distinction between surrendering his judgment and retaining some capacity to judge for himself: "but in divinity I love to keep the road; and, *though not in an implicit, yet an humble faith,* follow the great wheel of the church" (*Religio,* I.6; my emphasis). As portrayed by the Wilkin edition, Browne acknowledges human agency and the limited but important capacity of reason. His rejection of extreme skepticism and his avowal of a moderate skepticism were in fact noted and applauded by Melville's conservative Whig contemporaries; at about the time Melville was completing Mardi, an *American Whig Review* contributor commented:

> Sir Thomas Browne, then, did not waste his energies in a vain and endless chase after *absolute truth.* Clearly recognizing that man is but relative in his nature, and encompassed by no calculable course of events, nor influenced by the same unvaried causes, nor able, at all times and in all positions, to get a complete and reliable view of the elements on which his reason is exercised, he wisely abstained from a search he saw must be fruitless, and contented himself to attempt a discovery of his immediate relations, and of the wants arising therefrom. He thrust off every approach of skepticism, therefore, by a suppression of all doubts that

arose to disturb a belief which he had once deliberately settled, knowing that in this state of imperfect vision, many uncertainties and apparent contradictions will attach themselves to all the weightier conclusions of our reason.[22]

Although this Whig commentator was perhaps too confident of Browne's willingness to suppress all doubt, Browne's taxonomy of ways to err, in the opening chapters of *Pseudodoxia*, highlights the treacherousness of appearances as well as the tendency of the limited human mind to foist all too hastily the name of "certain" knowledge upon uninformed guesses and misunderstandings. After categorizing and illustrating the types of error, Browne insists, however, that the individual is nevertheless obliged to exercise the judgment of reason, not only as a means of participating in one's own salvation but also as a way of preventing the making of confident assertions that lead to both doctrinal and scientific dogmatism.[23] The tentative and provisional nature of human knowledge also ensures that Browne self-consciously regards his own limits and indicates the boundaries of his knowledge, acutely aware that the unintelligible may yet signify. And so while the subject of divine wisdom affords him the opportunity to repay the "debt" of "learned admiration" he owes God of "judicious inquiry into his acts, and deliberate research into his creatures" (*Religio*, I.13), it also compels him to confront his limitations, because "God hath not made a creature that can *comprehend* him" (*Religio*, I.11; my emphasis). Although Yahweh stipulates to Moses in Exodus 33:23 that "*thou shalt see my back parts*: but my face shall not be seen," Browne conveys – echoing also 1 Corinthians 13:12 – the wonder of contemplating the daunting attribute of divine wisdom, but magnifies to an infinite regress the partialness and mediated nature of human perception: "God is wise in all; wonderful in what we conceive, *but far more in what we comprehend not*: for we behold him but asquint, upon reflex or shadow; our understanding is dimmer than Moses's eye; we are *ignorant of the back parts* or lower side of his divinity; therefore, to pry into the maze of his counsels, is not only folly in man, but presumption even in angels" (*Religio*, I.13; my emphases).

Browne's tendency to intensify the partial and mediated quality of human knowledge would not have been lost on Melville. We are reminded of "The Tail" chapter in *Moby-Dick*, where Ishmael replaces the unequivocal stipulation in Exodus 33:23 about what will be permitted to be known with a revision of Browne's passage to draw out vividly the gradations of his own inability to "comprehend" (a word used repeatedly by Browne, but not in the Exodus text) the "mystic gestures" of the whale's tail, much less construe its face: "But if I know not the tail of this whale, how understand his head? much more, how *comprehend* his face, when face he has none? . . . But I *cannot completely make out his back parts;* and hint what he will about his face, I say again he has no face." Browne's oblique vision, which fails to penetrate and perceive acutely ("we behold him but asquint, upon reflex or shadow"), becomes literal and aggressive in Ishmael's "Dissect him how I may, I but go skin deep."

Yet the passage in *Religio,* no less than Ishmael's in *Moby-Dick,* bespeaks no sweeping condemnation of human knowledge: reason and judgment must be exercised, however partial they are. Browne insists that it is "for the contemplation of this [divine wisdom] only [I] do not repent me that I was bred in the way of study. The advantage I have of the vulgar [untutored masses] . . . is an ample recompense for all my endeavours" (*Religio,* I.13). And Ishmael's frustrated protestation, "I know him not, and never will," similarly stands alongside his chapter-long meditation demonstrating that human reason "comprehends" divinity and divine artifacts, if only equivocally, through acts of intellectual accommodation. Indeed, Browne tells us in *Religio,* "as in a portrait, things are not truly, but in equivocal shapes, . . . they counterfeit some real substance in that invisible fabrick" (*Religio,* I.12). (Elsewhere, in *Pierre,* Melville tells us "Far as we blind moles can see, man's life seems but an acting upon mysterious hints.")[24] As Browne eschews "a rigid definition" for "a description, periphrasis, or adumbration" (*Religio,* I.10), so Ishmael exhaustively searches for the most apt figurations and "curious similitude" to convey the power, lyricism, and signifying capacity of the whale's tail. According to Browne, though "no man can attain unto it [divine wisdom]: yet Solomon pleased God when he desired it" (*Religio,* I.13). In terms elaborated in *Pseudodoxia,* "credulity" (intellectual indiscriminateness), "supinity" (intellectual langour), and "obstinate incredulity" (skeptical willfulness) are misapprehensions or abdications of reason's cautious exercise, and it is to remedy these that *Religio Medici, Pseudodoxia Epidemica* – and *Mardi* and *Moby-Dick,* I – are offered.

Like many Anglican clergymen who were also pious virtuosi (practitioners of the Royal Society's method of "experimental" inquiry), Browne sought to exercise reason and build empirical knowledge, but he also sought, in Joseph Glanvill's words, "to destroy the confidence of assertions and establish a prudent reservedness and modesty in opinions." Glanvill may well be offering a gloss on Browne's limited confidence in human reason and Latitudinarian impulses in *Religio Medici* and *Pseudodoxia* when Glanvill explicitly relates the difficulty of progress in "experimental philosophy" (natural science) to the need for latitude in adjudicating the "subtleties" of doctrinal differences. Where Browne notes that "by acquainting our reason how unable it is to display the visible and obvious effects of nature, it becomes more humble and submissive unto the subtleties of faith" (*Religio*, I.10), Glanvill explains in *Philosophia Pia* (1671) that an active but chastened reason may not expect to decide among sophistical distinctions: "Converse with Gods works gives us to see the vast difficulties that are to be met with in the speculation of them; and thereby men are . . . at length brought to such an habitual modesty, that they are afraid to pass bold judgments upon those *opinions* in Religion, of which there is no infallible assurance" (my emphasis).[25] This perceived parallel between pursuits in theology and experimental philosophy (science) also underscores that no necessary conflict existed between their desire to believe and their will to know, for they assumed that the "revelation of Christian mystery came all at once, and perfectly . . . [whereas] the natural arts and sciences are still embryos that can be matured only by 'Times gradual accomplishments.' "[26]

Like many liberal Anglican experimentalists, Browne urges the careful practice of discrimination among all the qualitative categories of knowledge ranging from "opinion," to "faith," "moral certainty," "verities irrefragable," and knowledge "certain" and "infallible." According to Browne, that which is neither certain nor impossible must be entertained, since much of what is "known" is mediated and contingent. Actual knowledge must be carefully teased out of the masses of misperceptions, and Browne accordingly prefaces *Pseudodoxia* with the instruction that "*knowledge is made by oblivion; and to purchase a clear and warrantable body of Truth, we must forget and part with much we know*" (*PE*, "To the Reader"; my emphasis). Indeed, here and elsewhere, Browne takes great care to *distinguish* among the degrees of his uncertainty and to correlate that uncertainty with the precise quality of the evidence assessed as he judiciously weighs opinion, evidence, his own speculations, and historical examples and counterexamples. Accordingly, his expressions of doubt modulate with great frequency and variety. Inquiries often conclude with "it cannot escape some doubt," "we hold but a wavering conjecture," "it cannot pass without some question," "we do but palliate our determinations; until our advanced endeavours do totally reject, or partially salve their evasions." Such measured and deliberately antidogmatic expressions – ones frequently echoed by Ishmael at the conclusion of meditations such as those on water and the afterlife – have, on the basis of their frequency, been mistaken by modern critics as expressions of a thoroughgoing skepticism or a complete suspension of judgment on Browne's (or Ishmael's) part. Among pious experimentalists, however, no such resignation was countenanced. Browne represents instead the intersection of the Anglican probabilist theological method and the pious empiricist's "constructive," "creative," or "antidogmatic" skepticism,[27] which dismisses nothing as impossible until it becomes obviously untenable. In *Religio, Pseudodoxia,* and *Hydriotaphia,* an overlapping liberal Anglican theological method and "experimental" method (which would later be codified by the Royal Society) permit Browne to offer himself as a model of toleration, moderate skepticism, collective inquiry (assessing the quality of evidence in the historical records of testimonies), and consensual affirmation of contingent truths.[28] He presents himself as neither a thoroughgoing skeptic nor a promulgator of either positive doctrine or definitive conclusions in natural philosophy, for "We do but learn, to-day, what our better advanced judgements will unteach, to-morrow" (*Religio,* II.8).

Such uncertainty and contingency require considerable deference, and so Browne characteristically concedes to the proponent of an opposing argument that "because he hath probable reasons for it, and I no infallible sense, or reason against it, I will not quarrel with his assertion" (*PE,* I.5). Typical of Browne's empirical latitude and pious, antidogmatic skepticism is his observation: "That miracles are ceased, I can neither prove nor absolutely deny, much less define the time and period of their cessation" (*Religio,* I.27). From Melville's vantage point, all Browne's antidogmatic exertions – with the degree of certainty precisely proportioned to the quality of the available evidence – appeared to expand the range of the possible to include that which Locke discarded as highly improbable. In the gaps between revealed knowledge and human experimental endeavors, between probable human conceptual categories and yet-to-be-manifested divine fiats, Browne permits the possibility of unaccountable wonders – a position that Melville would find immensely attractive.

Locke exploited the separate yet compatible categories of reason and revelation to facilitate the investigation of extraordinary divine acts and enthusiast presumption by what increasingly became the antithetical presumption of empiricism, effectually, if inadvertently, reducing divine operations to natural law. Although Locke confidently insists that miracles, prodigies, and revelations may be "above reason" but not contrary to it, Browne more humbly affirms "that God can do all things: how he should work contradictions, I do not understand, yet dare not, therefore, deny" (*Religio*, I.27). But Browne is careful to distinguish his recognition of divine prerogative and reason's limits from the relinquishment of reason's operations, insisting that it "is no vulgar [credulous] part of faith, to believe a thing not only above, but contrary to, reason, and against the arguments of our proper senses" (*Religio*, I.10). The arguments of our senses and inferences of our reason, Browne suggests, tend only to be conversant with their sensuous or logical counterparts in this world, imposing their own standards of intelligibility and meaning upon the metaphysical world – standards that Browne intimates may be qualitatively distinct from those that obtain in the metaphysical realm. Unlike Locke, who valorizes the empirical and the probable against the enemy enthusiast, Browne insists against the seductions of both the devil and infidelity, that "to believe only possibilities, is not faith, but mere philosophy," offering not a fideistic credo of reason yielding to faith, but rather a pious probabilist's exhortation to extend the scope of "possibilities" to include improbable singularities by engaging different systems of reference and valuation, or at least imagining, through analogies, the existence of such alternatives. He explains that "many things are true in divinity, which are neither inducible by reason nor confirmable by sense; and many things in [natural] philosophy confirmable by sense, yet not inducible by reason." In offering the analogy of "the conversion of the needle to the north," Browne does not imply the need to relinquish reason, but rather the need to search for alternative and more appropriate systems of coherence, ones that may in fact supersede the available systems, for the magnetism of the north seems improbable by reason's explanations, but "possible and true, and easily credible, upon a single experiment unto the sense" (*Religio*, I.48).

Since Browne assumes an orderly, not a chaotic universe ("there is no liberty for causes to operate in a loose and straggling way" [*Religio*, I.18]), the existence of anomalies or prodigies suggests to him, in contrast to Locke, either the ongoing possibility of miracles or a "universal cause" as yet unapprehended or ever unknowable ("nor any effect whatsoever but hath its warrant from some universal or superiour cause" [*Religio*, I.18]). According to

Browne, one must seek out and examine all unyielding natural curiosities and even daunting material registers of spirit, no matter how extraordinary or obscure, for they may become the means of renovating our fallible conceptual categories. In his eagerness to pursue liminal phenomena, Browne might well have agreed with the spirit of renovation, if not the unlimited confidence in human reason and ideal natural laws, of Francis Bacon's aphorism: by pursuit of natural marvels, "the understanding is raised to the investigation of formes capable of including them."[29]

Yet Browne is ever vigilant against the temptation to an overweening confidence, either Aristotelian or empirical, in the reason's and sense's abilities to supply entirely what has not been divinely revealed or empirically supported. Indeed, Browne complains, "the villany of that spirit [the devil] takes a hint of infidelity from our [natural] studies; and, by demonstrating a naturality in one way, makes us mistrust a miracle in another," and so the devil "playd at chess with me, and, yielding a pawn, thought to gaine a queen of me," and "whilst I laboured to raise the structure of my reason, he strove to undermine the edifice of my faith" (*Religio,* I.19). Browne takes pleasure in the rising "structure of [his] reason," ever wary to distinguish the lure of natural explanations from demonic counterfeits and occult causes, and those from divine miracles. But his reason, which has "not only to combat with doubts, but always to dispute with the devil," is also chastened and hesitant to "mistrust a miracle" (*Religio,* I.19). Although one scholar of the early modern period suggests that the desire to remove oneself from the suspicion of being duped by demonic imposture led to the tendency to demonize the extraordinary, and then to demystify singularities altogether by substituting natural explanations,[30] Locke's *Essay* suggests that by the late seventeenth century, combating religious delusion was the abiding motive. Yet for Browne, the seductions of the devil in *Religio* (I.19) and *Pseudodoxia* (I.11.68) involve foisting upon the unsuspecting *natural* explanations for what are to Browne's mind divine miracles. Indeed, Browne's and Joseph Glanvill's notorious refusals to deny the existence of witches were attempts to promote in the discourse of empirical science the existence of finite immaterial beings in order to discredit those who would ascribe causation to mechanistic principles alone. And so Browne insists in *Religio* that it is a misapprehension of spirit "to ascribe his actions unto her [Nature], . . . to devolve the honour of the principal agent upon the instrument" (*Religio,* I.16). Browne's anxieties focus upon preserving divine prerogative by stopping the encroachments of the devil and atheistic materialism, and so the assigning of the proper "agent" to extraordinary phenomena is a crucial judgment to him – a judgment that Captain Ahab would also consider in "The Quarter-Deck" chapter.

While Browne prescribes pious discretion and learning to prevent the error of habitually ascribing natural explanations, so too he prescribes careful discrimination to prevent habitually attributing supernatural agency or portentous meaning to such natural phenomena as meteors, eclipses, and auroras, as do the credulous, "ignorant sort." (Francis Bacon's utopian vision in *The New Atlantis* also acknowledges such an anxiety by imagining its resolution: one of the members of Solomon's House prays, "Lord God of heaven and earth, thou hast vouchsafed ... to those of our order ... to discern ... between divine miracles, works of nature, works of art, and impostures and illusions of all sorts.")[31] Whereas Locke offers assurances of natural and regular laws governing the universe, Browne offers Melville only uncertainty: "True it is, and we will not deny, that although these [meteors] being naturall productions from second and settled causes, we need not alway look upon them as the immediate hand of God ... yet do they sometimes admit a respect therein ... a farther consideration." In Browne's age, the coincidence of unusual natural phenomena and momentous historical occasions often suggested portents of divine motives not yet understood. Browne may be alluding to Lilly's *Starry Messenger,* interpreting the "strange Apparition of three Suns seen in London, 19. Novemb. 1644. being the Birth Day of King CHARLES," or to his own son Edward's report in the Royal Society's *Philosophical Transactions* of seeing a double sun during his travels: in *Pseudodoxia,* Browne observes,

> that two or three suns or moons appear in any man's life or reign, it is not worth the wonder. But that the same should fall out at a remarkable time, or point of some decisive action; that the contingency of its appearance should be confirmed unto that time; that those two should make but one line in the book of fate, and stand together in the great ephemerides of God; beside the philosophical assignment of the cause, *it may admit a Christian apprehension in the signality.* (*PE,* I.11; my emphasis)

Such a providential "signality," though not yet intelligible, cannot be dismissed. And yet the equivocal intimations of divine portents or demonic counterfeits could be enlisted, as Browne – no less than Ahab – well knew, for purposes subversive of existing political or religious authority. Browne's *Religio Medici* and *Pseudodoxia Epidemica* thus made readily apparent to Melville the necessity of vigilance regarding partial human knowledge, as well as the radical instability of interpretations involving the extraordinary – a numinous instability by which the extraordinary could be rendered intelligible alternately (or simultaneously, as Melville would do in *Moby-Dick*) as divine supernatural "portents," demonic "counterfeit" marvels, human impostures, or rare "evidences" of natural laws more broadly conceived than human reason hitherto recognizes.[32]

In keeping with his unwillingness to secularize those phenomena for which there is no existing natural explanation, Browne will not confirm the cessation of miracles, for to do so is to domesticate and naturalize the transmundane, to "narrowly define the power of God, restraining it to our capacities" (*Religio*, I.27). He refuses to do so because of his keen awareness of the ongoing divine presence and because of the Protestant theological investment in the recent discoveries of early modern exploration and travel. Browne's *Pseudodoxia* and *Religio* share empirical probabilist assumptions with the early modern Protestant travel narratives, anatomies, and encyclopedias of errors that so fascinated Melville and that sought out the exotic and the remarkable in their attempts to demystify the world of Catholic credulity and mystifications, yet retain authentic wonders.[33] Miracles, according to early modern Protestants, were legitimate as instruments in Christian conversion, and so they might still be necessary for the conversion of newly discovered peoples. However reluctant to credit notoriously credulous Catholic sources, Browne concedes of miracles "That they survived Christ . . . that they outlived the apostles also, and were revived at the conversion of nations, many years after, we cannot deny . . .; therefore, that may have some truth in it, that is reported by the Jesuits of their miracles in the Indies" (*Religio*, I.27).

As a probabilist empiricist, Browne the physician and natural philosopher shares the interests and motives, as well as the methods of inquiry promoted and implemented by the Royal Society, of which his son Edward was an active member. Edward Browne, whose travels are detailed in Melville's Wilkin edition of Sir Thomas Browne, often reported his findings both to his father and to the Royal Society; thus he tells the readers of his published journeys through eastern Europe that he sought out such wonders as disappearing lakes and other "natural remarkables," par-

ticularly unusual metals and minerals. Moreover, an encomium
addressed to Edward reveals the high valuation of and intellectual
"commerce" in "rareties" in early modern England in which he
was a participant:

> Thus from a Foreign Clime rich Merchants Come / and
> thus unlade their Rareties at home / . . . they for themselves,
> for others you unfold / A Cargo swoln with Diamonds &
> Gold / with undefatigable Travels, they / The trading world,
> the Learned, you survey / and for renoun with great Colum-
> bus vye / In subterranean Cosmography.[34]

Sir Thomas Browne's *Pseudodoxia Epidemica* might in fact be usefully examined in conjunction with his son's travel narratives of
exotic customs and "natural remarkables," or, more particularly
with Samuel Purchas' *Hakluytus Posthumus, or Purchas his Pilgrimes,
contayning a History of the World in Sea Voyages and Land Travell by
Englishmen and others* (1625–6),[35] for both Browne and Melville
drew upon Purchas's twenty-volume compendium of travel narratives.

Pseudodoxia and *Purchas his Pilgrimes* share both an empirical
probabilist method of inquiry and a trope central to the Melvillean sea narratives that we will examine in the next sections, for
both seventeenth-century texts self-consciously figure the confrontation with epistemological opacity as an astonishing but perilous travel narrative, one in which the mission is to sort the
genuine wonders from the credulous fabrications in a receptive
and tractable way.[36] Like Purchas's encyclopedia of exploration
narratives, *Pseudodoxia* attempts to be a balanced, judicious assessment of historical testimonies, contemporary accounts by "ocular
Testators," and, in Browne's case, his own experiments and observations. In his preface Purchas boasts of having, in the empirical
discourse from which Browne also draws, "a World of Witnesses
for the Evidence," "knowledge from ey-witnesses," "probable conjectures of the Course taken in the Ophirian Voyage," and judgments deriving "from reasonable conjecture grounded on other
experiments."[37] Purchas explains that he deliberately retained a
certain amount of redundancy among accounts of various expeditions to the same location because the repetition "admitted for
more full testimonie the same things." Purchas's language, like
Browne's, reveals theological, judicial, commercial, and explora-
tional discourses all intersecting on the epistemological problem
of assessing probable truths when confronted with the unknown –

a nexus that Melville would find richly suggestive for his own more ambitious seafaring narratives.[38]

Purchas prefaces his vast encylopedia of explorers' peregrinations with the enticing caveat that only the "Far fetched and dear bought are the Lettice sutable to our lips." Like Browne, who concedes that he is "perhaps too greedy of magnallities [wonders]," and like Browne's son, who, disdaining "the common Road," instead "fetched a compass, and came about, passing from place to place, according as remarkable things or curiosities invited," Purchas discloses that "My Genius delights rather in bye-ways, then the high-wayes." He claims for his practice the confident Baconian "New way of Eye-evidence," and assumes an orderly universe. Yet in seeking out "the Rarities of Nature," he, like Browne, is careful to provide alternative natural, supernatural, and preternatural categories for marvelous phenomena: "such things also as are not against Nature, but either above, as Miracles, or *beside the ordinarie course of it, in the extraordinary Wonders.*"[39] In viewing Browne's *Pseudodoxia Epidemica* in relation to Purchas, we gain a sense of Browne's compendium as a narrative in which the unnatural natural world not only is acknowledged but serves, as it does in Melville's two novels, significantly to test epistemological assessment – to test the sufficiency of conceptual categories and interpretive judgment when confronted with the alien or the marvelous, and thereby to examine the process by which such judgments are made. Early modern travel narratives like Purchas's and Hakluyt's and encyclopedias like Browne's provide Melville with a concentration of just such epistemological challenges and instances of categorical instability. In advising the Royal Society to explore "the LAND OF SPIRITS," which "is a kinde of America, and not well discover'd Region,"[40] Joseph Glanvill, author of a treatise subtitled "full and plain evidence concerning witches and apparitions," further highlights the liminality that preoccupies this period, suggesting the necessity of pursuing one liminal enterprise (apparition narratives) in the discourse of another (travel narratives), for one emphasizes confrontations with wonders in the spiritual world, the other in the sensuous. We may link the epistemological speculations of *Pseudodoxia* (no less than those of *Mardi* and *Moby-Dick*) to the structure of Purchas's encyclopedic travel narrative, for if, as Purchas suggests, peregrination is the universal postlapsarian condition, then *Pseudodoxia Epidemica* may be viewed as a compendium of travel narratives without a single telos or continuous

trajectory (except in God's eye), but one in which each speculative foray, each probable assay, functions as one among many
expeditions, provisional and contingent, existing perpetually as,
in Purchas's words, "plantings, supplantings, Colonies and new
alterations of the face of the world in each part thereof."[41]

"Be Sir Thomas Brown our Ensample": The Melvillean Motive in Mardi

Employing Browne's modest skepticism and capacious method of
inquiry, and playfully exploiting at the same time such directives
as were given to seamen and voyagers "to keep an exact Diary . . .
to be perused by the R.[oyal] Society,"[42] Melville reveals in his
two novels the contingent nature of human knowledge not only
in exploration and "natural philosophy" but also in metaphysics
and politics. The narrator's exhortation at the beginning of
Mardi – "Be Sir Thomas Brown our ensample; who, while explod-
ing 'Vulgar Errors,' heartily hugged all the mysteries in the Pentateuch"(39) – signals that the Melvillean narrators' fascination
with the marvelous in both Mardi and Moby-Dick is an acknowledgment of the need to accommodate the divinity whose imperatives
brought forth the creation in Genesis, as well as the miracles and
scourges in the subsequent books of the Pentateuch, and whose
unimaginable power may yet rise up through his creations (perhaps even a white whale) to fulfill motives as yet unsurmised.
(Mardi's narrator exclaims, "Truly marvels abound. It needs no
dead man to be raised, to convince us of some things. Even my
Viking marveled full as much at those Pilot fish as he would have
marveled at the Pentecost" [53–4]). If Browne "heartily hugged
all the mysteries in the Pentateuch," it was less with a desire to
preserve all mysteries, though some, he admits, are intransigent,
and more to sift the range of all possible and probable answers:
"for the first chapters of Genesis," Browne himself writes, "I must
confess a great deal of obscurity; though divines have . . . endeavoured to make all go in a literal meaning, yet those allegorical
interpretations are also probable, and perhaps the mysticall
method of Moses" (Religio, 1.34). Browne's "ensample" also signals Melville's "method" in all the anachronistic and obsolete
splendor that the word "ensample" itself suggests – one engaged
in elaborately discriminating and sorting plausible truths from
such "vulgar errors" as credulous explorers' reports, sailors' superstitions, and such national "myths" as Manifest Destiny.

Stimulated by Browne's own attempts to make the unknown

and the ill-conceived usefully intelligible in *Pseudodoxia Epidemica,* Melville's speculations in *Mardi* and *Moby-Dick* suggest that human "knowledge" is rarely, if ever, certain. Yet the sheer abundance of speculations, the trustworthy as well as meretricious, also attests to a conception of human knowledge, and the language that articulates it, as necessarily involved in making judgments and expressing them. And so to characterize, as one recent scholar has done, Melville's Brownean "method of vulgar errors" as one that "consult[s] the best scientific or historical authorities" in order to "rejoice in the mysteries that they have failed to penetrate," is unaccountably to depict Browne's "method" as a celebration of intellectual abasement and to reduce the function of inquiry to ritual mystification.[43] By such an interpretation, the interpolated chapters in *Mardi* ("Time and Temples," "Faith and Knowledge," and "Dreams") – long recognized for their Brownean themes, prose rhythms, and anatomizing meditations – might be seen as little more than gratuitous interruptions of the narrative, redundant displays of antiquarian learning in which "irresolvable mysteries" become rhapsodic embellishments. The same might be said of the Brownean chapters in *Moby-Dick* ("The Whiteness of the Whale," "Of the Monstrous Pictures of Whales," "Of the Less Erroneous Pictures of Whales," "Of Whales in Paint; in Teeth," "The Honor and Glory of Whaling," "Does the Whale Diminish?").[44] On the contrary, the many speculations that constitute these Brownean chapters reveal the process and method of probabilist inquiry, one that functions to a significant extent as the structuring principle of the two novels. However theatrically heightened into playful overstatements of theme and method or unsettling enactments of excess, these manifold speculations and this method of inquiry also stand as reproaches to American culture by revealing the impoverishment of verisimilitude, vexing its equivalence with the predictable, and challenging the glib rationality and conservative ideology of Lockean antebellum America.

"To Wander in the America and Untravelled Parts of Truth": Verisimilitude and the Rejection of the Predictable

In the chapter "Of the Chondropterygii, and other uncouth Hordes infesting the South Seas," which initiates the exploration of the Mardian archipelago and marks the threshold of epistemological liberation, the appeal "Be Sir Thomas Brown our ensample" emphasizes the appropriation of *Pseudodoxia*'s central trope and anatomizing, probabilist method. Melville's chapter title clearly recalls headings in *Pseudodoxia* such as "Of the Amphisbaena or Serpent with two heads moving either way," "Of Gryphins," and "Of Sperma-Ceti, and the Sperma-Ceti Whale." The Melvillean narrator's enterprise is one in which the effort to adjudicate the truth claims of apparent wonders, probable truths, superstitions, prejudices, and human chicanery is figured as a journey without guidance to the margins of knowledge: one is compelled, Browne tells us in his preface to *Pseudodoxia*, "to wander in the America and untravelled parts of Truth." Indeed, Browne's *Pseudodoxia* and many of the early modern travel narratives read by Melville intersect on the issue of attempting to dispel superstitious wonders – the discourse of "vulgar errors."[45] Imperiling such an enterprise are the Scylla and Charybdis of human judgment, for on one side are the dangers of "vulgar errors" (popular credulity, untutored judgment), "whereby men often swallow falsities for truths, dubiosities for certainties,... and things impossible as possibilities themselves" (*PE,* I.5). But avoiding the other, the opposite danger of "wise men," which Browne defines as "not enjoying the truth" through "obstinate incredulity" and "sceptical infidelity," requires strenuous vigilance. Given the uneasiness occasioned by the anomalous and the unknown in antebellum American society, this danger is, not surprisingly, accorded considerable attention by the narrator of *Mardi.* And so literalizing Browne's trope "to wander in the America and untravelled parts of Truth," Melville's narrator extends to a further verge the map of the unknown, provoking the severe skeptic while rendering inference from the known hopelessly inadequate, and in so doing, opening the path toward the marvelous – and the imaginative:

> Though America be discovered, the Cathays of the deep are unknown. And whoso crosses the Pacific might have read lessons to Buffon. The sea-serpent is not a fable; and in the sea, that snake is but a garden worm. There are more wonders than the wonders rejected, and more sights unrevealed than you or I ever dreamt of. Moles and bats alone should be skeptics; and the only true infidelity is for a live man to vote himself dead. Be Sir Thomas Brown our ensample; who, while exploding "Vulgar Errors," heartily hugged all the mysteries in the Pentateuch. (*Mardi,* 39)

The presumptions of easy skepticism, the Melvillean narrator insists, must be curbed, even as the excesses of credulity are exposed. Melville upholds Browne's assessment in *Pseudodoxia* that "as credulity is the cause of error, so incredulity [is] oftentimes of not enjoying truth" (*PE,* I.5). Melville devotes much of both *Mardi* and *Moby-Dick* to these twin purposes, and to testing his readers' credulity as much as challenging their facile skepticism, both of which rest upon "neglect of enquiry." We too often prefer, according to Browne, "doubting with ease and gratis than believing with difficulty or purchase" (*PE,* I.5). The rejection of marvels by an empiricism that predicates credibility on predictability, the legacy of Locke's heirs, is inappropriate (and when unexamined reinforces consensus ideology) in these two antebellum American novels, for "there are more wonders than the wonders rejected." Yet extreme and willful incredulity, warns Browne in *Pseudodoxia,* makes a man "a fit companion for those who, having a conceit they are dead, cannot be convicted into the society of the living" (*PE,* I.29). Appropriating Browne's sense of "infidelity" as "sceptical infidelity against the evidence of reason and sense" (*PE,* I.5), as well as his stock example representing nonsense or insanity, Melville affirms in the above passage that for "a live man to vote himself dead" represents the "only true infidelity," the only ludicrous limit on the impossible and the only frivolous use of the senses and reason. All else, however unintelligible, ought not be easily rejected.

Confronting the prejudices and enigmas related to the extraordinary and "uncouth hordes" of the deep, the narrator of *Mardi* offers anatomizing elaborations of both the shark and beliefs about it, as Ishmael does the whale in the "Cetology" chapter of *Moby-Dick.* By investigating mistaken perceptions while attempting to characterize types of sharks (or whales), Melville's narrators combat not only "credulity" but also "supinity." The process is one of jocularly challenging received wisdom and the austere simplicity of "objective" travel reports by complicating and frustrating their truth claims. Similarly, Ishmael's "Cetology" offers a "contracted" definition of the whale as "a spouting fish with a horizontal tail" (*M-D,* 137), only to vex relentlessly that definition for the rest of the novel. Competing speculations about "strange monsters" in *Mardi* or whales in *Moby-Dick* ultimately deny the validity of each speculation. Accordingly, definitions become to differing degrees only "possible," "plausible," or "probable" approximations. In this way, Ishmael's rebelliousness through much of *Moby-Dick* is, as we shall see, exhibited by his reluctance to uphold the closure of "rigid definition" (Browne's phrase), aphorism, taxonomy, and certain knowledge (as much about cannibals as about the white whale), even as he searches for order and intelligibility. His famous comparison of his novel to a "draught of a draught," a candid comment on the task of constructing the narrative of *Moby-Dick,* resonates simultaneously with the resignation of inadequacy and the pride of a promise kept, "because any human thing supposed to be complete, must for that very reason infallibly be faulty" (*M-D,* 136).

With knowledge so utterly contingent, divine imperatives unguessed, and many "wonders unrevealed," the Melvillean narrator in *Mardi* feels obliged to assume Browne's charitable "latitude" in *Religio,* playfully converting Browne's tolerance toward ferocious sectarians and contentious heretics into a sardonic homage to (literal) sharks in this chapter on "Chondropterygii" in *Mardi.* Melville's narrator insists that even the "ghastly" white shark, among other extraordinary phenomena of the deep, deserves some charitable consideration, for there is "no Fury so ferocious, as not to have some amiable side" and you may "As well hate a seraph, as a shark. Both were made by the same hand" (*Mardi,* 40). We will also recall that with grotesque humor Fleece dilates upon this "latitude" as he "preaches" what Stubb calls "Christianity" to the sharks in *Moby-Dick;* Fleece observes, "for all angel is not'ing more dan de shark well goberned" (295). In *Mardi,* "spontaneous" "dislike" and uneasiness for the awesome monstrosity and "horrific serenity" of the Great White Shark is substituted for hate: as the narrator tells us, "we should hate naught . . . and disliking is not hating" (*Mardi,* 41). Despite his sharpness toward those who would disrupt the religious community, Browne's charity toward warring sectarians in *Religio* suggests his unswerving devotion to Latitudinarian inclusiveness and loving participation in the human community of postlapsarian limitation. Melville's Mardian narrator instead registers with nervous immediacy the precariousness of such magnaminity in the face of terror and imminent death. Melville's narrator cannot but scrutinize, and at times challenge, the very Brownean ethos he would embrace. So, although the chapter "The Hereafters of Fish" asks us to consider, in the empathetic but ironical language of *Hydriotaphia,* whether it does not "appear a little unreasonable to imagine, that there is any creature, fish, flesh, or fowl, so little in love with life, as not to cherish hopes of a future state?" (*Mardi,* 289), yet the equivocal charity of the narrator also asks us to consider that "True, the ["blood-bibbing"] Battas ["of Sumatra"] believe in a hereafter; but of what sort? Full of Blue-Beards and bloody bones. So, also, the sharks; who hold that Paradise is one vast Pacific, ploughed by navies of mortals, whom an endless gale forever drops into their maws" (*Mardi*, 289). Such nineteenth-century critics as Evert Duyckinck and Fitz-James O'Brien admired Browne for his self-possessed civility and stateliness, but Melville's narrator displays uneasiness toward a Brownean poise so implausibly secure and serene. Instead, Melville exploits Browne's capacity to probe difficult truths and to exaggerate sardonically in order to expose what passes for conventional wisdom.

Indeed, Melville turns all the more against his own critics' complacency – their easy skepticism and unexamined acceptance of predictable truths. As a wide-ranging reader of early modern travel narratives, Melville might well have come upon discourses resembling that of one seventeenth-century voyager to New England who indignantly complained of critics that "there be a sort of stagnant stinking spirits, who . . . never travelled . . . yet notwithstanding . . . will desperately censure the relations of the greatest Travellers," and so "it was a good *proviso* of a learned man, never to report wonders, for in so doing, of the greatest he will be sure not to be believed, but laughed at."[46] The Melvillean narrator ever so much more extravagantly ignores such a proviso and the expectations of verisimilitude it upholds, observing in *Mardi*'s "The Tale of a Traveler":

> stay-at-homes say travelers lie. Yet a voyage to Ethiopia would cure them of that; for few skeptics are travelers; fewer travelers liars . . . It is . . . true, as Bruce said, that the Abyssinians cut live steaks from their cattle. It was, in good part, his villainous transcribers, who made monstrosities of Mandeville's travels. (298)

Mindful of the nineteenth-century skeptical reappraisals of those travels, Melville here provocatively raises the comparison of *Mardi* with discredited travel narratives to flaunt before his own critics brazen extravagances of custom and bizarre events, testing the limits of his own credibility and their ostensible discernment with considerable boldness.

Whereas in "The Tale of the Traveler" and subsequent chapters Melville playfully exploits Brownean tropes in *Religio* and nineteenth-century accounts of bizarre customs in missionary and travel narratives to entice the reader into credulity, he also poses a more serious challenge to conservative Whig critics whose complacent and narrow-minded pursuit of "verity" and moral conventions in literature had frustrated his own writing career. Melville explains in his epigraph to *Mardi* that "having published two narratives of voyages in the Pacific, which, in many quarters, were received with incredulity, the thought occurred to me, of indeed writing a romance of Polynesian adventure . . . to see whether, the fiction might not, possibly, be received for a verity," (*Mardi*, xvii). He rejects the contempt shown by his critics for mere "romances"; instead, he exposes the misguided confidence of supposedly "discriminating" critics. Similarly, Melville's narrators in *Mardi* and *Moby-Dick* seem to challenge the "objective" discourse approved and codified by the Royal Society, one which recommends that travelers "make faithful *Records* of all the Works of *Nature,* or *Art*" in order "to put a Mark on Errors . . . to make the way more passable, to what remains unreveal'd." So too, the narrators sardonically exploit the discourse of rational Christian apologetics (we are reminded of Locke's *The Reasonableness of Christianity*), which offers rational glosses, personal testimonies, and corroborating historical evidences to certify and interpret revelation – "to take away incredulity," as Ishmael facetiously suggests in "The Affidavit," by "establishing in all respects the reasonableness of the whole story of the White Whale . . . For this is one of those disheartening instances where truth requires full as much bolstering as error" (*M-D,* 205).

To promote its ends, the Royal Society affirmed that some travelers "have endeavour'd, to separate the Knowledge of *Nature* from the colours of *Rhetorick* . . . or the delightful Deceit of *Fables*."[47] Yet an acknowledgment of the improbable, of "what remains unreveal'd," and perhaps sacred, lends itself to the suspicion of the "Deceit of *Fables*," as the narrator's own language in the passage from *Mardi* so clearly acknowledges, for he protests that "The sea-serpent is *not a fable*," and "there are . . . more sights unrevealed than you or I *ever dreamt of*," and Ishmael jestingly insinuates, in the language of literalist scriptural exegesis, that "without some hints touching the plain facts, historical and otherwise, of the fishery, they might scout at Moby Dick as a monstrous fable, or still worse and more detestable, a hideous and intolerable allegory" (205).[48] Yet Browne notes the folly of such hierarchies of exegetical interpretation, which give the literal priority, for "though divines have, to the power of human reason, endeavoured to make all go in a literal meaning, yet those allegorical interpretations [of the Creation and the Fall] are *also probable,* and perhaps the mystical method of Moses, bred up in the hieroglyphical schools of the Egyptians" (*Religio,* I.34; my emphasis). Whereas Browne in *Religio* asks his readers to acknowledge his own language of figuration, which must often stand in the place of actual knowledge ("there are many things to be taken in a soft and flexible sense"), Melville playfully both courts and resists the charge of the "Deceit of Fables" (the Sub-Sub-Librarian insists "you must not, in every case at least, take the higgledy-piggledy whale statements, however authentic, in these extracts, for verita- ble gospel cetology").[49] Much of what is known to mankind is known proximately and plausibly and articulated figuratively, not certainly and precisely ("unspeakable mysteries in the Scriptures are often delivered in a vulgar and illustrative way, and, being written unto man, are delivered, not as they truly are, but as they may be understood" [*Religio,* I.45]). If, as Browne suggests and Melville appears to affirm, our knowledge is constituted largely of plausible or probable truths of varying degrees of persuasiveness and much remains undiscovered, then the boundaries between "romance" and "verity," figuration and literalism, are less distinct and more fluid than the Lockean rationalist Whigs in America were willing to recognize. Moreover, the national "destiny," as radical Democrats or Southerners would have it, might be far less easy to discern than they would have Americans believe. Confrontations with the anomalous and the unknown in the two novels expose the fallible bases upon which such discriminations are determined, promulgated, and fought over.

Reconfiguring Categories: "Faith and Knowledge"

Melville devotes the entire chapter "Faith and Knowledge" in *Mardi* to an examination explicitly of the epistemological bound- aries between "faith" and "knowledge," but implicitly between "romance" and "verity," attempting to rehabilitate "faith," "ro- mance," and the marvelous in the process. This giddy chapter, at once exuberant and anxious, offers a Brownean defense of the marvelous, entreating one to doubt one's own skepticism in judg- ing the testimony related in the succeeding chapter, "The Tale of a Traveler." "Faith and Knowledge" is also a contemptuous caveat to "infidels [who] disbelieve the least incredible things" and "big- ots [who] reject the most obvious" that what they take to be "knowledge" is based on dubious inferences made from partial and benighted perspectives.

Melville's chapter clearly turns to seventeenth-century religio- philosophical apologia because of their intense engagement with the question of what is "knowledge" and what is known through "faith." Melville's "Faith and Knowledge" in fact recalls the clear divisions of Locke's chapter "Of Faith and Reason, and Their Distinct Provinces" (*Essay*, IV.18) in order to subvert what Browne shows to be only the false "antinomies" of faith and knowledge in *Religio Medici* (which means, "The Faith of a Physician"). Melville, moreover, summons up Locke's chapter title in order to replace, for his contemporaries, a Lockean esteem for knowledge gained by sensible "evidences" with an esteem for knowledge gained by the exertions of an active faith that acknowledges the demands of reason but that also acknowledges the less probable but no less true. As we have seen, Locke values most those evidences that Browne disdains as the elements of a facile devotion, for "to credit ordinary and visible objects," according to Browne in *Religio*, "is not faith, but persuasion ... 'Tis an easy and necessary belief, to credit what our eye and sense hath examined" (I.9). Instead, Browne most approves "believing with difficulty or purchase" (*PE*, I.5) and proclaims (to the chagrin of the Anglicans who wanted to embrace him in their more thoroughgoing rationalist fold) "there be not impossibilities enough in religion for an active faith" (*Religio*, I.9).

Melville's narrator clearly signals his position in this campaign to divest Lockean epistemology of its undeserved credit by reformulating Browne's infamous "resolution" borrowed from Tertullian, *"Certum est quia impossibile est"* ("It is certain because it is impossible") (*Religio*, I.9). This is appropriated and revised by the Mardian narrator, who prefaces a testimony of a marvelous event by insisting that "a thing incredible is about to be related; but a thing may be incredible and still be true; sometimes it is incredible because it is true" (296). Browne's frame of reference was that of a compromised reason and a divine prerogative well protected, one which underwrote the possibility that an anomaly, an "impossibility," indeed what might be deemed a "romance," was more apt to be "true" than what we usually take to be "verity." Like Browne's formulation ("it is certain because it is impossible"), Melville's reformulation ("it is incredible because it is true") underscores the necessity of grappling with a weak apprehension given to easy skepticism. Perhaps Melville also appropriates Browne's substitution of the term signaling a premise ("because") for the term more properly signaling a conclusion ("therefore") in order to underscore, however jovially, the inefficacy of logical constructions.

Melville's narrator further signals his efforts in the design to divest Lockean epistemology of its undeserved credit and dispel its suspicions of the improbable by appropriating Browne's trope in *Religio* depicting the encroachment on faith. Browne envisions it as the battle of pious Christians defending faith with "gauntlet," "sword," or St. Paul's "buckler" against Turkish "infidels," triumphing against the Turkish fleet in a "battle of Lepanto" (*Religio,* I.6,10; II.7). Elsewhere, in a chapter of *Pseudodoxia* clearly read by Melville, Browne interprets a picture of St. George fighting the dragon as "A horseman armed *cap à pié,* intimating the *panoplia* or complete armour of a Christian combating with the . . . devil, in defence of . . . the Church of God" (V.17). Similarly, the Melvillean narrator entreats: "Panoplied in all the armor of St. Paul, morion, hauberk, and greaves, let us fight the Turks inch by inch, and yield them naught but our corpse" (*Mardi,* 296). We must, like Browne, "hold fast to all we have; and stop all leaks in our faith" (*Mardi,* 296). Yet neither Browne nor Melville suggests crediting a naive faith. Instead, they seek to avert an unexamined and dogmatic skepticism.

In a series of conspicuous allusions to the obsolete theological crises and seventeenth-century conundrums raised in *Religio Medici,* the Mardian narrator further exhorts his audience to imagine an active human reason enhanced by the intimations of an equally active faith. By an analogy with angelic knowledge, we might, for example, imagine such an enhanced human knowledge, for "probabilities to us may be demonstrations unto them," notes Browne (*Religio,* I.33); and according to the Mardian narrator's comparison, "The higher the intelligence, the more faith, and the less credulity: Gabriel rejects more than we, but outbelieves us all" (296).

According to Melville's narrator, however, the realities of human knowledge suggest that although our true "foes" are skeptics and dogmatic unbelievers, we tend, in the midst of our epistemological uncertainties, to insist upon doctrinal and institutional certainty, and misguidedly exclude even those who would believe ("But let us not turn round upon friends, confounding them with foes" [296]). And so, according to Browne, mere opinions become dogmas, "sects usurp the gates of heaven, and turn the key against each other" (*Religio,* I.56), and "even in the doctrines heretical there will be superheresies; and Arians, not only divided from the church, but also among themselves" (I.8). Browne accentuates the difficulty of distinguishing the heretical from the holy, insisting "I believe many are saved who to man seem reprobated, and many are reprobated who in the opinion and sentence of man stand elected. There will appear, at the last day, strange and unexpected examples, both of his justice and his mercy; and, therefore, to define either is folly in man, and insolency even in the devils" (I.57). Similarly, Babbalanja later in *Mardi* inquires, "Where [is] our warrant . . . to justify the killing, burning, and destroying, or far worse, the social persecutions we institute in his behalf? Ah! how shall these self-assumed attorneys and vice-gerents be astounded, when they shall see all heaven peopled with heretics and heathens, and all hell nodding over with miters!" (428). Perceptions of heterodoxy, then, must be revised into those of comprehensiveness, "for dissenters," according to the Melvillean narrator, "only assent to more than we" (296). In an earlier chapter of *Mardi*, it is even imagined that "Christian shall join hands between Gentile and Jew . . . and monk Luther, over a flagon of old nectar, talk over old times with Pope Leo" (12). Melville, in fact, seems to adopt Browne's assessment of dissenters. The nature of Anglican reform was such that "in calling for the old, and *desiring that which was novel and crept in might be rejected*, and the Church of Rome refusing it, we have *reform'd from those upstart novel Doctrines, but against none of the old*."[50] Yet Browne's latitude apparently permits doctrinal and ritual accretions because of his unwillingness to cause divisiveness on issues "indifferent" to salvation. Browne more comprehensively insists: "There are, questionless, both in Greek, Roman, and African churches, solemnities and ceremonies, whereof the wiser zeals do make a Christian use" (*Religio,* I.3). Browne's greater latitude prompts him to examine and make pious use of the truths that variations and innovations may contain – as do the questors in *Mardi* when they confront religious differences, or Ishmael when he reflects upon the exotic rites of Queequeg ("I was . . . born and bred in the bosom of the infallible Presbyterian Church. How then could I unite with this wild idolator in worshipping his piece of wood? But what is worship? thought I. Do you suppose now, Ishmael, that the magnanimous God of heaven and earth – pagans and all included – can possibly be jealous of an insignificant bit of black wood?" (*M-D,* 52). Indeed, Ishmael's eccentric but genial deliberations about joining Queequeg in worship may well have behind them that section of *Religio* (I.3) which shows Browne's uncommon tolerance in uniting in worship with others, particularly Catholics, whom his contemporaries scorned ("I am not scrupulous to converse and live with them, to enter their churches in defect of ours, and either pray with them, or for them. I could never perceive any rational consequence from those many texts which prohibit the children of Israel to pollute themselves with the temples of heathens"). Believing that he is doing "the will of God," Ishmael decides to "unite with him [Queequeg] in his [form of worship]." Melville parodies what may be any literalist ceremony, Catholic or pagan: Ishmael graciously "kindled the shavings; helped prop up the innocent little idol; offered him burnt biscuit with Queequeg; salamed before him twice or thrice, [and] kissed his nose" (52). Similarly both skeptical and gracious, Browne also insists that many ceremonies (including genuflection) and religious objects ("Holy water and crucifix" ["dangerous to the common people"]) that to Browne's Protestant contemporaries were little more than idolatrous, "deceive not my judgment, nor abuse my devotion at all," for "there is something in it of devotion." Instead, these acts and objects, for Melville as much as for Browne, may "stand condemned by us, not as evil in themselves, but as allurements and baits of superstition to those vulgar heads that look asquint on the face of truth" (*Religio,* I.3).

The believer of active faith and high intelligence, according to the Melvillean narrator in *Mardi,* assents to truths expressed in doctrines and rituals that to the institutions of men are otherwise without traditional precedent, or improbable. That person is capable of transcending doctrinal differences born of the failure of human reason adequately to accommodate and human judgment adequately to discern divine truths in their own representations. Indeed such discriminations are so problematic that later in the novel Babbalanja intimates that an all-pervading divine immanence appears to make God responsible for evil (427): "But this is a heresy; wherefore, orthodoxy and heresy are one. And thus is it . . . that upon these matters we Mardians all agree and disagree together and kill each other . . . Think you he [Oro/God] discriminates between deist and atheist? . . . The universe is all of one mind" (428). For Melville's narrator, the person of high intelligence and active faith neither needs nor misinterprets the creeds or sensible evidences buttressing faith: "Though Milton was a [Arian] heretic to the [trinitarian] creed of Athanasius, his faith exceeded that of Athanasius himself; and the faith of Athanasius that of Thomas, the disciple, who with his own eyes beheld the mark of the nails" (296). Alluding in *Religio* to doubting Thomas in John 20:29, Browne announces that "I . . . am thankful, that I lived not in the days of miracles; . . . then had my faith been thrust upon me; nor should I enjoy that greater blessing pronounced to all that believe and saw not" (I.9). But since Christians in his latter day have the advantage of historical testimonies, Browne insists that the exertions of his active faith are comparatively little: "Nor is this much to believe" compared to those "who lived before his coming, who, upon obscure prophesies and mystical types, could raise a belief, and expect apparent impossibilities" (*Religio,* I.9). Echoing Browne, Melville's narrator observes that assent like Thomas's, which is granted only in accordance with the "evidence" of miracles, and even more so ours, based on the numerous testimonies of history, is an "easy" faith that offers no exertions of its own, relying all too heavily on demonstrations to the senses and reason: "Whence it comes that though we be all Christians now, the best of us had perhaps been otherwise in the days of Thomas" (*Mardi,* 296).

Melville's narrator highlights the disjunction between divine wisdom and partial human knowledge in a series of typically Brownean paradoxes ("the greatest marvels are first truths; and first truths the last unto which we attain. Things nearest are furthest off" [296]).[51] He intimates that the highest levels of human knowledge enhanced by an active faith could show us that "the greatest marvels" appear to be abrogations of the natural order or rational understanding because they exist outside the logic of coherence that we have constructed to explain them. Whereas Browne reverently asks, "who can speak of eternity without a solecism?" (*Religio,* I.11), Melville rambunctiously calls attention to the incidentals that can distort knowledge ("Though your ear be next-door to your brain, it is forever removed from your sight") and to the apparent illogic of paradox ("It is only because we are in ourselves, that we know ourselves not") so as to remind us that greater truths, "universe-old truths," are often unjustly dismissed by partial and arbitrary human knowledge. Thus Melville's narrator challenges complacency by calling attention to the precariousness of human knowledge, especially when confronting transmundane truths. Just how precarious and fragile that knowledge is, the narrator intimates in his confession that "I, it was, who suppressed the lost work of Manetho, on the Egyptian theology, as containing mysteries not to be revealed to posterity, and things at war with the canonical scriptures" (*Mardi,* 297).

On a single epistemic scale, Locke extended the threshold of what is considered "knowledge" from that which is mathematically "demonstrable" and compels assent to encompass that which is not quite demonstrable but is "morally certain" (highly probable based on reason, precedent, and sensible evidence), and even to that which is "probable."[52] With greater reservations about the capacities and caprices of unaided reason, Browne – from Mel-

ville's retrospective vantage point – appears to expand the threshold of "knowledge" still more to include that which is surmised by
an active "faith" but which may be less probable, or even improbable according to the usual standards of reference. By allowing
what is "known" by faith greater comprehensiveness (in Locke's
terms, "above probability" or "beyond certainty"), Melville's narrator, like Browne, provides the model and then challenges the
reader similarly to question and reconfigure received categories,
yet carefully to avoid credulity.

This challenge to received categories continues in the meditation on reincarnation concluding this chapter of *Mardi* (ch. 97),
while the test of credulity, as we shall see later in this discussion,
is preferred in the succeeding chapter, "The Tale of a Traveler."
F. O. Matthiessen interpreted the meditation on reincarnation as
evidence of Melville's fascination with the "scholastic strain" in
Browne, as well as his "ventriloquism" of "one of Browne's "favorite topics, metempsychosis."[51] The meditation depicts instead the
narrator witnessing historical events from the vantage point of a
"higher intelligence" and a more active faith. From this perspective, he believes he discerns in himself scores of historical innova-
tors, conspirators, and "dissenters," such as the one who hid "in
the old oak at Hartford" the Charter for Massachusetts from the
king's "minions"; the one who authored American Revolutionary
tracts called the *Junius Papers;* and the one who led "the Mohawk
masks, who in the Old Commonwealth's harbor, overboard threw
the East India Company's Souchong" (297). Yet this meditation,
like Browne's in *Religio,* employs reincarnation tropically. Browne
uses reincarnation as a metaphor to illustrate the hardiness and
periodic recurrence of "opinions," that is, heresies: "One general
council is not able to extirpate one single heresy . . . it will flourish till it be condemned again. For, *as though there were a metempsychosis,* and the soul of one man passed into another, opinions do
find, after certain revolutions, men and minds like those that first
begat them" (*Religio,* I.6; my emphasis), and so "every man is not
only himself; there have been many Diogeneses, and as many
Timons, though but few of that name" (I.6). Prefaced by a lament
about flaccid "faith" that the Mardian narrator articulates in the
Brownean idiom ("it is only of our easy faith, that we are not
infidels throughout; and only of our lack of faith, that we believe
what we do" [297]), the meditation in *Mardi* similarly employs
the trope of reincarnation both to illustrate the resilience of
dissent throughout history and to enfranchise the exertions of
an active faith and high intelligence. As if from the universal

perspective of divinity, Melville's narrator depicts himself witnessing or aiding the Israelites, Solomon, Columbus, and the English regicide conspirators Goffe and Whalley. The Mardian narrator intimates that such dissenters of active faith and probing intelligence transgress as often as councils, creeds, and institutions make their transgressions necessary. His exhaustive enumeration of such moments, moreover, implicitly underscores the tenuousness and inadequacy of human schemes, edicts, and orthodoxies to adjudicate worldly issues appropriately and even less the marvelous and the supernal.

The Artifice of Conceptual Categories and the Mediation of Art: Mardi's "Time and Temples" and "Dreams"

Whereas "Faith and Knowledge" asks us to reconceive these respective epistemological categories in order to encompass a greater range of "truths," Melville's Brownean chapter on "Time and Temples," recalling both *Hydriotaphia* and *Religio Medici,* challenges our apprehension of "time," "eternity," and "creation." Much like Browne's "gorgeous metaphysical" prose style, paradoxical expressions, and swelling amplifications in *Hydiotraphia*'s ironic tribute to time and funerary monuments, Melville's "Time and Temples" calls attention – through elaborate intensifications of its own artifice on the thematic and stylistic levels – to the contingent relationship between the artifacts that human reason has wrought to render divine truths intelligible (time as *chronos* and temples designed as calendars) and those divine truths themselves (eternity and creation).[54]

Gleaned from the Melvillean narrator's reading in the "Oriental Pilgrimage of the pious old Purchas, and in the fine old folio Voyages of Hakluyt, Thevenot, Ramusio, and De Bry," "wondrous" narratives and "wild eastern tale[s]" depict "glorious old Asiatic temples, very long in erecting" (*Mardi,* 228). The narrator explicitly associates the Eastern architectural wonders with attempts to symbolize chronological time (the "three-hundred-and-sixty-five-pillared Temple of the Year" [228]). These remarkable structures are also associated with the paradox of how we calculate age and duration ("though a strong new monument be builded to-day, it only is lasting because its blocks are old as the sun" [228]). They are connected too with the power to mold, which we equivocally call "originality" and "creativity" ("For we are not gods and creators; and the controversialists have debated, whether indeed the All-Plastic Power itself can do more than mold" [229]).[55] And finally, the wondrous piles are associated with the long lapse of time required to perfect these finite edifices (architectural and literary) so that they approach the infinite ("No fine firm fabric ever yet grew like a gourd; Nero's House of Gold was not raised in a day; nor the Mexican House of the Sun; nor the Alhambra . . . and from its first founding, five hundred years did circle, ere Strasbourg's great spire lifted its five hundred feet into the air . . . Nor were the parts of the great Illiad put together in haste; though old Homer's temple shall lift up its dome, when St. Peter's is a legend" [229]). Using a Brownean vocabulary (itself echoing Ecclesiastes) that contemptuously dismisses mankind's "vanity," as well as the "folly of posthumous memory,"[56] Melville's narrator in these examples exposes the critics' "folly" and false logic in determining what constitutes originality, and what will create an enduring artifact (architectural, but with intimations of literary artifacts). When we remember Melville's self-conscious analogy between the edifice of his novel *Moby-Dick*, his "cetological System," and "the great Cathedral of Cologne . . . left, with the crane still standing upon the top of the uncompleted tower," we realize that Melville's stance on this issue of creativity is self-referential, "for small erections may be finished by their first architects," he claims in *Moby-Dick*, but "grand ones, *true ones*, ever leave the copestone to posterity" (*M-D*, 145; my emphasis).

Through paradox and tautology, Melville's narrator repeatedly challenges the demand for original creations quickly produced, as he does even more explicitly in a later chapter (*Mardi*, ch. 181). Indeed, he questions the notion of creativity itself:

> that which long endures full-fledged, must have long lain in the germ. And duration is not of the future, but of the past; and eternity is eternal, because it has been . . . For to make an eternity, we must build with eternities; whence, the vanity of the cry for any thing alike durable and new; and the folly of the reproach – Your granite hath come from the old-fashioned hills. (228–9)

At this moment, when Melville's voice is clearly distinguishable from that of the narrator's, Melville dismisses his critics' censure by capturing the resonance and cadence of Browne's *sententia* in *Hydriotaphia*, which expose the artifice of time and tenses as well as the mistake of expecting immortality from any human artifact: "There is nothing strictly immortal, but immortality. Whatever hath no beginning may be confident of no end" (*Hy*, V. 494).

Similarly, both Melville and Browne note the disjunction between the temporal and the eternal in the failed expectations of humanity ("his whole mortal life brings not his immortal soul to maturity"). But whereas Browne reposes in the assurance of being "recalled" to "the perfect state of men," Melville dwells upon the problem of intelligibility that the eternal and the perfect pose to the human mind. Temporal markers and liberal Christian assumptions about mankind's steady amelioration are irrelevant in this chapter of *Mardi:* "Even man himself lives months ere his Maker deems him fit to be born," observes Melville's narrator, "And his whole mortal life brings not his immortal soul to maturity; nor will all eternity perfect him" (229).

If Melville insists "nor will all eternity perfect him," it is to emphasize that completion and perfection are divine attributes, to be neither applied to human beings nor demanded of their artifacts. "The difference betwixt *Eternity* and *Time*," as Browne's annotator in the 1686 edition (the edition Melville purchased in England) explains, is not one of quantity, not "duration perpetual consisting of parts." Rather, it is one in which eternity is, according to Browne, "without succession, parts, flux, or division" (*Religio*, I.11). Endlessness and perfection refer, according to Plato's *Timaeus*, cited by Browne's annotator, to an *"eternal thing, a Divine substance*, by which he meant *God*, or his *Anima mundi:* and this he did, to the intent to establish this truth, That no mutation can befall the Divine Majesty, as it doth to things subject to generation and corruption." Browne's commentator explains the problem of intelligibility in presenting those opposed to this notion of eternity. He paraphrases those who contend that "Plato . . . intended not to define or describe any species of duration: and they say *it is impossible to understand* any such species of duration that is . . . but one *permanent point*." But divine attributes cannot always be made to conform to human comprehension, and so the eternity of God "is according to Boetius his definition, *interminabilis vitae tota simul & perfecta possessio* [full and perfect possession of endless life always present in its entirety]" – "to which opinion," the annotator suggests, "it appears by what follows in this Section [on eternity in *Religio*], [Browne] adheres."[57]

Accordingly, the exaggerated redundancy of the Mardian narrator's vertiginous list of architectural feats requiring great lapses of time for completion vividly displays the artifice by which quantitative increase of the finite in time and space is made to serve as an approximation of that which is actually infinite in power, extension, and time. In this way, Melville not only underscores the tenuous relation between epistemological constructions and the eternal and ineffable they are meant to represent, but also mimetically recapitulates the act of accommodation to human understanding. The accumulation of hundreds of examples of human funerary rites and monuments in Browne's *Hydriotaphia* serves to show the redundant but futile exertions in the temporal domain to emulate the eternal and confer duration in eternity. Similarly, Melville's amassing of some thirty-seven examples of magnificent edifices negating the possibility of swift completion builds, on the syntactic level, in artificial imitation of the infinite ("nor . . . nor . . . nor"), yet on the substantive level negates sublime creation within time. Here Melville has demonstrated the artifice and inadequacy of qualitatively distinguishing time from eternity in terms of quantitative accretion or division ("duration perpetual consisting of parts"). This distinction "doth not at all difference *Eternity* from the nature of *Time*," writes Browne's 1686 annotator, summarizing Browne's putative objection, "for they say if it be composed of many *Nunc*'s, or many instants, by the addition of one more it is still increased; and by that means *Infinity* or *Eternity* is not included, nor ought more than *Time*."[58]

The Mardian narrator proceeds explicitly to acknowledge the disjunction between such divine attributes as the infinite, eternal, and perfect and conceptions that are intelligible to the human mind: "Yea, with *uttermost reverence, as to human understanding,* increase of dominion *seems* increase of power; and day by day new planets are being added to elder-born Saturns, even as six thousand years ago our own Earth made one more in this system; so, *in incident, not in essence,* may the Infinite himself be not less than more infinite now" (229 – 30; my emphases). Melville makes a distinction by using the accumulation of "incidents" figuratively in an attempt to convey the unimaginable dimensions of infinite "essence." Moreover, in his analogy accommodating the notion of the infinite to his contemporaries in the age of Manifest Destiny and the Mexican War, Melville pointedly chooses the vocabulary of empire building ("as . . . increase of dominion seems increase in power"), yet signals in the syntactic and logical collapse of the sentence's conclusion the inadequacy of quotidian values and temporal logic to render the infinite intelligible ("so . . . may the Infinite himself be not less than more infinite now"). He may also be intimating that it is a delusion to think that power increases with domain.

In an effort to convey to human reason the immensity of divine power and dimension, Melville's narrator continues the trope of empire, employing an analogy between the discovery and conquest of new lands and the divine creation of the material universe:

> if time was, when this round Earth, which to innumerable mortals has *seemed an empire never to be wholly explored;* which, in its seas, *concealed all the Indies* over four thousand five hundred years; if time was, when *this great quarry of Assyrias and Romes* was not extant; then, time may have been, when the whole material universe lived its Dark Ages; yea, when the Ineffable Silence, proceeding from its unimaginable remoteness, *espied it as an isle in the sea.* (230; my emphases)

The language here creates an analogy that already signals figuration as a convenience ("seemed an empire," "quarry of Assyrias and Romes," "espied it as an isle") and conditional logic as highly tentative ("if . . . then time may have been"). Yet the Melvillean narrator is still more careful to emphasize the divine nature's intractability to human representations: "And herein is no derogation" (detraction), the narrator insists of the preceding analogy, "For the Immeasurable's altitude is not heightened by the arches of Mahomet's heavens; and were all space a vacuum, yet would it be a fullness; for to Himself His own universe is He" (230). In this passage, the typically Brownean stylistic hallmarks – the latinate and archaic diction, as well as the use of litotes ("herein is no derogation") – clearly designate Melville's engagement with the Brownean issue of verbal and conceptual tentativeness in the task of representing metaphysical truths. In *Religio,* Browne self-consciously admits that the language he must employ is only slightly more than nominal ("Now for that immaterial world . . . which *if I call* the ubiquitary and omnipresent essence of God, *I hope I shall not offend divinity*" [I.35; my emphasis]), and is accordingly critical of those who mistake figural approximations for literal representations ("Men commonly set forth the torments of hell by fire, and the extremity of corporal afflictions, and describe hell in the same method that Mahomet doth heaven" [I.51]). One note in the Wilkin edition, commenting on Browne's attempt to depict creation in *Religio,* expressly warns that acts of divine accommodation must themselves be understood properly:

> If God [in the Bible] sometimes represents himself with feet, with hands, with eyes, he means in the portraits rather to give to us emblems of his attributes, than images (properly speaking) of any parts, which he possesseth: therefore

when he attributes these to himself, he gives to them so vast an extent, that we easily perceive that they are not to be grossly understood.[59]

But still Browne (and as we also see Melville) must resort to depicting the act of creation, like the attempts to represent time, as a process by which undistinguished unity is transformed into discernible parts that are intelligible to man, for creation, writes Browne, is "that which is truly contrary unto God: for he only is; all others have an existence with dependency, and are something but by a distinction . . . God, being all things, is contrary unto nothing; out of which were made all things, and so nothing became something, and *omneity* informed *nullity* into an essence" (*Religio*, I.35). Melville's rendition ("were all space a vacuum, yet would it be a fullness; for to Himself His own universe is He") signals its own representational provisionality not only by its conditional mood and the subversion of logic in its tautological structure but also by the discontinuous perspectives of divinity and humanity presented, ones in which informing divine immanence ultimately pre-empts any human perception. But whereas Browne piously assents to such pre-emption, Melville's philosopher, in two later chapters of *Mardi*, "Babbalanja Discourses in the Dark" (ch. 135) and "L'Ultima Sera" (ch. 185), articulates the more unsettling implications of divine immanence for his own sense of human identity and intellection: "those orthodox systems which ascribe to Oro [God] almighty and universal attributes every way, those systems, I say, destroy all intellectual individualities but Oro, and resolve the universe into him" (427–8). Babbalanja the philosopher, moreover, entertains the disturbing notion – one that Browne never considers but that consistently troubles Melville – that human epistemological limitations may extend to moral discernment: "Yet what seems evil to us, may be good to him . . . He lives content; all ends are compassed in Him" (620).

Melville concludes this chapter on time and temples in part by appropriating Browne's trope of falconry. In the section of *Religio* that pronounces his allegiance to figuration rather than definition, Browne acknowledges the difficulty of comprehending divinity (I.10), and by this acknowledgment he finds the means to "teach my haggard [wild hawk] and unreclaimed [untamed] reason to stoop unto the lure of faith." Browne's trope emphasizes the necessity of taming the wild and uncontrolled reason to seek the desired quarry proffered by faith. Contrastingly, the

Melvillean narrator's metaphor of the soul as a "wild" "night-hawk" that has, like the Ineffable, "espied" the "great quarry of Assyrias and Romes," emphasizes no such desire for domestication but rather stresses the stunning power and perspective enabled by such a flight, one concluding in an infinite regress:

> Thus deeper and deeper into Time's endless tunnel, does the winged soul, like a night-hawk, wend her wild way; and finds eternities before and behind; and her last limit is her everlasting beginning.
>
> But sent over the broad flooded sphere, even Noah's dove came back, and perched on his hand. So comes back my spirit to me, and folds up her wings. (230)

Given the glimpses of true limitlessness and perfection in this chapter, it is no surprise that Melville concludes, "Thus, then, though Time be the mightiest of Alarics [plunderers], yet is he the mightiest mason of all" (230), for it has become clear from "Time and Temples" that the artifacts of creation in the temporal world, including Melville's own verbal "edifice," though they aspire to the immortal, are in fact endlessly repeated acts of accommodation, fables and figurations like the "temples" of *Mardi* and the great "cathedral" of *Moby-Dick* standing ever so tenuously in place of the eternal.

These earlier chapters experiment with imagining human intellection and language eclipsed in vast cosmic perspectives. They are also meditations on ways to acknowledge and accommodate human limits – epistemological, spiritual, and aesthetic. The later chapter "Dreams" (ch. 119), however, imagines the difficulty of testing (and even surpassing) human limitations – the loneliness, the fears, the internal trepidation amidst the exhilaration. In *Religio Medici*, Browne playfully but reverently depicts the contemporaneity of God's perspective: " 'Before Abraham was, I am,' is the saying of Christ, yet is it true in some sense if I say it of myself; for I was not only before myself but Adam, that is, in the idea of God" (I.59). But in the "Dreams" chapter of *Mardi*, Melville's narrator, increasingly Promethean in his boldness ("my own mad brood of eagles devours me"), "blanches" at his own quasi-divine thoughts:

> In me, many worthies recline and converse. I list to St. Paul who argues the doubts of Montaigne; . . . and though Democritus laugh loud and long, and the sneer of Pyrro be

seen; yet, divine Plato, and Proclus, and Verulam are of my
counsel; and Zoroaster whispered me before I was born . . .
My memory is a life beyond birth; my memory, my library of
the Vatican, its alcoves all endless perspectives. (367–8)

Commentators have suggested that "Dreams" reveals the grandiose delusions of the increasingly "meglomaniacal," self-deluded
character Taji. I suggest instead that this embodiment of supernal
knowledge is the artist-philosopher's vision of human limits surpassed and epistemological obstacles overcome. Its dauntlessness
contrasts with the timidity of human metaphysical speculation
indicted in the next chapter (ch. 120).[60] (This passage, in fact,
bears some resemblance both to the Sub-Sub-Librarian's heroic
efforts in *Moby-Dick* and to Pierre's fantasies of power in the novel
of the same name, and suggests something about Melville's own
preoccupations.) In ch. 120, the dialogue between the "mortal"
philosopher Babbalanja and the demigod King Media ends with
the king's lament (perhaps Melville's own searching and anguished voice only thinly disguised):

> Meditate as much as you will . . . but say little aloud, unless
> in a merry and mythical way. Lay down the great maxims of
> things, but let inferences take care of themselves . . . And if
> doubts distract you, in vain will you seek sympathy from your
> fellow men . . . Discourse with them, and it is mostly formu-
> las, or prevarications, or hollow assumption of philosophical
> indifference, or urbane hypocrisies, or a cool, civil defer-
> ence to the dominant belief; or still worse, but less common,
> a brutality of indiscriminate skepticism . . . The free, airy
> robe of your philosophy is but a dream, which seems true
> while it lasts; but waking again into the orthodox world,
> straightway you resume the old habit. And though *in dreams*
> you may hie to the uttermost Orient, yet all the while you
> abide where you are. (369–70; my emphasis)

King Media's trope of traveling to the "uttermost Orient" as a
lonely movement toward grand, heterodox speculation articulates the novel's own daring structure. Whereas most awake to
"resume the old habit" and "abide where you are," the quester
takes up the challenge and continues the flight of the "night-
hawk" soul, "find[ing] eternities before and behind." *Mardi* in
fact traces a tour through the defamiliarized yet still recognizable
world of the Mardian archipelago long enough to provide a

satirical political allegory of the European revolutions of 1848, then leaves those islands behind for increasingly unfamiliar destinations and ever bolder metaphysical speculation.

Navigating a Mardian Archipelago of "Vulgar Errors"

In such Brownean chapters as "Of the Chondropterygii," "Faith and Knowledge," "Time and Temples," and "Dreams," Melville poses a challenge to existing epistemological paradigms and human orthodoxies as he depicts travels through the South Seas. Yet he also achieves, much as Browne does in *Religio Medici, Hydriotaphia,* and *Pseudodoxia Epidemica,* an intensely chastened attitude toward the variations of customs and conceptions humanity has fashioned to render comprehensible the as yet unintelligible. From the uncertain and ephemeral nature of human knowledge ("final, last thoughts you mortals have none; nor can have; and, at bottom, your own fleeting fancies are too often secrets to yourselves"[370]) as well as from the condemnation of speculative timidity, we can see that well-considered but undaunted assessment is the only genuine alternative. Concentrating upon Brownean themes, appropriating Brownean stylistic features, and using Brownean methods of seeking out liminal phenomena upon which moderately skeptical, probabilist apprehension and figural accommodation are self-consciously practiced, each of these chapters in *Mardi,* then, can be seen as procedural instructions to chapters on encounters with exotic or uncommon social, political, or theological systems.[61]

Thus "Time and Temples" (ch. 75), for example, both probes and provides a gloss on the Mardian prince Donjalolo's extraordinary scheme (chs. 76–7) to control time and make himself eternal. (Among his many epithets in the chapter with the pointedly Augustinian title "The Center of Many Circumferences" are the divine attributes of the "indivisible" and "the insphered sphere of spheres" [240].) By having himself daily transported from his House of the Morning to his House of the Afternoon, "thereby anticipating the revolution of the sun," the absolute ruler of this Mardian isle attempts to evade the cycle of mortality, for in "dodging day's luminary through life, the prince hied to and fro in his dominions; on his smooth, spotless brow Sol's rays never shining" (235). In the following chapter (ch. 78), the novel's philosopher meditates on death and mortality in the House of the Afternoon (decorated with the remains and reliquary of past rulers), then pauses to dwell, in the manner of both Browne's meditation on urns in *Hydriotaphia* and Hamlet's soliloquy about Yorick's skull, on the abiding flux of the ephemeral world. In the context of "Time and Temples," Prince Donjalolo's extraordinary and luxuriant organic palaces and singular scheme become intelligible and not improbable; indeed, they take their place beside the many other human efforts that prompted Browne ironically to call man "a noble animal, splendid in ashes, and pompous in the grave" (*Hy*, V. 494).

If we are asked to modify our skepticism when reading of uncommon behavior and singular places, we are also asked to reform and chasten the excesses of our naive and "vulgar" credulity – as much concerning island demigods and surgical miracles as concerning political myths. So, although the chapter "Faith and Knowledge" (ch. 97) challenges us to reconceive what we consider knowledge in order to "believe with difficulty or purchase" (*PE*, I.5), it does so in part to test us in the following chapter, "The Tale of a Traveler" (ch. 98). This latter chapter gives us the task of evaluating the probability of extraordinary phenomena, an evelution based not strictly upon testimony or predictability, but upon a close examination of the criteria used and inferences made in the reports of extraordinary phenomena we judge. The apparently miraculous event borrowed from William Ellis's *Polynesian Researches* (1833), quoted at length in the Wilkin edition of Browne[62] and recounted in "The Tale of a Traveler," poses the challenge of judging its possible veracity in a scene of Lockean assessment based on supporting testimonies ("But let not the truth be postponed. To the stand, Samoa" [298]). But although the chapter begins with a Brownean exhortion to reconsider the plausibility of wonders recounted in travel narratives, the tale itself flirts with the fictive in its opening formula of "Once upon a time." And although the tale concludes with an assertion that "this anecdote was credited by some present" (299), the chapter ends with a teasingly literal intimation of the difficulty of swallowing, as it were, Samoa's "tale of a traveler," for if the incredible and vaguely cannibalistic practice of Abyssinians who "cut live steaks from their cattle" cited from an earlier travel narrative is difficult to credit, then all the more "Tough the thews [muscles], and tough the tales of Samoa" (299). Samoa's own testimony is itself rendered suspect in that he tells the tale "as a traveler," and travelers, the chapter tells us, are sometimes reputed to be liars (298) – and this despite what we are told in "Samoa a Surgeon" (ch. 96), that "there is testimony to show that it [his story] involves nothing at variance with the customs of certain barbarous tribes" (295). Through these conflicting cues, then, the reader, who is positioned to be the adjudicator, is deliberately poised between credulity and incredulity.

At this point Melville identifies for us, and comically exploits, the problem of crediting the excessive literalism of Samoa's anecdote and the syllogistic extrapolation of Babbalanja's musings that follows it – the objects of both Melville's and Browne's procedural critiques here. In Samoa's tale, Melville playfully literalizes the imbruting effect of an injured warrior's trepanning surgery infusing the essence of a pig along with its brains ("But from being a warrior of great sense and spirit, he became a perverse-minded and piggish fellow, showing many of the characteristics of his swinish grafting" [299]). In *Religio*, Browne offers just such a droll enactment of the same "vulgar error," that of extrapolating the literal from the figurative: "As for those wingy mysteries in divinity, and airy subtleties in religion, which have unhinged the brains of better heads, they never stretched the *pia mater* ["The inmost skin which incloseth the braine"] of mine" (I.9). Here Browne satirically imagines his own mind's failure of intellection in attempting to solve theological conundrums. He imagines the task as having the potential to do actual violence to the human brain, just as Samoa depicts the transformation of human character attending the "swinish grafting."

Babbalanja's own musings heighten the literalism of Samoa's tale still further:

> "Yet, if this story be true," said he, "and since it is well settled, that our brains are somehow the organs of sense; then, I see not why human reason could not be put into a pig, by letting into its cranium the contents of a man's. I have long thought, that men, pigs, and plants, are but curious physiological experiments; and that science would at last enable philosophers to produce new species of beings, by somehow mixing, and concocting the essential ingredients of various creatures; and so forming new combinations. My friend Atahalpa, the astrologer and alchymist, has long had a jar, in which he has been endeavoring to hatch a fairy, the ingredients being compounded according to a receipt of his own. (299)

The reference to hatching a fairy from a recipe has long been attributed to a footnote in the Wilkin edition of *Religio*.[63] But what deserves attention here is the "vulgar error" of remarkable literalism, of attempting to work from such a formal definition as "Man is a rational animal" or "men, pigs, and plants are but curious physiological experiments," which permits false inferences from the general category to the particular, so as to make conceivable a combination of "essential ingredients" creating new forms of life. "The deepest mysteries," according to Browne, "have not only been illustrated, but *maintained,* by syllogism and the rule of reason" (*Religio,* I.9; my emphasis). Melville's depiction above acknowledges Browne's empirical, as well as scholasticism's and occult science's, literal-minded attempt to understand how and where the "incorruptible and immortal" soul that distinguishes man from animals enters and inheres in the human body. "I am not of Paracelsus's mind, that boldly delivers a receipt to make a man without conjunction," notes Browne, yet "I find not . . . organ or instrument for the rational soul; for in the brain, which we term the seat of reason, there is not any thing of moment more than I can discover in the crany of a beast" (*Religio,* I.36). So based on reports of "equivocal and monstrous productions in the copulation of a man with a beast," Browne himself credulously infers that reason and the soul are probably transmitted by the parents, otherwise "why are not those [monstrous] productions merely beasts, but have also an impression and tincture of reason in as high a measure, as it can evidence itself in those improper organs?" (I.36). Finally, however, the "equivocal and monstrous productions," which seem to fascinate both Melville and Browne, become tropes – grotesque conflations of that which characterizes humanity and the rational (though fallacious) extrapolations of occult science or the empirical efforts of anatomical study. And so Browne's failure to locate the site of the soul or track the point of its infusion concludes with a self-ironizing acknowledgment of his own literalist folly, enacted by prepositions that resist and scatter precise spatial location: "Thus we are men, and we know not how; there is something *in* us that can be *without* us, and will be *after* us, though it is strange that it hath no history what it was *before* us, nor cannot tell how it *entered* in us" (I.36; my emphases). Similarly, Babbalanja's "little . . . heeded" parodic disquisition on making new species based on syllogistic and definitional inferences makes Melville's critique of literalism in Samoa's tale inescapable. In the context of the chapter on "Faith and Knowledge," not only Samoa's tale, which "he told . . . as a traveler," but also Babbalanja's reflections warn against the fallacy of imposing a self-consistent logic that fulfills its own requirements but explains nothing beyond itself, and of drawing analogies and inferences too literally and indiscriminately from the known to the naturally, culturally, or metaphysically opaque. Samoa's "surgery," after all, is a failure: his "equivocal and monstrous production" dies. And we as readers, despite the testimonies we are offered, are asked to reflect upon our own process of crediting and judging accounts of the extraordinary and unfamiliar.

These self-conscious reflections are, moreover, to be carried into the social and political realms. From the letter about Melville and that "crack'd Archangel" Browne that Evert Duyckinck wrote to his brother George (who witnessed the overthrow of the French monarchy in Paris), we can infer that Browne's presence may well have entered *Mardi* at largely the same phase of composition as the extended political allegory surveying mid-century politics and the European revolutions of 1848 (chs. 145–68).[64] It is possible to infer that Browne's writings provided Melville with a method of assessment that enabled him to structure his challenges not only to epistemological complacency about natural myths and supernatural events, but also to unexamined ideological beliefs. Browne's own method of challenging the "vulgar errors" of credulity in *Pseudodoxia Epidemica* in fact extends to social, racial, and national opinions, which he assesses for their probable truths and possible prejudices according to the evidence of natural philosophy, his own observations, and an exhaustive list of authorities which he frequently consults with a critical eye. So, for example, in "Of Many Popular and Received Tenets Concerning Man" (Book IV) and "Of Popular and Received Tenets, Cosmographical, Geographical, and Historial" (Book VI), Browne evaluates and disputes many common prejudices about "Jews," "Gypsies," and "Negroes." We also know that at least one of Melville's contemporary Democratic reviewers (and a "Young American") saw *Mardi* as a novel calculated to challenge the social and political status quo, particularly the Whig status quo, for in July 1849 William A. Jones wrote in the *U.S. Magazine and Democratic Review* that "To those who believe that ours is the best of all possible worlds, this book will be a senseless homily, as impertinent as it is to them untrue. To those who believe that the world is bad, and cannot be made better, and that they have only to take care of themselves and their families, and thus prove that they are orthodox in faith and practice, Mardi will have been written in vain."[65]

In the novel, Melville alternates between echoing *Religio* in moments of high fellow feeling and appropriating the method and probing language of *Pseudodoxia* to evaluate political beliefs.

In the former, charitable mode, the Mardian narrator assumes a Brownean latitude. Accordingly, whereas Browne insists that "I wonder not at the French for their dishes of frogs, snails, and toadstools, nor at the Jews for locusts and grasshoppers; . . . I am averse from nothing: my conscience would give me the lie if I should say I absolutely detest or hate any essence, but the devil; or so at least abhor any thing, but that we might come to composition" (*Religio*, II.1), the Mardian narrator assumes, in the frame of reference of a South Seas sailor, that we "one and all, brothers in essence . . . All things form but one whole . . . Away with our stares and grimaces. The New Zealander's tatooing is not a prodigy; nor the Chinaman's ways an enigma. No custom is strange; no creed is absurd; no foe, but who will in the end prove a friend" (12–13). But it is the idiom of *Pseudodoxia* that Melville employs in "They hearken unto a Voice from the Gods" (ch. 161) to articulate a thinly disguised challenge to zealous American nationalist belief and Jacksonian Manifest Destiny, and (perhaps) to disarm American antimonarchical prejudices. One of Melville's modern critics has interpreted the political commentary in the anonymously authored scroll in "A Voice from the Gods" as informed by conservative impulses – either Melville's own or as a conciliatory gesture toward more conservative friends.[66] Yet in the context of Browne's efforts in *Pseudodoxia,* the scroll can be seen less as signaling a positive political position and more as an assumption of a pose attempting to be extrinsic to the political ideology it would appraise. So it is that the curiously "anonymous" scroll, deemed a "voice from the gods" (ch. 161), is equivocally attributed either to the "conservative" monarch King Media or to the more liberal Babbalanja, for it purports to align itself with neither position but rather to emulate Browne in his moderately skeptical but undogmatic enterprise of challenging mistaken beliefs and notions even at the risk of dismantling existing systems of belief. Accordingly, a Democratic reviewer could also find enough to praise in the novel's political challenges to those who would complacently accept the bounty of America.[67] Exploiting Browne's typical procedure of surveying pertinent historical examples for instances that confirm, disprove, or complicate the opinion being appraised (in this case one concerning the Roman, English, and French republics), the Melvillean scroll exposes the prejudices of Whig Puritan providential, Jacksonian Democratic, and "Young American" myths of American exceptionalism as respectively the "grand error of this age" (525), "the grand error of your nation" (525), and the "superstitious notions you [Americans] harbor" (529). As an implicit critique of the beliefs of the politically active Young Americans who were celebrating the overthrow of European monarchies in 1848, the scroll's commentary intimates darkly that the United States' apparent exemption from the decay and corruption of earlier republics is illusory, a vulgar error. The nation is itself credulous and "young" – that is, impetuous, at an early stage in its political development, and oblivious to history – for its empire building, its so-called Manifest Destiny, has temporarily provided sufficient land to allow the inhabitants to think themselves all "sovereign-kings" (526). But based in part on probable inferences from the vast perspective of history ("not more infallible the ponderings of the Calculating Machine than the deductions from the decimals of history" [527]), including the short-lived English Commonwealth (526–7)– and despite the magical and often dignifying power that the vocabulary of republicanism seems to confer ("Names make not distinctions" [528]) – the American republic is not, as popularly believed, miraculously singular or providentially elect. Having demystified American exceptionalism, exposed its symbolism ("that bloody hawk may hereafter be taken for the eagle" [527]),[68] and challenged its catechetical creed ("It is not the prime end, and chief blessing, to be politically free" [527]), the scroll suggests that Young American prejudices against monarchies are baseless and unconsidered: "in themselves, monarchies are not utterly evil. For many nations, they are better than republics . . . And better, on all hands, that peace should rule with a scepter, than that the tribunes of the people should brandish their broadswords" (527).

Although historical precedents are consulted in determining probable truths, the possibility of a unique nation is not dismissed simply because it is unprecedented. Evaluations of economic and political dynamics are introduced, and geographic advantages and human nature are reckoned in the scroll's assessment. But in an age when patriotic enthusiasm is applauded and the myth of American exceptionalism dignifies its imperialism, the Melvillean scroll issues an audacious challenge to the nation's ideology as it is buttressed by the (Whig) Puritan providential myth and the (Jacksonian Democratic) Manifest Destiny agenda. As the meditations of Babbalanja repeatedly warn, unconsidered "Faith is to the thoughtless, doubts to the thinker" (428). And as we follow the questers in *Mardi* who move through a seascape that could have been assembled from the wonders in Browne's *Pseudodoxia Epidemica,* we are reminded that "Our very axioms, and postulates are far from infallible" (574). Accordingly, Melville cautions us to test and challenge both our easy skepticism and our naive credulity, for, as the glib but still trenchant "Ponderings of old Bardianna" suggest in *Mardi*, "Supine we can only be annihilated" (575).

Moby-Dick, *"Of Monstrous Pictures of Whales," and Monstrosities of Interpretive Practice*

Melville may see himself as beginning in *Moby-Dick* where Browne concludes *Pseudodoxia Epidemica* – with a catalogue of "some relations whose truth we fear" (*PE*, VII.19), monstrosities of human behavior that Browne managed to detail despite his fear that "they do enlarge the theory of wickedness in all" and his wish that there not "remain any register, but that of hell" (VII.19). Melville's "crack'd Archangel" fears to suggest to the susceptible imagination the endlessly proliferating "errors" that Satan, who peers from the edges of *Pseudodoxia*, introduces into the world, and from which Melville in part draws the "classification of the constituents of a chaos." Melville in fact disobeys Browne's warning – he too supplements the "register . . . of hell." As we shall see in the next section, *Moby-Dick* has much in common with *Mardi* in the way Browne's *Pseudodoxia* and its method are exploited – particularly its critique of types of interpretive errors. But as we shall see in the last section, *Moby-Dick* contrastingly pursues the implications and dwells upon the terrors – metaphysical as well as political – to which Browne's chastened assessment of human knowledge is liable without its assurances.

Particularly in such cetological chapters of *Moby-Dick* as "Ambergris," "The Heidelberg Tun," "Cetology," "The Nut," and "The Honor and Glory of Whaling," Melville draws directly, both verbally and substantively, upon the sensuous particularity and arcane details of Browne's "Of Sperma-Ceti, and the Sperma-Ceti Whale" in *Pseudodoxia*. Browne, for example, observes that "But upon breaking up, the *magazine of spermaceti,* was found in the head, *lying in folds and courses,* . . . in form of honeycombs, very white and full of oil" (III.26). In "The Great Heidelberg Tun" and "The Nut," Ishmael reveals to the uninitiated "one immense honeycomb of oil, formed by . . . elastic white fibres" (*M-D*, 339), and when "the operator's instrument is . . . forced into the *spermaceti magazine*" (340), it is mistakenly believed, even by some whalemen, to be the vast store of the whale's brains, but is instead "the cubic-yards of his sperm magazine. *Lying in strange folds, courses,* and convolutions, to their apprehensions, it seems more in keeping with the idea of his general might to regard that mystic part of him as the seat of his intelligence" (348). Citing Rondeletius, Browne further observes, "a fatness, more liquid than oil, runs from the brain of that animal . . . which *melting with heat, [is] again concreted by cold*" (*PE,* III.26, and a note by Wilkin adds, "when completely *concrete, it is crystallized* and brilliant" (III.26). Similarly, Ishmael details, "Though in life it remains perfectly fluid yet, upon exposure to the air, after death, it soon begins *to concrete;* sending forth beautiful *crystalline shoots"(M-D,* 340). Like Browne's semiserious attempt to find the actual site of the soul in the human brain, the speculations in *Moby-Dick* about whale brains and whale intelligence conjoin the literal and the figurative in grotesque and sardonic ways.

   Yet it is more particularly the self-conscious, self-reflexive irony and metaphorical vividness with which types of "vulgar" errors are characterized and exposed by Browne that fascinate Melville and enable him to provoke doubt even as his Ishmael makes ever more exuberant claims upon our credulity.[69] In Browne's "Of Pictures of Mermaids, Unicorns, and some others" (*PE,* V: "Of Many Things Questionable As They Are Commonly Described in Pictures"), these painted marvels are exposed as ridiculous hybrids of the imagination and are characterized metaphorically: "And therefore these pieces [depictions of mermaids], so common among us, do rather derive their original, or are indeed the very descriptions of Dagon, which was made with human figure above, and fishy shape below; whose stump, or, as Tremellius and our margin render it, whose fishy part only remained, when the hands and upper part fell before the ark" (*PE,* V.19). Browne's rendition of 1 Samuel 5:2–4 dwells upon the heterogeneity of Dagon (not remarked upon in 1 Samuel 5), focuses on his "fishy shape" and "fishy part" (not mentioned in 1 Samuel 5:4), and highlights Dagon's disintegration in contrast to the Bible's rendering of his active dismemberment.[70] Browne's droll version reworks the destruction of a false idol (which was both the literal and figurative source of the error he lamented in "Of Credulity and Supinity") into a trope that depicts satirically both the absence of integrity in the pagan god and the promiscuous mixing of incongruous elements in many erroneous myths and "vulgar" interpretations. The trope also suggests Browne's own larger efforts in *Pseudodoxia* to expose the fantastic enshrined in common opinion, as is suggested by such chapter titles as "Of Many Popular and Received Tenets Concerning Man, Which Examined, Prove Either False or Dubious" and "Of Many Things Questionable As They Are Commonly Described in Pictures." Browne sees his own efforts in *Pseudodoxia Epidemica* as promoting the skill of discriminating the forgery and sham of vulgar "verisimilitude" (defined as "commonly received opinion") from the "probable" and the true, which is the domain of the learned initiate.[71] "Verisimilitude and Opinion are an easie purchase," notes Joseph Glanvill, a member of the Royal Society,

> and these counterfeits are all the Vulgars treasure: But true Knowledge is as dear in acquisition, as rare in possession. Truth, like a point or line, requires an acuteness and intention to its discovery; while verisimility, like the expanded superficies, is an obvious sensible on either hand, and affords a large and easie field for loose enquiry.[72]

Melville himself, particularly in *Mardi,* challenged the lack of discrimination among the verisimilar, the predictable, and the probable in his contemporary milieu. Though even more playfully, Ishmael, like Browne, similarly evaluates the relative merits of popular depictions of marvelous sea creatures and exposes their deficiencies in the chapters of *Moby-Dick* entitled "Of the Monstrous Pictures of Whales," "Of the Less Erroneous Pictures of Whales, and the True Pictures of Whaling Scenes" and "Of Whales in Paint; in Teeth; in Wood; in Sheet-Iron; in Stone; in Mountains; in Stars."

Ishmael insists that we must reconsider the false clarity of many modern interpretations of St. George and the Dragon ("Let not the modern paintings of this scene mislead us" [*M-D,* 362]), for there may be another reason why "in many old chronicles whales and dragons are strangely jumbled together." Then Ishmael glibly asserts the authenticity of the "fishy" part of his own reading of the dragon as a whale and reflects ironically upon the doubtful integrity of his own redaction – and perhaps upon his whole narrative: "In fact, placed before the strict and piercing truth, this whole story will fare like that fish, flesh, and fowl idol of the Philistines, Dagon by name; who being planted before the ark of Israel, his horse's head and both the palms of his hands fell off from him, and only the stump or fishy part of him remained.[73] Like Browne, Melville envisions the dramatic enactment of his own iconoclastic efforts, the destruction, when "placed before the strict and piercing truth," not only of erroneous myths, but also of Ishmael's fallible and "monstrous" interpretive practices, which eclectically join literal and figurative elements in a grotesque narrative.

In fact, when Ishmael surveys historical chronicles, natural philosophers' compendia, and travelers' eyewitness accounts with an aim toward dispelling myths and prejudices about whaling, as the chapter on the "Honor and Glory of Whaling" suggests, he also *demonstrates* how erratic interpretive practices are constructed and exploited for ulterior motives. Appropriately for Ishmael the naturalist and the initiate in the priesthood and ceremony of whaling, *Pseudodoxia*'s investigative procedure represents to some degree the conjunction of empiricism in natural philosophy and the Anglican theological method. That Anglican method searched historical sources and testimonies closest to the primitive church not only for justification in repudiating accretions and erroneous corruptions but also for precedents establishing the authenticity and integrity of its own organization, principles, ceremonies, and creeds. The efforts by Ishmael in "The Honor and Glory of Whaling" can in fact be seen as Melville's ironic commentary on institutional religion's dubious procedures for asserting legitimacy: "The more I . . . push my researches up to the very spring-head of it [whaling], so much the more am I impressed with its great honorableness and antiquity; and especially when I find so many great demi-gods and heroes, prophets of all sorts, who one way or other have shed distinction upon it, I am transported with the reflection that I myself belong . . . to so emblazoned a fraternity" (*M-D,* 361). Melville, moreover, may well have read the footnote to the chapter "Of the Picture of St. George" in the Wilkin edition of *Pseudodoxia,* which comments on the effort of Browne's successors in "vindicating the honor of the patron saint of these realms [England], and of that society; asserting that he was a Christian saint and martyr . . . distinct from the Arian bishop George of Alexandria" (*PE,* V.17). In this chapter of *Pseudodoxia,* which equally attempts to discredit the legend but vindicate the honor of fraternal allegiances and Christian institutions built upon them, Browne demonstrates that in all probability "the literal acception [of the emblem of St. George and the dragon] to be a misconstruction of the symbolical expression" (V.17). But as he restores the image entirely to the realm of Christian symbolism, he insists that his strictly figural interpretation "doth not disparage the knights and noble order of St. George: whose cognisance is honourable in the emblem of the soldier of Christ ["combating with the devil, in defence of . . . the

Church of God"], and is a worthy memorial to conform unto its mystery. Nor, were there no such person at all, had they more reason to be ashamed, than the noble order of Burgundy, and knights of the golden fleece; whose badge is a confessed fable" (V.17). Like Browne, who turns St. George into the emblem or type of the Christian soldier, Ishmael appropriates St. George as the type of the noble and victorious whaleman: "Thus then, one of our own noble stamp, even a whaleman, is the tutelary guardian of England; and by good rights, we harpooners of Nantucket should be enrolled in the most noble order of St. George. And therefore, let not the knights of that honorable company . . . eye a Nantucketer with disdain, since . . . we are much better entitled to St. George's decoration than they"(*M-D*, 362). Yet despite exploiting the modesty of Browne's probabilist language ("it is not indisputable" [*PE*, VI.10]), Ishmael extends the antiquity and nobility of his vocation to the Perseus and St. George myths by proposing increasingly far-fetched, literal-minded interpretations of their depictions, so that dragons may be construed as whales ("it will not appear altogether incompatible with the sacred legend and the ancientest draughts of the scene" [*M-D*, 362]). So whereas Browne rescues a dignified and plausible figurative interpretation from the myth of St. George, Ishmael both implies the legerdemain of his own interpretive practices in his reference to Dagon in the same chapter and wrests an ancient and noble lineage from implausible interpretations and dubious inferences.

The temptation to indulge in interpretive eclecticism can be seen again in the very next chapter, "Jonah Historically Regarded." With the figurative interpretations of "German," "continental," and other "learned exegetists," Ishmael challenges a skeptic's denial of the Jonah story based upon an overly literal, vulgar evaluation of it (it "only evinced his foolish pride of reason – a thing still more reprehensible in him, seeing that he had but little learning" [*M-D*, 365]). Yet Ishmael's own more informed literal computations and alternative readings end in greater improbabilities and inconsistencies, forcing Ishmael back on figurative interpretations or requiring him to leap to the conclusion of a miraculous intervention. Melville's chapter cautions us about the difficulty of determining when such a marvel as Jonah's experience is in fact a divine act that defies human reckoning (a tack to which Ishmael hastily resorts at the chapter's conclusion) and when such an anomaly should be assessed literally and discounted as erroneous (a tack that obliquely commends itself as worthy of our attention). But it also cautions us against the seductions of indiscriminately fashioning "a fish, flesh, and fowl idol" out of figurative and literal interpretations, as Ishmael implicitly does here in his polemical debate with the skeptic's arguments and implies he has done in the previous chapter.

As part of their procedural critiques, Browne and Melville also caution that when presented with the numerous and often contradictory sources cited in *Pseudodoxia* and *Moby-Dick,* we are neither to assume that all the enigmas are unresolvable nor are we to submit utterly to authority, for "our advanced beliefs," Browne reminds us, "are not to be built upon dictates, but having received the probable inducements of truth, we become emancipated from testimonial engagements, and are to erect upon the surer base of reason" (*PE,* I.7). Browne and Melville's Ishmael instead perform upon these sources numerous tasks of probabilist judgment, frequently reminding us, as much through their successes as their inadvertent failures, of the complexity of such judgments, in which so many particular facts and circumstances must be weighed, and exhorting us to examine the process by which we arrive at our own conclusions. On closer examination, Ishmael often stands as a fallible proxy for the reader.

"Of the Blackness of Negroes"
and "The Whiteness of the Whale":
America's "Vulgar Errors"

In the age of the Missouri Compromise and the Fugitive Slave Law, Melville's chapter on "The Whiteness of the Whale" draws tellingly upon Browne's three chapters concerning "the Blackness of Negroes" in *Pseudodoxia.*[74] Melville does so in order to ask us to examine self-consciously the process by which we ascribe significance to color ("giving the white man ideal mastership over every dusky tribe" [*M-D,* 189]),[75] and to question the hastiness with which we resort to explanations of supernatural agency ("the instinct . . . of the demonism in the world," or the curse upon the tribe of Cham) as a way to render intelligible that which seems alien or unfamiliar, but with the inadvertent effect of confirming our own fears or aversions.[76] Assaulted by the thought of "indefinite" whiteness "shadow[ing] forth heartless voids," Ishmael, as the reader's fallible proxy, becomes here an allegory of interpretive error, heightening instead of overcoming the very indistinctness that baffles perception and intellection and that so terrifies him – and imperils the Pequod as a ship of state.

This chapter on whiteness is not the only place in *Moby-Dick* where Melville turns to *Pseudodoxia* to dispel social prejudices. For the chapters that attempt to dispel prejudices against whalemen, Melville turns to *Pseudodoxia*'s Book IV ("Of Many Popular and Received Tenets Concerning Man, Which Examined, Prove Either False or Dubious"), where Browne, for example, surveys the existing myths and arguments and insists, "That Jews stink naturally, that is, that in their race and nation there is an evil savour, is a received opinion we know not how to admit." Later in the chapter, Browne notes sardonically of those who might stand to gain by such a myth, "could they be smelled out, [it] would much advantage, not only the church of Christ, but also the coffers of princes," since renunciation of worldy goods was expected upon conversion (*PE,* IV.10). "Owing to [his] anxiety to repel a charge often made against whalemen," Ishmael similarly surveys sources and notes the probable origins of the "odious stigma" against whales and whalemen, and having already appropriated Browne's comments on the odor of ambergris as the epigraph to ch. 91, he concludes his chapter of the same name by asserting, "The truth is, that living or dead, if but decently treated, whales as a species are by no means creatures of ill odor; nor can whalemen be recognised, as the people of the middle ages affected to detect a Jew in the company, by the nose" (*M-D,* 410).

Browne devotes three chapters to an examination of the causes, significance, and myths associated with the blackness of Negroes and blackness in general in Book VI of *Pseudodoxia* ("Of Popular and Received Tenets Cosmographical, Geographical, and Historical"). In the first of these chapters, Browne examines theories of color and light, explaining,

> Thus of colours in general, under whose gloss and varnish all things are seen, few or none have yet beheld the true nature, or positively set down their incontrollable causes. Which while some ascribe [color] unto the mixture of the elements, others to the graduality of opacity and light ["the receptions, refraction, or modification of light"], they have left our endeavours to grope them out by twilight, and by darkness almost to discover that whose existence is evidenced by light. (VI.10)

Browne's first trope ("gloss and varnish") emphasizes the painterly artifice of color that enables our perception. Ishmael similarly considers general theories of color ("the visible absence of color, and at the same time the concrete of all colors" [*M-D,*

195]), noting with mounting anguish "that other theory of the natural philosophers" in which the beguiling but false and superficial veneer of color enables vision: "all other earthly hues . . . are . . . only laid on from without; so that all deified Nature absolutely paints like the harlot; . . . and when we . . . consider that the mystical cosmetic which produces every one of her hues, the great principle of light, for ever remains white or colorless itself . . . – pondering all this, the palsied universe lies before us a leper" (195). And as Browne plays ironically upon the metaphor of knowledge as light and muses upon the paradox of attempting to make discriminations about the origin and meaning of blackness in the near-darkness of undifferentiated ignorance ("left to grope them out by twilight, by darkness almost to discover"), so too Ishmael pursues the paradox that the undifferentiated light and whiteness of the "palsied universe" obliterates rather than enables vision and knowledge, and effaces the individuation that results from divine creation, so that "the wretched infidel gazes himself blind at the monumental white shroud that wraps all the prospect around him" (195). While Ishmael suggests the blanching properties of light as it renders the very universe utterly "appalling," and "if operating without medium upon matter, would touch all objects, even tulips and roses, with its own blank tinge" (195), Browne explores the chemistry of "denigration," proposing a correction to the mistaken common association of blackness with hell: "by reason of the drying and penetrating quality of sulphur, which will make red roses white . . . to conceive a general blackness in hell, and yet therein the pure and refined flames of sulphur, is no philosophical conception" (*PE*, VI.12). (Here we are reminded of Ishmael's "erroneous" depiction of the "negro church" congregation: "It seemed the great Black Parliament sitting in Tophet . . . and the preacher's text was about the blackness of darkness, and the weeping and wailing and teeth-gnashing there" [*M-D*, 9–10].)

After abandoning his quest for the reason of blackness as beyond human resolution, Browne investigates the physical causes of blackness, but unlike Ishmael, he challenges superficial resemblances and reductive reasoning as he distinguishes probable optical and chemical from improbable climatic and supernatural causes. Browne refutes the argument that blackness is the consequence of a divine curse upon the tribe of Cham[77] in the second of the three chapters ("Of the Same") – a refutation in part based upon a discussion of beauty and deformity.[78] Working from details gathered from various travel narratives, particularly the study of Ethiopians in *Purchas his Pilgrimes,* Browne argues that cultural relativism in standards of beauty undermines the possibility of a supernatural fiat or universal consensus on the meaning of blackness: "whereas men affirm this colour was a curse, I cannot make out the propriety of that name, it neither seeming so to them, nor reasonably unto us, for they take so much content therein, that they esteem deformity by other colours, *describing the devil and terrible objects white*" (*PE,* VI.11). Yet Ishmael dwells upon the historical and global ubiquitousness of "the thought of whiteness, when ... coupled with any object terrible in itself, to heighten that terror to the furthest bounds" (*M-D,* 189). And whereas Browne warns "the two foundations of beauty, symmetry and complexion, receiving such various apprehensions, ... no deviation will be expounded so high as a curse or undeniable deformity, without a manifest and confessed degree of monstrosity" (*PE,* VI.11), Ishmael consistently attempts to assess the horrific power of whiteness in conjunction with objects already confirmed in their ferocity or monstrosity. Furthermore, after consulting various definitions of beauty, Browne infers that "we shall not apprehend a curse, or any deformity" in blackness, and so "the Moors are not excluded from beauty, there being in this description no consideration of colours, but [rather] an apt connection and frame of parts and the whole" (*PE,* VI.11). Ishmael's analogue to the Moor appears to be "the Albino [who] is as well made as other men – has no substantive deformity," (*M-D,* 191). But Ishmael breaks down the very distinction Browne takes pains to make, conflating the albino's color with monstrosity: "and yet this mere aspect of all-pervading whiteness makes him more strangely hideous than the ugliest abortion" (*M-D,* 191).

Even within Western culture, beyond standards of beauty and deformity, Browne can point to contradictory associations with blackness, thereby casting doubt upon the possibility of universal interpretation or inherent significance: "howsoever Cerberus, and the furies of hell be described by the poets under this complexion, yet in the beauty of our Saviour, blackness is commended ... his locks are bushy and black as a raven" (*PE,* VI.11). Yet Ishmael's many examples of whiteness, even in its "kindlier associations," suggest a transcultural, transhistorical, indeed a universal and inherent power and meaning – one especially terrifying "when exhibited under any form at all approaching to muteness or universality" (*M-D,* 193).

Indeed, whereas Ishmael's survey of examples enables him to

associate the horror of whiteness with "the instinct of the knowledge of demonism in the world," Browne's survey leads him to lament "the conceit" that blackness is a curse, for it represents a type of error that prevents rational inquiry by adducing a single and supernatural cause: "it is a very injurious method unto philosophy, and a perpetual promotion of ignorance, in points of obscurity . . . to fall upon a present refuge unto miracles; or recur unto immediate contrivance from the unsearchable hands of God . . . [so that] by a final and satisfactory discernment of faith, we lay the last and particular effects upon the first and general cause of all things" (*PE*, VI.11). Earlier in *Pseudodoxia,* Browne had warned against resorting unnecessarily to such explanations for unfamiliar phenomena: "these [meteors] being natural productions from second and settled causes, we need not alway look upon them as the immediate hand of God" (I.11). If he insists upon the possibility of divine prerogative unsettling the predictable and "natural order," he also warns against precipitous conclusions of supernatural causation. Morever, he points out the common aversion to difference in standards of beauty: "beauty is determined by opinion, and seems to have no essence that holds one notion with all . . . according as custom hath made it natural, or sympathy and conformity of minds shall make it seem agreeable . . . Thus we that are of contrary complexions accuse the blackness of the Moor as ugly" (VI.11). Browne suggests that ascribing supernatural curses or blessings seems only to literalize and confirm our fears, suspicions, or aversions (like "describing the devil and terrible objects white"). And so in a chapter on the blackness of negroes, he reminds us that "in the conceit of the evil odour of the Jews, Christians, without a further research into the verity of the thing, or enquiry into the cause, draw up a judgment upon them from the passion of their Saviour" (VI.11).

In the context of Browne's efforts in "Of the Blackness of Negroes," Melville's chapter attempting to come to terms with whiteness and the anomaly of a white whale may be seen both as a cautionary tale about the difficulty of making intelligible that which seems alien and as a compendium of judgmental errors with both political and metaphysical implications. Indeed, we can recall that before Ishmael befriends Queequeg, Ishmael's response to his appearance and "unearthly complexion" concludes with the disclosure "Ignorance is the parent of fear, and being completely nonplussed and confounded about the stranger, I confess I was now as much afraid of him as if it was the devil himself" (*M-D,* 21–2). This chapter, then portrays the collapse or failure of Ishmael's own discernment when confronting the mysterious other.

Divine Portents, Demonic Counterfeits, and Human Deceits

The power of *Moby-Dick* – its frantic and horrified confrontation with all that lies outside orthodoxy and conventional categories of thought and value, its wrenching discovery that that which one confronts cannot always be made intelligible (not even whiteness's "dumb blankness, full of meaning"), much less explained away – owes much to Browne's moderate skepticism, which charges him with the obligation to entertain an ever-changing and expanding range of possibilities. But for Ishmael as for Browne, the terror is not that signs fail altogether to have signification, nor that the human mind lacks all capacity for making the universe at least tentatively intelligible. Rather, Ishmael's trials demonstrate the urgent need for active discernment in worlds that are fraught with meaning but also are fraught with counterfeits and snares that baffle and misguide apprehension. Standing as a caveat to a too complacently rational, post-Lockean America is Ishmael's perilous dilemma – that even his probing but not sufficiently wary and discriminating mind will fail to distinguish genuine wonders from demonic delusions, and those from human myths, doubts, prejudices, fears, and deceits.

In the chapter entitled "The Chapel" we gain a glimpse of these perils and their implications. In Ishmael's speculations before the cenotaphs of whalemen, Melville employs *Hydriotaphia*'s meditation on funerary monuments, its moderate skepticism, and its associated prose style to explore the anarchic potential ushered in by the systematic dismissal of dogmatism. Here, in a distinctly Melvillean revision of Browne, he seizes the opportunity to challenge Christian "myths" that Browne's skeptical vision of human knowledge allows. Melville associates Ishmael's meditations with the uncertainties of an afterlife but also with the genre of funeral orations. Through Ishmael's meditations, Melville reveals that Brownean antidogmatic inclusiveness does not allow for the imposition of a single theological narrative. Melville turns to Brownean speculation to reveal the unsettling, to show the limited and fragmented vision of the future that is the son's only true inheritance.

During Ishmael's meditation on cenotaphs in the whalemen's chapel, Melville suspends the dramatic action and dispenses with

Ishmael's "free and easy genial desperado philosophy" – though he resumes it at the conclusion, perhaps in an attempt to suppress the terrors opened up by the inquiry. In his meditations, Ishmael, like Browne, confronts the limits of human knowledge about death and the afterlife elicited by the monuments of what had once been meaningful lives. We see in both "The Chapel" and *Hydriotaphia* the same mounting tension between the desire to adjudicate among the bewildering diversity of religious customs and practices as they were thought to affect immortality, and the features of a skeptical inquiry that attempts to comprehend the manifold possibilities but in this case falls far short of resolving them. Browne observes in *Hydriotaphia* that "since the religion of one seems madness unto another, to afford an account or rational of old rites requires no rigid reader" (*Hy*, IV.482). Yet although the interpreter of customs and rites who exercises such latitude may render intelligible and even reconcilable the variety of funerary rites practiced throughout time, ultimately human reason must acknowledge its funerary rites as well as its efforts to commemorate the dead in monuments or language as at best equally plausible, and ultimately self-contained, efforts at "accommodating" to itself the intractable metaphysical domain.

In Ishmael's reflections on cenotaphs, we can hear resonances of Browne's highly patterned and alliterative prose, which deliberately calls attention to itself as an ironic commentary on the failed power, "even by everlasting languages," to procure immortality or achieve anything beyond language's own logic and syntax. Browne's sensuous, eloquent, self-conscious prose displays its own richness but also its inescapable inefficacy, as it is employed to comment on language: "To be read by bare inscriptions . . . To hope for eternity by enigmatical epithets or first letters of our names, to be studied by antiquaries, . . . and have new names given us like many of the mummies, are cold consolations unto the students of perpetuity, even by everlasting languages" (*Hy*, V.491). Similar to these "bare inscriptions," "enigmatical epithets," and "cold consolations" are Ishmael's "bitter blanks" and "immovable inscriptions," which expose, in all the sonority that language offers, the inability of words to redeem emotions, "recollect" lost lives in a Christian burial, or compensate for the failed consanguinity of cenotaphs that "cover no ashes": "What bitter blanks in those black-bordered marbles which cover no ashes! What despair in those immovable inscriptions! What deadly voids and unbidden infidelities in the lines that seem to gnaw upon all Faith, and refuse resurrections to the beings who have placelessly perished without a grave" (*M-D*, 36). Both Ishmael and Browne connect the artifacts that are words with those that are commemorative monuments, for while Ishmael comments upon the "bitter blanks in those black-bordered marbles" and "deadly voids . . . in the lines that seem to gnaw upon all Faith," Browne connects (in his own footnote) the configuration of tombs and urns with the "theta, character for death": "Circles and right lines limit and close all bodies, and the mortal right lined circle [theta] must conclude and shut up all" (*Hy*, V.491). Yet both are also struck by the ineffectuality and deceptiveness of monuments compared with the "truth" of death: Browne notes that "The certainty of death is attended with uncertainties, in time, manner, places. The variety of monuments hath often obscured true graves; and cenotaphs confounded sepulchres. For beside their real tombs, many have founded honorary and empty sepulchres" (*Hy*, III.475). Indeed, it is especially the physical emptiness of such cenotaphs and questions of the existence and location of "spirit" that most trouble Ishmael as he confronts the possibility of "placelessly" perishing on the forthcoming whaling expedition.

As Ishmael continues his meditation, he, like Browne, illustrates the contradictions between belief and funerary practices, and recognizes the contradictions as symptoms of the uncertain knowledge about the nature of the afterlife. For both Ishmael and Browne, burial customs and practices are, in Browne's words, necessarily "questionable, . . . discordant, or obscure" (*Hy*, IV.485). Ishmael asks, "In what census of living creatures, the dead of mankind are included," and speculates upon the discrepancies by which "Life Insurance Companies pay death-forfeitures on immortals" and the contradictions by which "we still refuse to be comforted for those who we nevertheless maintain are dwelling in unspeakable bliss" (*M-D*, 36–7). Browne is likewise struck by contradictions in practice and belief: "to extend our memories by monuments, whose death we daily pray for, and whose duration we cannot hope, without injury to our expectations in the advent of the last day, were a contradiction to our beliefs" (*Hy*, V.491).

Moreover, in both Ishmael's long series of speculative questions and Browne's catalogue of speculations, the considerations arising from their moderate and probabilist skepticism overlook no details, no matter how insignificant, trivial, or peculiar. Ishmael wonders about the nature of "antique Adam's" "deadly hopeless trance," while Browne wonders whether Periander's wife is justified in her complaint about the freezing tortures she must

suffer for want of a funeral burning (*Hy*, IV.485). Ishmael wonders about payment of death forfeitures and Browne about the
menu for funeral suppers (*Hy*, IV.485). Both sets of inquiries
proceed through a seemingly arbitrary and endless series of predicaments involving death, duration, the afterlife, and attenuated
states in between. Browne, in fact, seems to open up a whole
range of inquiries that Ismael pursues to imply new terrors hitherto undreamt of by most.

Both texts are indeed exhaustive compendia of equally uncertain superstitions, signaled stylistically by the omission of logical
connectives and by punctuation creating the effect of equal yet
syntactically disjunct members that ironically amplify the uncertainties but fail to resolve them. In both Ishmael's reflections
and Browne's meditation, all remains "discordant or obscure."
Closure on the syntactic, semantic, and structural levels tends to
be partial. Tentative closure comes in the form of such modest
refrains as "it cannot escape some doubt" (Browne), "it cannot
pass without some question" (Browne), or "all these things are
not without their meanings" (Melville) and "Surely all this is not
without meaning" (Melville). These summary comments, however, are only momentary pauses before the next round of speculations. Browne's accretive and suggestive seventeenth-century
prose style is in fact well suited to Ishmael's probabilist inquiries
in a way that the logical progressions and transparencies of an
Addisonian style tailored to Lockean rationalist pursuits would
not be.

Yet the absence of resolution in Browne's *Hydriotaphia* is meant
to underscore the vanity of such ambitions of duration, or of
knowledge that extends beyond what God has chosen to reveal.
Browne abandons questions about the location of remains, for it
is sufficient that among the dead "many are not like to err in
the topography of their resurrection" (*Hy*, III.481). Instead, he
celebrates the "recollection" of all men in the Resurrection, and
the subsidence "of all things which are but a colony" back into
the "mother element [which] will have . . . their primitive mass
again" (*Hy*, III.477). But the language of Ishmael's meditation
points only to fragmentation with no hope of reunification ("refuse resurrections to those who have placelessly perished"), and
to unrest, for the "deadly voids" of the cenotaphs "gnaw upon all
Faith," and the commotion among the dead ("why all the living
so strive to hush all the dead") is intimated in the "rumor of a
knocking in a tomb [which] will terrify a whole city" (*M-D*, 37).
Ishmael initiates Browne's habit of exhaustive speculation but

concludes without the assurances of any providential design (beneficent or otherwise). In the world of *Moby-Dick,* no paternal God gathers up his children, nor does his presence provide the *telos* that makes sense of human history. Instead, "Faith, like a jackal, feeds among the tombs, and even from these dead doubts she gathers her most vital hope," and the "devious-cruising Rachel . . . only found another orphan," whom she carries onto yet another unending voyage. When Ishmael concludes his speculations in the chapel with the comment that "all these things are not without their meanings," there is a certain terror in the obscurity of those meanings – "why all the living so strive to hush all the dead" – that is not quite suppressed by his assertion of Christian belief and his platonizing effusions at the chapter's conclusion. Indeed, Ahab's power to induce the otherwise skeptical Ishmael to ascribe to him supernatural power and to join the hunt for the white whale has its basis in Ishmael's earlier unsettling suspicions, which suggest the problem of discerning the agent of such turbulent natural or supernatural forces lying beneath humanly constructed myths that obscure more than they explain. Ishmael's chapel meditation hints at an insurgent world of spirit of which no systems of human belief – myths, religions, superstitions, rituals – have taken adequate account and over which they exercise no power.

Indeed, it is the "myths" alone – Christian or otherwise – that are most often commemorated by such monuments. Although the cenotaphs of the lost whalemen record private losses, Ishmael, in "The Honor and Glory of Whaling," would have us remember the service to their nation of these otherwise unacknowledged heroes. But for Ishmael, whose meditation begins with an apostrophe to survivors, the cenotaphs betray those heirs and survivors because they emphasize the absence of connection, kinship, and continuity. Here, as in "The Gilder," we are asked to acknowledge loss, abandonment, and broken kinship ("Where is the foundling's father hidden? Our souls are like those orphans whose unwedded mothers die in bearing them: the secret of our paternity lies in their grave, and we must there to learn it" [*M-D,* 492]. Once the Brownean pandora's box of speculation is opened, it cannot be closed, however much Ishmael may assert his belief, and Starbuck insist, "Let faith oust fact; let fancy oust memory; I look deep down and do believe," (*M-D,* 492).

Through his appropriation of Browne's moderate skepticism and probabilist methods, Melville sought to unsettle his contemporaries from the reductive certainties to which they too often resorted. Yet he also insisted on the necessity of engaged judgment, and tried to accommodate those phenomena not readily recognizable or immediately intelligible. But Melville did not always respond in this way; rather, in his readings of Milton's poetry, his response to the inexplicit phenomena – particularly the divine – was one of angered frustration.

6

SURMISING THE INFIDEL:

MELVILLE READS MILTON

━━━━━

As seen in Chapter 1, Evert Duyckinck and Fitz-James O'Brien were uneasy with Melville's Brownean "extravagant speculations." In the way that Melville reads John Milton, as we shall see next, their suspicions seem well founded. In fact, in responding to Milton (perhaps at a later date than his reading of Browne), Melville himself seems increasingly frustrated with the instances of epistemological opacity he encountered, and now vindictively heightens the instances of inscrutability of which he thinks Milton was also aware. In Melville's annotations of Milton's poetry,[1] we are confronted with a curious reading of Milton's ambitions and agenda, one that seems to be significantly self-reflexive for Melville. Indeed, these annotations offer the opportunity of viewing some of Melville's own subversive techniques as they are projected onto another author, and confirm, to some extent, his contemporary critics' suspicions of him.[2] Dating from his readings of Milton in 1849, 1860, and 1868, Melville's unpublished annotations reveal that he was a highly engaged and frequently ingenious reader of the poetry.[3] From these annotations it is possible to infer that Melville rather startlingly regards Milton himself as the "Sampson," who, in Andrew Marvell's famous words, "grop'd the temple's posts in spite," intent upon bringing down the entire Christian theological edifice.[4] Neither an orthodox Calvinist, a radical Puritan revolutionary, nor a heretical Manichean, Milton, according to Melville's annotations, covertly displays a much darker, more doubting, and more insinuating investment in Christian theology than the Anglican editor of Melville's edition, the Reverend John Mitford, ever guesses.

Melville suggests that Milton's heretical beliefs were in fact justly surmised by Andrew Marvell in "On Paradise Lost," and most clearly expressed by Satan in *Paradise Lost* and *Paradise*

Regained, as well as by Dalila in *Samson Agonistes.*[5] Melville infers from the speeches of these characters a deflective narrative strategy employed by Milton to voice his own most profound theological criticisms and doubts.[6] Deflected through such doubting and provocative characters as Dalila and Satan, Milton's sentiments do not, however, take on the conviction of their alien or inverted values, but instead gain a skeptical and ironic edge, complicating, vexing, and at times posing an affront to the values Melville's Milton would interrogate.[7] Upon reflection, we can see too that Melville himself employed just such a character – Ishmael, who is more skilled in Browne's skeptical probabilism, rather than the deluded Taji or Ahab – to deliver his most decisive blows and to offer his most incisive criticisms of his culture's ideology.

Melville is immediately struck by Andrew Marvell's suspicions in his prefatory poem "On Paradise Lost" (printed along with the epic in the Mitford edition) that Milton deliberately "would ruine . . ./ The sacred truths to Fable and old song." Melville scores in the margin lines 6 through 9 of Marvell's poem and partly underscores Marvell's words "the argument / Held me awhile misdoubting his intent, / That he would ruine (for I saw him strong) / The sacred truths to Fable and old song: / (So Sampson grop'd the temple's posts in spite) / The world o'erwhelming to revenge his sight." Replying to Marvell's words, Melville asserts that

> It is still misdoubted by some. First impressions are generally true, too, Andrew.

Melville's confident tone here reveals an esteem for his own acuity in detecting Milton's subtle but profound heterodoxy, and perhaps, a certain complicitous sympathy with Milton. According to this annotation, which distinctly echoes Marvell's word "misdoubting," Melville implies that Marvell has misguidedly resolved or suppressed his own well-justified doubts about Milton's destructive intent ("That he would ruine . . . The sacred truths"). Marvell initially portrays Milton as the blind Samson whose rage is enacted in his cataclysmic destruction of the "sacred truths" figured as the "temple" and the "world" (and whose awful sense of "heaven's desertion" Milton allows his own Samson to utter in *Samson Agonistes* [line 632]). Marvell's second allusion in "On Paradise Lost," however, revises this rendering of Milton as a Samson, for this time Milton is depicted as the blind Tiresias whose "loss of sight" is appropriately compensated by a "Just heav'n" with the gift of prophecy as well as inspired poetry (line

43). Marvell's shift from Samson to Tiresias serves not only to dispel the specter of bewildered rage raised by the image of Samson but also to mute all murmuring against divine injustice. But in dismissing Marvell's second, more pious rendering in favor on an ongoing "misdoubt" about Milton's motives, Melville reveals that he himself is convinced of Milton's intent to shake the "temple" and its "sacred truths." And so although Marvell begs Milton's "pardon" for his "causeless, yet not impious, surmise" (lines 23–4), Melville refuses to relinquish Marvell's "first impression," his "surmise" that Milton is indeed a Samson incensed to rage and destruction by a perceived injustice or frustrated sense of abandonment. It may be that Melville prefers the image of a powerful and accomplished but frustrated and impious Milton because of his own identification with the poet. And Melville's precarious career and difficult artistic development may have similarly informed his impulse to compute and note Milton's age at the time he composed many of the early poems.[8]

If we explore, moreover, the possibility that Melville read Walter Savage Landor's dialogues between Milton and Marvell in Landor's immensely popular *Imaginary Conversations,* what emerges is Melville's intense identification with a Samson-like, embittered, and impious Milton. Melville's familiarity in addressing Marvell as "Andrew" in the above annotation may in fact mimic the intimacy between authors in the dialogues created by Landor. Although we do not know for certain that Melville was acquainted with the particular edition containing the dialogues between Milton and Marvell (Landor republished and expanded the *Imaginary Conversations* periodically),[9] we do know that the *Conversations* was greatly admired and often imitated by many contemporary American writers, including Ralph Waldo Emerson and by Margaret Fuller in her imaginary conversation between George Herbert and Lord Herbert of Cherbury. In the *Imaginary Conversations,* Landor portrays both the embittered Milton of post-Restoration England and the admiringly protective Marvell, whom Milton repeatedly addresses as "Andrew" throughout their conversations. Melville's wary, slightly patronizing tone toward Marvell in his annotation may well be echoing – indeed impersonating – the tone of Milton's own voice in these fictive conversations. Melville's and Milton's voices are certainly consonant in their disappointment with Marvell's too orthodox assessment of Milton's impious intentions and achievements.[10]

As we have seen from this annotation to "On Paradise Lost," Melville resists Marvell's rehabilitation of Milton's heterodox intent. Perhaps Melville found in another of Landor's imaginary conversations a more compelling account of Milton – one that emphasizes his impious rage. In this fictive conversation between "Andrew Marvel and Bishop Parker," Landor's Bishop Samuel Parker, like Melville, sardonically affirms rather than dismisses Marvell's figuration of Milton as a destructive Samson: "Your Samson had shaken its [the Anglican church's] pillars by his attack on Prelaty."[11] Referring to Milton's antiprelatical tracts, Parker angrily and slanderously accuses Milton of an overwhelmingly destructive intent in his engagement with the Anglican church. Melville may well have found this depiction of a vengeful Milton hostile to the church more persuasive or more suited to his own temperament than Marvell's orthodox Milton, for Melville often relished the irreverent or the atheistic in his favorite writers.[12] And yet through historical contextualizations of Milton's defeated hopes, Marvell's sympathies, and Parker's hostile motives, Landor is careful to distinguish Milton from Samson. In his poem, Marvell also distinguishes the "mighty poet" and his triumphs from the loss and rage of the Samson figure. Melville, however, seizes upon and confirms Marvell's initial "misdoubt," which conflates Milton with the bound, provoked, and violent Samson (in "On Paradise Lost" and perhaps *Samson Agonistes*). In so doing, Melville intimates a narrative about Milton and his God more far-reaching in its theological pessimism than either Marvell or Landor depicts.

We can gauge the extent of the theological pessimism that Melville ascribes to Milton when we note the absence of either typological resonance or historical context in Melville's association of Milton with Samson. In Melville's reading, there is no desire to emphasize the "typological distance" between the type of the deluded, violent Samson and the antitype of the inspired, nonviolent Milton.[13] Melville overlooks or eschews the ameliorative force of typological schemes, which typically placed Samson's latter-day antitype in the position of one favored by God. It seems that for Melville, the blind poet has been granted neither grander revelations nor heroic fortitude in the face of adversity. Instead, Melville's certainty about the correctness of Marvell's "first impression" securely collapses the cunningly vindictive Samson and Milton into one figure. Nor does Melville's reading reveal an historical consciousness. One critic has suggested that Milton laments the role of Puritan fanaticism in the outcome of the Puritan Revolution through his depiction of a Samson deluded in believing his destructiveness divinely inspired. Melville's annotation implicating Milton as Samson, however, suggests an eternal drama removed from any actual political devastations. Such devastations may, as this critic suggests, at least serve to ignite new millennial fervor, allowing the projection of the *regnum Christi* into a real if distant future. Melville's annotation confirming Marvell's suspicions suggests the furious rage of Samson and Milton equally locked in changeless roles, and heightens the sense that Melville perceived an *ongoing* human tragedy in which both figures (and perhaps Melville himself) are caught.[14] This is a tragedy of a God so inscrutable to his followers that they cannot distinguish inspiration from delusion, paternal chastisement from abandonment and betrayal. Melville's Samson-like Milton at times seems close to the Milton who prays for deliverance in *Of Reformation:* "I doe now feele my selfe in wrapt on the sodaine into those mazes and *Labyrinths* of dreadfull and hideous thoughts, that which way to get out, or which way to end I know not."[15] But whereas Milton expects succor and prays for deliverance from the discord of the ecclesiastical strife he has internalized, Melville's Milton seems to dwell in perpetual darkness and bewilderment about divine intent. Indeed, Melville's perceptions of a dark, distant, mysterious God are consonant with those depicted in *Samson Agonistes* and may inform his perceptions of God in both *Paradise Lost* and *Paradise Regained.* Marvell's words ("The world o'erwhelming to revenge his sight") posit as the source of Milton's vengeful anger the personal anguish of blindness. The annotations examined next suggest instead that Melville assumed Milton consciously sought opportunities to intensify the already inherently equivocal status of those "sacred truths" and, in so doing, attempted to surpass God at his own game. A case in point singled out by Melville is Dalila's last speech in *Samson* (lines 960–996).

Milton's *Samson Agonistes* is a text fraught with equivocal betrayals. Samson's betrayal by Dalila resonates with preceding betrayals – not only that of Samson's first Philistian wife but also those of the Israelites themselves, who had so forsaken their vows to their God (lines 265–70) that they neither remembered to cry out to him in their oppression nor recognized in Samson the "judge" whom God raised up to deliver them (lines 245–6, 272), and so in giving Samson to the Philistines, they had ironically, as one critic observes, "delivered themselves of their own deliverer."[16] Yet among all the betrayals, Melville's eyes were drawn most to those (apparent) betrayals by God. Early in the drama, Melville marks on the same page lines that reveal the appalling insufficiency of God's "gift" to Samson: first Melville marks Samson's lament "But what is strength without a double share / Of wisdom? vast, unwieldy, burthensome" (lines 53–4); then he marks and underscores the cruel paradox of Samson's gift from God: "Suffices that to me strength is my bane, / and proves the source of all my miseries" (lines 63–4, Melville's underscoring). Through Melville's identification with Milton – and, by the extrapolation he intimates, with the character of Samson – we gain a sense not only of Melville's own anguish but also that of the branded, "moody stricken Ahab [who] stood before them with a crucifixion in his face; [and] in all the nameless regal overbearing dignity of some mighty woe."[17]

And if vows of allegiance are shown not to be binding in *Samson*, Melville finds most curious of all a God who blurs or contravenes his own laws. Attempting to exculpate God from such charges, the Chorus first asserts the justness of the God "Who made our laws to bind us, not himself" (line 309), and then tries to make sense of God's curious arrangement – to "prompt" a marriage that goes against Samson's "vow of strictest purity" – by assuming it part of God's greater plan "To set his people free." While the Chorus seeks to avert the "vain reasonings" of those who would "confine th'Interminable, / And tie him to his own prescript" (lines 317–322, 307–8), Melville calls the Chorus's assertion ("laws to bind us, not himself") not "vain reasonings," but rather, ironically echoing Milton's words,

Noble rhetoric but vile reasoning.

The Chorus suggests that attempts to render intelligible the ways of God are both futile and presumptuous ("vain"). But Melville's word "vile," a word Samson repeatedly associates with his own moral degradation and corruption (lines 376–7, 1361), implies the corruption or distortion of reason, a sophistry in the service of a theology of incommensurability. (Here the Chorus reminds us of such a character as Starbuck, who could assert against all experience and all logic, though with more self-conscious awareness of what doubts he must suppress and what rationale he must resort to, "Tell me not of thy teeth-tiered sharks, and thy kidnapping cannibal ways. Let faith oust fact; let fancy oust memory; I look deep down and do believe" [*M-D*, 492].) Presumably Melville is troubled either by the single-minded logic of the Chorus, which insists upon a plan of divine benevolence, or by the dubious logic that calls a scheme "just" that is in fact a unilaterally flexible covenant. This annotation suggests that Melville finds Milton's Chorus unconvincing in its attempt to acquit God, and the Chorus's failure, to his mind, seems to leave the supreme deity vulnerable to the charges of insidious betrayal, contrariety, or complete opacity.

From Melville's annotation of Dalila's last words to Samson, which we will next examine, it seems he believes that Milton intended to leave God undefended. Melville intimates that Milton establishes the credibility of Dalila in order to discredit Samson's God. His eye is drawn to Dalila's final speech (lines 960–96). Melville marks, with an X for annotation, the words in which Dalila attempts to vindicate both her actions and especially her legacy according to the exigencies and values of her own Philistian culture, claiming that she will be "Not less renown'd than in Mount Ephraim / Jael, who with inhospitable guile / Smote Sisera sleeping through the temples nail'd" (lines 989–90). Melville, who knew the Bible intimately, apparently feels pleased and vindicated in surmising Milton's heterodox intent, for in this passage in which Milton depicts Dalila comparing herself with Jael, Melville finds the conclusive evidence he sought:[18]

> There is basis for the doubt expressed by A. Marvel in his lines to Milton on the publication of P. Lost. There was a twist in Milton. From its place, the above marked passage has an interesting significance. (Melville's underscoring)

William Empson, a critic known for his hostility toward Christianity and especially for his antagonism to Milton's God, remarked of these particular lines that "To recall the Israelite Jael is a telling stroke; Shelley could have said here too that the decisive proof of Milton's genius is that he alleged no moral superiority for Jehovah's religion over Dagon's."[19] In explicating the association of Jael with Dalila, Empson is of course both echoing and extrapolating from Shelley's assessment in *A Defence of Poetry* (a passage that Melville later [in 1873] marked in his personal copy of Shelley's *Essays, Letters from Abroad, Translations and Fragments*) that "Milton has so far violated the popular creed . . . as to have alleged no superiority of moral virtue to his God over his Devil. And this bold neglect of a direct moral purpose is the most decisive proof of the supremacy of Milton's genius."[20] Given the Dalila/Jael passage in *Samson Agonistes*, Empson rightly calls attention not only to Shelley's belief that Milton subverts didactic expectations but also to the doubt cast on both theological and cultural systems by their juxtaposition.

Yet for Melville, Milton's parallel between Jael and Dalila is neither a token of (Satanic) Promethean heroism that dares to defy the tyranny of monotheism or of an unjust god, nor the sign of a Manichean universe divided equally between contending forces of good and evil.[21] Rather, given that Melville associates Milton's comparison of the two women with Marvell's suspicion about his intent to "ruine the sacred truths" and given that Melville also underscores the line "God sent her to debase me" (line 999), which precedes his annotation on the same page, Melville, it seems, finds the "twist in Milton" here to be a bias or bent of mind that insists upon desecrating the sacred truths already mysteriously desecrated by God. In claiming that the Dalila/Jael passage becomes particularly remarkable "from its place" in the text, Melville may well be suggesting that Dalila's comparison with Jael is her attempt to wrest for herself a legend of virtue and dutifulness from Samson's sarcastic, cursing omen about her legacy ("Bewail thy falsehood, and the pious works / It hath brought forth to make thee memorable / Among illustrious women, faithful wives!" [lines 955–7]). Samson alludes to a Jael-like figure (herself a prophesied deliverer of her nation in Judges 4:14) as the exemplum of commendable womanly behavior, but Dalila appropriates this paragon of illustrious womanhood and serves it back to him utterly transformed. And so whereas Dalila appears to dignify her actions by comparing herself with Jael, her analogy may function for Melville as a kind of reverse typological scheme in which her antitypic misdeed actually contaminates the ostensible deed of the type, Jael. It may seem to Melville that, in having Dalila compare herself with Jael, Milton's desire is to render opaque, doubtful, or substantially vitiated any supposed moral clarity or triumph attaching to Jael's deed. The nobility of Jael's "deed" is illusory because Milton's comparison of the two women (a comparison not made in the Book of Judges) aggravates the already dubious nature of Jael's brutal deed of "inhospitable guile." The dubious nature of both women's deeds is highlighted further in the ironic symmetry Milton creates by deliberately and explicitly connecting their stories: Jael is the "illustrious" Israelite woman who betrays a Canaanite for her nation; Dalila, a Canaanite/Philistine, is the "memorable" woman who betrays an Israelite for her nation.

In the betraying action of Dalila, Milton could be said to be only mirroring an already obscure, God-inspired act – one that also has far-reaching implications for Samson's own final act of violence. For Melville here, Milton's depiction of Dalila does not quite offer the clarity needed to support a Shelleyan accusation of divine malice or injustice. Rather, Milton "would ruine the sacred truths" by amplifying the already equivocal, by exacerbating the tension between what are deemed to be morally unambiguous, God-inspired acts and what are actually clouded, difficult, and uncertain moral and spiritual discriminations. And Melville here – and in his *Mardi* and *Moby-Dick* – seems less concerned with a contest of cultures and religions that effectually privileges one over the other or cancels both in atheistic neutrality. Rather, given the passages and lines he singles out on this page of *Samson* as the "basis" for Marvell's "doubt" about Milton's motives, it seems Melville is more concerned with the nearly unbridgeable epistemological chasm between humankind and the insurgent but inscrutable forces of the metaphysical world. It may be that the rage of Milton's Samson so fascinates Melville not because it is the idiom of righteous anger that embraces God's plan, however uncomprehendingly, but because it is the expression of poignant frustration and devastating bewilderment of the sort both Ishmael and Ahab at times experience. Significantly too for Melville, Dalila as the cultural "other" serves to vex what are supposed to be clear moral, cultural, and theological values and hierarchies – a role that we saw Queequeg, and more pervasively, Ishmael, fulfill in Chapter 5 of this book.

I have suggested that Melville believed Milton himself to be a provoked and perplexed Samson figure, and that several of Melville's annotations attest to his view of Milton's cunning and vindictive opacity – an opacity that mimetically reproduces that which seems to remain obscure by divine intent. These preceding annotations have suggested a Milton disinclined to conclude injustice from divine inscrutability. Yet some of Melville's other comments do recall the acerbic criticism of Christianity and the Christian God in Shelley's *Defence of Poetry* and *Queen Mab*, Byron's *Cain,* and Blake's *Marriage of Heaven and Hell*. But even these annotations in one way or another move away from the English Romantic poets' angered certainty of divine sadism. Instead, Melville ascribes to Milton a strongly skeptical theological bias from which, much to his apparent satisfaction, Melville is prompted to pursue inferences and implications altogether devastating to Christian theology and theodicy alike.

Melville's eyes, for example, are drawn to Satan's criticism of God's motives in Book IX of *Paradise Lost*. Melville scores in the margin or underlines on the same page three different, potentially atheistic arguments made by Satan in tempting Eve. First

Melville scores the lines that could be read as an argument from the limitation or incompleteness of God's creation that no infinite God exists, for Satan claims that "life more perfect have [I] attain'd than fate / Meant me, by vent'ring higher than my lot" (line 689–90). Then Melville underscores the line that (like Samson's words "the contradiction / Of their own deity, / Gods cannot be") could be viewed as an argument refuting the existence of an omnipotent God who is perfect in His goodness: "Not just, not God" (line 701). Finally Melville scores, marks for annotation, and partly underscores the words of Satan's that seem to refute an infinite God, deny human agency, and depict a mean-spirited, trivialized deity: "Why then was this forbid? Why but to awe, / Why but to keep ye low and ignorant,/His worshippers" (lines 703–5). In a partially erased comment, Melville responds to Satan's words:

> This is one of the many profound atheistical hits of Milton. A greater than Lucretius since he always teaches under a masque, and makes the Devil himself a Teacher & Messiah.

It is likely that in Melville's view, Satan's announcement of his intentions at the beginning of his temptation speech ("not only to discern / Things in their causes, / but to trace the ways of highest agents, deemed however wise" [lines 681–3]) clearly invites a comparison with the Lucretian project both to demystify religion and to explain the workings of a universe in which the divine is irrelevant. Melville's comparison of Milton with Lucretius, I suggest, significantly modifies the otherwise Romantic tenor of his comment. Accordingly, while Blake's words in *The Marriage of Heaven and Hell* may resonate in the phrase "makes the Devil himself a Teacher & Messiah," the authentic, powerful contrarieties of Devil and Messiah in Blake's cosmogony seem to be belied by the satiric disposition Melville ascribes to a Milton who would offer a "greater" "atheistical hit" than Lucretius by "always teach[ing] under a [demonic] masque."[22] In this annotation, Melville, in referring to Milton's concealing "masque," may be echoing Shelley's *Defence of Poetry:* "The distorted notions of invisible things which Dante and his rival Milton have idealised, are merely the mask and mantle in which these great poets walk through eternity enveloped and disguised."[23] But more particularly, he seems to intimate in his comment that Milton consciously employs his "masque" as a provocative affront ("makes the Devil himself a Teacher & Messiah") to the prevailing orthodoxy. Moreover, Melville reveals here his supposition that authors teach and even prophesy by exploiting the disguise of their characters – "masques" (Landor's of Milton and Marvell; Milton's of Samson, Dalila, and Satan; and Melville's of Ahab and Ishmael) that encode or render ironically some mediated version of the author's own thoughts, doubts, or anxieties. Indeed, Chapter 5 discussed how Melville exploited a double "masque" in the character of Ishmael and his appropriation of Sir Thomas Browne's probabilist methods.

Melville's associations of Milton's own beliefs with Satan's do not ascribe to Milton a forthright allegiance to Satan (either acknowledged or unacknowledged by Milton). Rather, Melville ascribes to Milton an ironic stance toward Satan that should not be overlooked. Neither in the annotation just quoted nor in the ones to follow does Melville suggest, as Blake did, that Milton was "of the Devils party without knowing it," nor does Melville locate the vitality of Milton's imagination in the counterpoint of the demonic. Instead, here and in the annotations discussed later in this chapter, Melville attributes to Milton an imaginative vehemence more directed at God and Christian theology than displayed in his depiction of Satan's character – the "energy and magnificence" that Shelley, by contrast, claimed would never be exceeded. Melville intimates that in choosing as his spokesman the very symbol of terror (which, according to Lucretius, was fostered by priestcraft), Milton ridicules and makes a mockery of the entire Christian theological system. Melville ascribes to Milton calculated, highly self-conscious interrogations of the divine scheme that Milton (according to Melville) cleverly and often ironically camouflages by ascribing to the character of Satan. Melville's vocabulary of theatrical disguise and *dramatis personae* in both the annotation just quoted ("always teaches under a masque") and the next one ("Put into Satan's mouth, but spoken with John Milton's tongue") highlights his sense that Milton employs artifice and ironic mediation to articulate his challenges – a tactic that constrains and probably forecloses the speculation that Melville is clearly ascribing to Milton a belief in an inverted theology of diabolism or in Manicheanism. Here we might be tempted to recall Captain Ahab's blasphemous challenges and the taunting "pasteboard mask" that drives Ahab to a frenzy because he would know the malicious, "unknown but still reasoning thing [that] puts forth the mouldings of its features from behind the unreasoning mask" (*M-D*, 164). And yet the spirit of the annotations discussed here comes closer to Ishmael's thinly veiled, skeptical affront to religion in the Whaleman's Chapel.

There Ishmael posits no "reasoning thing" behind the mask but rather seems to dwell on the inscrutable mask itself, and so provocatively acknowledges the legerdemain of cenotaphs as well as that of "Faith, [that] like a jackal, feeds among the tombs, and even from these dead doubts . . . gathers her most vital hope" (*M-D*, 37).

In his comment on Satan's words in *Paradise Regained,* Melville similarly casts Milton as the ventriloquist who exploits Satan to tarnish the monotheistic injunction ("Thou shalt worship / The Lord thy God, and only him shalt serve") by showing it harshly reflected in the (Satanic) son's own desire to subordinate Christ and be worshiped ("if thou wilt fall down / And worship me as thy superior lord" [IV.166–7]). About Satan's words challenging the unique status of Christ as the created Son of God ("Be not so sore offended, Son of God, / Though sons of God both angels are and men" [IV.197]), Melville remarks:

> Put into Satan's mouth, but spoken with John Milton's tongue; – conveys a strong controversial meaning.[24]

Melville's response does not so much aim to show, as Byron's *Cain* asserts, that "the snake spoke *truth*" and therefore offers a plausible, inverted orthodoxy,[25] as that the Satanic character provides Milton with the means to display further the self-evidently dubious nature of the God of Christian theology.[26]

Even when Melville's comments sound like Byron's *Cain* and his own Ahab when they are most convinced of God's divine malice, the certainty of Melville's conviction is mitigated by his own emendation or by the language he uses to articulate his point. In Book X of *Paradise Lost,* for example, Melville scores the lines (8–16) where the narrator asserts the wisdom and justness of God in permitting Satan to "attempt the mind / Of man," for Adam and Eve were "with strength entire, and freewill arm'd, / Complete to have discover'd and repuls'd / Whatever wiles of foe or seeming friend!" To this justification Melville responds:

> The fall of Adam did not so much prove him weak, as that God had made him so. From all that is gatherable from Milton's theology the Son was created. Now, had the Son been planted in the Garden (instead of Adam) he would have withstood the temptation; – Why then he & not Adam? Because of his created superiority to Adam. [At some later point Melville adds:] Sophomoricus

What is striking about Melville's initial response (in addition to his curious effacement of Eve) is his unequivocal belief in the Fall as God's house of cards. Melville finds the argument for human agency no more plausible than Byron's Cain, who similarly asks, though with more belligerence, "The tree was planted, and why not for him? / If not, why place him near it, where it grew, / The fairest in the centre?" (I.i.72–4). The logic of Melville's annotation (like Ahab's conviction) seems to move toward Cain's doubt: "Because / He is all-powerful, must all-good, too follow?" (I.i.76–7). And yet from this stifling necessitarian argument and implicit condemnation of God's omnipotent malice, Melville eventually withdraws at some later time, for the self-judgment "Sophomoricus" suggests a mind that now perceives the theological issues with greater complexity, or perhaps with less certainty of divine culpability.

Melville's imagination does seem to find the inscrutable omnipotence and omniscience of Milton's God more compelling and more troublesome than the apparently hollow assertions of free will in *Paradise Lost*. And yet the more Melville is able to imagine an omnipotent, inescapable God, the more he attempts to find ways to circumscribe and demystify him. From God's assertions in Book X of *Paradise Lost* (lines 43–7) that "no decree of mine / Concurring to necessitate his fall, / Or touch with lightest moment of impulse / His free will, to her own inclining left / In even scale," Melville concludes:

> All Milton's strength & rhetoric suffice not to satisfy, concerning this matter – free-will. Doubtless, he must have felt it himself; & looked upon it as the one great unavoidable flaw in his work. But, indeed, God's alleged omnipotence and foreknowledge are insuperable bars to his being made an actor in any drama, imagined.

Since this annotation echoes the long talks Melville reports having with German philosopher George Adler on "Fixed Fate, Free-will, fore-knowledge absolute" (Melville's journal entry for October 12, 1849 [*Paradise Lost,* II.560]), this comment probably dates from the period of Melville's sea voyage to England in the fall of 1849 (from which he returned to begin *Moby-Dick*). As with the "Noble rhetoric but vile reasoning" of the Chorus in *Samson Agonistes,* Melville is thoroughly unpersuaded by Milton's "rhetoric" attempting to exculpate God or to render plausible the dynamic of meaningful human agency in the context of divine omnipotence and omniscience. The general sense of Melville's comment is one of defeat (Milton's, his own, and perhaps Ahab's) in the face of either doctrinal consistency or, more particularly, the desire to harness divine power and knowledge for one's own purposes. The concession, however, is tinged with skepticism and entertains judicial doubt, since God's omnipotence and fore-knowledge are only "alleged," not proven. Melville in fact tries Milton in court, claiming in formal and legalistic language that despite Milton's abilities, they "suffice not to satisfy, concerning this matter" due to "God's alleged omnipotence" and the "insu-perable bars to his being made an actor in any drama." Although Melville distances himself from Milton in judging him, there is yet a sense here of collegial compassion: Melville commiserates with the aesthetic problems, if not the doctrinal conundrums, that Milton attempts to "justify," confirming, as if from Melville's own artistic experience, "But, indeed, God's alleged omnipotence and foreknowledge are insuperable bars." Melville retreats from the theological implications of this divine drama by instead focus-ing upon the aesthetic problems with which Milton was forced to grapple – with the tensions between theological requirements and aesthetic effectiveness, between divine foreknowledge and the writer's attempt to construct an affecting and plausible narra-tive: "Doubtless, he must have felt it himself; & looked upon it as the one great unavoidable flaw in his work." As seen in his com-ments on Milton's more compliant "actors," Melville has shown himself disposed toward making characters complex disguises for his own skeptical challenges and interrogations. Yet here Melville, no less than the Milton he portrays, is confounded as an artist by this unmanageable "Actor" at the center of the drama, for whom no plausible script of positive doctrine can be written.

And so the drama revealed by these annotations is also one of a tension within Melville projected upon Milton – between the impulse toward Ahab's Samson-like powerful frustration but also certainty of divine malice and consequent desire to defy, and the impulse toward the skeptical Ishmael who at times, like Dalila and Satan, mockingly mirrors the equivocation elicited by a deity so inscrutable that his very existence must be inferred from the questions he raises. In 1856, Nathaniel Hawthorne described Melville himself as wavering: "he can neither believe, nor be comfortable in his disbelief; and he is too honest and courageous not to try to do one or the other."[27] Not surprisingly, Melville responds to Milton's numerous denominational realignments de-scribed in the prefatory biography – from Puritanism to Calvinism to "an esteem for Arminius" to an accordance with Independents and Anabaptists to a final antipathy toward all ecclesiastical institutions – with empathy for Milton's restless unease. Hawthorne believed that Melville himself "will never rest until he gets hold of a definite belief," and yet "it is strange how he persists – and has persisted ever since I knew him, and probably long before – in wandering to-and-fro over these deserts."[28] A similar restlessness led Milton, according to Melville, to more daring and more troubling speculations than those elicited by the search for the ideal ecclesiastical institution. On the biography of Milton prefacing the poetry, Melville inscribes the knowing affirmation,

> He who thinks for himself never can remain of the same mind. I doubt not that darker doubts crossed Milton's soul, than ever disturbed Voltair. And he was more of what is called an Infidel.

NOTES

Abbreviations of Works Cited

CA	Izaak Walton, *The Complete Angler,* ed. Jonquil Bevan (London: Everyman, 1993).
CPW	John Milton, *The Complete Prose Works of John Milton,* ed. Don M. Wolfe et al. (New Haven: Conn.: Yale University Press, 1953–82).
CS	Ralph Waldo Emerson, *The Complete Sermons of Ralph Waldo Emerson,* ed. Albert J. von Frank et al., 4 vols. (Columbia, Mo.: University of Missouri Press, 1989-92).
"Discourse"	John Locke, *"The Reasonableness of Christianity" with "A Discourse of Miracles"* . . . , ed. I. T. Rawsey (Stanford: Stanford University Press, 1958).
EL	Ralph Waldo Emerson, *The Early Lectures of Ralph Waldo Emerson, 1833–1836,* ed. Stephen E. Whicher and Robert E. Spiller, 3 vols. (Cambridge, Mass.: Harvard University Press, 1966–72).
EPGH	George Herbert, *The English Poetry of George Herbert,* ed. F. E. Hutchinson rev. ed. (1941; Oxford: Clarendon Press, 1945).
Essay	John Locke, *An Essay Concerning Human Understanding,* ed. Alexander Campbell Fraser, 2 vols. (1894; rpt. New York: Dover, 1959).
Hy	Sir Thomas Browne, *Hydriotaphia, Urn Burial, or a Discourse of the Sepulchral Urns Lately Found in Norfolk* in *Sir Thomas Browne's Works,* ed. Simon Wilkin, 4 vols. (London: William Pickering, 1835-6).
JMN	Ralph Waldo Emerson, *The Journals and Miscellaneous Notebooks of Ralph Waldo Emerson,* ed. William H. Gilman, Alfred R. Ferguson et al., 16 vols. (Cambridge, Mass.: Belknap Press of Harvard University Press, 1963–80).
Letters	Margaret Fuller, *The Letters of Margaret Fuller,* ed. Robert N. Hudspeth, 5 vols. (Ithaca: Cornell University Press, 1983–).
M	*The Memoirs of Margaret Fuller Ossoli,* ed. Ralph Waldo

Emerson, James Freeman Clarke, and William Henry Channing (Boston: Phillips, Sampson, 1852).

M-D   Herman Melville, *Moby-Dick, or The Whale,* ed. Harrison Hayford, Hershel Parker, and G. Thomas Tanselle (Evanston: Northwestern University and Newberry Library, 1988).

PE   Sir Thomas Browne, *Pseudodoxia Epidemica or Enquiries into Very Many Received Tenets and Commonly Presumed Truths,* in *Sir Thomas Browne's Works, Including His Life and Correspondence,* ed. Simon Wilkin, 4 vols. (London: William Pickering, 1835–6).

Religio   Sir Thomas Browne, *Religio Medici* in *Sir Thomas Browne's Works, Including His Life and Correspondence,* ed. Simon Wilkin, 4 vols. (London: William Pickering, 1835–6).

Reform Papers   Henry David Thoreau, *Reform Papers,* ed. Wendell Glick (Princeton, N.J.: Princeton University Press, 1973).

W   Ralph Waldo Emerson, *The Complete Works of Ralph Waldo Emerson,* Centenary Edition, 12 vols. (Boston: Houghton Mifflin, 1903–4).

Walden   Henry David Thoreau, *Walden,* ed. J. Lydon Shanley (Princeton, N.J.: Princeton University Press, 1971).

Week   Henry David Thoreau, *A Week on the Concord and Merrimack Rivers,* ed. Carl F. Hovde, William L. Howarth, Elizabeth Hall Witherell (Princeton, N.J.: Princeton University Press, 1980).

Writings   Henry David Thoreau, *The Writings of Henry David Thoreau,* Walden Edition, 20 vols. (Boston: Houghton Mifflin, 1906).

Introduction: Antebellum America & 17th-cent. England

1. F. O. Matthiessen, *American Renaissance: Art and Expression in the Age of Emerson and Whitman* (New York: Oxford University Press, 1941), pp. 100–32.

2. For example, Sherman Paul, *The Shores of America: Thoreau's Inward Exploration* (Urbana: University of Illinois Press, 1958); Merton M. Sealts, Jr., "Melville and the Platonic Tradition" (1980), in *Pursuing Melville: 1940–1980* (Madison: University of Wisconsin Press, 1981); editors' "Explanatory Notes" in Herman Melville, *Moby-Dick,* ed. Luther S. Mansfield and Howard P. Vincent (New York: Hendricks House, 1962).

3. Donald E. Pease, *Visionary Compacts: American Renaissance Writings in Cultural Context* (Madison: University of Wisconsin Press, 1987), p. 269.

4. Yvor Winters, *Maule's Curse: Seven Studies in the History of American Obscurantism* (New York: New Directions, 1938); Perry Miller, *The New England Mind: The Seventeenth Century* (New York: Macmillan,

1939); Sacvan Bercovitch, *The Puritan Origins of the American Self* (New Haven, Conn.: Yale University Press, 1975); Richard Chase, *The American Novel and Its Tradition* (Garden City, N.Y.: Doubleday, 1957); Harold Bloom, *The Anxiety of Influence: A Theory of Poetry* (New York: Oxford University Press, 1973); Harold Bloom, *A Map of Misreading* (New York: Oxford University Press, 1975); Robert Weisbuch, *Atlantic Double-Cross: American Literature and British Influence in the Age of Emerson* (Chicago: University of Chicago Press, 1986); Leon Chai, *The Romantic Foundations of the American Renaissance* (Ithaca, N.Y.: Cornell University Press, 1987). Weisbuch does acknowledge the importance of English writers of the Renaissance, but devotes his demonstrations to the Romantic and Victorian periods.

5. Sacvan Bercovitch, "How the Puritans Won the American Revolution," *The Massachusetts Review* 17 (1976), 597–630; Sacvan Bercovitch, *The Rites of Assent: Transformations in the Symbolic Construction of America* (London: Routledge, 1993); Keith W. F. Stavely, *Puritan Legacies: "Paradise Lost" and the New England Tradition, 1630–1890* (Ithaca, N.Y.: Cornell University Press, 1987); K. P. Van Anglen, *The New England Milton: Literary Reception and Cultural Authority in the Early Republic* (University Park: Pennsylvania State University Press, 1993). Both Stavely and Van Anglen depict the conservative motive to accommodate in such a way as to suppress "antinomian" impulses in a culture otherwise rational, orderly, law-abiding, and "Arminian."

6. For an example of the Democratic Party's interest in seventeenth-century English culture as a source of political ideas and strategies, see the series of papers by a Young American radical Democrat, William A. Jones, "Political Theories of the English Commonwealth" (including discussions of John Milton, James Harrington, Andrew Marvell, Algernon Sidney, and Andrew Fletcher), *Democratic Review* 11 (September 1842).

7. Perry Miller, *New England Mind: Seventeenth Century;* Miller, *The New England Mind: From Colony to Province* (New York: Macmillan, 1953); Miller, ed., *The Transcendentalists: An Anthology* (Cambridge, Mass.: Harvard University Press, 1950); Bercovitch, *Puritan Origins*.

8. Bernard Bailyn, *The Ideological Origins of the American Revolution* (Cambridge, Mass.: Harvard University Press, 1967). See also Stanley Elkins and Eric McKitrick, *The Age of Federalism: The Early American Republic, 1788–1800* (New York: Oxford University Press, 1993), p. 6.

9. Russell Reising, in *The Unusable Past: Theory and Study of American Literature* (New York: Methuen, 1986), criticizes American studies as over-aestheticized and divorced from social and political connections. He does not, however, explore nationalist issues.

10. Albert J. von Frank, *The Sacred Game: Provincialism and Frontier Consciousness in American Literature, 1630–1860* (Cambridge University Press, 1985).

11. For a discussion of the radical Democratic Young American literary agenda, particularly as it was presented in the *United States Magazine and Democratic Review,* see John Stafford, *The Literary Criticism of*

"Young America" (1952; rpt. New York: Russell and Russell, 1967), and Michael Paul Rogin, *Subversive Genealogy: The Politics and Art of Herman Melville* (Berkeley and Los Angeles: University of California Press, 1979), ch. 2. For a discussion of the Whigs' literary and social values, see Stafford, as well as Perry Miller, *The Raven and the Whale: The War of Words and Wits in the Era of Poe and Melville* (New York: Harcourt Brace, 1956).

12. Thomas Gustafson, in *Representative Words: Politics, Literature, and the American Language, 1776–1865* (Cambridge University Press, 1992), has attempted to historicize attitudes toward language theories and rhetoric, correlating a perceived relationship between corrupt language and political corruption. See also Michael P. Kramer, *Imagining Language in America: From the Revolution to the Civil War* (Princeton: Princeton University Press, 1992), on alternative canons; Donald Weber, *Rhetoric and History in Revolutionary New England* (New York: Oxford University Press, 1988), on revolutionary rhetoric; and Philip Gura, *The Wisdom of Words* (Middletown, Conn.: Wesleyan University Press, 1981), on language practice in antebellum America.

13. Stavely, *Puritan Legacies;* Van Anglen, *New England Milton;* David S. Reynolds, *Beneath the American Renaissance: The Subversive Imagination in the Age of Emerson and Melville* (Cambridge, Mass.: Harvard University Press, 1989).

14. Orestes A. Brownson, "Literary Notices," *Boston Quarterly Review* 1 (January 1838), 126.

15. Some of the studies mentioned earlier, particularly Michael Kramer's, do attempt to acknowledge the aesthetic dimensions of texts as well.

16. On the Americans' familiarity with Madame de Staël's study, as well as Edward Everett's discussion of the relation between government and the cultivation of letters, see Jared Sparks, review of Edward Everett's "Oration pronounced at Cambridge, before the Phi Beta Kappa Society, August 27, 1824" and "Oration delivered at Plymouth, December 22, 1824," *North American Review* 20 (April 1825), 435. See also "The Life and Writings of Madame de Stael," *Christian Examiner,* new ser. 3 (July 1820), 129–31. On nationality and literature, see also William Ellery Channing's "Remarks on National Literature," a review of "The Influence of America on the Mind," an oration by C. J. Ingersoll (1823), in *The Works of William E. Channing, D. D.,* 8th ed., 6 vols. (Boston: James Munroe, 1848), 1:245–80.

17. "Nationality in Literature," *Democratic Review* 20 (March 1847), 267. John Stafford, in *Literary Criticism of "Young America,"* pp. 87, 138, ascribes the authorship to Evert Duyckinck.

18. James Freeman Clarke, *Autobiography, Diary and Correspondence,* ed. Edward Everett Hale (Boston: Houghton Mifflin, 1891), pp. 38–39.

19. *The Memoirs of Margaret Fuller Ossoli,* ed. Ralph Waldo Emerson, James Freeman Clarke, and William Henry Channing, 2 vols. (Boston: Phillips, Sampson, 1852), 1:204.

20. "Sir Thomas Browne," *American Review: A Whig Journal Devoted to Politics and Literature* 8 (July 1848), 15–23, esp. p. 20.

21. The occasion was the meeting on February 3, 1865, of Lincoln with the Confederate commissioners on the Union steamer *River Queen*. From Alexander H. Stephens, *A Constitutional View of the Late War Between the States* (Philadelphia: National Publishing Company, 1868), 2:613.

22. See, for example, the long review "History of the English Revolution of 1640," *Democratic Review* 21 (August 1847), 33–44; 141–9. For a conservative view, see W. Dowe, "The Puritan Revolution in England," *North American Review* 76 (April 1853), 336–69, esp. p. 367. On the new scope given to language and originality by the English Revolution, see W. H. Prescott, "Chateaubriand's Sketches of English Literature: The Influence of the Reformation upon Eloquence," *North American Review* 49 (October 1839), 324–38. On the conservative motive in the English Revolution, see C. C. Smith, review of "On the Causes of the English Revolution of 1640–1688," *Christian Examiner* 49 (September 1850), 287–9. See also Samuel Osgood, "Milton in our Day," *Christian Examiner* 57 (November 1854), 327.

23. Edward Everett, *Catalogue of the Private Libraries of William Everett, and his father Hon. Edward Everett* (Boston, C. F. Libbie, Book and Art Auctioneers, 1910). In the catalogue, *Eikon Basilike* (1648–9) is listed under its subtitle *The Portraiture of His Sacred Majesty in His Solitudes and Sufferings*.

24. Another American reviewer also mentions Mrs. Hutchinson's memoirs approvingly, complaining that Clarendon's, Whitlock's, and Baxter's royalist biases made them unfit to give a final estimate of Cromwell or Laud. See the review of Carlyle's life of Cromwell and edition of his letters, "Cromwell and His Times," *Democratic Review* 18 (May 1846), 339. Lucy Hutchinson is quoted in Emerson, "Woman," in *The Complete Works of Ralph Waldo Emerson* (Boston: Houghton, Mifflin, 1903–4), 11: 407, and "Courage," in *Works*, 7:273. *The Complete Works of Ralph Waldo Emerson* is here after cited in the text as *W* with volume and page numbers. Hutchinson is quoted in Fuller, *Woman in the Nineteenth Century*, in *The Essential Margaret Fuller*, ed. Jeffrey Steele (New Brunswick, N.J.: Rutgers University Press, 1992), p. 279. (Steele and previous editors of Fuller's work misidentify Colonel Hutchinson as Col. Thomas Hutchinson, the eighteenth-century American royalist. Fuller, however, in *Woman* quotes a comment from Lucy Hutchinson's *Memoirs* [c. 1670] about companionate marriages: " 'on this side idolatry' because it was religious." Moreover, the English context and the mention of the Tower [of London] can only refer to the English regicide John Hutchinson [1615 – 64].)

25. J. Sullivan Cox, "Imaginary Commonwealths," *United States Magazine and Democratic Review* 19 (September 1846), 175–85. Hereafter cited in the text as "Cox" with page numbers. Citations from the

writings of John Milton will refer to the *Complete Prose Works of John Milton*, ed. Don M. Wolfe et al., 8 vols. (New Haven, Conn.: Yale University Press, 1953–82). Hereafter cited in the text as *CPW*, with volume and page numbers. Cox substitutes "their" for "her" and "scaling" for Milton's "unscaling."

26. Cox quotes Edward Everett, who echoes Berkeley's verse, "Westward the course of empire takes its way." On the notion of *translatio* as it moves from eighteenth-century English Country party ideology into Augustan American ideology, see William C. Dowling, *Poetry and Ideology in Revolutionary Connecticut* (Athens: University of Georgia Press, 1990), pp. 47–8.

27. Bercovitch, *Rites of Assent*, ch. 5, esp. pp. 151–6.

28. See Bailyn, *Ideological Origins*, pp. 34–5; and the discussion on the American republic in J. G. A. Pocock, *The Machiavellian Moment* (Princeton: Princeton University Press, 1975). Although George F. Sensabaugh's *Milton in Early America* (New York: Gordian Press, 1979) extensively treats Milton's poetry, it omits discussion of his polemical prose altogether.

29. Daniel Walker Howe, *The Political Culture of the American Whigs* (Chicago: University of Chicago Press, 1979), p. 88. For the British Real Whigs, the Stuarts also provided cautionary tales against tyrants. See the history that was popular in America, Catharine Graham Macaulay's *The History of England from the Accession of James I to the Elevation of the House of Hanover*, 2d ed. (London, 1766), 1:ix.

30. Bercovitch, *Rites of Assent*, esp. ch. 6; David Levin, *History as Romantic Art: Bancroft, Prescott, Motley, and Parkman*, (Stanford, Calif.: Stanford University Press, 1959); Reginald Horsman, *Race and Manifest Destiny: The Origins of American Racial Anglo-Saxonism* (Cambridge, Mass.: Harvard University Press, 1981).

31. On Harrington's political system, see J. G. A. Pocock, *The Political Works of James Harrington* (Cambridge University Press, 1977), pp. 6–76; Charles Blitzer, *An Immortal Commonwealth: The Political Thought of James Harrington* (New Haven, Conn.: Yale University Press, 1960). On the transmission of Harrington's political ideas to American colonists, see H. F. Russell Smith, *Harrington and His Oceana* (Cambridge University Press, 1914).

32. Daniel Webster, "The First Settlement of New England" (presented at Plymouth, Mass., in 1820), and "The Basis of the Senate" (presented at the Massachusetts Constitutional Convention of 1820), in *Writings and Speeches* (Boston: Little, Brown, 1903), 1:210–16; 5:14–16.

33. David Simpson, *The Politics of American English 1776–1850* (New York: Oxford University Press, 1986).

34. Orestes A. Brownson, "American Literature," *Boston Quarterly Review* 3 (January 1840), 70.

35. In his review of "Norton on the *Evidences of Christianity [The Genuineness of the Four Gospels]*," Orestes A. Brownson uses "opaque" as the

term the "the disciples of Locke" (Whigs) might use to impugn the social and political views of the "people." See *Boston Quarterly Review* 2 (January 1839), 111. In Brownson's review of Francis Bowen's "Locke and the Transcendentalists," he calls Locke's writing and philosophy, by contrast, "transparent" (meaning facile but immediately intelligible). See Brownson, "*The Christian Examiner,* No. LXXXIII. November, 1837, Article II., 'Locke and the Transcendentalists,'" *Boston Quarterly Review* 1 (January 1838), 87. Emerson frequently used both terms in his essays, particularly *Nature.*

36. See, for example, Gura, *Wisdom of Words.*

37. On Scottish Common Sense realism's subscription to elite values imported from Britain, especially Kames's *Elements,* see William Charvat, *The Origins of American Critical Thought, 1810–1835* (Philadelphia: University of Pennsylvania Press, 1936), p. 42; see also Daniel Walker Howe, *The Unitarian Conscience: Harvard Moral Philosophy, 1805–1861* (Cambridge, Mass.: Harvard University Press, 1970), pp. 83–114.

38. Edward Everett, "Advantage of Knowledge to Workingmen, An Address Delivered as the Introduction to the Franklin Lectures in Boston, November 14, 1831," in *Orations and Speeches on Various Occasions,* 8th ed., 4 vols. (Boston: Little, Brown, 1870), 1:315.

39. S. Margaret Fuller, "The Two Herberts," *Papers on Literature and Art* (London: Wiley & Putnam, 1846), pp. 18, 22–3, 21.

40. Orestes A. Brownson, "The Currency," *Boston Quarterly Review* 3 (January 1840), 107.

41. Henry David Thoreau, *Walden,* ed. J. Lyndon Shanley (Princeton, N.J.: Princeton University Press, 1971), p. 11.

1: Cultural Predicaments, Authorial Responses

1. These cries may well have been public signals showing sympathy with the Democratic Party's Young American agenda for a nativist culture. Emerson, Fuller, Thoreau, and Melville were being sympathetically reviewed in the 1840s by the Young American editorial staffs of the *Democratic Review* and the *Literary World.* See John Stafford, *The Literary Criticism of "Young America": A Study in the Relationship of Politics and Literature, 1837–1850* (1952; rpt. New York: Russell & Russell, 1967).

2. Orestes A. Brownson, "American Literature," *Boston Quarterly Review* 3 (January 1840), 70.

3. J. S. Buckminster, "The Dangers and Duties of a Man of Letters," *Monthly Anthology* 7 (September 1809), 146, 149–50, 156.

4. James Russell Lowell, "Thoreau" (1865) and "Milton's Areopagitica" (1890) in *The Prose Works of James Russell Lowell* (Boston: Houghton Mifflin, 1957), 1:362, 1:97.

5. Orestes A. Brownson, review of "*The Christian Examiner,* No. LXXXIII November, 1837, Article II, *Locke and the Transcendentalists,*" *Boston*

Quarterly Review 1 (January 1838), 96. Hereafter cited in the text as "Locke and the Transcendentalists" with page numbers.

6. For an opposing view on jeremiads related to verbal expression, see Thomas Gustafson, *Representative Words: Politics, Literature, and the American Language, 1776–1865* (Cambridge University Press, 1992); see also his extended discussion of Locke's treatment of language as contractual and liable to abuse, esp. pp. 156–68.

7. Myra Jehlen, *American Incarnation: The Individual, the Nation, the Continent* (Cambridge, Mass.: Harvard University Press, 1986), p. 77. Carolyn Porter also interprets American writers according to this paradigm; see *Being and Seeing: The Plight of the Participant Observer in Emerson, James, Adams, and Faulkner* (Middletown, Conn: Wesleyan University Press, 1981).

8. Alexis de Tocqueville, *Democracy in America,* trans. Henry Reeve, rev. Francis Bowen, ed. Phillips Bradley, 2 vols. (1835, 1862; rpt. New York: Random House, 1945), 2:4–5. I use this translation because it is the one Melville is likely to have read.

9. For a biographically based analysis of what is proposed as Melville's two cultural choices – the Unitarian optimism of his father or the anguished Dutch Calvinist resentment of his mother – see T. Walter Herbert, *"Moby-Dick" and Calvinism: A World Dismantled* (New Brunswick, N.J.: Rutgers University Press, 1977).

10. Citing Scottish Common Sense philosopher Dugald Stewart, Robert D. Richardson, Jr., suggests that Locke's epistemology (which included knowledge gained by reflection) has been mistaken for the simplified versions of his followers (Gassendi, Condillac, and Diderot), whose epistemologies were based more strictly on sense impressions. See Richardson, *Emerson: The Mind on Fire* (Berkeley and Los Angeles: University of California Press, 1995), pp. 30–1. However, on the issue of supernatural phenomena, Locke's requirements for authentication were more narrowly restricted to verifiable sense perceptions.

11. A. A. Livermore, "Reason and Revelation" (1838), reprinted in Sydney E. Ahlstrom and Jonathan S. Carey, *An American Reformation: A Documentary History of Unitarian Christianity* (Middletown, Conn.: Wesleyan University Press, 1985), p. 23; Henry Whitney Bellows, "The Suspense of Faith, A Discourse on the State of the Church" (1859), p. 5. See also F. H. Hedge's "Antisupernaturalism in the Pulpit" (1864): he finds it necessary to define for his audience the differences between science and religion, and laments the encroachments of empiricism and historical biblical criticism without a "corresponding effort to reinstate spiritual truths" (14). These essays are reprinted in Ahlstrom and Carey, *An American Reformation.*

12. Robert Burton, *The Anatomy of Melancholy,* ed. Holbrook Jackson (New York: Vintage Books, 1977), pt. 3, member 2, subsection 1 ("Religious Melancholy in Defect"), p. 384.

13. Andrews Norton, "Two Articles from the Princeton Review, Concerning the Transcendentalist Philosophy of the Germans and of Cousin, and its Influence on Opinion in This Country" (Cambridge, Mass.: J. Owen, 1840), p. 3. J. W. Alexander and Albert Dod, review of "*Elements of Psychology* by Victor Cousin; *Introduction to the History of Philosophy* by Cousin; *An Address* by Ralph Waldo Emerson," *Biblical Repertory and Princeton Review* 11 (January 1839), 37–101, esp. 88. Hereafter cited in the text as "Two Articles" with page numbers.

14. Francis Bowen, "Kant and His Philosophy," reprinted in *Critical Essays on a Few Subjects Connected with the History and Present Condition of Speculative Philosophy* (Boston: Williams, 1842), p. 65.

15. On the connection seen by Whigs between irreverence for tradition, the French Revolution, and Kantian transcendental metaphysics, see "More Gossip from a New Contributor," *American Whig Review* 6 (September 1847), 321. For Whig associations of Bostonian values with a "bee-hive of notions," with Fourierism, and with transcendentalism, see, for example, the "Religious Union of Associationists," *American Whig Review* 5 (May 1847), 492, 498.

16. On the importance of Locke's epistemology and Scottish Common Sense philosophy in eighteenth- and nineteenth-century American society, see Perry Miller, "The Rhetoric of Sensation" in *Errand in the Wilderness* (Cambridge, Mass.: Harvard University Press, 1956), pp. 167–83; Daniel Walker Howe, *The Unitarian Conscience: Harvard Moral Philosophy, 1805 – 1861* (Cambridge, Mass.: Harvard University Press, 1970); Philip F. Gura, *The Wisdom of Words: Language, Theology, and Literature in the New England Renaissance* (Middletown, Conn.: Wesleyan University Press, 1981); Terence Martin, *Instructed Vision: Scottish Common Sense Philosophy and the Origins of American Fiction* (Bloomington: Indiana University Press, 1961) pp. 17–18, 30–1. For discussion of the recoil on the part of conservatives away from the incipient skepticism of the later realists and back toward Locke, see William Charvat, *Origins of American Critical Thought, 1810 – 1835* (Philadelphia: University of Pennsylvania Press, 1936), pp. 39–40, 84–5. On the importance of Locke's political theory in early America, see Bernard Bailyn, *The Ideological Origins of the American Revolution* (Cambridge: Harvard University Press, 1967).

17. On the American Whigs' acceptance of Locke's epistemology, and the "new commercial, industrializing social order they were trying to introduce," see Howe, *Political Culture*, pp. 30–2. For a recent reassessment of the ideological biases in Locke's epistemology, suggesting that Locke's political biases in his own time were largely "populist" in nature, see Richard Ashcraft, *Revolutionary Politics and Locke's "Two Treatises of Government"* (Princeton: Princeton University Press, 1986), p. 458.

18. George Bancroft, "On the Progress of Civilization, or Reasons why the Natural Association of Men of Letters is with the Democracy," *Boston Quarterly Review* 1 (October 1838), 390. For Bancroft's asser-

tion of a democratic aesthetic ("Who are the best judges in matters of taste? Do you think the cultivated individual? Undoubtedly not; but the collective mind"), see "The Office of the People in Art, Government, and Religion, Oration August, 1835," in *Literary and Historical Miscellanies by George Bancroft* (New York: Harper & Brothers, 1855), p. 417. "On the Progress of Civilization" appears to be a revised version of the oration, given at Williamstown College in 1835.

19. Bancroft hoped to write a conciliatory narrative of America's history. Yet despite his larger political ambitions and his family's Whig affiliations, the more radical Democratic impulses in his *History* may still be discerned, however coded and camouflaged. For a contrasting opinion, see Sacvan Bercovitch's interpretation of Bancroft's *History:* his characterization of the *History* makes it virtually indistinguishable from Whig histories. See Sacvan Bercovitch, *The Rites of Assent: Transformations in the Symbolic Construction of America* (London: Routledge, 1993), ch. 6. Edward Pessen characterized Bancroft as an opportunist with aristocratic tastes and romantic notions about "the people" in *Jacksonian America: Society, Personality, and Politics,* rev. ed. (New York: Dorsey, 1978).

20. George Bancroft, *The History of the United States,* 3d ed., (Boston, 1838), 2:377–80 (ch. 16). Hereafter cited in the text as *History* with volume and page numbers. (Bancroft continued to revise and supplement this work for the next forty years.)

21. Letter of July 10, 1840, in *The Life and Letters of George Bancroft,* ed. Mark Antony DeWolfe Howe (New York: Scribner's, 1908), p. 234. Bancroft refers to a new chapter, "Of Enthusiasm" (IV. 19), added to the fourth edition of *Locke's Essay Concerning Human Understanding* in 1700. For the long foreground of this chapter in America, see Perry Miller on Jonathan Edwards's *Divine and Supernatural Light,* in *Jonathan Edwards,* new intro. Donald Weber (1949; rpt. Amherst: University of Massachusetts Press, 1981), pp. 52–68.

22. For a discussion of the radical heritage in American thought, see Staughton Lynd, *Intellectual Origins of American Radicalism* (1968; rpt. Cambridge, Mass.: Harvard University Press, 1982), esp. ch. 4.

23. For a different interpretation of Bancroft's solution to the uncertainties of Lockean contractualism, see Bercovitch, *Rites of Assent,* p. 177. He argues that Bancroft replaced the uncertainties of contractualism with the certainties of filial obedience to the New England fathers, and ultimately, with a model of ideological consensus.

24. On Scottish Common Sense philosophy as a (theological) reaction to the dismissal of innate ideas, see Sydney E. Ahlstrom, "The Scottish Philosophy and American Theology," *Church History* 24 (1955), 257–72.

25. On Scottish Common Sense adaptations "restoring faith in Lockean empiricism," see Howe, *Unitarian Conscience,* pp. 36–44. It has been argued that "moral relativism" was an accurate depiction of Locke's position toward the end of his life, and especially in his *Paraphrase,*

but not an accurate characterization of his earlier work, when he believed that natural reason alone might adequately discern moral obligation. See David Wooton, "John Locke: Socinian or natural law theorist?" in *Religion, Secularization and Political Thought*, ed. James E. Crimmins (London: Routledge, 1990), pp. 39–67.

26. "The Future Policy of the Whigs," *American Whig Review* 1 (April 1848), 330.

27. Orestes A. Brownson, "Norton on the Evidences of Christianity," *Boston Quarterly Review* 2 (January 1839), 110. Hereafter cited in the text as "Norton on the Evidences" with page numbers. The words he quotes are "the author of the History of the United States" – presumably George Bancroft.

28. See, for example, Livermore's widely read tract, "Reason and Revelation" (cited in note 11 to this chapter), pp. 210–20, for references to Locke – explicitly his *Reasonableness of Christianity* (p. 213). Andrews Norton, in "A Discourse on the Latest Form of Infidelity, July, 1839" (Cambridge, Mass.: John Owen, 1839) (hereafter cited in the text as "Infidelity" with page numbers), pp. 23–30, also argued from the premises of that work. For Locke's presence in the Harvard curriculum in 1743 and after, see Conrad Wright, *The Beginnings of Unitarianism in America* (Boston: Beacon Press, 1955) pp. 136–7.

29. Norton, "Infidelity" pp. 32–3. For an illuminating discussion of Unitarian exegesis and epistemology, see Gura, "*Wisdom of Words,* ch. 1.

30. See, for example, the evidentialist language in Norton's "Infidelity," pp. 5–15.

31. [Richard Hildreth], *A Letter to Andrews Norton on Miracles as the Foundation of Religious Faith* (Boston: Weeks, Jordan, 1840), pp. 3–4, 7.

32. For a discussion of the value of internal evidence for Unitarians, see Wesley T. Mott, "*The Strains of Eloquence": Emerson and His Sermons* (University Park: Pennsylvania State University Press, 1989), pp. 54–60. See also Lawrence Buell, "The Literary Significance of the Unitarian Movement," in *American Unitarianism, 1805–1865*, ed. Conrad Edick Wright (Boston: Northeastern University Press, 1989), pp. 174–9. Buell suggests that Channing's "The Evidences of Revealed Religion," often regarded as a classic Unitarian defense of miracles, when taken in its entirety, shows that "Channing hurries through his direct defense, referring his audience to Paley (3:131) and lingers on arguments that would minimize the non-natural of what he fundamentally feels constrained to admit are departures from the natural order" (p. 179, n. 25).

33. David S. Reynolds, *Faith in Fiction: The Emergence of Religious Literature in America* (Cambridge, Mass.: Harvard University Press, 1981), pp. 39, 215.

34. Francis Bowen, *Critical Essays,* p. 322.

35. For a Unitarian example, one might cite Henry R. Bellows, *Restatements of Christian Doctrine: In Twenty-Five Sermons* (New York,

1860), p. 93, who asks, "Will the day ever come when the sacredness we now superstitiously confine to the Scriptures shall be extended to the soul of man, his reason, his affections, his conscience; and to Nature herself – each of them a book of God, all volumes of one work, truly coherent, equally divine, and not intelligible except in connection and harmony with each other?"

36. Ralph Waldo Emerson, *The Journals and Miscellaneous Notebooks of Ralph Waldo Emerson*, ed. William H. Gilman et al., 16 vols. (Cambridge, Mass.: Belknap Press of Harvard University, 1960–82). Hereafter cited in the text as *JMN* with volume and page numbers.

37. Sampson Reed, "Miracles," *New Jerusalem Magazine* 1 (January 1828), 149, transcribed by Emerson in *JMN*, 2:216. On William Furness's contribution of a naturalistic theory of miracles to Transcendentalism in his *Remarks on the Four Gospells* (1836), see William R. Hutchison, *The Transcendentalist Ministers: Church Reform in the New England Renaissance* (New Haven, Conn.: Yale University Press, 1959), pp. 45–6. On the narcissistic element in the Transcendentalist naturalizing of miracles, see Jonathan Bishop, "Emerson and Christianity," *Renascence* 38 (1986), 183–200, esp. 194–6.

38. William Ellery Channing, *The Works of William E. Channing, D. D.*, 8th ed., 6 vols. (Boston: James Munroe, 1848), 3:233. It is but a short distance, too, from Unitarian James Walker's assertion that "When we say that God is wise and just and benevolent . . . we mean that he is wise and just and benevolent as men sometimes are, only in an infinitely higher degree," and Emerson's axiom that "All the attributes of the Deity are attributes of human nature . . . extended to infinity" (*JMN*, 2:24).

39. William Ellery Channing, "On the Character and Writings of Milton," in Channing, *Works*, 1:54. Clearly, Emerson's argument in the Divinity School "Address" and his familiarity with this essay suggest that the "Address" has one of its antecedents here.

40. Still other Unitarians employed the metaphors of the seventeenth-century Cambridge Platonists, describing human reason as the mediating rather than self-authenticating light, "the candle of the Lord" (Emerson calls it "a prior revelation" in 1824 [*JMN*, 2:250]), and scriptural revelation as the "after-revelation." They also described God's ideas, in neoplatonic terms, as "the archetypes of all things." See Daniel Walker Howe, "The Cambridge Platonists of Old England and the Cambridge Platonists of New England," in Wright, *American Unitarianism, 1805–1865*, pp. 95–8. Orestes Brownson hailed the republication of Ralph Cudworth's *The True Intellectual System of the Universe*, 2 vols. (Andover: Gould & Newman, 1837 and 1838), as "a favorable sign of the times, as a proof that there is springing up among us a taste for sound learning, profound erudition, and spiritual philosophy." See *Boston Quarterly Review* 1 (July 1838), 386.

41. Cited in Mott, "*Strains of Eloquence*," p. 72.

42. See Lawrence Buell's "Literary Significance" (cited in note 32) for a discussion of figurative interpretation suggesting that Unitarian defenses of miracles "have the effect of trying to lessen the alterity of the miraculous" (p. 174). See also Wesley T. Mott's argument describing another Unitarian strategy, that of creating a typological relationship between the historically valid but foreshadowing external evidence of miracles and the fulfilled new dispensation of internal evidence. See "*Strains of Eloquence,*" p. 88.

43. On Anglo-American rationalist theology, see Norman Fiering, "The First American Enlightenment: Tillotson, Leverett, and Philosophical Anglicanism," *New England Quarterly* 54 (1981), 315ff; Henry S. Stout, *The New England Soul: Preaching and Religious Culture in Colonial New England* (New York: Oxford University Press, 1986) pp. 127–47, esp. pp. 128–37; Sydney E. Ahlstrom, *A Religious History of the American People* (New Haven, Conn: Yale University Press, 1972), p. 389. For an account by a nineteenth-century contemporary, see Samuel Osgood, *Evert Augustus Duyckinck, His Life, Writings and Influence* (Boston: David Clapp & Son, 1879), pp. 14, 4.

44. Octavius Brooks Frothingham, *Transcendentalism in New England* (1876; rpt. Philadelphia: University of Pennsylvania Press, 1972), p. 110.

45. "Burnet's *Life of Sir Matthew Hale* with Baxter's *Recollections of Hale,*" *American Monthly Review* 2 (1832), 387.

46. On rationalist apologetics in antebellum America, see Ahlstrom, "Scottish Philosophy and American Theology," pp. 257–72, esp. 267–9.

47. Jonathan Bishop, "Emerson and Christianity," p. 196. Bishop argues that the Transcendentalists' sense of the "otherness" of miracles is based upon their relegation to the historical past. Bishop assumes clearer divisions between the Unitarians and Emerson than Mott, Buell, and Howe have recently argued.

48. Duyckinck was also Margaret Fuller's editor at Wiley & Putnam.

49. Evert Duyckinck, "Melville's *Moby-Dick; or The Whale* ('Second Notice')," *Literary World* (November 22, 1851), 404.

50. Osgood, *Duyckinck,* pp. 5, 13, 14; see also, William Allen Butler, *Evert Augustus Duyckinck: A Memorial Sketch, Read before the New York Historical Society, January 7, 1879* (New York: Trow's Printing, 1879), p. 12. On the *New York Review,* see Frank Luther Mott, *History of American Magazines, 1741–1850* (New York: Appleton, 1930), 1:671.

51. George Long Duyckinck later wrote biographies of such Anglican "worthies" as Herbert and Jeremy Taylor for an Episcopalian church society.

52. Evert A. Duyckinck, "George Herbert of Bemerton," *New York Review* 2 (January 1838), 124.

53. Osgood, *Duyckinck,* p. 7.

54. Duyckinck, "Melville's *Moby-Dick,*" p. 404.

55. Duyckinck, "Melville's *Moby-Dick,*" p. 404. Cf. Duyckink's response

with Whig Francis Bowen's similar denunciation in *Christian Examiner* 23 (November 1837), 170–94. The Whig editor of the New York *Knickerbocker,* Lewis Gaylord Clark, was similarly "contemptuous of Thomas Carlyle and the New England transcendentalists."

56. Joseph Hartwell Barrett, "Sir Thomas Browne," *American Whig Review* 8 (July 1848), 22–3.

57. F. O. Matthiessen, *American Renaissance: Art and Expression in the Age of Emerson and Whitman* (New York: Oxford University Press, 1941), pp. 100–30. In "Herman Melville and the Example of Sir Thomas Browne," Brian Foley, *Modern Philology* 81 (February 1984), 265–77, working from the earlier thesis of Millicent Bell, depicts Browne as an extreme skeptic and Melville's use of Browne as his way of pointing to the severe limitations of the human mind. I suggest that Browne was not an extreme skeptic, and Melville's use of Brownean elements was instead an attempt to entertain the improbable and to arrive at a considered judgment of phenomena that lie outside familiar experience. See also the numerous references to Browne in the editors' "Explanatory Notes" to *Moby-Dick,* ed. Luther S. Mansfield and Howard P. Vincent (New York: Hendricks, 1962).

58. On Duyckinck in relation to Jacobus Arminius and the Remonstrant tradition, see Osgood, *Duyckinck,* pp. 3–7.

59. Archbishop William Laud, *A Relation of the Conference betweene William Lawd, then Lrd. Bishop of St. Davids, . . . and Mr. Fisher the Jesuite* (London: printed by Richard Badger, 1639), Preface, sig. *3.

60. Channing, "Milton," *Works,* 1:22. Hereafter cited in the text with page numbers.

61. For a discussion of the aesthetics of Scottish philosophy, see Verle D. Flood, " A Study of the Aesthetics of Taste in America: The Role of Common Sense Philosophy in the Literary Criticism of the Boston Anthologists," Ph.D. diss., State University of Iowa, 1959, p. 228. For a more extensive discussion, see Martin, *Instructed Vision,* (cited in note 16).

62. "Review of the Eighteenth Century," *Monthly Anthology, and Boston Review* 4 (September 1807), 43–4.

63. John Quincy Adams, *Lecture on Rhetoric and Oratory,* 2 vols. (Cambridge, Mass.: Hilliard and Metcalf, 1810). J. S. Gardiner, "The Old English Pulpit," *Democratic Review* 18 (May 1846), 346. Gardiner, a High Church Episcopalian minister for Trinity Church in New York (as well as a frequent contributor to the *North American Review,*) may well have had an ideological investment, like Evert Duyckinck, in promoting some of the religious writers of the earlier seventeenth century praised in his article (at the expense of the authors of the Queen Anne period). Perhaps his praise of the earlier writers was enough to get his article published (uncharacteristically) by the *Democratic Review.*

64. Thomas P. Miller, Introduction, *The Selected Writings of John Witherspoon* (Carbondale: Southern Illinois University Press, 1990), pp. 9, 24, quoted in Gregory Clark and S. Michael Halloran, *Oratorical*

Culture in Nineteenth-Century America: Transformations in the Theory and Practice of Rhetoric (Carbondale: Southern Illinois University Press, 1993), p. 40.

65. For an illuminating discussion of the informing aspects of civic humanism and legal eloquence in the writings of certain American authors, see Robert A. Ferguson, *Law and Letters in American Culture* (Cambridge, Mass.: Harvard University Press, 1984). On the relationship between language and politics in America, see also Gustafson, *Representative Words.*

66. Howe, *Unitarian Conscience,* p. 8. For a survey of the curricula of American colleges before the Civil War, see George Schmidt, *The Old Time College President* (New York: Columbia University Press, 1930).

67. Hugh Blair, *Lectures on Rhetoric and Belles-Lettres,* ed. Harold F. Harding, 2 vols. (Carbondale: Southern Illinois University Press, 1965), 1:395. Subsequent citations are to this edition and will be given in the text with volume and page numbers.

68. Albert J. von Frank, *The Sacred Game: Provincialism and Frontier Consciousness in American Literature, 1630–1860* (Cambridge University Press, 1985).

69. Unitarians dominated local institutions to such an extent that Harriet Beecher Stowe commented, "all the literary men of Massachusetts were Unitarian. All the trustees and professors of Harvard College were Unitarians. All the elite of wealth and fashion crowded Unitarian churches." Quoted in Howe, *Unitarian Conscience,* p. 318.

70. Andrews Norton, "Observations on the *Literary Miscellany*," *Monthly Anthology* 2 (1805), 170.

71. Hon. B. F. Porter, "The Principles of Rhetoric," *American Whig Review* 9 (June 1849), 597–603. Hereafter cited in the text by page number.

72. Barrett, "Browne," p. 20. Like those Americans who valued Browne's distinctiveness, Coleridge remarked, "Sir Thomas Browne . . . had a genuine idiom; and it is the existence of an individual idiom in each, that makes the principal writers before the Restoration the great patterns and integers of English style." Quoted in *Coleridge and the Seventeenth Century,* ed. Roberta F. Brinkley (Durham: Duke University Press, 1955), p. 414.

73. Fitz-James O'Brien, "Our Young Authors – Melville," *Putnam's Monthly* 1 (February 1853), 156. Hereafter cited in the text as "Our Young Authors" with page numbers.

74. Hans Frei, *The Eclipse of Biblical Narrative: A Study in Eighteenth and Nineteenth Century Hermeneutics* (New Haven, Conn.: Yale University Press, 1974), p. 78.

75. Fitz-James O'Brien, "Our Authors and Authorship: Melville and Curtis," *Putnam's Monthly* 9 (April 1857), 389. Hereafter cited in the text as "Our Authors and Authorship" with page numbers.

76. O'Brien may be referring to Melville's appropriation of seventeenth-

century anatomies. Among nineteenth-century reviewers, see, for example, the review in the London *Morning Advertiser,* October 24, 1851: "Now we have a Carlylism of phrase, then a quaintness reminding us of Sir Thomas Brown [*sic*], and anon a heap of curious out-of-the-way learning after the fashion of Burton who 'anatomised' 'melancholy.' " Among modern critics, see Northrop Frye, *The Anatomy of Criticism* (Princeton, N.J.: Princeton University Press, 1957). On Burton's *Anatomy of Melancholy* in relation to Melville, see Edgar Dryden, *Melville's Thematics of Form: The Great Art of Telling the Truth* (Baltimore: Johns Hopkins University Press, 1968), pp. 189–91.

77. For extended discussions of conservative (Whig) aesthetic, philosophical, and moral values, see Howe, *Unitarian Conscience;* Lawrence Buell, *New England Literary Culture: From Revolution through Renaissance* (Cambridge University Press, 1986). On Unitarian aesthetics, see Buell, *Literary Transcendentalism: Style and Vision in the American Renaissance* (Ithaca, N.Y., Cornell University Press, 1973), ch. 1.

78. Ralph Waldo Emerson, "On the Best Mode of Inspiring a Correct Taste in English Literature," *The Early Lectures of Ralph Waldo Emerson,* ed. Stephen Whicher and Robert E. Spiller, 3 vols. (Cambridge, Mass.: Harvard University Press, 1959), 1:215.

79. [Sidney Willard,] "Locke on the Epistles of St. Paul" *American Monthly Review* 2 (October 1832), 265, 272, 270, 269. See Sidney Willard, *Memories of Youth and Manhood* (Cambridge, Mass., 1855).

80. For a useful discussion of Emerson's changing theory of rhetoric, see Sheldon W. Liebman, "The Development of Emerson's Theory of Rhetoric, 1821–1836," *American Literature* 41 (May 1969), 178–206.

81. John Milton, *The Doctrine and Discipline of Divorce,* vol. 2 of *The Complete Prose Works of John Milton,* ed. Ernest Sirluck (New Haven, Conn.: Yale University Press, 1959), 2:241. Hereafter cited in the text as *CPW* with volume and page numbers. On Milton's problematic hermeneutical practice in this tract, see Stanley Fish, "Wanting a Supplement: The Question of Interpretation in Milton's Early Prose," in *Politics, Poetics, and Hermeneutics in Milton's Prose,* ed. David Loewenstein and James Grantham Turner (Cambridge University Press, 1990), pp. 41–68.

82. For a discussion of woman's "domestic sphere," see Barbara Welter, "The Cult of True Womanhood: 1820–1860," in *The American Family in Social-Historical Perspective,* 2d ed., ed. Michael Gordon (New York: St. Martin's Press, 1978), pp. 313–33; Nancy F. Cott, *The Bonds of Womanhood: "Woman's Sphere" in New England, 1780–1835* (New Haven, Conn.: Yale University Press, 1977); and Ann Douglas, *The Feminization of American Culture* (New York: Knopf, 1977).

83. Sarah Josepha Hale, "Eve," in *Woman's Record: or Sketches of All Distinguished Women from the Creation to A.D. 1854* (New York, 1855), pp. 38–9; Hale, "Margaret Fuller Ossoli," *Woman's Record,* pp. 666–7;

Hale, "Preface," *Woman's Record,* p. ix: Hale's volume, with slightly different titles, was repeatedly republished in revised and enlarged editions through 1876. My interpretation of Hale's essay on Adam and Eve extends and modifies that of Ann Douglas in *Feminization of American Culture,* p. 152. For an interpretation of Hale's text as somewhat more sympathetic to feminist concerns, see Nina Baym, *Feminism and American Literary History: Essays* (New Brunswick, N.J.: Rutgers University Press, 1992), pp. 176–80.

84. Mrs. L. H. Sigourney, *Letters to Mothers* (Hartford, 1838), p. 10.

85. Letter 244 in *The Letters of Margaret Fuller,* ed. Robert N. Hudspeth (Ithaca, N.Y.: Cornell University Press, 1983–), 2:109–10. Hereafter cited in the text as *Letters* with volume and page numbers.

86. Margaret Fuller, "Children's Books," in *Woman in the Nineteenth Century and Kindred Papers by Margaret Fuller Ossoli,* ed. Arthur Buckminster Fuller (Boston: John P. Jewett, 1855), pp. 313, 311, 312.

87. William Ellery Channing, "Remarks on National Literature" (1823), in Channing, *Works,* 1:245.

88. James Russell Lowell, "Kavanagh, a Tale by Henry Wadsworth Longfellow" *North American Review* 69 (July 1849), 198. Hereafter cited in the text by page number.

89. For a full account of this cultural situation, see Benjamin Spencer, *The Quest for Nationality: An American Literary Campaign* (Syracuse, N.Y.: Syracuse University Press, 1957).

90. Asher B. Durand, "Letters On Landscape Painting" (Letter 1), *Crayon* 1 (January 1855), 2.

91. Durand, "Letters On Landscape Painting" (Letter 1), p. 2.

2: Emerson, Milton, Apocalyptic Eloquence

1. Ralph Waldo Emerson, from his working notes to his lecture "John Milton," in *The Early Lectures of Ralph Waldo Emerson, 1833–1836,* ed. Stephen E. Whicher and Robert E. Spiller, 3 vols. (Cambridge, Mass.: Harvard University Press, 1966), 1:450. Hereafter cited in the text and notes as *EL* with volume and page numbers. Emerson used both the widely available Charles Symmons edition, *Prose Works with a Life of the Author, Interspersed with Translations and Critical Remarks,* 7 vols. (London, 1806), and the Francis Jenks American edition, *A Selection from the English Prose Works of John Milton,* 2 vols. (Boston, 1826). See Kenneth Walter Cameron's *Ralph Waldo Emerson's Reading,* corrected ed. (Hartford: Transcendental Book, 1962).

2. Ralph Waldo Emerson, *The Journals and Miscellaneous Notebooks,* ed. William H. Gilman, Alfred R. Ferguson, et al., 16 vols. (Cambridge, Mass.: Belknap Press of Harvard University Press, 1963–80), 4:103 (1833). Hereafter cited in the text and notes as *JMN* with volume and page numbers. The editors of Emerson's journals give Plutarch's "On Isis and Osiris" from his *Morals* as Emerson's source, but Emerson's mention of Milton's *Lycidas* in this journal entry, his early

knowledge of *Areopagitica* (*JMN*, 1:12 [1820]), and his frequent reference to this tract as his favorite among Milton's prose works all point to *Areopagitica* as his source.

3. The "Masters second comming" is from Milton's *Areopagitica*, quoted from *The Complete Prose Works of John Milton*, ed. Don M. Wolfe et al., 8 vols. (New Haven, Conn.: Yale University Press, 1953–82), 2:549. Subsequent citations of Milton's prose are to this edition and will be given in the text and notes as *CPW* with volume and page numbers. On Emerson's association of Orpheus with ordering civility, see Thomas Gustafson, *Representative Words: Politics, Literature, and the American Language, 1776–1865* (Cambridge University Press, 1992), pp. 70–1.

4. For a brief mention of Emerson's early and deep immersion in Milton's prose, see G. R. Elliott, "On Emerson's 'Grace' and 'Self-Reliance' " *New England Quarterly* 2 (1929): 93–104. See also Richard Pettigrew, "Emerson and Milton," *American Literature* 3 (1931): 45–59.

5. Michael J. Colacurcio, " 'Pleasing God': The Lucid Strife of Emerson's 'Address;'" *ESQ* 37 (1991): 140–212.

6. B. L. Packer, *Emerson's Fall: A New Interpretation of the Major Essays* (New York: Continuum, 1982), and "Origin and Authority: Emerson and the Higher Criticism," in *Reconstructing American Literary History*, ed. Sacvan Bercovitch (Cambridge, Mass.: Harvard University Press, 1986); Julie Ellison, *Emerson's Romantic Style* (Princeton, N.J.: Princeton University Press, 1984). For Emerson's words, see *The Complete Works of Ralph Waldo Emerson*, Centenary Ed. (Boston: Houghton Mifflin, 1903), 1:29. Subsequent references to Emerson's published essays will appear in the text as *W* with volume and page numbers.

7. In this he diverged sharply from Coleridge, who suggest that Milton's attacks were neither personal nor historical but "hypothetical" and abstract. See Joseph Wittreich, *The Romantics on Milton* (Cleveland: Press of Case Western Reserve University, 1970), pp. 213–15. Cf. also Coleridge's emphasis on "Milton's platonizing Spirit" and "Ideality" (pp. 166, 183).

8. See K. P. Van Anglen's " 'That Sainted Spirit' – William Ellery Channing and the Unitarian Milton," *Studies in the American Renaissance, 1983* (Charlottesville: University of Virginia Press, 1983), and *The New England Milton: Literary Reception and Cultural Authority in the Early Republic* (University Park: Pennsylvania University Press, 1993), chs. 1–2.

9. For a discussion of Milton's moral character as a Unitarian focus, and of Channing's appreciation in particular, see Van Anglen, *New England Milton*, chs. 1–2. The reviewer of the newly discovered *Christian Doctrine* commented in the *North American Review*, "For ourselves, we can truly say that we never knew Milton, till we were acquainted with his prose writings. We never knew the man till

then." See F. W. P. Greenwood, "Milton's English Prose Works" (a review of *A Selection from the English Prose Works of John Milton*), *North American Review* 25 (July 1827), 74.

10. Although some critics have suggested that the Unitarian William Ellery Channing's magisterial essay of 1826 celebrating the discovery of Milton's *Christian Doctrine* drew Emerson's attention to Milton, Emerson's earliest journal writing suggests a thorough knowledge of Milton's apocalyptic prose tracts preceding Channing's essay by at least six years. Cf. Packer, *Emerson's Fall*, p. 54; Phyllis Cole, "The Purity of Puritanism: Transcendentalist Readings of Milton," *Studies in Romanticism* 17 (1978): 129–48; R. A. Yoder, *Emerson and the Orphic Poet in America* (Berkeley and Los Angeles: University of California Press, 1978), pp. 14–16.

11. For Emerson's transcriptions of or references to *Church-Government,* see *JMN,* 1:8, 41–42, 374 (1820); 2:107, 109, 170 (1823); and 2:221, 240, 280 (1824); and *EL,* 1:363 (1835). Emerson also knew *An Apology* as early as 1820, and returned to it periodically over at least fifteen years. See *JMN,* 1:39, 40 (1820); 4:57 (1832); 4:379 (1834); and 6:385 (1835); and *EL,* 1:150, 153, 155 (1835).

12. Ellison (in *Emerson's Romantic Style,* p. 22) suggests Emerson is here "reworking" the culminating judgment scene in Henry Hart Milman's Romantic poem *Samor, Lord of the Bright City,* but Emerson alludes to the judgment scene only as an example of a public occasion of some importance. In Milman's scene, Samor neither has priestly functions nor is capable of eloquence.

13. Emerson cites Luther's words in EL, 1:129. "The world turned upside down" was a popular phrase among radicals during the English Civil War and Interregnum: see Christopher Hill, *The World Turned Upside Down: Radical Ideas during the English Revolution* (Harmondsworth, England: Penguin, 1972). For Milton's apocalyptic use of Hebrews 12:26–29 in *Lycidas,* see Michael Lieb, *The Sinews of Ulysses: Form and Convention in Milton's Works* (Pittsburgh: Duquesne University Press, 1989), p. 56. For Emerson's use of the King James translation, see Harriet Rodgers Zink, *Emerson's Use of the Bible* (1935; rpt. Folcraft, Pa.: Folcraft Library Editions, 1977), p. 4.

14. In chs. 2 and 4 of *"The Strains of Eloquence": Emerson and His Sermons* (University Park: Pennsylvania State University Press, 1989), Wesley T. Mott also emphasizes the importance of eloquence in Emerson's vocational decision but depicts a pious, earnest Emerson concerned solely with attaining moral purity in his (sermonic) eloquence.

15. These distinctions were also clear in Milton's earlier allusion to Isaiah in "On the Morning of Christ's Nativity" (lines 25–7). See *John Milton: Complete Poems and Major Prose,* ed. Merritt Y. Hughes (Indianapolis: Odyssey Press, 1957).

16. For recent discussions contextualizing Emerson's oratorical concerns, see Lawrence Buell, *New England Literary Culture: From Revolution through Renaissance* (Cambridge University Press, 1986), pp.

137–65; and Packer, *Emerson's Fall,* pp. 1–21. See also Colacurcio, " 'Pleasing God,' " pp. 162–71, for Emerson's oratorical rivalry with William Ellery Channing.

17. See Barbara Kiefer Lewalski, *Protestant Poetics and the Seventeenth-Century Religious Lyric* (Princeton, N.J.: Princeton University Press, 1979), ch. 2.

18. O. W. Firkins, *Ralph Waldo Emerson* (1915; rpt. New York: Russell and Russell, 1965), p. 270.

19. *The Complete Sermons of Ralph Waldo Emerson,* ed. Albert von Frank (Columbia: University of Missouri Press, 1991), 3:122. Hereafter cited in the text as *CS* with volume and page numbers.

20. Channing wrote, "To a man of a literal and prosaick character, the mind may seem lawless in these workings [of "creative energies," "poetry"]; but it observes higher laws than it transgresses, the laws of the immortal intellect," p. 33. William Ellery Channing, "Milton" (a review of *A Treatise on Christian Doctrine, compiled from the Holy Scriptures alone,* trans. Charles R. Sumner), *Christian Examiner and Theological Review* 3 (January–February 1826), 29–77. All subsequent citations of Channing will be from a reprint of the *Examiner* article entitled "Remarks on the Character and Writings of John Milton," in *The Works of William E. Channing, D.D.,* 8th ed. (Boston: James Munroe, 1848). Citations refer to volume 1 of this edition and will be cited in the text by page number.

21. On the importance of Channing's essay in "prepar[ing] the way for the Emersonian synthesis of religion and art," see Lawrence Buell, *Literary Transcendentalism: Style and Vision in the American Renaissance* (Ithaca, N.Y.: Cornell University Press, 1973), pp. 36–37; see also Van Anglen, "That Sainted Spirit," pp. 101–28, and, in its revised version, ch. 2 of *New England Milton.*

22. In a letter to his brother Edward, Emerson suggests that Milton (*Paradise Lost,* V.486–90), as well as Coleridge, distinguishes between the "discursive" Understanding and the "intuitive" Reason. *The Letters of Ralph Waldo Emerson,* ed. Ralph L. Rusk, 6 vols. (New York: Columbia University Press, 1939) 1:412.

23. Barbara Packer ("Origin and Authority," pp. 68–9), citing the lessons Emerson learned from debates about Scriptural textual transmission, argues for his skepticism about the authority (inspired or otherwise) that inheres in a text. Yet Emerson's journals suggest that he entertained the possibility that prophetic authority could be attained *and* conveyed, though more particularly through the spoken word rather than the written text.

24. Citing Milton's anguish in *Church-Government,* Emerson reveals in his journals that he himself, by contrast, finds incomprehensible the burden of prophetic foreknowledge (*JMN,* 2:280). For Emerson's familiarity with *Of Reformation,* see his citation from the tract in his Sermon 56, dated November 21, 1829, in *Complete Sermons,* 2:91. He cites the same phrase from *Of Reformation* in his 1835 lecture "John

Milton" (*EL,* 1:156). For a discussion of the emotional and aesthetic dimensions of Milton's involvement with the historical process in his prose, see David Loewenstein, *Milton and the Drama of History: Historical Vision, Iconoclasm, and the Literary Imagination* (Cambridge University Press, 1990).

25. For a discussion of Milton's (as well as Emerson's own) "hagiography," see Joel Porte, *Representative Man: Ralph Waldo Emerson in His Time* (New York: Oxford University Press, 1979), pp. 7, 73–4, 76, 132.

26. See Van Anglen, *New England Milton,* ch. 3.

27. This seems to be the basis of Van Anglen's conclusion (*New England Milton,* ch. 3) that Emerson's self-fashioning after Milton was conventionally Unitarian in his early years. My view that Emerson's evolving sense of inspired language was based upon Milton's apocalyptic prose tracts is another key difference between our arguments.

28. At self-lacerating moments, Emerson vies with Milton in tabulating the lost hours of an unproductive youth. Cf. Milton's sonnet "How soon hath Time" with Emerson's entry in *JMN,* 1:133.

29. In a letter to Caroline Sturgis (dated January 24, 1841), Fuller writes about her poetic ambitions, and insists that she, unlike Milton in Sonnet 19, is not able to "*stand* and wait" for divine inspiration. Margaret Fuller, *Letters,* ed. Robert N. Hudspeth (Ithaca, N. Y.: Cornell University Press, 1983–), 2:199. See also my discussion in Chapter 3 of the present study.

30. Ten years later, however, in his sermon on sacrifice (Sermon 87, 1830), Emerson could urge churchgoers to submit to God's will, to be willing in their illness "to be left out of the race, to send up thanksgivings to him that has stricken us, to feel glad that he doth not need our service, . . . [though] [']thousands at his bidding *speed.*[']" Emerson, *Complete Sermons,* 2:250.

31. Cf. Emerson's "The American Scholar," *Works,* 1:94. Responding to Milton's Romantic biographer, William Haley, who claims that "The ambition of Milton was as pure as his genius was sublime," Coleridge decries the "fondness of ingrafting a good sense on the word 'ambition,' [for it] is not a Christian impulse in general." Quoted in Wittreich, *Romantics on Milton,* p. 177.

32. See Milton's *Of Reformation, CPW,* 1:583–4. On the political nature of Milton's own revision of the trope for the body ecclesiastic and politic, see Janel Mueller, "Embodying Glory: The Apocalyptic Strain in Milton's *Of Reformation,*" in *Politics, Poetics, and Hermeneutics in Milton's Prose,* ed. David Loewenstein and James Grantham Turner (Cambridge University Press, 1990), pp. 25–34.

33. Colacurcio, "Pleasing God," pp. 152 – 4.

34. See Christopher Grose, *Milton and the Sense of Tradition* (New Haven, Conn.: Yale University Press, 1988), pp. 18–20, 70–80, for the centrality of *An Apology* to Milton's sense of his literary vocation.

35. Packer, "Origin and Authority," p. 92.

36. Although Van Anglen, in "That Sainted Spirit," depicts Channing's appreciation of Milton's politics as charitably tending toward transhistorical "libertarian" values rather than partisan issues (pp. 122–3), we can see that in his essay on Milton, Channing does suggest a desire for reforming formulaic preaching.

37. John Calvin, *Commentaries on the Epistles of Paul to the Galatians and Ephesians,* trans. William Pringle (Edinburgh, 1854), 19:280.

38. In "Milton," Channing, in contrast to other Unitarians, announces, "who will blame him [Milton] for binding himself to them [interests of infinite moment] . . . and for defending with fervor and vehemence?" (p. 24).

39. Several modern historians and literary critics have challenged Emerson's perception of Unitarian culture. See Daniel Walker Howe, *The Unitarian Conscience: Harvard Moral Philosophy, 1805–1861,* (Cambridge, Mass.: Harvard University Press, 1970) esp. pp. 151–73; and Conrad Wright, *The Liberal Christians: Essays on American Unitarian History* (Boston; Beacon Press, 1970), pp. 41–61. See also Buell, *Literary Transcendentalism,* pp. 21–55.

40. David Simpson, *The Politics of American English, 1776–1850* (New York: Oxford University Press, 1986), pp. 230–59.

41. Hugh Blair, *Lectures on Rhetoric and Belles-Lettres:* ed. Harold F. Harding, 2 vols. (Carbondale: Southern Illinois University Press, 1965), 1:395. Subsequent citations of Blair are to this edition and will be given in the text with volume and page numbers.

42. The words are those of John Quincy Adams, *Lectures on Rhetoric and Oratory, Delivered to the Classes of Senior and Junior Students in Harvard University,* 2 vols. (Cambridge, Mass.: Hilliard and Metcalf, 1810), 2:127.

43. Verle D. Flood, "A Study of the Aesthetics of Taste in America: The Role of Common Sense Philosophy in the Literary Criticism of the Boston Anthologists," Ph.D. diss., State University of Iowa, 1959, p. 228. See also Terence Martin, *The Instructed Vision: Scottish Common Sense Philosophy and the Origins of American Fiction* (Bloomington: Indiana University Press, 1961).

44. William Kerrigan, *The Prophetic Milton* (Charlottesville: University of Virgina Press, 1974), p. 172.

45. An 1825 advertisement, quoted in Barbara Owen, *The Organ in New England* (Raleigh, N.C., 1979), p. 56; "Self-Acting Musical Instruments," quoted in A. W. J. G. Ord-Hume, *Clockwork Music* (New York, 1973), p. 199.

46. Joseph Hall, "Bishop Hall's Account of the Sacrilegious Prophanation of this Church [Norwich Cathedral], in the Time of the Civil Wars," from *Bishop Hall's Hard Measure,* quoted in *The Posthumous Works of Sir Thomas Browne: Miscellanies Written by Sir Thomas Browne, Kt. M.D. Late of Norwich' Published from his Original Manuscripts* (Norwich, 1712), pp. 42, 32.

47. For a discussion of changing lyceum cultures and their regional and

ideological expectations, see Mary Kupiec Cayton, "The Making of an American Prophet: Emerson, His Audiences, and the Rise of the Culture Industry in Nineteenth-Century America," in *Ralph Waldo Emerson: A Collection of Critical Essays,* ed. Lawrence Buell (Englewood Cliffs, N.J.: Prentice Hall, 1993), pp. 77–100. See also Cayton, *Emerson's Emergence: Self and Society in the Transformation of New England, 1800–1845* (Chapel Hill, N.C.: University of North Carolina Press, 1989), ch. 6.

3: Fuller, Emerson, the Herberts

1. All three passages are from *The Memoirs of Margaret Fuller Ossoli,* ed. Ralph Waldo Emerson, James Freeman Clarke, and William Henry Channing, 2 vols. (Boston: Phillips, Sampson, 1852), 1:294–5, 230. Hereafter the *Memoirs* will be cited in the text as *M* with volume and page numbers. The first quotation is originally from a letter of December 26, 1842, believed to have been addressed to Emerson. The last quotation comes from a letter to Caroline Sturgis dated January 24, 1841. See Margaret Fuller, *The Letters of Margaret Fuller,* ed. Robert N. Hudspeth, 5 vols. (Ithaca: Cornell University Press, 1983–), 3:81, 2:199. Hereafter the *Letters* will be cited in the text as *L* with volume and page numbers.

2. See Albert J. von Frank, *The Sacred Game: Provincialism and Frontier Consciousness in American Literature, 1630–1860,* ch. 7; Ann Douglas, *The Feminization of American Culture* (New York: Knopf, 1977), ch. 8; and Jeffrey Steele's "Introduction" to *The Essential Margaret Fuller* (New Brunswick, N.J.: Rutgers University Press, 1992), pp. xi – xlvi. For a documentary depiction of Fuller based on excerpts from her writings and letters and on commentaries by contemporaries, see Bell Gale Chevigny, *The Woman and the Myth: Margaret Fuller's Life and Writings,* rev. and exp. ed. (1976; rpt. Boston: Northeastern University Press, 1994).

3. It is likely that Fuller was reading *The Life of Edward Lord Herbert of Cherbury; Written by Himself: and Continued to his Death* (London: Saunders & Otley, 1826). This edition contains the two abridged Latin poems, as well as his English poem "An Ode: Upon the Question Moved, Whether Love Should Continue For Ever?," which she quotes in *Woman in the Nineteenth Century* and also in a letter to Frederick Hedge (L, 3:108–9). Although Robert Hudspeth, the editor of Fuller's letters, conjectures that she read the Walpole first edition of 1764, that edition (of only two hundred copies) was privately distributed, was relatively rare, and does not contain all three poems – the Latin as well as the English one that she quotes.

4. S. Margaret Fuller, "The Prose Works of Milton," *Papers on Literature and Art* (London: Wiley & Putnam, 1846), p. 38. Fuller's "Two Herberts" was first published in *The Present* 1, nos. 9–10 (March 1844), 301–12; this short-lived journal (no more issues were pub-

lished) was edited by William Henry Channing. "The Two Herberts" was then reprinted in *Papers,* pp. 15–34. The second quotation is from p. 17 of this essay. Subsequent citations of "The Two Herberts" are to this edition and will be given in the text by page number. Like Emerson and Melville, Fuller greatly admired the work of Walter Savage Landor, who wrote sixteen volumes of *Imaginary Conversations.*

5. Theophilus Parsons, Review of "Notices sur le Caractère et les Écrits de Madame la Baronne de Stael Holstein, par Madame Necker. Paris, 1819," *North American Review* 11 (July 1820), 131.

6. For a general account of Emerson's and Fuller's difficult relationship, see Gay Wilson Allen, *Waldo Emerson: A Biography* (New York: Viking, 1981), pp. 354–6. See also Anne C. Rose, *Transcendentalism as a Social Movement, 1830–1850* (New Haven, Conn.: Yale University Press, 1981), pp. 182–3. For a discussion of Fuller's insistence on "idealism that is concerned with ideas only as they can be lived, . . . with the spiritual only when it animates the material" and her effect on Emerson, see Robert D. Richardson, Jr., *Emerson: The Mind on Fire* (Berkeley and Los Angeles: University of California Press, 1995), pp. 240–1. My account emphasizes their intellectual competition, whereas the other accounts focus on the mismatch of temperaments and their thwarted intimacy. For an illuminating discussion of Fuller's feminism as it is exhibited in and shaped by language, see Julie Ellison, *Delicate Subjects: Romanticism, Gender, and the Ethics of Understanding* (Ithaca, N.Y.: Cornell University Press, 1990), chs. 7 and 8. For Fuller's and Emerson's exchange, see Emerson, *The Letters of Ralph Waldo Emerson,* ed. Ralph L. Rusk, 6 vols. (New York: Columbia University Press, 1939), 2:326–41.

7. Margaret Fuller, *Woman in the Nineteenth Century,* in *Essential Margaret Fuller,* pp. 279, 281.

8. From a letter to Caroline Sturgis dated January 24, 1841 (*L,* 2:199). The context of the letter makes it clear that this moment of arrest is not informed solely by outward circumstance, but also and more clearly by her momentary lack of inspiration.

9. Quoted in Edward W. Emerson, note to "Grace," in Ralph Waldo Emerson, *The Complete Works of Ralph Waldo Emerson,* Centenary Ed. 12 vols. (Boston: Houghton Mifflin, 1903), 9:510. The poem was reinstated without title or attribution; see *Memoirs,* 2:117.

10. For a more recent discussion of Lord Herbert's epistemology, one highlighting the skeptical elements, see Richard H. Popkin, *The History of Skepticism from Erasmus to Spinoza* (Berkeley and Los Angeles: University of California Press, 1979), 151–71.

  The indirect line of transmission from Lord Herbert to the Transcendentalists includes Common Sense philosopher Thomas Reid and the Unitarians themselves. Lord Herbert's *De Veritate,* however, shows him to hold more of a probabilist and empiricist view (despite his insistence on innate "common notions") than Transcendentalists would accept. See his ch. 11, "On Probability," in *De Veritate*, trans. Meyrick H. Carre (Bristol: for University of Bristol, by J. W. Arrowsmith, 1937), p. 314ff.

11. For a discussion of the Transcendentalist value of self-culture as Fuller shapes it for feminist concerns, see David Robinson, "Margaret Fuller and the Transcendentalist Ethos: *Woman in the Nineteenth Century*," *PMLA* 97 (January 1982), 83–98.

12. Douglas, *Feminization of American Culture*, chs. 1–7.

13. Review of "Notices sur le Caractère," p. 125.

14. Emerson, *Works*, 8:186.

15. "Miss Fuller's Papers on Literature and Art," *Democratic Review* 19 (September 1846), 198–202.

16. George Herbert, *The English Poetry of George Herbert*, rev. ed., ed. F. E. Hutchinson (1941; Oxford: Clarendon Press, 1945), p. 37. Subsequent quotations of George Herbert's poetry are from this edition and will be cited in the text as *EPGH* with page numbers. Fuller's citations of these poems will be cited as "Fuller," with the page number from "The Two Herberts."

17. On George Herbert's self-representation, see Barbara Leah Harman, *Costly Monuments: Representations of the Self in George Herbert's Poetry* (Cambridge, Mass.: Harvard University Press, 1982); on his theology, see Richard Strier, *Love Known: Theology and Experience in George Herbert's Poetry* (Chicago: University of Chicago Press, 1983), and Barbara Kiefer Lewalski, *Protestant Poetics and the Seventeenth-Century Religious Lyric* (Princeton: Princeton University Press, 1979), ch. 9. For a discussion emphasizing self-abnegation, see Joseph Summers, *George Herbert: His Religion and Art* (London: Chatto & Windus, 1954).

18. For a discussion of Emerson's rewriting of Herbert's poem "Sin" in Emerson's poem "Grace," see Michael J. Colacurcio, " 'The Corn and the Wine': Emerson and the Example of George Herbert," *Nineteenth Century Literature* 42 (June 1987), 12–13.

19. Colacurcio, " 'The Corn and the Wine,' " pp. 6, 15, 21.

20. See her January 24, 1841, letter to Caroline Sturgis, *L*, 2:199.

21. Christina Zwarg, "Emerson as 'Mythologist' in *Memoirs of Margaret Fuller Ossoli*," *Criticism* 31 (Summer 1989), 213–33. Zwarg argues that Fuller caused Emerson to rethink his own sometimes unconsidered cultural assumptions as he attempted to write essays that represented human experience (especially his essay "Fate").

22. Americans prided themselves on having eschewed primogeniture and its associated liabilities. See J. Sullivan Cox, "Imaginary Commonwealths," *United States Magazine and Democratic Review* 19 (September 1846), 181.

23. Fuller does not cite these lines, but I provide them to make explicit the context of the lines she does use.

24. For the suggestion that Fuller accedes to (was "seduced" by) her culture's portrayal of woman's superior sensitivities, see Mary P.

Ryan, *The Empire of the Mother: American Writing about Domesticity* (New York: Haworth Press, 1982), p. 37.

25. For a discussion of how Fuller in *Woman in the Nineteenth Century* exploits the sermonic form for her feminist agenda, see Marie Mitchell Olsen Urbanski, *Margaret Fuller's "Woman in the Nineteenth Century": A Literary Study of Form and Content, of Sources and Influence* (Westport, Conn.: Greenwood Press, 1980).

26. For a discussion of Fuller's deployment of "translation" for her own feminist purposes, see Christina Zwarg, "Feminism in Translation: Margaret Fuller's *Tasso*," *Studies in Romanticism* 29 (Fall 1990), 463 – 90.

27. Lord Herbert was one of Emerson's favorites; see his "Society and Solitude": "Among the best books are certain Autobiographies: as St. Augustine's Confessions . . . Montaigne's Essays, Lord Herbert of Cherbury's Memoirs" (*Works*, 7:208).

28. For a discussion of *De Religione,* see *Lord Herbert of Cherbury's De Religione Laici,* ed. and trans. Harold R. Hutcheson (New Haven, Conn.: Yale University Press, 1944), pp. xxi – xxx.

29. On the tensions created by the exertions of opposite forces in nineteenth-century American culture, see Mary Kelley, *Private Woman, Public Stage: Literary Domesticity in Nineteenth-Century America* (New York: Oxford University Pres, 1984).

30. Fuller, *Woman,* in *Essential Fuller,* p. 257.

31. William A. Jones, "Female Novelists," *Democratic Review* 14 (May 1844), 484.

32. Jones, "Female Novelists," pp. 488, 489.

4: Thoreau's 17th-Century Landscapes

1. Henry David Thoreau, *A Week on the Concord and Merrimack Rivers,* ed. Carl F. Hovde, William L. Howarth, Elizabeth Hall Witherell (Princeton: Princeton University Press, 1980), p. 104. Hereafter cited in the text as *Week* with page numbers.

2. Particularly in *A Week,* Thoreau has little tolerance for the encroaching industrialization that turns rivers into stagnant marshes and makes river transportation outmoded. John Conron, for example, states that "For the mills of Lowell and Manchester [Thoreau] has no pictorial imagination at all. They are blank spaces on his mental map." See "Bright American Rivers: The Luminist Landscapes of Thoreau's *A Week on the Concord and Merrimack Rivers,*" *American Quarterly* 32 (1980), 156. Cf. Leo Marx, who argues that Thoreau aestheticizes the railroad, indeed naturalizes it as an artistic production that constitutes an intrinsic part of *Walden.* See *The Machine in the Garden: Technology and the Pastoral Ideal in America* (New York: Oxford University Press, 1964), pp. 220–1. But this too needs qualification, for the "grotesque vegetation" created by the

railway cut in the "Spring" chapter remains clearly a conjunction of the artificial and the natural – the grotesque.

3. In *Thoreau: A Naturalist's Liberty* (Cambridge, Mass.: Harvard University Press, 1983), John Hildebidle acknowledges that Thoreau's ambivalence toward history – both his denial of it and his use of it in "*Walden* and *Cape Cod* – are more often than not full of the old, of facts, personages, documents, events, and literary remains" (p.4).

4. James Lyndon Shanley's study of the genesis of the *Walden* text shows that it is a pastiche of observations and allusive meditations collected from various times, texts, and locations – not at all the precise chronicle of two years condensed into one that it purports to be. See Shanley, *The Making of Walden* (Chicago: University of Chicago Press, 1957). For a similar assessment of *A Week,* showing its heterogeneous sources, see C. Linck Johnson, *Thoreau's Complex Weave: The Writing of "A Week on the Concord and Merrimack Rivers"* (Charlottesville: University of Virginia Press, 1986), chs. 2 and 5.

5. For a detailed analysis of Thoreau's development based on his reading, see Robert Sattelmeyer, *Thoreau's Reading: A Study in Intellectual History* (Princeton: Princeton University Press, 1988). See also Robert D. Richardson, Jr., *Henry Thoreau: A Life of the Mind* (Berkeley and Los Angeles: University of California Press, 1986); Walter Harding, *Thoreau's Library* (Charlottesville: University of Virginia Press, 1957); and "A New Checklist of Books in Thoreau's Library," in *Studies in the American Renaissance, 1983,* ed. Joel Myerson (Boston: Hall, 1983), pp. 151–86.

6. For example, see William Bysshe Stein, "Thoreau's *A Week* and *OM* Cosmography," *American Transcendental Quarterly* 11 (1971), 26. For a more positive account of Thoreau's interpolations, see Lawrence Buell, *Literary Transcendentalism: Style and Vision in the American Renaissance* (Ithaca, N.J.: Cornell University Press, 1973), p. 210–11.

7. Among those who read Thoreau as a Romantic naturalist are Frederick Garber, *Thoreau's Redemptive Imagination* (New York: New York University Press, 1977); James McIntosh, *Thoreau as Romantic Naturalist: His Shifting Stance Toward Nature* (Ithaca, N.Y.: Cornell University Press, 1974); Sharon Cameron, *Writing Nature: Henry Thoreau's "Journal"* (Cambridge, Mass.: Harvard University Press, 1987).

8. Here I agree with Hildebidle (*Thoreau: A Naturalist's Liberty,* p. 8) that Thoreau regularly interrupts progressions backward or forward in time. I think the implication of this is that it is difficult to posit a consistent Romantic nostalgia on Thoreau's part.

9. Henry David Thoreau, *Maine Woods,* ed. Joseph J. Moldenhauer (Princeton, N.J.: Princeton University Press, 1972), p. 70. Henry David Thoreau, *Walden,* ed. J. Lyndon Shanley (Princeton, N.J.: Princeton University Press, 1971), p. 318. Hereafter citations are to this edition and will be given in the text as *Walden,* followed by page numbers.

10. See F.O. Matthiessen, *The American Renaissance* (New York: Oxford University Press, 1941), pp. 100–19, for a discussion of Thoreau's familiarity with the metaphysical poets and with Sir Thomas Browne's writings. Similarly, Sherman Paul argues that Thoreau used what he gleaned from reading "to prove the indifference of time and place": see *The Shores of America* (Urbana: University of Illinois Press, 1972), p. 111. Paul, like Matthiessen, notes Thoreau's interest in Browne's *Religio Medici* for "the conception of the microcosm," "friendship," "the metaphysics of sound," Thoreau's exploration of self, and his use of a "correspondential method" akin to Browne's metaphysical habit of mind.

11. Robert Sattelmeyer chronicles Thoreau's never-completed project to assemble an anthology (with some introductory and critical commentary) of early modern English lyric and dramatic poetry. For this project, Thoreau embarked upon a three-year course of reading and note taking (1841–4) at Harvard and in New York. See "Thoreau's Projected Work on the English Poets," *Studies in the American Renaissance, 1980,* ed. Joel Myerson (Boston: Twayne, 1980), pp. 239–57, esp. p. 254.

12. For a socioeconomic evaluation of Concord's problems, see Philip R. Yannella, "Socio-Economic Disarray and Literary Response: Concord and *Walden,*" *Mosaic* 14 (1981), 2–24. Yannella confirms the accuracy of Thoreau's perceptions regarding the shift in how the land was used in farming, but insists upon the conservatism of Thoreau's social remedies for a culture attempting to deal with poverty, capitalist agriculture, and large-scale immigration. For a detailed account of the way land use changed, see also Robert A. Gross "Culture and Cultivation: Agriculture and Society in Thoreau's Concord," *Journal of American History* 69 (June 1982), 42–61. These studies require that we significantly qualify what now seems to be Leo Marx's excessive focus on technology and industrialization as causes of Thoreau's discontent.

13. Lawrence Buell, *New England Literary Culture: From Revolution through Renaissance* (Cambridge University Press, 1986), p. 320.

14. Stanley Cavell, *The Senses of Walden,* expanded ed. (San Francisco: North Point Press, 1981), p. 50. Focusing on the scriptural and American folkloric mediations, Cavell offers a compelling depiction of the speaker's aesthetic distance from the experiment at the pond. Also important for my chapter has been Cavell's reading of Thoreau's enterprise in *In Quest of the Ordinary: Lines of Skepticism and Romanticism* (Chicago: University of Chicago Press, 1988).

15. Sacvan Bercovitch, *The Puritan Origins of the American Self* (New Haven: Yale University Press, 1975), ch. 5.

16. Similarly, in *Walking,* Thoreau relates of his townsmen who "can remember . . . some walks which they took ten years ago, in which they were so blessed as to lose themselves for half an hour in the woods," that "No doubt they were *elevated for a moment as by the*

reminiscence of a previous state of existence, when even they were forest-ers and outlaws." After next quoting two stanzas from the Robin Hood Ballads in which the outlaw voices his wildness, Thoreau then voices his own participation in "the wild" by rejecting the life of the cities and presenting a recuperated archaic landscape and corres-ponding archaic, heroic self. See *Walking,* in *"Walden Edition," The Writings of Henry David Thoreau,* 21 vols. (Boston: Houghton Mifflin, 1906), 5:207.

17. Thoreau suggests another interstitial world in *Walking,* where the focus is upon the attenuation of "the wild" in his contemporary New England: "There are some intervals which border the strain of the wood thrush, to which I would migrate – wild lands where no settler has squatted; to which, methinks, I am already acclimated." *Writings,* 5:225.

18. The quotation from Izaak Walton is from "How to fish for, and to dress the Chavender or Chub," in *The Complete Angler,* ed. Jonquil Bevan (London: Everyman, 1993), p. 105. Subsequent citations are to this edition and will be given in the text as *CA* with page numbers. The standard edition is *The Compleat Angler, 1653–1676,* ed. Jonquil Bevan (Oxford: Clarendon Press, 1983).

19. Ralph Waldo Emerson, *The Letters of Ralph Waldo Emerson,* ed. Ralph L. Rusk, 6 vols. (New York: Columbia University Press, 1939), 3:338. Bronson Alcott, journal entry for March 16, 1847, in F. B. Sanborn and William T. Harris, *A. Bronson Alcott: His Life and Philosophy,* 2 vols. (Boston: Roberts Brothers, 1893), 2:446.

Given the March dates of Emerson's and Alcott's comments about the Waltonian elements in *A Week,* given the relatively late date (February of 1847) of editor George Washington Bethune's preface to the first American edition of *The Complete Angler,* and given the chaotic separation of the Wiley Press from Putnam's near the time of Walton's American publication, this edition probably appeared late in 1847 and was not the edition Thoreau used for *A Week* or *Walden.* On the delay of Walton's text, see John Hammond Moore, *One Hundred and Seventy Five Years of Publishing* (New York: John Wiley & Sons, 1982), p. 54. Instead, I conjecture that Thoreau used *The Complete Angler . . . with Original Memoirs and Notes,* ed. Sir Nicholas Harris Nicolas, 2 vols. (London: William Pickering, 1836). To this edition is prefixed a "Life of Walton," including documents and details about his religious and political allegiances. Nicolas published the 1676 version as his standard text, but also appended the 1653 edition. Since hundreds of editions of Walton were in print by the mid-nineteenth century, it is ultimately impossible to know which Thoreau read.

20. I refer here to Wordsworth's famous "spots of time." Thoreau may have known Wordsworth's sonnet on Izaak Walton, first published in 1819; however, the sonnet offers no such collocation of memories but rather emphasizes Walton's meek piety.

21. John R. Cooper, *The Art of "The Compleat Angler"* (Durham, N.C.: Duke University Press, 1968), p. 47. Jonquil Bevan, the most recent editor of *The Compleat Angler*, also suggests that Walton's audience was composed of the tolerationists and believers in moderation in religious controversy – Anglicans and, quite probably, the Great Tew Circle ("Introduction," *Complete Angler*, pp. xviii–xix). Bevan suggests that the "real-life Brotherhood of the Angle, and Anglers are an obvious metaphor in Walton's book for Anglicans" (p. xix).

22. "To the Reader of the Complete Angler," by Christopher Harvey, in *Complete Angler*, Nicolas edition, 1: xcv–xcvi.

23. Note 6 in volume 2 of the Nicolas edition comments on the lines about the Book of Common Prayer: "These verses were written at or near the time when the Liturgy was abolished by an ordinance of parliament, and while it was agitating, as a theological question, whether, of the two, *preconceived* or *extemporary* prayer be most agreeable to the sense of Scripture?" (p. 157).

24. *Complete Angler*, Nicolas edition, 1:xcvii, my emphasis.

25. Bevan, ed., "Introduction," *Complete Angler*, p. xviii.

26. Cooper, *Art of "The Compleat Angler,"* p. 71. For a book-length study of this topic (exclusive of Walton), see Leah S. Marcus, *The Politics of Mirth* (Chicago: University of Chicago Press, 1986).

27. See Cliff Tolliver, "The Recreation of Contemplation: Walton's *Angler* in Thoreau's *Week*," *ESQ* 38 (1992), 293–313.

28. This poem is identified and quoted in the Nicolas edition, 2:159: "a poem which occurs in a Collection of Poems entitled the "Phoenix Nest" publ. in 1593": "Like to a Hermite poor, in place obscure, / I mean to spend my daies of endles doubt, / To waile such woes as time cannot recure / Where none but Love shall ever finde me out."

29. For a nuanced and informed discussion of the pastoral mode – particularly its exclusivities, discontinuities, and artifice – see Thomas Rosenmeyer, *The Green Cabinet: Theocritus and the European Pastoral Lyric* (Berkeley and Los Angeles: University of California Press, 1969).

30. Several critics have characterized the opening dialogue of the "Brute Neighbors" chapter in *Walden* as an imitation (satiric or otherwise) of Walton's dialogues in *The Compleat Angler:* see Robert R. Hodges, "The Functional Satire of Thoreau's Hermit and Poet," reprinted in *Critical Essays on Henry David Thoreau's Walden*, ed. Joel Myerson (Boston: Hall, 1988), pp. 106–10. See also Thomas Blanding, "Walton and Walden," *Thoreau Society Bulletin* 107 (1969), 3. Whereas I emphasize stylization as the means to satirize pastoralism, they focus on the dialogue as a satiric portrait of Transcendentalism.

31. Cf. *Dark Thoreau* (Lincoln: University of Nebraska Press, 1982), where Richard Bridgman argues that these brute neighbors are

manifestations of nature's intransigence, its unwillingness to admit the frustrated Thoreau into its "brotherhood" (pp. 123–7).

32. The three commentaries on Milton's poetry that Thoreau had before him in 1837 were: *Milton, Poems Upon Several Occasions, with notes by Thomas Warton*, 2d ed. (London, 1791); *The Poetical Works of John Milton, ed. with Life by Henry John Todd*, 6 vols. (London, 1801); and *The Poetical Works of John Milton with Notes of Various Authors*, ed. Thomas Newton, 3 vols. (London, 1752–4).

33. The first comment ("[Milton's] design . . .") is Thoreau's, about an observation by William Warburton; the second is by Thomas Newton, transcribed by Henry John Todd and by Thoreau. Both appear in "Miscellaneous Extracts" (February 1837), Pierpont Morgan Library, Ms. 594. Thoreau was also well aware that *Lycidas* contained self-conscious allusions to Milton's engagement with the writing of poetry.

34. John Crowe Ransom is the most famous instance. See his seminal article "A Poem Nearly Anonymous," *American Review* 4 (1933), 179–203, reprinted in C. A. Patrides, ed., *Milton's Lycidas* (New York, 1961), pp. 64–81.

35. For Thoreau's transcription of a section of the tribute to Charles Diodati, see "Miscellaneous Extracts."

36. I quote Milton's poetry from Merritt Y. Hughes, ed., *John Milton: Complete Poems and Major Prose* (Indianapolis: Odyssey Press, 1957). Subsequent references will be to this edition and will be given in the text.

37. For a detailed discussion of Thoreau use of *Lycidas* in *A Week*, see Johnson, *Thoreau's Complex Weave*, ch. 2, "The Elegiac Mode." For a view that coincides with Johnson's on the inefficacy of Thoreau's consolation but contrasts in regarding the elegiac echoes of Milton's poem as a distraction from the larger conservative ideological message of *A Week*, see K. P. Van Anglen, *The New England Milton: Literary Reception and Cultural Authority in the Early Republic* (University Park: Pennsylvania State University Press, 1993), pp. 200–2. My emphasis is upon Thoreau's use of *Lycidas* in *Walden* and *Walking*, and I suggest that his impulses are less personal but more denunciatory and more prophetically hopeful as public expressions.

38. Thoreau, *Writings*, 5:220, Thoreau's emphasis. Subsequent citations of *Walking* are to the edition cited in note 16 and will be given in the text as *Writings* with volume and page number.

39. I agree with Bercovitch that the movement in Thoreau (in *Walking* and *Walden*) is neither toward "an aesthetic withdrawal nor a romantic-antinomian declaration of superiority to history" but rather toward an engagement with a "social ideal." But I disagree with Bercovitch's idea that *Walden* is ultimately a text giving vent to rebellious impulses as part of the process of acculturation, of preserving conservative values – a jeremiad that allows "Thoreau simul-

taneously to berate his neighbors and to safeguard the values that undergird their way of life." See Sacvan Bercovitch, *The American Jeremiad* (Madison: University of Wisconsin Press, 1978), pp. 185–6. Moreover, in light of recent work on the English Revolutionary period, I disagree that only American Puritans actually believed in merging the city on the hill with earthly institutions and national settlements. Certainly the Milton of the 1640s thought in terms of an earthly millennium.

40. See Michael T. Gilmore, *American Romanticism and the Marketplace* (Chicago: University of Chicago Press, 1985), pp. 18, 38.

41. He copies from Book IV of *Paradise Lost:* "soft downy Bank damaskt with flow'rs," "irriguous valley," "umbrageous grots," "mantling vine," "ambrosial fragrance," "mellifluous dews"; and from Book VIII, "liquid lapse of murmuring streams." He also copies phrases from several other books of *Paradise Lost* and from *Lycidas, Comus,* and *Paradise Regained.* See Henry David Thoreau, "Index Rerum," Huntington Library, Ms. HM.945. Thoreau rehearses the use of the Miltonic idiom in a brief exercise called "Gratitude," written in 1838, not long after he copied these excerpts.

42. Cf. Kevin Van Anglen's reading of these passages in Milton and Thoreau, which, contrary to my own, emphasizes the conservative impulse in both authors, *New England Milton,* pp. 209–12. Although he acknowledges the antiauthoritarian impulse in *Walden* (p. 212), Van Anglen emphasizes that, like the Christian Milton who asserts the "superiority" of the biblical garden over the Arcadian, Thoreau uses the comparison of gardens to affirm "the same ideologically moderate, dominant-class values of order, modified hierarchy, and limited liberty as Milton had in Book IV" (p. 211).

43. Henry David Thoreau, "Slavery in Massachusetts," in *Reform Papers,* ed. Wendell Glick (Princeton, N. J.: Princeton University Press, 1973), p. 108. Subsequent citations are to this edition and will be given in the text as *Reform Papers,* followed by page numbers.

44. See Milton, *De Doctrina Christiana,* in *The Complete Prose Works of John Milton,* gen. ed. Don M. Wolfe, 8 vols. (New Haven: Yale University Press, 1953–82), 6.351–2 (my emphasis).

45. Robert A. Gross, "The Great Bean Field Hoax: Thoreau and the Agricultural Reformers," in *Critical Essays on Henry David Thoreau's "Walden,"* ed. Joel Myerson (Boston: Hall, 1988), pp. 196–205.

46. For a discussion of melancholy as signaling the limits of the pastoral in the classical and Renaissance periods, see Rosenmeyer, *Green Cabinet,* pp. 229–31.

47. Cowley appears on Thoreau's dated list of books that he read at Staten Island, New York, for April 15, 1841; however, the dates of the Cowley excerpts in his literary notebook suggest that Thoreau may have read him as early as sometime between 1837 and 1839. An examination of the *Prose Works of Abraham Cowley, esq., Including his Essays in Prose and Verse* (London: William Pickering, 1826) sug-

gests that this is probably the edition Thoreau read. Further citations to Cowley will refer to this edition and appear in the text as "Cowley, *Prose Works*" followed by page numbers. See also Sattelmeyer, *Thoreau's Reading,* p. 159. For a facsimile of his Cowley transcriptions, see Kenneth Walter Cameron, *Thoreau's Literary Notebook in the Library of Congress* (Hartford: Transcendental Books, 1964), pp. 28, 63.

48. For a discussion of the essays, including their composition, literary sources, and biographical connections, see Arthur H. Nethercot, *Abraham Cowley: The Muses Hannibal* (London: Oxford University Press, 1931), pp. 261ff.

49. Quotation from Cowley, "A Discourse By Way of Vision Concerning the Government of Oliver Cromwell," in *Prose Works,* p. 82.

50. For his lecture, see "Thomas Carlyle and His Works" (1846), in Henry David Thoreau, *Early Essays and Miscellanies,* ed. Joseph J. Moldenhauer and Edwin Moser, with Alexander C. Kern. (Princeton: Princeton University Press, 1975), pp. 316–55. For his significantly expanded version of his lecture, see his review, "Thomas Carlyle and His Works," *Graham's Magazine* 30 (1847), no. 3, 142–52, and no. 4, 238–45. Subsequent citations are to this expanded version and will be given in the text as "Carlyle" (1847), followed by page numbers. For his comparison of John Brown with Cromwell, see "A Plea for Captain John Brown" (1859), in *Reform Papers,* pp. 113–15.

51. The Digger movement began on St. George's Hill in Surrey and was led by Gerrard Winstanley: see F. D. Dow, *Radicalism in the English Revolution, 1640–1660* (Oxford: Blackwell, 1985), pp. 74–80.

52. On the interconnection between Cowley's royalist politics, his involvement in the royalist underground, and his poetry, see Thomas N. Corns, *Uncloistered Virtue: English Political Literature, 1640 – 1660* (Oxford: Clarendon Press, 1992), pp. 250–68. Thoreau may have read the biography by Thomas Sprat, "An Account of the Life and Writings of Mr. Abraham Cowley," included in the 1826 *Prose Works of Abraham Cowley,* pp. vii–xxix.

53. Cowley was seen by fellow royalists as too fully surrendering to the enemy in the following passage from the preface to his 1656 poems: "we must lay down our *Pens* as well as *Arms,* we must *march* out of our *Cause* it self, and *dismantle* that, as well as our *Town* and Castles, of all the *Works* and *Fortifications* of *Wit* and *Reason* by which we defended it." This passage was suppressed by Sprat in his edition of Cowley. I quote here from Cowley's "Unmutilated Preface of 1656" in *The Complete Works in Verse and Prose of Abraham Cowley,* ed. Alexander B. Grosart (1881; rpt. New York: AMS Press, 1967), "Memorial-Introduction," appendix C, p. cxxviii.

54. Samuel Johnson, *Rambler,* "No. 6," in *Essays from the "Rambler, Adventurer, and Idler,"* ed. Walter Jackson Bate (New Haven: Yale University Press, 1968), p. 18.

55. On the West Indian slave trade, see Eric J. Sundquist, *To Wake the Nations: Race in the Making of American Literature* (Cambridge, Mass: Harvard University Press, 1993), pp. 135–7.

56. On the politics of the georgic mode in seventeenth-century England, and especially Cowley's involvement with the new science and land reform, see Anthony Low, *The Georgic Revolution* (Princeton: Princeton University Press, 1985), esp. chs. 4 and 6; my quotation is from Low, p. 153. Low points out that political alignment over land reform was "never quite one of Puritan against Cavalier" (p. 222).

57. On reification in nineteenth-century America, see Carolyn Porter, *Seeing and Being: The Plight of the Participant Observer in Emerson, James, Adams, and Faulkner* (Middletown, Conn.: Wesleyan University Press, 1981).

58. In *Machine and the Garden* and "Pastoralism in America," Leo Marx makes a similar case for Jefferson's pastoralism rather than "economic" agrarianism (Machine, pp. 125–28. "Pastoralism in America" in *Ideology and Classic American Literature,* ed. Sacvan Bercovitch and Myra Jehlen (Cambridge University Press, 1986), p. 51. Cowley's devotion to scientific improvements in land use, however, makes him a pastoralist in the midst of civil wars, and an economic agrarianist in the midst of a scientific revolution.

59. The edition Thoreau read was Thomas Jefferson, Query 19 of *Notes on the State of Virginia. With an Appendix,* 8th American ed. (Boston: David Carlisle, for Thomas & Andrews, 1801). Of course Jefferson later modified his views on agrarianism.

60. For a discussion of the Whig predominance in antebellum New England, see Daniel Walker Howe, *The Unitarian Conscience: Harvard Moral Philosophy, 1805–1861* (Cambridge, Mass.: Harvard University Press, 1970) and *The Political Culture of the American Whigs* (Chicago: University of Chicago Press, 1979).

61. Samuel Johnson, in "The Life of Abraham Cowley," in *The Lives of the Most Eminent English Poets; with Critical Observations on their Works,* 4 vols. (London: Bathhurst & Buckland, 1783), 1:10–11. Thoreau checked out the first volume from Harvard University Library in the spring of 1837.

62. Sprat, "An Account," in *Prose Works of Abraham Cowley,* p. xiv.

63. Henry David Thoreau, *Journal,* John C. Broderick, gen. ed., ed. Elizabeth Hall Witherell et al., 4 vols. (Princeton, N.J.: Princeton University Press, 1971) 4:468.

64. For a discussion of such tensions among Americans artists, see Albert J. von Frank, *The Sacred Game: Provincialism and Frontier Consciousness in American Literature, 1630–1860* (Cambridge University Press, 1985). Although von Frank sees Thoreau as choosing the "liberal" solution to American cultural identity in celebrating nativism (p. 113), I think his comment about Washington Irving is more apt for Thoreau: "The predicament in which he also placed himself – that of resorting to provincial material for the vital strength of

his art while at the same time having to overcome it with style and culture – is among the most persistent of the problems confronted by American artists in the nineteenth century" (p. 73). On Thoreau's *A Week*, see also Eric J. Sundquist, *Home as Found: Authority and Genealogy in Nineteenth-Century America* (Baltimore: Johns Hopkins University Press, 1979), ch. 2.

65. For what remains the most comprehensive treatment of Browne's reputation in nineteenth-century England and America, see Ruth M. Vande Kieft, "The Nineteenth Century Reputation of Sir Thomas Browne," Ph.D. diss., University of Michigan, 1957. Based on the anthology selections and belles-lettres essays available to the nineteenth-century American audience, *Hydriotaphia* was as least as familiar to that audience as was Browne's *Religio Medici*. For a fuller discussion of antebellum Americans' responses to Browne's thought, style, and motifs, see Chapter 5 of the present volume.

66. For a discussion of the attempt by American writers to define the national identity, see Benjamin T. Spencer, *The Quest for Nationality: An American Literary Campaign* (Syracuse: Syracuse University Press, 1957), and Robert Weisbuch, *Atlantic Double-Cross: American Literature and British Influence in the Age of Emerson* (Chicago: University of Chicago Press, 1986), ch. 1.

67. William Ellery Channing, "Remarks on National Literature" (1823), in *The Works of William E. Channing*, 8th ed., 6 vols. (Boston: James Munroe, 1848), 1:245.

68. Channing, "Remarks," 1:245–6.

69. By 1872, Trinity Church was considered enough of a landmark to be remarked upon in *Picturesque America, or The Land We Live In: A Delineation by Pen and Pencil*, ed. William Cullen Bryant, 2 vols. (New York: D. Appleton, 1872), 2:353.

70. See Orestes A. Brownson, "Sub-treasury Bill," *Boston Quarterly Review* 1 (July 1838), 333–60; "The Currency," *Boston Quarterly Review* 2 (July 1839), 298–326; "The Currency," *Boston Quarterly Review* 3 (January 1840), 86–116, esp. 113–16; and his review of a *New System of Paper Money* by a Citizen of Boston (I. R. Butts, 1837), 128. Thoreau met and began to work for Brownson in 1836 and continued the connection with him through the 1840s. The *Boston Daily Courier* also carried a series of articles on the United States Bank in 1838. For a discussion of the Bank War and banking policies in this period, see, among others, Ronald P. Formisano, *The Transformation of Political Culture, Massachusetts Parties, 1790s–1840s* (New York: Oxford University Press, 1983), pp. 251–6; Eric Foner, *Free Soil, Free Labor, Free Men: The Ideology of the Republican Party before the Civil War* (New York: Oxford University Press, 1970), pp. 165–78; Marvin Meyers, *The Jacksonian Persuasion: Politics and Belief* (Stanford: Stanford University Press, 1957), pp. 10–14, 24–28, 103–11.

71. Sir Thomas Browne, "Hydriotaphia; Urn Burial, or A Discourse of the Sepulchral Urns Lately found in Norfolk," in *Sir Thomas Browne's*

Works, Including His Life and Correspondence, ed. Simon Wilkin, 4 vols. (London: William Pickering, 1835–6), 3:489, 490, 496. Subsequent references to Browne's writings will be to this edition and will be given in the text with title, volume, and page number.

72. Jonson insists that the patrons of his masques be more "curious after the most high and hearty inventions to furnish the inward parts, and those grounded upon antiquity and solid learnings." Thoreau read Thomas Warton's *History of English Poetry,* ed. Richard Price, 4 vols. (London: T. Tegg, 1824). For a discussion of the history and function of masques, including individual masques, see vol. 2, sec. 16.

73. An examination of *The Works of Thomas Carew* (Edinburgh: W. and C. Tait, 1824) suggests that this reprint of the original 1640 edition might be the edition Thoreau read. There were, however, numerous other seventeenth-century editions of the masque and poetry available to him at Harvard. My citations from *Coelum Britannicum* are taken from *The Poems of Thomas Carew,* ed. Rhodes Dunlop (Oxford: Clarendon Press, 1959). Mercury's speech on "The Pretensions of Poverty" appears in Cameron, *Thoreau's Literary Notebook in the Library of Congress,* and in Thoreau's journal for September of 1843 (*Journal,* 1:466). Thoreau's transcriptions from *Coelum* include Poverty's speech (lines 609–16), the speech by Mercury (lines 642–68), another by Mercury condemning Pleasure (lines 628–9), and biographical and stylistic comments on Carew and his writings.

74. For a discussion of this protean Gamecock figure, see Constance Rourke's classic study *American Humor* (New York: Harcourt, Brace, 1931), ch. 2. For a discussion of Chanticleer as a Jeremiah figure, see Cavell, *Senses of Walden,* pp. 36–40.

75. Cameron, *Thoreau's Literary Notebook in the Library of Congress,* p. 28. Moreover, in his notes to Milton's *Comus,* Thoreau shows a detailed knowledge of the political occasion and the personages involved. See Kenneth Walter Cameron, *The Transcendentalists and Minerva: Cultural Backgrounds of the American Renaissance,* 3 vols. (Hartford: Transcendental Books, 1958), 1:193.

76. Nina Baym, Wayne Franklin, Ronald Gottesman, et al., eds., *The Norton Anthology of American Literature,* 4th ed. (New York: Norton, 1989) 1:1,760. These editors are following the more equivocal comment by Walter Harding, *The Variorum Walden* (New York: Washington Square Press, 1963), p. 172.

77. The particulars of Orestes Brownson's article on "Ultraism" in the first volume of the *Boston Quarterly Review* (1838) may well be resonating in this section against reformers in *Walden.* We know from Thoreau's correspondence with Brownson that he read at least the first issue of the *Review.*

78. The character of Carew's Momus is based in part on a character in Giordano Bruno's *Spaccio de la Besta Trionfante.*

79. Shanley, *Making of Walden,* p. 123. No other sources for the Momus

figure have been identified: see Robert D. Richardson, Jr., *Myth and Literature in the American Renaissance* (Bloomington: Indiana University Press, 1978), and Ethel Seybold, *Thoreau: The Quest and the Classics* (New Haven: Yale University Press, 1951).

80. As the supreme adjudicator, or Lord-Chancellor ("Woollsacke god"), Momus cannot vote as do the other gods (lines 146–7) in Parliament, which in any case had already been dissolved by Charles I by the time *Coelum* was written.

81. For a discussion of how Charles's consolidation of power (and equivocations about this power) are revealed in the masque, see Stephen Orgel and Roy Strong, *Inigo Jones: The Theatre of the Stuart Court*, 2 vols. (Berkeley and Los Angeles: University of California Press, 1973), 1:64–70; Kevin Sharpe, *Compliment and Criticism: The Politics of Literature in the England of Charles I* (Cambridge University Press, 1987), pp. 239–43; and Jennifer Chibnall, " 'To that secure fix'd state': The Function of the Caroline Masque Form," in *The Court Masque*, ed. David Lindley (Manchester, England: Manchester University Press, 1984), pp. 78–93.

82. For a recent account of Charles I's belief in his God-given authority and power, see Ann Hughes, *The Causes of the English Civil War* (London: Macmillan, 1991), ch. 4.

83. For a discussion of Thoreau's troubles in the literary marketplace, see Gilmore, *American Romanticism and the Marketplace*, ch. 3. On the problems of authorship in antebellum America, see William Charvat, *Literary Publishing in America, 1790–1850* (Philadelphia: University of Pennsylvania Press, 1959).

84. Cameron, *Thoreau's Literary Notebook in the Library of Congress*, p. 23.

85. This is noted by Shanley, *Making of Walden*, p. 136, n. 29. It seems from the order of the three phrases – obviously notes made by Thoreau to himself – cited by Shanley as constituting leaf 36v ("Mercury's Reply to Poverty in Carew," "End of *Economy*," "S about Hollowell Farm"), that Thoreau viewed Mercury's speech as the conclusion to the "Economy" chapter rather than the preface to "Where I Lived, and What I Lived for," where Hollowell's farm is the focus.

86. For a discussion of Thoreau's notion of "creative poverty," see Thomas Woodson, "Thoreau on Poverty and Magnanimity," *PMLA* 85 (January 1970), 21–34. In "Socio-Economic Disarray and Literary Response," Yanella takes issue with the accuracy of Thoreau's (and Woodson's) perceptions of those who were said to be the creative poor (p. 15).

87. In "Thoreau on Poverty and Magnanimity," Woodson correctly suggests that Thoreau uses these verses to "complete the argument of 'Economy,' and especially his attack on the practice of philanthropy in Concord" (p. 24). However, Woodson does not remark upon a complementary relationship between Momus and Mercury. Instead, he argues that since the heroic virtues of poverty Thoreau sees in certain poor men are not appropriately called "regal," Thoreau's

notion comes primarily from Greek mythology and Aristotle's *Nicomachean Ethics.* I suggest that Thoreau has his own example in mind, one to which "regal" does apply.

88. For a discussion of Thoreau's shifting attitudes toward heroism and soldiery, see Linck C. Johnson, "Contexts of Bravery: Thoreau's Revisions of 'The Service' for *A Week,*" in *Studies in the American Renaissance, 1983,* ed. Joel Myerson (Charlottesville: University of Virginia Press, 1983), 281–96.

89. Thoreau's gradual retreat from a social agenda in *Walden* has been argued by a variety of critics, including Gilmore in *American Romanticism and the Marketplace,* ch. 2; Robert Gross, "'The Most Estimable Place in All the World': A Debate on Progress in Nineteenth-Century Concord," in *Studies in the American Renaissance, 1978,* ed. Joel Myerson (Boston: Twayne, 1978), pp. 90–105; Marx, *Machine in the Garden,* ch. 5. For complementary discussions focusing on Thoreau's impulses divided between "reclamation" and retreat into pristine landscapes, see Garber, *Thoreau's Redemptive Imagination;* Buell, *New England Literary Culture,* ch. 14; Bercovitch, *American Jeremiad,* pp. 181–2. For a discussion of Thoreau's reliance on the imagery of Ovid's *Metamorphoses,* specifically in the thawing-sand section of the "Spring" chapter and as "a master image of the workings of nature," see Richardson, *Myth and Literature,* p. 137.

90. Orgel and Strong, *Inigo Jones,* 1:68.

91. Cavell, *Senses of Walden,* p. 8; Bercovitch, *American Jeremiad,* p. 186; Buell, *New England Literary Culture,* p. 326.

92. He transcribes from *Love Freed from Ignorance and Folly* (lines 302–10) and also from *The Masque of Queens* ("Who, Virtue, can thy power forget?" [lines 515–27]); *The Golden Age Restored. In a Masque at Court, 1615* (Act 3, lines 282–3); and *Victorious Men of Earth,* "From a masque by James Shirley presented in 1653," all in Cameron, *Thoreau's Literary Notebook in the Library of Congress,* p. 28.

93. For Thoreau's familiarity with Sir Thomas Browne's writings, see Thoreau's commonplace book (Morgan Library, Ms. 594) for the period of 1837–9; see also Sattelmeyer, *Thoreau's Reading,* p. 140. For a discussion of the theatrical element in Browne's narrative persona in *Religio,* see Marta Straznicky, "Performing the Self in Browne's *Religio Medici,*" *Prose Studies* 13 (1990), 211–29; and more generally, Joan Webber, *The Eloquent "I": Style and Self in Seventeenth-Century Prose* (Madison: University of Wisconsin Press, 1968). The excerpts from Browne in the *Journal* and *A Week* suggest that Thoreau was drawing from his Wilkin edition of Browne rather than from desultory gleanings collected from such Browne popularizers as Coleridge, Lamb, or DeQuincey; see Thoreau, *Journal,* 1:446–7, 1:532, n. 446.6–16.

94. For an extended discussion of the political character of *Religio Medici,* see Jonathan F. S. Post, *Sir Thomas Browne* (Boston: Hall, 1986), pp. 76–94. See Anne Drury Hall, "Epistle, Meditation, and Sir

Thomas Browne's *Religio Medici*," *PMLA* 94 (1979), 234–46, for a discussion of his use of several genres and his characteristic sense of modesty, restraint, and decorum in *Religio*. See Anna Nardo, "Sir Thomas Browne: Sub specie Ludi," *Centennial Review* 21 (1977), 311–20, for a discussion of playful wit as an alternative to the seriousness and ferocity of sectarian conflicts in Civil War England.

95. Thoreau would have read Johnson's "The Life of Sir Thomas Browne" in the Wilkin edition of *Sir Thomas Browne's Works*, 1:xvii–liv.

96. Cf. Henry Golemba's rhetorical reading of Thoreau's dilations as a way to fill the inevitable lacunae created by language: see *Thoreau's Wild Rhetoric* (New York: New York University Press, 1993).

5: Melville & Marvelous Travel Narratives

1. In addition to James Duban's *Melville's Major Fiction: Politics, Theology, and Imagination* (DeKalb: Northern Illinois University Press, 1983) and Michael Paul Rogin's *Subversive Genealogy: The Politics and Art of Herman Melville* (Berkeley and Los Angeles: University of California Press, 1979), see Lawrence Buell, *New England Literary Culture: From Revolution through Renaissance* (Cambridge University Press, 1986); Wai Chee Dimock, *Empire for Liberty: Melville and the Poetics of Individualism* (Princeton: Princeton University Press, 1989); and David S. Reynolds, *Beneath the American Renaissance: The Subversive Imagination in the Age of Emerson and Melville* (Cambridge, Mass.: Harvard University Press, 1989).

2. Herman Melville, *Moby-Dick, or The Whale*, ed. Harrison Hayford, Hershel Parker, and G. Thomas Tanselle (Evanston, Ill.: Northwestern University and Newberry Library, 1988), p. 327. All subsequent references to *Moby-Dick* and to *Mardi, A Voyage Thither* (Evanston, Ill.: Northwestern University and Newberry Library, 1970) are to the Northwestern–Newberry editions and will be given in the text as *M-D* and *Mardi*, respectively, with page numbers.

3. For a discussion of the connections between New England theology and seventeenth-century English theology, see Daniel Walker Howe, "The Cambridge Platonists of Old England and the Cambridge Platonists of New England," in *American Unitarianism: 1805 – 1865*, ed. Conrad Edick Wright (Boston: Massachusetts Historical Society and Northeastern University Press, 1989), pp. 87–119. Howe documents two "intertwining" strains of American rationalist theology (Charles Chauncy's and Benjamin Colman's), the former traced to the empirical and utilitarian, to "Locke and the Latitudinarians of the Tillotson school," and the latter, upon which he focuses, to the more pietistic Cambridge Platonists.

On Anglicanism and American liberal Christian Arminianism, see Sydney E. Ahlstrom, *A Religious History of the American People* (New Haven, Conn.: Yale University Press, 1972), pp. 343–59, esp.

p. 357. See also William R. Hutchison, *Transcendental Ministers: Church Reform in the New England Renaissance* (New Haven, Conn.: Yale University Press, 1959), who notes that the American Unitarian movement "drew its inspiration . . . from rationalistic and Arian writers such as Chillingworth, Milton, and Clarke, who represented the liberal element in the English Churches during the seventeenth and eighteenth centuries" (p. 7).

4. Although I acknowledge that some Whigs advocated more broadly conceived attitudes toward race relations and women's rights, most notably William Ellery Channing, as well as more "progressive" responses to industrialization and universal education, I am roughly equating Whiggery with conservatism. Whigs saw their own efforts as "conservative" in their emphases upon "protecting property rights, maintaining social order, and preserving a distinct cultural heritage" and because of their "moral absolutism, paternalism, and preoccupation with discipline." See Daniel Walker Howe, *The Political Culture of the American Whigs* (Chicago: University of Chicago Press, 1979), pp. 210–37, quotation on p. 210.

5. On Melville's knowledge of Browne, see Merton M. Sealts, Jr., *Melville's Reading*, rev. ed. (Columbia: University of South Carolina Press, 1988), items 89–90 and also pp. 38–9, 42–3, 159. On Browne's probabilism, see Victoria Silver, "Liberal Theology and Sir Thomas Browne's 'Soft and Flexible' Discourse," *English Literary Renaissance* 20 (1990), 69–103. Although I had previously discovered Browne's modest use of reason and his limited confidence in individual agency, I owe my awareness and interpretation of his probabilism to Silver. Silver premises her discussion of the rhetorical implications of human agency in Browne's prose style and theology on the Arminian doctrines underlying liberal Anglican theology.

6. On Melville's response to rationalist theology and empiricist epistemology in relation to the verification of the miraculous and supernatural in *Moby-Dick*, see also Duban, *Melville's Major Fiction*, pp. 117–25. On Melville's knowledge of Locke's *Essay Concerning Human Understanding*, see Robert Zoellner, *The Salt Sea Mastodon: A Reading of "Moby-Dick"* (Berkeley and Los Angeles: University of California Press, 1973), pp. 1–28. For an argument that focuses on Locke's sensationalist epistemology, see David Hirsch, "The Dilemma of the Liberal Intellectual: Melville's Ishmael," *Texas Studies in Literature and Language* 5 (1963), 182–6.

7. For Locke's reading in and personal acquaintance with Boyle and his high esteem for Chillingworth's and Tillotson's writings, see John Marshall, "Locke and Latitudinarianism," in *Philosophy, Science, and Religion,* eds. Richard Kroll, Richard Ashcraft, and Perez Zagorin (Cambridge University Press, 1992), pp. 253–4, 265. See also Barbara J. Shapiro, *Probability and Certainty in Seventeenth-Century England: A Study of the Relationship Between Natural Science, Religion, History, Law and Literature* (Princeton: Princeton University Press, 1983), ch. 3.

8. Shapiro, *Probability and Certainty*, esp. p. 12.

9. See Shapiro, *Probability and Certainty*, pp. 27–73; Henry Robert McAdoo, *The Spirit of Anglicanism: A Survey of Anglican Theological Method in the Seventeenth Century* (London: Adam & Charles Black, 1965), chs. 7–8; Michael McKeon, *The Origins of the English Novel 1600–1740* (Baltimore: Johns Hopkins University Press, 1987), pp. 100–5; Henry G. van Leeuwen, *The Problem of Certainty in English Thought, 1630–1690* (The Hague: Martinus Nijhoff, 1963); Richard S. Westfall, *Science and Religion in Seventeenth-Century England* (New Haven, Conn.: Yale University Press, 1958); and R. M. Burns, *The Great Debate on Miracles: From Joseph Glanvill to David Hume* (Lewisburg, Pa.: Bucknell University Press, 1981), ch. 2.

10. John Locke, *An Essay Concerning Human Understanding*, ed. Alexander Campbell Fraser, 2 vols. (1894; rpt. New York: Dover, 1959), Book IV, ch. 1, paragraph subsection 1. Subsequent citations are to this edition and will be given in the text as *Essay* with book, chapter, and paragraph subsection number.

   Though Locke was a moderate empiricist in the broad tendencies of his thought, his "egocentric predicament," which he shares with the Cartesians, positions him closer to Hume and the Deists than earlier probabilists such as Joseph Glanvill and Robert Boyle; see Burns, *Great Debate on Miracles*, pp. 59–69. On Locke, see also Douglas Lane Patey, *Probability and Literary Form: Philosophic Theory and Literary Practice in the Augustan Age* (Cambridge University Press, 1984), pp. 27–34.

11. Patey, *Probability and Literary Form*, p. 27.

12. *A Discourse of Miracles*, in *John Locke: "The Reasonableness of Christianity" with "A Discourse of Miracles" and part of "A Third Letter Concerning Toleration,"* ed. I. T. Ramsey (Stanford: Stanford University Press, 1958), p. 84. Subsequent citations are to this edition and will be given in the text as *Discourse* with page number.

13. See I. T. Ramsey's discussion of Locke on intuition, power, and the mysterious element of "reasonable" Christianity in *John Locke: "Reasonableness of Christianity,"* pp. 15–18.

14. Sir Thomas Browne, *Pseudodoxia Epidemica: or Enquiries Into Very Many Received Tenets and Commonly Presumed Truths*, in *Sir Thomas Browne's Works, Including His Life and Correspondence*, ed. Simon Wilkin, 4 vols. (London: William Pickering, 1835–6), vol. 2, book I, chapter 3. Hereafter citations of *Pseudodoxia* will refer to this edition and will be given in the text as *PE* with book and chapter numbers. Books 4 to 7 are in volume 3 of the Wilkin edition.

15. On Melville's association of Browne with thoroughgoing skepticism and fideism, see Bruce L. Grenberg, *Some Other World to Find: Quest and Negation in the Works of Herman Melville* (Urbana: University of Illinois Press, 1989), p. 165; Brian Foley, "Herman Melville and the Example of Sir Thomas Browne," *Modern Philology* 81 (1984) 265–77; and Ruth M. Vande Kieft, " 'When Big Hearts Strike Together': The Concussion of Melville and Sir Thomas Browne, *Papers on Lan-*

guage and Literature 5 (1969), 39–50. On Browne's fideism, see Achsah Guibbory, "Sir Thomas Browne's *Pseudodoxia Epidemica* and the Circle of Knowledge," *Texas Studies in Literature and Language* 18 (1976), 486–99. On Melville, Browne, and the Platonic tradition, see Merton M. Sealts, Jr., *Pursuing Melville: 1940–1980* (Madison: University of Wisconsin Press, 1982), pp. 282–4, 298. On Browne's "Christian Platonism," see Leonard Nathanson, *The Strategy of Truth: A Study of Sir Thomas Browne* (Chicago: University of Chicago, 1967).

16. For Browne's epistemology, characterized by a partly efficacious human agency and a resemblance to some aspects of the liberal Anglican position, see Victoria Silver, "Liberal Theology," pp. 69–103. On Browne's modest skepticism and Latitudinarian tendencies, see also Nathanson, *Strategy of Truth,* pp. 111–41.

17. Sir Thomas Browne, *Religio Medici,* in *Sir Thomas Browne's Works,* Wilkin ed., vol. 2. Subsequent citations of *Religio Medici* are to this edition and will be given in the text as *Religio* with book and subsection number.

18. In the "Man-of-War Library" (ch. 41) of *White-Jacket,* Melville mentions that this library includes "a folio of Tillotson's Sermons – the best of reading for divines, indeed, but with little relish for a maintop-man; and Locke's Essays – incomparable essays, every body knows, but miserable reading at sea." *White-Jacket,* ed. Harrison Hayford, Hershel Parker, and G. Thomas Tanselle (Evanston, Ill.: Northwestern University and Newberry Library, 1970), p. 167.

19. John Jortin, quoted in the "Supplementary Memoir" of the Wilkin edition of *Sir Thomas Browne's Works,* 1: lxiii–lxiv. These quotations are also duplicated in the footnotes to Sir Kenelm Digby's *Observations on Religio Medici* in the Wilkin edition of *Browne's Works,* 2:122.

20. van Leeuwen, *Problem of Certainty,* pp. 14–48; McAdoo, *Spirit of Anglicanism,* chs. 7–10; Silver, "Liberal Theology," pp. 85–91.

21. Sir Kenelm Digby, *Observations on Religio Medici,* in the Wilkin edition of *Browne's Works,* 2:120.

22. James Hartwell Barrett, "Sir Thomas Browne," *American Whig Review* 8 (July 1848), 23.

23. Excluding the issue of scientific dogmatism, this is Silver's argument with respect to *Religio Medici* in "Liberal Theology," pp. 69–103. On the moderate skepticism of Latitudinarians and the similarities between them and Arminians, see John Marshall, "Locke and Latitudinarianism," pp. 262, 269. More generally, see van Leeuwen, *Problem of Certainty;* and McAdoo, *Spirit of Anglicanism.*

24. Herman Melville, *Pierre, or The Ambiguities,* ed Harrison Hayford, Hershel Parker, and G. Thomas Tanselle (Evanston, Ill: Northwestern University and Newberry Library, 1971), p. 176.

25. Joseph Glanvill, *Philosophia Pia* (1617), in *Works,* ed. Bernhard Fabian (1671; facsimile, Hildesheim: Olms Verlag, 1970), 5:89. See

also Joseph Glanvill, Essay 1 ("Against Confidence in Philosophy and Matters of Speculation") and Essay 2 ("Of Scepticism and Certainty") in *Essays on Several Important Subjects in Philosophy and Religion,* ed. Bernhard Fabian (1676; facsimile, Hildesheim: Olms Verlag, 1979), 6:1; 6:39ff.

26. Herschel Baker, *The Wars of Truth: Studies in the Decay of Christian Humanism in the Earlier Seventeenth Century* (1952; rpt. Gloucester, Mass.: Peter Smith, 1969), p. 358.

27. Browne, however, does not quite share the optimism that some of these virtuosi expressed for ultimate resolutions or for achieving through natural studies the same degree of knowledge as had been divinely revealed. See Margaret L. Wiley, *The Subtle Knot: Creative Scepticism in Seventeenth-Century England* (London: George Allen & Unwin, 1952), pp. 75, 137–60. More generally on "constructive or mitigated scepticism," see Richard H. Popkin, *The History of Scepticism from Erasmus to Spinoza* (Berkeley and Los Angeles: University of California Press, 1979), ch. 7.

28. For a discussion characterizing the Anglican method, see McAdoo, *Spirit of Anglicanism,* pp. 240–355.

29. Bacon's *Novum Organon,* Book II, aph. 21. Cf. Bacon's comment, "Nor should we desist from inquiry, until the properties and qualities of those things, which may be deeemed miracles, as it were, of nature, be reduced to, and comprehended in, some form or certain law; so that all irregularity or singularity may be found to depend on some common form." See Francis Bacon, *Novum Organum* (1620), in *The Works of Francis Bacon,* ed. Basil Montagu, 17 vols. (London, 1825–34), 14:137.ii.29.

30. Lorraine Daston, "Marvelous Facts and Miraculous Evidences in Early Modern Europe," *Critical Inquiry* 18 (1991), 93–124, esp. 107–8.

31. Bacon, *New Atlantis,* in *Works,* 2:336.

32. For a discussion of this categorical instability see Daston, "Marvelous Facts," pp. 93–124, esp. pp. 98–113. See also Katharine Park and Lorraine Daston, "Unnatural Conceptions: The Study of Monsters in Sixteenth- and Seventeenth-Century France and England," *Past and Present* 92 (1981), 20–54.

33. See Loren Pennington, *Hakluytus Posthumus: Samuel Purchas and the Promotion of English Expansion,* Emporia (Kans.) State Research Studies, vol. 14, no. 3 (March 1966) pp. 12–13.

34. "Out of Mr Flatmans Poems," (*Poems and Songs, by Thomas Flatman,* 4th ed. [London: 1686], p. 168), copied into *The Commonplace Book of Elizabeth Lyttelton, Daughter of Sir Thomas Browne,* ed. Geoffrey Keynes (Cambridge University Press, 1919).

35. Melville's knowledge of Samuel Purchas's *Hakluytus Posthumus, or Purchas his Pilgrimes* appears to be in some instances independent of Browne's; see *Moby-Dick,* ed. Luther S. Mansfield and Howard Vincent (New York: Hendricks House, 1962), pp. 738, 782. Samuel

Purchas, *Hakluytus Posthumus, or Purchas his Pilgrimes: Containing a History of the World in Sea Voyages and Lande Travells by Englishmen and Others* (1625–6; rpt Glasgow: James MacLehose and Sons, 1905). For other discussions of Purchas in Melville's writings, see Howard P. Vincent, *The Trying Out of Moby-Dick* (Boston: Houghton Mifflin, 1949) pp. 377–79; and for Melville's knowledge of Purchas's earlier text, *Purchas his Pilgrimage, or Relations of the World and the Religions observed in all Ages* (1613), see Dorothea M. Finkelstein, *Melville's Orienda* (New Haven, Conn.: Yale University Press, 1961), pp. 46–9, 150, 161, 177–87.

36. See Mary B. Campbell, *The Witness and the Other World: Exotic European Travel Writing, 400–1600* (Ithaca, N.Y.: Cornell University Press, 1988), for a discussion of how "to the extent of the editor's ability to distinguish (an admittedly problematic limit), there is no imaginative or marvelous literature in Hakluyt, de Bry, or Purchas" (p. 221). For a recent study of the "colonizing of the marvelous" and the issue of appropriation as it defines identity and informs mimesis in medieval and Renaissance European societies, see Stephen Greenblatt, *Marvelous Possessions: The Wonder of the New World* (Chicago: University of Chicago Press, 1991).

37. Purchas, *Purchas his Pilgrimes,* 1:xliv, 66, 108.

38. Browne himself moves fluidly from theological to geographical probability when he asserts in *Religio Medici* (I.59) the probability of his own salvation as equivalent to the probable existence of the far-off Constantinople which he has never seen.

39. Browne, *Pseudodoxia Epidemica*, I.105; Purchas, *Purchas his Pilgrimes,* 1:xlii, xxxvii, xliii.

40. Cited in the introduction to Joseph Glanvill, *Saducismus Triumphatus; or, Full and Plain Evidence Concerning Witches and Apparitions,* introd. Coleman O. Parsons (1689; facsimile, Gainesville: Scholars' Facsimiles and Reprints, 1966), p. xvi.

41. *Purchas His Pilgrimes,* 1:184–5.

42. Philosophical Transactions of the Royal Society of London (London: Royal Society of London, 1666), 1 (1665–6), 141.

43. Foley, "Herman Melville and the Example of Sir Thomas Browne," pp. 265–77, esp. 271–2. Not surprisingly, Foley explains (p. 272, n. 26) that his "working hypothesis" for what constitutes Browne's "method of vulgar errors" came from a remark in an article on fideist Pierre Bayle by Millicent Bell, "Pierre Bayle and *Moby-Dick*," *PMLA* 66 (1951), 630. Many have detected a more thoroughgoing skepticism in Bayle.

44. See the Hendricks House edition of *Moby-Dick* and *Mardi*, ed. Nathalia Wright (Putney, Vt.: Hendricks, 1990), for the copious allusions to Browne. For the particular Brownean resonances in these chapters, see also F. O. Matthiessen, *American Renaissance: Art and Expression in the Age of Emerson and Whitman* (New York: Oxford University Press, 1941); John Wenke, "Melville's *Mardi:* Narrative Self-

Fashioning and the Play of Possibility," *Texas Studies in Literature and Language* 31 (1989), 406–25; Richard Dean Smith, *Melville's Complaint: Doctors and Medicine in the Art of Herman Melville* (New York: Garland Press, 1991), pp. 17–24, 27, 30.

45. For the discourse of travel narratives, see R. W. Franz, *The English Traveller and the Movement of Ideas: 1660–1732* (1934; rpt. Lincoln: University of Nebraska Press, 1967), pp. 32–70. On Melville and John Harris's travel narratives, see John M. J. Gretchko, "New Evidence for Melville's Use of John Harris in *Moby-Dick*," *Studies in the American Renaissance, 1983*, ed. Joel Myerson (Charlottesville: University of Virginia Press, 1983), 303–11.

46. John Josselyn, *An Account of Two Voyages to New England* (1674; rpt. Boston, 1865), pp. 30–1.

47. Thomas Sprat, *The History of the Royal Society* (1667), 3d, rev. ed. (London, 1722), pp. 61–2.

48. Melville may have in mind John Calvin commenting on "Allegori-makers," saying that it is "an euill thing to dally with the holie scripture by transforming of it into allegories," in *Sermons . . . upon the Booke of Job*, trans. Arthur Golding (London, 1574), p. 733, quoted in C. A. Patrides, *"Paradise Lost* and the Theory of Accommodation," in *Bright Essence* (Salt Lake City, 1971), p. 161, n. 4.

49. Cf. Duban, *Melville's Major Fiction*, who notes the use of rational Christian apologists such as William Paley and Bishop Butler to suggest that Ishmael is availing himself of the testimonial documentation for the *same* purpose as such rationalists – that "the more credible will be his final description of Moby-Dick staving the *Pequod*" (pp. 120–1).

50. Thomas Keck, "Annotations to *Religio Medici*," in *The Works of the Learned Sr Thomas Brown, Kt.*, ed. Archbishop Tenison (London, 1686), p. 55. This is an annotation to *Religio*, I.iii: "Yet I have not so shaken hands with those desperate Resolutions."

51. Although these distinctions were frequently made by Transcendentalists such as Theodore Parker in his "Discourse on the Permanent and Transient in Christianity" and Emerson in his Divinity School "Address," the presence of frequent paradoxes and tautologies, as well as verbal echoes, signals Browne as his immediate source.

52. Shapiro, *Probability and Certainty*, p. 42.

53. Matthiessen, *American Renaissance*, p. 123.

54. In "Herman Melville and the Example of Sir Thomas Browne," Foley notes Melville's use of Brownean stylistic features (pp. 270–1).

55. Obviously, Melville borrows the term "All-Plastic Power" from Coleridge. For a discussion of Melville on the topic of originality, see Charlene Avallone, "Vast and Varied Accessions . . . From Abroad': Herman Melville and Edward Young on Originality," in *Studies in the American Renaissance, 1984* (Charlottesville: University of Virginia Press), pp. 409–24. For a discussion of the American critics' desire

for originality as part of a quest for national authorization and cultural autonomy, see Benjamin T. Spencer, *The Quest for Originality: An American Literary Campaign* (Syracuse: Syracuse University Press, 1957).

56. Sir Thomas Browne, *Hydriotaphia, Urn Burial, or a Discourse of the Sepulchral Urns Lately Found in Norfolk,* in Wilkin ed. of *Works,* vol. 3, chapter V, p. 494. Subsequent citations will be to this edition, and will be given in the text as *Hy* with chapter and page number.

57. All preceding annotations in this paragraph are by Keck, "Annotations," p. 58.

58. Keck, "Annotations," p. 58.

59. From *Saurin's Discourses,* trans. Robert Robinson, in the Wilkin edition of *Browne's Works,* 2:51, n. 5.

60. See Wenke, "Melville's *Mardi:* Narrative Self-Fashioning and the Play of Possibility," for a discussion of this chapter as expressing the character Taji's "megalomaniacal" and "solipsistic isolationist" delusions. He describes Taji's experience here as "states of existence outside the diachronic movement of the narrative" (p. 418). I am less certain that it is Taji's dreams that are depicted – at least King Media also seems to have intimations of these thoughts when he comments about "dreams" in the next chapter.

61. For a discussion of Browne's own procedural instructions to his readers relating specifically to religious judgment and salvation, of which I am suggesting Melville selectively partakes and revises, see Silver, "Liberal Theology," pp. 94–105.

62. See David Jaffe, "Some Sources of Melville's *Mardi," American Literature* 9 (1937–8), 68. Extended excerpts from William Ellis, *Polynesian Researches* (1829; rpt. London: Dawsons, 1967), on superstitions about sorcery and witchcraft (including passages Jaffe suggests are sources for ch. 144 of *Mardi*) are also quoted at length in the Wilkin edition of *Browne's Works,* 1:lxxxv–lxxxvi.

63. Merton M. Sealts, Jr., notes that in Babbalonja's "receipt" "to hatch a fairy" Melville made imaginative use of a footnote to *Religio;* see "Melville's 'Friend Atahalpa,' " *Notes and Queries* 194 (1949), 37–8.

64. See Merrell R. Davis's discussion of the genesis of the novel between January and June of 1848, in *Melville's "Mardi": A Chartless Voyage* (1952; rpt. Archon Press, 1967), pp. 60–99, esp. p. 83.

65. William A. Jones, "Melville's Mardi," *U.S. Magazine and Democratic Review* 25 (July 1849), 48–9.

66. See Rogin's assessment in *Subversive Genealogy,* pp. 70–6.

67. Jones, "Melville's Mardi," pp. 49–50.

68. For the eagle as a symbol of American expansionism, see Alan Heimert, "*Moby-Dick* and American Political Symbolism," *American Quarterly* 15 (1963), 504, 507–8.

69. For a discussion of Ishmael's narratological self-consciousness, see Edgar A. Dryden, *Melville's Thematics of Form: The Great Art of Telling the Truth* (Baltimore: Johns Hopkins University Press, 1968).

70. Cf. the Authorized Version translation of 1 Samuel 5:4: "Dagon was fallen upon his face to the ground before the ark of the Lord; and the head of Dagon and both of his hands *were cut off upon the threshold;* only the stump of Dagon *was left to him*" (my emphasis).

71. For an historical survey of the changing definitions of verisimilitude and the probable, see Patey, *Probability and Literary Form,* pp. 77–83.

72. Joseph Glanvill, *The Vanity of Dogmatizing: or Confidence in Opinions manifested in a Discourse of the Shortness and Uncertainty of our Knowledge* (London, 1661), p. 64.

73. In "Herman Melville and the Example of Sir Thomas Browne," Foley also notes the verbal resemblances here (p. 275) but stops short of examining the implications.

74. These chapters in Browne are noted as a possible source for Melville by Mansfield and Vincent in their "Explanatory Notes" to *Moby-Dick* in the Hendricks House edition, p. 706, as well as by Foley, "Herman Melville and the Example of Sir Thomas Browne," p. 273. However, none examine the critical or cultural implications.

    The chapters on blackness were commented upon by Melville's contemporaries: Barrett, for example, in "Sir Thomas Browne," remarks that Browne "expends much eloquence and research on the blackness of negroes," *American Whig Review* 8 (July 1848) p. 17.

75. For a recent study of Melville (esp. *Benito Cereno*), race, and the intertwining of black and white cultural expression, see Eric J. Sundquist, *To Wake the Nations: Race in the Making of American Literature* (Cambridge, Mass.: Harvard University Press [Belknap Press], 1993), pp. 135–224. For an extended discussion of Melville, race, and slavery, see also Carolyn L. Karcher, *Shadow over the Promised Land: Slavery, Race, and Violence in Melville's America* (Baton Rouge: Louisiana State University Press, 1980), esp. pp. 62–91. Karcher suggests that Melville countered racial bigotry by relying upon "ingenious techniques of subverting his readers' racial prejudices and inducing them to identify with victims of oppression, regardless of race" (p. xi).

76. Cf. Foley, "Herman Melville and the Example of Sir Thomas Browne," who concludes, somewhat beside Melville's or Browne's procedural points, that "the contradictions leave Melville unable to assign the color [white] any definite meaning . . . Both the whiteness of the whale and the blackness of the Negro must remain irresolvable mysteries" (p. 274).

77. In the political critique of the United States in *Mardi*, Melville refers ironically to "the tribe of Ham," to whom the privileges of liberty seem not to apply. See *Mardi*, pp. 513, 535.

78. Cf. Karcher's discussion, in *Shadow over the Promised Land*, of nineteenth-century "ethnocentric standards of beauty and innate intelligence" (p. 22). She draws largely upon Josiah Clark Nott and George R. Gliddon, *Types of Mankind: or, Ethnological Researches, Based upon the Ancient Monuments, Paintings, Sculptures and Crania of Races,*

and upon their Natural, Geographical, Philological, and Biblical History . . . (1854; rpt. Miami: Mnemosyne Pub. 1969).

6: Melville, Milton, & Heresy

1. These annotations, not known to exist until the mid-1980s, are still unpublished. I would like to thank jointly Stephen Ferguson, Curator of Rare Books and Assistant University Librarian for Rare Books and Special Collections at Princeton University, and a private endowment for their kind permission to inspect the original annotations.

2. Henry Pommer, without definite knowledge of the existence of Melville's annotated Milton, rightly surmised that Melville read Milton for confirmation of his own ideas but inaccurately supposed that Melville generally read Milton as an orthodox Christian, confirmed in his belief in God. Pommer, however, describes Melville's response as "Romantic" where depictions of Ahab are concerned. See Henry Pommer, *Milton and Melville* (Pittsburgh: University of Pittsburgh Press, 1950), pp. 13, 90, 107.

   John T. Shawcross has recently traced Milton's importance to many other American writers in both the colonial period and the nineteenth century; see *John Milton and Influence: Presence in Literature, History and Culture* (Pittsburgh: Dusquesne University Press, 1991). Kevin P. Van Anglen has sketched the importance of Milton for the Unitarian and Transcendentalist circle in *The New England Milton* (University Park: Pennsylvania State University Press, 1993). Both supplement and extend George Sensabaugh's *Milton in Early America* (Princeton: Princeton University Press, 1964).

3. I offer here a composite interpretation rather than a palimpsest of Melville's three separate readings, since the date of each penciled annotation and marking (as well as several partial erasures) cannot, without further investigation, be ascertained with certainty. The argument I offer here, moreover, pursues the implications of one important vein of thought offered by Melville's annotations, and is by no means intended as a comprehensive survey of his numerous markings, underscorings, and annotations.

4. Throughout this chapter I will quote from *The Poetical Works of John Milton*, ed. John Mitford (Boston: Hilliard, Gray, 1836), which is the edition owned by Melville. This edition reads "temple's posts" for "temple's post."

5. William Braswell noted that Melville "significantly marked passages in his copy of Shelley's *Essays* which relate to anti-Christian argument in *Paradise Lost.*" See Braswell, *Melville's Religious Thought* (Durham, N.C.: Duke University Press, 1943), p. 13. Melville's copy of Shelley, however, is inscribed with a date much later (1873) than any of his readings of Milton in his Hilliard and Gray 1836 edition.

6. For a discussion of the techniques Melville employs for expressing

theological doubts, see T. Walter Herbert, Jr., *"Moby-Dick" and Calvinism: A World Dismantled* (New Brunswick, N.J.: Rutgers University Press, 1977). For an extended discussion of the devices of "artistic deception and hoodwinking" employed by Melville throughout his career because "of his embarrassment over the heretical and blasphemous nature of his views," see also Lawrence Thompson, *Melville's Quarrel with God* (Princeton: Princeton University Press, 1952), p. 423.

7. See Charlene Avallone, " 'Vast and Varied Accessions ... From Abroad': Herman Melville and Edward Young on Originality," *Studies in the American Renaissance 1984,* ed. Joel Myerson (Charlottesville University of Virginia Press, 1984), for the assessment that Melville reveals "a definition of the writer's role as an active, insistent, not always successful essay to obtain a spiritual revelation from an established book-authority to coincide with and 'elucidate' the writer's vision" (p. 417).

8. Melville's literary ambitions were significantly frustrated and impeded by his family's and his own financial difficulties, as well as by increasingly hostile critical responses. For very different versions of Melville's (and his family's) frustrations, see Leon Howard, *Herman Melville: A Biography* (Berkeley and Los Angeles: University of California Press, 1967), and Michael Paul Rogin, *Subversive Genealogy: The Politics and Art of Herman Melville* (Berkeley and Los Angeles: University of California Press, 1979).

9. Landor's first imaginary conversation between Marvell and Milton was published in 1824 and again in his *Works* (1846); the second and third conversations were published in 1862 and added to a new edition of his works in 1876. Merton M. Sealts, Jr., in *Melville's Reading,* rev. ed. (Columbia: University of South Carolina Press, 1988), has noted that Melville quotes from Landor's *Pentameron* (an early set of "imaginary dialogues") in an annotation in his copy of Dante (p. 192). On the same page (p. xlviii) is Melville's dating of his reading of Dante: "Pacific Ocean Sunday afternoon Sep. 22, 1860" (p. 171). Since this is only one day later than the date he inscribes in volume 2 of his *Poetical Works of John Milton* ("Sep. 21st, 1860, Pacific Ocean N.L. 15°."), it is probable that Melville had some version of Landor's *Conversations* with him at sea in the fall of 1860.

10. Walter Savage Landor, *Imaginary Conversations,* ed. T. Earle Welby, 16 vols. (London: Chapman & Hall, 1927–34), 4:175–98.

11. Landor, *Imaginary Conversations,* 4:216. For a discussion of the Marvell – Parker controversy and Parker's libelous references to Milton in *The Transposer Rehearsed* (1673; attributed to Parker by Marvell) and *A Reproof to the Rehearsal Transposed* (1673), see William Riley Parker, *Milton: A Biography,* 2 vols. (Oxford: Clarendon Press, 1968), 1:629 – 31.

12. Melville often relished the savagely impious in his favorite authors. His friend Evert Duyckinck noted, after spending an evening with

him, that he "instanced old [Robert] Burton as atheistical" and that he was "charged to the muzzle with his sailor metaphysics and jargon of things unknowable." Duyckinck deemed the evening "an orgy of indecency and blasphemy" (quoted in Sealts, *Melville's Reading*, p. 102).

In the lines he copied from Landor into his Dante, Melville quotes Landor (speaking in the voice of Petrarcha) on Dante: "what execrations! what hatred against the human race! what exultation and merriment at eternal sufferings! In this view, the "Inferno" is the most immoral and impious book ever written." Melville comments, with some appreciation, it seems, "Thus savagely writes Savage Landor of the still more savage Tuscan" (facsimile in Sealts, *Melville's Reading*, p. 106).

13. On the typological tensions and dissociations, see Joseph Wittreich, *Interpreting "Samson Agonistes"* (Princeton: Princeton University Press, 1986), pp. 316–28. On the Samson story and its contemporary political and ideological associations, see pp. 359–70.

14. On Melville's Calvinist, heretical, and atheistic preoccupations, see T. Walter Herbert, Lawrence Thompson, and H. Bruce Franklin, *In the Wake of the Gods: Melville's Mythology* (Stanford: Stanford University Press, 1963).

15. Milton, *Complete Prose Works of John Milton*, ed. Don M. Wolfe et al., 8 vols. (New Haven, Conn. Yale University Press, 1953–82), 1:613.

16. Wittreich, *Interpreting "Samson Agonistes,"* p. 363. Wittreich contends, moreover, that Samson himself betrays his God or transgresses the law of the Old Dispensation by his "patently unlawful marriages . . . [and] his indiscriminate slaughtering not once but many times" (p. 360). For the Samson narrative's departure from the "cyclical pattern of sin, oppression, repentance, and salvation" established in the Book of Judges, see David M. Gunn, "Joshua and Judges," in *The Literary Guide to the Bible,* ed. Robert Alter and Frank Kermode (Cambridge, Mass.: Harvard University Press, 1987), pp. 114, 118–19.

17. Herman Melville, *Moby-Dick, or The Whale,* ed. Harrison Hayford, Hershel Parker, and G. Thomas Tanselle (Evanston, Ill.: Northwestern University and Newberry Library, 1988), p. 124. Subsequent citations are to this edition and will be given in the text as *M-D* with page numbers.

18. On Melville and the Bible, see Natalia Wright, *Melville's Use of the Bible* (Durham: Duke University Press, 1949). See also Wilson Walker Cowen, "Melville's Marginalia," 11 vols., Ph. D. diss., Harvard University, 1965.

19. William Empson, *Milton's God* (London: Chatto & Windus, 1961), p. 221. Empson is referring to Percy Bysshe Shelley's *Defence of Poetry.* For a modern edition, see *Shelley's Critical Prose,* ed. Bruce McElderry, Jr. (Lincoln: University of Nebraska Press, 1967), p. 24.

20. Percy Bysshe Shelley, *A Defence of Poetry,* in *Essays, Letters from Abroad,*

Translations and Fragments, ed. Mrs. Shelley, 2 vols. (London: Moxon, 1852), 1:33. Melville's marked copy is in the Houghton Library at Harvard University; vol. 1 bears the inscription "H. Melville 1873 N.Y." There was also an annotated copy of Shelley's *Poetical Works* owned by Melville and dated "April 9, 1861 Pittsfield," Massachusetts (present location unknown). Both the publication dates and the inscription dates of these two editions of Shelley's poetry suggest that the *documented* evidence for Shelley informing Melville's reading of Milton is later than the publication of *Moby-Dick,* and possibly later than all but his last (1868) reading in the Milton volumes under discussion. If Melville had access to the 1840 Moxon edition (the first edition), then of course Shelley must be considered as an influence on Melville's reading of Milton.

21. According to Pommer, Melville marks the following sentences in his copy of Shelley's *Defence* (in the *Essays, Letters from Abroad, Translations and Fragments*): "Milton's poem contains within itself a philosophical refutation of that system [of rewards and punishments], of which, by a strange and natural antithesis, it has been a chief popular support. Nothing can exceed the energy and magnificence of the character of Satan as expressed in 'Paradise Lost.' " "Milton's Devil as a moral being is as far superior to his God, as one who perseveres in some purpose which he has conceived to be excellent in spite of adversity and torture, is to one who in the cold security of undoubted triumph inflicts the most horrible revenge upon his enemy." Pommer, *Milton and Melville,* p. 107.

    For an informed and sensitive discussion of Manicheanism in *Mardi* and *Moby-Dick,* see Thompson, *Melville's Quarrel with God,* see pp. 28–9, 65–6, 139–40.

22. Melville's knowledge of Blake was sketchy. Sealts (in *Melville's Reading,* p. 178) records that Melville had a copy (inscribed "H. Melville, June 4, '70") of Alexander Gilchrist's *Life of William Blake.*

23. Shelley admits in the next sentence of the *Defence of Poetry* that "It is a difficult question to determine how far they [Dante and Milton] were conscious of the distinction which must have subsisted in their minds between their own creeds and that of the people." It is unlikely that Melville would have known Shelley's early work, *The Necessity of Atheism.*

24. Milton's doctrinal anti-Trinitarianism may only be a part of the issue in Melville's words about "a strong, controversial meaning." (Melville's father was a Unitarian.) It seems more likely that Melville is insinuating doubt about matters more fundamental to monotheistic religion and, specifically, Christianity.

25. George Gordon, Lord Byron, *Cain,* in *The Poetical Works of Byron,* rev. ed., ed. Robert F. Gleckner (Boston: Houghton Mifflin, 1975), Act I, scene i, line 36. Subsequent citations will be given in the text with act, scene, and line numbers.

26. If anything, Melville's Satan, judging from other passages that Mel-

ville underlines in *Paradise Lost,* is a tragic figure who is remorseful while vengeful, serving at times as a model for Captain Ahab at his most complex, humane, and compelling. Milton's powerful dramatic depictions of Satan's character have interest for Melville largely as they reveal the tension in Satan between his former glory and virtue and his present degradation and viciousness.

27. Nathaniel Hawthorne, *The English Notebooks,* ed. Randall Stewart (London: Oxford University Press, 1941), pp. 432–3.

28. Hawthorne, *English Notebooks,* pp. 432–3.

INDEX

Continued from the front of book